MEMOIRS OF GENERAL SIR HENRY DERMOT DALY

G.C.B., C.I.E.

SOMETIME COMMANDER OF CENTRAL INDIA
HORSE, POLITICAL ASSISTANT FOR WESTERN
MALWA, Etc., Etc.

BY MAJOR H. DALY

LONDON
JOHN MURRAY, ALBEMARLE STREET
1905

PREFACE

THE criticisms and strictures upon leading men and current policy, which appear in the extracts from Sir Henry Daly's correspondence and diaries, were frequently modified by him in the light of fuller information or subsequent events. They have been allowed to stand as interesting examples of the feeling of the hour.

HUGH DALY.

THE RESIDENCY,
INDORE, *August* 1905.

CONTENTS

CHAPTER I

EARLY LIFE (1823-1848)

CHAPTER II

MULTAN (1848-1849)

CHAPTER III

GUJERAT AND PESHAWAR

CHAPTER IV

RAISING OF THE IST PUNJAB CAVALRY (1849-52)

PAGE

CHAPTER V

MARRIAGE, 1852-1856

CHAPTER VI

RAISING OF THE IST OUDH IRREGULAR CAVALRY
1856-1857

CHAPTER VII

THE GUIDES AND DELHI—1857

CONTENTS

CHAPTER VIII

LUCKNOW—1858

CHAPTER IX

SIR HOPE GRANT'S OPERATIONS IN OUDH, 1858-1859

CHAPTER X

CENTRAL INDIA HORSE AND GWALIOR, 1861-1869

CONTENTS

CHAPTER XI

ADMINISTRATION OF CENTRAL INDIA, 1869-1881

CHAPTER XII

1881-1895

LIST OF ILLUSTRATIONS

SIR HENRY DALY

CHAPTER I

EARLY LIFE (1823-1848)

Parentage; voyage to, and early days in, India; first staff appointment; Kaira; early friends; invalided; return to Sind; Sir
Charles Napier; a sketch of the three Lawrence brothers.

HENRY DERMOT DALY was born at Kirkee, near
Poona, in the Bombay Presidency, on the 25th
October 1823; the second of the two children of
Francis Dermot Daly by his marriage with Mary,
only child of Captain Hugh McIntosh, who served in
the Peninsular War in the 16th Light Dragoons
(taking part in the battle of Salamanca, and in the
actions of Llerna, Castrajon, La Serna, Tudela, and
Torquemado), and subsequently in the 101st Foot.

The pedigree of the Daly family is traced far back
into the twilight of Irish history. In the beginning
of the eighteenth century, the branch from which
Henry Daly sprang possessed estates in West Meath.
They were dispossessed in the penal times, and
settled in Connaught on old family lands at Clan-
baniffe (now Daly's Grove); here Francis Daly was
born and brought up. As a mere lad, Ensign Francis
Daly joined Wellington's army in the Peninsula, in
company with a still younger brother who was killed
in the storming of San Sebastian. Francis served the
campaigns of 1813 and 1814 in the 84th Foot, being
wounded in the action near Bayonne on the 13th

A

December 1813. In June 1814, he was transferred to the 76th Foot, with which corps he served in the American War, and was present at the siege and battle of Plattsburg. After a short period on half-pay he was posted in 1818 to the 4th* Light Dragoons, with whom he proceeded to India at the end of 1821 ; he commanded a wing of the regiment during Sir John (afterwards Lord) Keane's operations in Afghanistan, including the siege and capture of Ghazni in 1839, his services being rewarded by a brevet lieutenant-colonelcy. He subsequently held command of the regiment, with which he returned to England in 1842, until he sold out in January 1846.

In the absence of their parents in India, Henry Daly, who had been sent home as an infant, and his brother Francis Hugh, who became a barrister, and died unmarried in 1871, were brought up at Newport, Isle of Wight, by their maternal grandmother, Mrs McIntosh. In 1840, Henry was given a nomination to the East India Company's service, and was posted to the 1st Bombay European Fusiliers (now the 1st Dublin Fusiliers). The regiment was then at Aden, having formed part in the previous year of the force which first occupied the Aden Peninsula ; but Daly proceeded direct to India to join his father. Ten years later he wrote a brief sketch of his early life :—

" On looking back I see a confused mass of impressions, with little worthy of record, less worthy of selection. Not but perhaps I have, when reflecting on days gone, felt something akin to pride and gratitude. Amidst all, my chief desire has been to become what some in their love and partiality thought I was, and though I may have fallen short of this, I doubt not the very thought of climbing has made me shun the ground.

* Now the 4th Hussars.

"I was out of sight of England on the 3rd September 1840. The steamer ploughed away until we reached Gibraltar, where we landed. Since then I have wandered in many lands, have mixed with many strange people, but the memory of that first evening at Gibraltar is clear and *distinct;* the faces and costumes betokening every race; the Turk and the Christian, the Jew and the Arab, all mingled together in the narrow streets, with grim houses towering up on either side. 'The Rock,' the Galleries, the hundreds of steps, the tongues of this mass of people, the gestures and grimaces to be equalled in a French Bourse only. On reaching Malta, we are told that Alexandria was in blockade by our fleet; so at Malta we remained four or five days. When eventually we arrived at Alexandria, we found one noble British ship riding at anchor at the mouth of the harbour (a very narrow mouth it is), preventing the egress of the splendid *Turkish fleet* moored within. After some communication with the shore it was announced that Mehemet Ali * would allow us to pass through Egypt; accordingly we landed. In those days arrangements for travel were not as they are now (1850). Vehicles of every whimsical kind may at this time be seen in Cairo. Steamers and tug boats now darken the Nile. Then there was but one steamer, which, from its extreme smallness, some wag said was of three donkey power. After many delays on the mud banks of the Nile we entered Cairo. We wished to cross the desert to Suez at once. No horses or camels were to be had; donkeys were brought out to be our chargers. These animals are extraordinary creatures, not less so than their attendants, the 'donkey boys.' Without his attendant the pony of Jerusalem moves not. The Arab boy shouts and shrieks; at this signal the donkey rushes on his route quite independent of his rider. As no change was to be had in the desert, two donkeys were assigned to each of us. We traversed the distance to Suez, 78 or 80 miles, in less than twenty-four hours; there we found the steamer. On the 23rd September we went

* An excellent sketch of Mehemet Ali and his career is given in Chapter XVIII. of *The Cross and the Crescent*, by Eliot Warburton, a book to which Daly frequently referred in his earlier letters.

puffing down the Red Sea, and reached Bombay on the 10th October. I was driven to Sir Henry Roper's house; he was a great friend of my father's, and from him I met with a most kind and warm reception. That evening I started for my father's house at Kirkee, about 100 miles from Bombay; the following evening I reached the cantonment at dusk. I continued with him about a month, when he was ordered with his regiment, as was then supposed, on service to Afghanistan.

"My own regiment was at Aden, but to enable me to study the language, father got me attached to a corps at Poona. I remained at Poona till May 1841; then I went to Bombay to try my chance before the Committee of Examination. When the General Orders were published I had the gratification of seeing my name, Ensign Daly, first on the list of 'Qualified Interpreters.' I returned to Poona. Two months after this I was directed to join a detachment of my regiment at a cantonment 70 miles distant. A few months more and my father's regiment was ordered home. I galloped down to spend a week ere the time of departure drew very near; then I saw him no more* till my return to England. I now

* It was shortly after this that the first news of the Kabul disasters were received. In January 1842, Daly wrote to his brother: "An order has arrived suspending all movements. The deadly outbreak at Cabool has been the cause of this change. Fancy, since father sailed from Bombay, 22 officers have been killed and upwards of 30 wounded, and amongst these some of the wisest and best—Sir A. Burnes and Sir W. Macnaghten. I have this instant seen an extract from a letter from Cabool, detailing some of the terrible events. It is thought that without delay an army will be sent up to clear the country of every cut-throat who breathes in it, treacherous villains all. The Chief has offered our regiment to Government. I hope and trust the offer may be accepted, but I fear not.

" About three weeks since an express was received by the Brigadier here from Mallegaum, about 120 miles hence, saying that a Madras † regiment there was in a state of mutiny and calling for aid from here as soon as possible. Accordingly, 150 European artillerymen, 4 guns and 150 Sepoys were ordered to march the next day. I wrote to the Brigadier, volunteering to go; he accepted and put me in orders to

† The 52nd N. I. : see footnote at page 290 in *Kaye's Sepoy War*, vol. i.

deliberately composed myself to overcome a second language; that of the Mahratta. In May 1842, I again appeared before the Committee and with success. At that time I knew the Commander-in-Chief, Sir T. M'Mahon,* and his family well. Lady M'Mahon was kindly interested about my passing. Laughingly, I had obtained a promise from her that, if I got through my trial, she would obtain from Sir Thomas two months' leave for me to the hills, for my health. The day of passing I saw her; that evening I received a note from an A.D.C. directing me to wait on the Chief the following morning. I concluded it was anent the hills leave; having been but eighteen months in the army, I had not dreamt of an appointment. Accordingly, I went to Sir Thomas, who congratulated me, and said, 'I have a reward for your industry,' and added something kind. I was appointed Adjutant of an Irregular Infantry Regiment. I was but an ensign at the time; it changed my pay from 200 to upwards of 500 rupees a month. Strange coincidence, the 'Provincial† Battalion' to which I was appointed was stationed at the very place where formerly had been a large cantonment, which had been abandoned from its unhealthiness to Europeans; Kaira: there had been the 4th Dragoons; there too was my mother's grave! So we met. For months every day I passed the spot where she lies. My poor mother! I was a child when she died, but so often had I read her beautiful letters that her memory was a living feeling.

"There were three European officers in the corps, commandant, adjutant, and doctor. The commandant, a captain of some standing, was married. So was the doctor. I have seen no spot in any march with the detachments, and away we went, but alas! our hopes of glory! were doomed to die a sudden death, for, when we had arrived within 30 miles of Mallegaum, we received an order to retrace our steps as all was quiet."

* Lieut.-General Sir Thomas M'Mahon, Bart., K.C.B., was Commander-in-Chief in Bombay from 1840 to 1847.

† The "Guzerat Battalion," which was raised in 1824, and was some 1200 strong; it was chiefly employed on civil and police duties in Kaira, Ahmedabad, Broach, and Surat. The Adjutant was also Interpreter and Quarter-master.

country more luxuriantly beautiful than Kaira.
Verdure and culture on all sides. Trees of great
magnificence, which had been planted by the
Muhammadans when the tide of conquest bore them
there. The society was limited; two or three
civilians besides the regiment; yet was I very happy
there. Here commenced a friendship between
Anderson and myself which ended with his death
at Multan. He belonged to my regiment. I had
known him before. It so chanced that three of us of
the same corps had staff appointments far away from
the regiment but near each other :—Grant, the
adjutant of a cavalry regiment (like mine), Anderson
in the quarter-master general's department. These
two were at a large station 20 miles from mine;
we became constant associates and were always at
each other's houses. Poor Grant, I can scarcely
write his name without a tear. Noble and high-
minded, he died young, a year after the time I allude
to. Of Anderson I knew even more. Being in the
same regiment, possessing many similar inclinations
and studies, we were much together. We both
entertained ambitious hopes of rising in the service,
and for many an hour did we sit of a night at Kaira,
dreaming dreams of days to come, breathing hopes
of success, alas how suddenly cut short in his case;
at a time too when they were being fast realised.
Scarce of my own brother's mind and capacity did
I so well know the workings as of Anderson's. After
a year near me he joined Sir Charles Napier's staff
in Sind.* He won the regard and esteem of the

* In October 1843 Daly wrote home to his brother :—"You will
have heard of the rebellion in the Punjab; I should trust now that
we shall place the country in leading strings; under our sway the
Valley of Cashmere would prove the richest and most productive in the
world : we are all deeply anxious to know what Lord Ellenborough
will do, but it is not probable he will let slip so favourable an opportunity of annexing a gem so precious to our possessions. Should he
do this, it will require a strong force and some sharp fighting, for the
Sikhs can bring into the field an army 80,000 strong, composed of
well-disciplined brave soldiers, and 120 pieces of cannon. All the
fighting will, I fancy, fall to the good luck of the Bengal Army. Sind
is not to be occupied by Bombay troops any longer. The order for a
Bengal Force to march to relieve the Bombay Force is out, but the

general, who gave him an appointment of honour. Severe fever overtook him in the jungle of Sind, and he was obliged to seek home for his health in December 1843. Our correspondence had been regular, for we were *much to each other*.

"About the time he went to England, or a little earlier, I was seized with fever. I struggled with it for some months, till at last in February 1844, much weakened by its repeated attacks, I went to try the change and sea breeze of Bombay. The first week in Bombay revived me and I saw visions of returning to Kaira, but these were not to remain long. The attacks were renewed; I was recommended to proceed home, and sailed on the 1st March 1844. I thus relinquished a good appointment and good interest, and the latter could not easily be renewed, as my father had left India. Many said, 'You'll sorely regret this in days to come. At twenty-two resigning a soldierly appointment worth £700 a year. Try the Cape or Egypt; your health will be restored there.' (By the rules of the service an officer might go to the Cape or Egypt without losing his Indian pay and Staff appointment, whereas by going home both were sacrificed.) However I cared little for this sound advice. We underwent quarantine at Malta, whence I travelled with a friend through Sicily, Naples, Civita Vecchia, Leghorn, and Pisa to France. There Anderson and I became again united. I spent some weeks amidst his family in Scotland, and was treated by them as one of themselves. My days passed joyously, and by and by I began to realise mentally the prophecies of those who warned me against going. I knew I ought not to remain the full length (three years) of my leave. It was waste if I thought of climbing. When happily, to save me the decision and free me from the responsibility, came the order in March 1846, during the Sutlej campaign, 'Rejoin your regiment ordered on service.' In fifteen days I was off. I joined my regiment. The adjutancy became vacant; I was offered it. A month later I should have lost it, and

Punjab row will probably prevent its being carried into execution for some time; I hope so, for it would lose me my present appointment."

I have ever been a Republican in literature, following
a most desultory course. I never drew up a system
in my life, never followed that of anyone. I confess I
have occasionally repented the not having done so.
I find I have collected a considerable quantity of
knowledge, for I have read much of general literature
—History, Travels, Biographies, Reviews. I have
never attempted to master any scientific subject,
know nothing of any of the *ology* family. But I hold
the information a man gets from books very inferior
towards educating the mind to that which is obtained
from observation and reflection. Yet is there no
more ardent lover of books than I am ; none so lonely
without them. Biography has ever been a favourite
branch of reading with me. There is no study so
ennobling, more instructive, more consolatory ; perseverance and self-culture—no ability can claim immunity from these and still perform its course.
Touching languages, I can always cover my reputation with the mantle of Eastern tongues, which I
hope will always be to me what the earth is to the
physician, covering all civilised blunders. German I
can speak tolerably (read that last word slowly, it is
not intended to imply vast things) ; three or four
weeks in Germany would, I think, make me perfectly
fluent in the language. Not so French ; I have had
less practice there in conversation."

At Karachi Daly was first introduced to Sir
Charles Napier, from whom in later years he received
much kindness, and whom he ever regarded with the
deepest respect and affection. In 1847 he recorded
in his journal :—

" Sir Charles has quitted 'his own won' country,
bearing with him as much affection and respect from
all employed under him as ever great man had on
relinquishing a high command in which, of necessity,
he had frequently to apply the curb in an autocratic
government. Even those who at times spoke lightly
of the hero that's gone, felt deeply at his going ; as
he placed his foot upon the boat which was to bear
him away, the hearts of those around were too full to

cheer; no one spoke, but many instinctively un-
covered their heads. He too was deeply affected.
Never did I feel prouder than as he passed down the
line of troops, where with dropped sword I sat on
horseback at the end of our formation, he recognised
me and said, 'Ah, Daly, is that you?' and turned his
horse and shook me by the hand with 'Goodbye,
good luck to you, my boy.' I bade God bless him,
and felt at that moment that good must befall me
after his wish."

Shortly after this Daly was also much affected by
the departure of his commanding officer, Colonel
Cumming :—

"We have lost the dear old Colonel. I knew not
how much we were attached to him until the time of
parting. I have never met such a character. He
had mingled much with the world, and from being of
an inquisitive temper and fond of the study of men,
had seen and thought much of feelings and dispositions. In some things he had an intuitive knowledge of what a man would think and do. His
simplicity was wondrous, as pure and high in his own
ideas and in his appreciation of the 'right' as on the
day he left his father's house. He possessed more
charity than any man I ever knew. He judged more
kindly of acts perhaps than they at all times deserved ;
but, by his interpretations of men's motives, he raised
the standard in the mind of each, and many who
heeded little of morality before strove to win the
Colonel's regard. Falsehood he held as the lowest
and meanest act a man could commit ; without truth,
rigid truth, no character could prosper, no talents
could support a man lacking it."

Daly's health had not been fully restored by his
sojourn in Europe. It was in opposition to strong
medical advice that he returned to India in the spring
of 1846; at Malta he was so ill that he was almost
sent back to England. Soon after his arrival in
Karachi his regiment was decimated by a terrible

outbreak of cholera ; the rest of that year was spent
in tents, and in May of the following year he was
dangerously ill. He recovered sufficiently to avoid
being invalided, but his health remained unsatisfactory for several years. He was at this time
exceedingly anxious to obtain employment in the
Punjab, but was not successful, being then unknown
to the Lawrences, or to anyone with local influence.
His friend Anderson, who had been more fortunate,
kept up a close correspondence from the Punjab, and
early in March 1848 wrote the following sketch of the
famous brothers who then formed the most interesting
group on the stage of Indian history :—*

"First for Henry : a thin face ; an expansive, but
not massive, forehead ; widely apart grey eyes, that
seem to look always on a distant object, even when
observing *you*, and which suggest ideas of abstracted-
ness and contemplation. An expression wonderfully
benevolent. Let me, however, dwell on the mouth,
which is perhaps the most sympathetic organ we
have. The mouth of Colonel Lawrence shows you at
once that he is desirous to please and to avoid hurting
a single feeling. The shyness of vanity is unknown
to him ; but the shyness of modesty, which sits well,
though not very elegantly, on a great man, is his
failing, his demon. He is, as of course he must be,
an entertaining companion ; his voice is the personi-
fication of *entre-nous-ness*, if I may be bold enough
such a word to try. Still he shirks literature as
literature, and sticks to Indian subjects, where no
immediate personal feeling or taste, beyond what is
referable to justice and truths and facts, is developed.
He does not think it advisable or becoming to open

* Henry Lawrence was at this time Resident at Lahore, with
control of the Council of Administration, which was formed under the
treaty of December 1846 ; John was Commissioner of the Jalandar
Division, which included the territory annexed after the first Sikh
War ; George was Political Agent on the North-West Frontier, with
headquarters at Peshawar.

his mind upon any personal subject; but throws
away all affectation of superior talent or dignity in
discoursing on matters where the welfare of India, the
state of the English world, or anything connected in
short with the sort of practical knowledge you would
expect to find in a man in his position is concerned.
But he avoids soliloquies, and shuns opinions without
a sound bottom; and you would say, if you had not
read his novel,* had not a grain of romance in his
disposition.   He provokes opinions from others, and
is as sharp as the Spanish Prime Minister in *Gil
Blas* in detecting the gold from the dross.   He
surpasses Outram† and all men I have seen as a
perfect knower of men.

"One kind of greatness is common to all the
three brothers—decision of character, unsurpassable
and dauntless courage.   The Major is brisk, jolly,
less solid than John and the Colonel, but capable of
great deeds in a crisis by his pluck, talent, honesty,
and decision.   John, whom I did not appreciate till
I learnt from his acts what a splendid creature he is,
is original, plain-spoken, playful and even prantic in
conversation; is one of the first civil servants in
India; knows natives like A B C; notes humbug;
pulls out your most secret wishes by an apparent
artlessness; is fond of billiards and cigars; writes
splendid reports and letters; does immense *naukri*
(service), and has a very nice wife.   The Colonel
surpasses the brothers by having all their decision,
all their experience, but with a refined, sensitive
nature.   I do not doubt that great part of his life
has been spent in study, in nurturing grand resolves,
and carrying them out."

A few weeks after this sketch was written, the
whole situation in India was changed by the outbreak
at Multan, and the great events to which it was the
prelude.

---

* *Adventures of an Officer in the Service of Ranjeet Singh*, by
Major H. M. Lawrence.

† Sir James Outram, the "Bayard of India," whose wife was
Anderson's sister.

CHAPTER II

MULTAN (1848-1849)

Peaceful condition of the Punjab early in 1848; Multan affairs; the outbreak; voyage up the Indus; the first siege of Multan; general condition of the Punjab; George Lawrence a prisoner; defection of Sher Singh; reinforcements from Bombay; storm and capture of Multan; burial of Agnew and Anderson.

SIR GEORGE LAWRENCE, in his *Forty-Three Years in India*, especially notices (p. 240) the profoundly peaceful condition of the entire Punjab at the end of January 1848, when he returned from leave and resumed his appointment as Political Agent at Peshawar. On the 22nd March 1848 the Governor-General in Council informed* the Secret Committee of the Board of Control that "the perfect tranquillity which prevails in the Punjab is enabling the Darbar, with the assistance of the Resident, to promote reforms in the administration of the Lahore State, calculated to relieve its finances, and to ameliorate the condition of the people." Sir Henry Lawrence had proceeded to England on sick leave in November 1847, handing over charge to his brother John, who officiated as Resident at Lahore until the arrival of Sir Frederick Currie early in March 1848. While John Lawrence was thus officiating, he received a visit from Mulraj,† the

* Despatch No. 25, dated 22nd January 1848: Parliamentary Papers, India, 1849, vol. xli., p. 104.

† For details as to Mulraj, see despatch from the Governor-General in Council to the Secret Committee, No. 43, dated 11th May 1848, at page 116: Parliamentary Papers, India, 1849, vol. xli.

MULTAN.

Struggle in the streets—Capture of two Sikh standards.

[*To face p.* 14.

Dewan of Multan, who expressed his desire to resign the government of that province, a desire in which he persisted, in spite of Mr Lawrence's endeavours to dissuade him from the step. By Mulraj's request, the matter was treated as secret, until Sir Frederick Currie reached Lahore; the latter then communicated the proposal to the Sikh Darbar, and, after a further unsuccessful attempt to induce Mulraj to retain his charge, decided to send two British officers to accept the Dewan's resignation, and to instal his successor.

The great Multan province, as then constituted, may be roughly described as covering, on the east of the Indus, the present Multan and Muzaffargarh districts, with cis-Indus Dera Ismael Khan and portions of the present Bannu, Jhelum, Shahpur, Jhang, and Montgomery districts; on the west of the Indus, it included practically the whole of what is now the Dera Ghazi Khan district, and a very considerable tract of the adjacent tribal country. The city of Multan is of remote antiquity, and has been the scene of repeated struggles: it fell before Alexander the Great; it was taken by Mahmud of Ghazni at the beginning of the eleventh, and by Tamerlane at the end of the fourteenth century; it was besieged in 1810 by Ranjit Singh, who was then bought off by the Afghan governor,* but he stormed it in 1818, and annexed the province to the Punjab. Three years later he appointed as Governor Dewan or Sawan Mull, a man of distinguished ability, who belonged to a banking family of Lahore. Sawan Mull ruled the province for twenty-three years, during which he amassed

* Sir H. Lawrence's *Adventures of an Officer, etc.*, vol. i., p. 256.

great wealth and became almost independent of the Darbar. He it was who constructed at Multan the fortifications which, improved as they were by Mulraj after April 1848, the British were to find so formidable. Dying in 1844, from the effects of a wound inflicted by one of his own guard, he was succeeded by his son, Mulraj, whose appointment was confirmed by the Regency on the conclusion of the first Sikh war in 1847, and again by the British Resident after the downfall of the Regency.

Vans Agnew, of the Civil Service, and Daly's friend, Anderson were selected to accompany the new Governor designate, Sardar Khan Singh, to Multan. Vans Agnew was described by Sir Frederick Currie as "the oldest political officer on this frontier, and a man of much ability, energy, and judgment"; Anderson had the benefit of local knowledge, as he had travelled through the whole of the Multan province, and was "an excellent Oriental scholar, who had been employed with credit under Sir Charles Napier in Sind." The escort consisted of 1400 Sikh infantry, a Gurkha regiment, 700 cavalry, and 100 artillerymen with 6 guns.

In a letter written *en route*, Anderson said :—

"I am enjoying, in company with my senior, Agnew, the pleasure of a boat on the Ravi. Such a bumping voyage I never knew. Sardar Khan Singh, the future Governor of Multan, accompanies us in another boat. The Sardar is a fine fellow, has been through all the wars, and has lots of pluck. We do not yet know precisely what our duties are to be; but I fancy I shall be obliged to disband some 3000 or 4000 irregular troops of Mulraj, the late Ijaradar,* and

* *Ijara* signifies lease, and *ijaradar* leaseholder. The Dewan, or Governor, was in fact a farmer of the revenues, paying a fixed annual quit-rent to the Darbar.

keep on some 2000 for regular regiments, and also to superintend the discipline and equipment of two Sikh regiments and a battery. My other duties will be to help Agnew as much as possible in his revenue and magisterial transactions. To say that I am a lucky fellow, Daly, is less than the truth. I could not in all India have had a better appointment given me than the present one. Agnew is a first-rate and most distinguished man. The country we are appointed to has never been directly governed by the Sikhs; but by Ijara. It is very rich, and it is expected that an increase of 6 to 8 lakhs will accrue to Government by the new system.

"We expect in the cold weather to have to use the strong arm against the Baluch and Afghan tribes on the west of the Indus, and hence the military preparations; but Agnew will not resort to arms without great necessity, and he managed so well in Hazara that it is to be hoped we shall avoid fighting.

"I am indebted to John Lawrence for my present berth, and to Napier * having given me a good character at the right time. The *vera causa* was Outram's letter to Mr Clark. Outram is much more known here than in Bombay. There is no one in the whole Residency who does not thoroughly support him, from Currie to myself."

The party reached Multan on the 18th April 1848. On the 19th, when returning from the fort of which they had taken formal charge, the British officers were attacked without warning and both wounded, Anderson very seriously; Agnew was actually riding at the time by the side of Mulraj, who made no effort to help or protect them. They were brought back by Khan Singh to the Idgah † where their escort was quartered; but next morning the escort went over to

* The late Lord Napier of Magdala, then employed as a civil engineer in the Punjab.

† An Idgah is a place where the Muhammadans worship on certain festival days, which are termed Id. This Idgah was a partially enclosed building, a short distance outside the walls of Multan.

B

the rioters and that evening the two officers were murdered by a fanatical mob. Sardar Khan Singh, with
some eight or ten faithful horsemen, stood by them
to the last; he was made prisoner and insultingly
treated by Mulraj, who now displayed himself as in
open revolt against the established administration.

On the 22nd April, Herbert Edwardes,* who was
engaged on revenue work in the Dera Ismael Khan
district, some 90 miles from Multan, received a letter
from Agnew, informing him of the attack made on
himself and Anderson, and calling for assistance.
The letter was written before the mutiny of the
escort. Edwardes at once made arrangements to
cross the Indus and proceed towards Multan with
such forces as he could muster, but it was not long
before he learnt that the worst had happened. This
is not the place to recount his brilliant performances.
It will suffice to say that with the help of local levies, of
the forces of the Nawab of Bahawalpur, and of some
loyal Darbar troops, mostly Muhammadans, under
the command of General Cortlandt,† he not only
kept the field against Mulraj until the arrival of the
British troops, but that his operations had the
successful results which are summed up in the
following passage from his own book‡ :—

"Mulraj rebelled on the 20th April 1848. On the
20th May, the battle of Dera Ghazi Khan lost him
all his Trans-Indus dependencies. On the 18th of
June, the battle of Kineyree deprived him of the
country between the Indus and the Chenab, and nearly

* The late Colonel Sir Herbert Edwardes, K.C.S.I., C.B.

† Cortlandt was an officer of mixed parentage, holding the rank
of general under the Sikh Darbar. After the annexation he was made
a Deputy Commissioner in the Punjab. He did excellent service in
the Mutiny.

‡ *A Year on the Punjab Frontier, in* 1848-49, vol. ii., p. 483.

[From a lithograph.

THE IDGAH, WHERE MR VANS AGNEW AND LIEUTENANT ANDERSON WERE MURDERED.

[To face p. 18.

all between the Chenab and the Sutlej. On the 1st July, the battle of Suddoosam shut him up in the city and fortress of Multan, whence he never issued again except to resist the siege of a British army."

When the news of the Multan outbreak reached Lahore, it was at first determined to despatch a Sikh force, with a British brigade, to suppress it. But, when intelligence of the deaths of Agnew and Anderson had been received, it was considered best, in view of the season of the year, to postpone active operations until October. Uneasiness, however, soon began to spread through the Punjab, manifesting itself first in Hazara, where Chattar Singh, an old and influential Sikh chief, was governor; and Edwardes' success at Suddoosam decided the acting Resident to move at once against Multan, partly in the hope that it might now be possible to finish off the rebellion at one blow, and partly to check the widespread conspiracy which was known to exist. Accordingly, in July 1848, a force under General Whish started in two columns from Lahore and Ferozpur and concentrated before Multan soon after the middle of August. The force included Her Majesty's 10th and 32nd Regiments, with three companies of fort artillery, 32 pieces of siege ordnance, and 12 horse artillery guns. The strength was a little over 200 British officers and 7800 men. Co-operating with them were the irregular forces * under Lieutenant Edwardes and General Cortlandt; the native aids †
of Bhawal Khan, Nawab of the Bhawalpur State, who were commanded by Lieutenant Lake; and the

* Cavalry, 7700; infantry, 3100; H.A. guns; mortars, 2; camel-guns, 25.

† Cavalry, 1900; infantry, 5700; H.A. guns, 14; camel-guns, 18.

Sikh force* under Sher Singh, which represented the Lahore Darbar; Sher Singh was the son of the Chattar Singh above mentioned. Edwardes estimated Mulraj's force at the beginning of September 1848 at 10,000 men, of whom 1200 were cavalry, with about 54 guns and 4 mortars.

News of the Multan outbreak reached Karachi, where Daly was serving with the 1st Bombay Fusiliers, early in June. As soon as General Whish's force was organised, Daly obtained permission to join it as a volunteer. Travelling on the Indus was in those days uncertain and difficult. He left Karachi on the 16th August, and embarked on the steamer *Napier* at Tatta on the 19th with four other officers, including Captain Brown, formerly secretary to Sir Charles Napier, and Major Gordon of the 60th Rifles.

"We steamed the next day through some of the most beautiful scenery eye ever saw—glorious trees, resplendent with foliage and blossom, forming shades and knolls which realise what one imagines from Percy's Ballads the woods and forests of old England must have been—such as Robin Hood would have delighted to travel in. Tatta is some 70 miles from Hyderabad, which we reached about 8. This being the headquarters of the flotilla, all the preparations for the voyage immediately commenced—coal, arms, ammunition, spare funnels, sails, tents, provisions, and a doctor.

"At 9 the following morning we were again under steam; all day we were running past beauteous woods, trees hanging down with yellow blossom. The rolling rage of the river during this month carries all before it, often from some unaccountable freak it turns its force on a bank where trees have risen to beauty and age in security and sweeps all

---

* Cavalry, 3400; infantry, 900; H.A. guns, 10; mortars, 2; camel-guns, 115.

away in one swoop; a bubble and no more is seen, the undercurrent burying all.   We had a strange example of this while at Tatta Bunder (May)—the boatmen had placed a large pile of wood for the steamer some 10 yards from the bank; about an hour after they had done so, the water began to suck in the bank by feet; the boatmen hurriedly removed it farther back—an hour sufficed to carry away the ground on which it had been; this, however, did not suffice the hungry current—again they were obliged to move the heap, and ere six hours were over, 60 feet had been swept away.   On the 20th we anchored 40 miles up the river.   In places there is naught to divest one of the idea of being in the wide seas save that the water is dark and dirty in colour; here and there grand old trees rising with their richly covered heads, the trunks being under water.   It reminds me much of my first impressions on coming up the Nile in boyhood.

"I hardly know what expectations I have formed for this expedition; under any circumstances I am glad of the opportunity of seeing the Indus; I have an inexpressible feeling to look on the spot where he (Anderson) was wounded and where he lay; it may be something for good may arise from it; I cheer myself up with this: such hopes are apt enough to creep in, and may be I am too much inclined to indulge in high ones for the future and to bask in fancies which can never be realised—at any rate such dreamings do one no harm.   D'Israeli says to think the heroic make heroes; sure I am that high thoughts and aspirations raise the standard of conduct in life, and that alone is fruit.   I do indeed despair when I read the characters and abilities of those who have filled prominent places in the world.

"About 5 P.M., 26th, we came in sight of Sukkur, the rise of the river and consequent increased strength of the current had delayed us more than we had expected.   The passage rounding Sukkur Fort being somewhat difficult and doubtful, it was joyously carried to attempt it at once without stopping at Sukkur, so on we went—the view of the fort on one side and Roree opposite, with temples and palm trees rising high, was more picturesque and 'eastern,'

according to our ideas than anything I remember.
The currents run down through two mouths, their
violence even all that I had heard and the experience
I had from Tatta did not prepare me for. It was
indeed the battle of the floods, a strife of currents and
undercurrents meeting in three different places, and
roaring and boiling in very whirlpools; the space
between which this mass of waters rolls and the scene
of this contention can scarcely be a width of 100
yards. The boat was steamed to full power, she
slowly but steadily breasted the first embankment,
on to the second with the same success; the third
and last, as we approached, was visibly a bridge of
eddies: her pace, slow as it had been before,
slackened; when she met the full force of the torrent,
she paused, reeled under it, sheered slightly away,
one slight effort more would have carried her head
round and taken us far down the stream, if we had
escaped contact with the projecting walls of the town
—but that did not occur—we escaped, and she
steamed through.

"*27th and 28th.*—We have been running on with
indifferent luck. The first pilot we brought with us
was not very well informed as to the channels; but,
as he truly remarked, this ignorance might be
accounted for by the fact of his never having been so
high up before.

"Yesterday morning we came upon a boat containing an elderly gentleman and his family: these,
our pilot told us, had no other place of residence.
Deeming that such an one would know something of
the channel and course of the river on which he
'moved and had his being,' we stopped to take him
in. The banks of the river, since leaving Sukkur,
have lost the wooded clothing; trees do appear, but
far in the distance, not in masses as before, but
separately or in small clumps. The inhabitants,
when there are any, rush to the banks and stare in
wonderment, yet in fear; these children of the jungle,
like rabbits passing out of a warren.

"*29th to 3rd.*—The past days have been full of
misfortunes: first, at Mithankot an attempt was
made to run up a creek and so get into the Panjnad
by a cut—the adage was verified of the shortest road

being the longest way. We ran hard-and-fast upon
a sandbank a couple of miles above Chacha, and
there, though shallow and broad the stream, it was so
violent that we did not get afloat until the sand had
drifted completely under the vessel, and so made a
completely new channel, by forming an embankment
on the other side. Then through some blundering
we backed onto the bank the current had formed,
and the probability appeared of our being left high
and dry, the river fast falling, and the creek was
merely a temporary ebullition of the river. However,
by daylight the next morning she was swinging; we
started down the stream and took the long route:
this was on the 1st morning. We were now in the
Panjnad;* on the 2nd, by 10 A.M., we came to very
shallow water. The course recommended by the
gentleman who represented the pilot, was found at its
mouth to contain but 4 feet of water; the stream ran
down this with such violence that the boat twice
slewed round and refused to enter; unhappily, this
was held a sufficient reason for eschewing that
channel. The pilot said he didn't know the other
course, and feared that though deep now, we should
find not enough of water. Albeit, away we steamed
for about two hours, when his prophecy became too
true; it was discovered that there was no *débouche*
by that course. We were obliged to steam back to
the old entrance—there, after some difficulty, we were
successful, the depth gradually greater as we
advanced; we passed through a beautiful country
better cultivated and better populated than any I
have seen in Sind.

"*3rd September.*—Last night we were joking at
the results of our experiments in attempting channels
and cuts not recommended by the pilot, yet this
morning at 6 A.M. we found the same enormity had
been perpetrated. We were again obliged to turn
back. No man of sense will say there is a sandbank
between this and Karachi with which we are not
intimately acquainted. Here at 2 P.M. on the 3rd we

---

* Panjnad (Five Streams) is the name sometimes given to the
united rivers of the Punjab immediately below the junction of the
Chenab with the Indus.

are at the mouth of the Chenab, where we ought to have been on the 30th or 31st. Most conflicting rumours have reached us, gathered from the different villages, respecting Mulraj's fate. No letters; so on we go in fear and trembling, hoping much, yet I fear scarcely trusting that we are in time.

"We arrived at the Raj Ghât at 6 A.M., 6th. Information was immediately sent off, and we soon discovered that General Whish's camp was some 10 miles distant, though that of the irregular troops lay between us and him. An answer came from Brown's friend to the effect that no operations had yet taken place, but that a consultation was to be held that morning to decide the point of attack, and probably, the result would be the removal of the General's camp from its present to a nearer position, in which case there would be difficulty in procuring carriage for our kit. No guns were heard, and this news made us somewhat easy in mind. About 7 P.M. three elephants and some tattoos [ponies] arrived for our conveyance with a guard of sowars, as it appears the fort is not completely invested. We resolved to remain till 2 the following morning and so reach camp at daylight. Accordingly, we started at 2 on the 7th, and well was it that our journey began so soon. We passed through Edwardes' camp, which, with that of a native prince adjoining, from the appearance of the men with their matchlocks and mottled accoutrements and dress resembled an Indian Fair— a more ragged lot man never eyed. We did not reach the position till 7 A.M., just in time to see the skirmishers clearing the ground, and driving the enemy from the space where the first parallel was to run. We went up to the skirmishers at a place which since that it has been my lot to become intimately acquainted—the 'Ramtirat.' There I stood under my first fire of heavy shot. Brown and I had walked out in front to look at a battery the Sikhs were busy erecting, a sound indescribable was heard just over our head, and about 10 feet in our rear a ball, a cross between an 18 and 24-pounder, fell slap between the horses of an artillery waggon; the shock floored one, but killed none. The distance from which this came could not have been less than $1\frac{3}{4}$ miles. It is a gun

which, from his constant visits since, has obtained
great celebrity in camp under the title of 'Long
Tom,' 'John Long'; his voice and range are alike
peculiar: after the Sikh artillerymen had succeeded
in obtaining the range of the 'Ramtirat,' during the
whole day he fell about in a manner most unpleasing
to gents who love their ease and comfort, some two
or three sepoys being cut to pieces by him; yet 100
shot from him must have fallen within a space of 50
square yards."

"Siddons, Brown's friend, shortly after my arrival,
went to Napier,* the Directing Engineer; on his
return he said Napier had offered to make me an
Assistant Field Engineer, if so inclined—assuredly I
was willing. By 5 P.M. I was in the trenches, cutting
out with some 400 Europeans of the 32nd the first
parallel, and many a salute did we receive during the
night from the enemy's ordnance in the fort, and
their matchlocks and zamburaks (camel-guns) fired
from under cover of the bushes and irregular ground.
About 10 a rush was made by them on our picket,
and the firing became so heavy that the men were
obliged to be withdrawn from the right of the work.
I was relieved at 1 A.M., 8th, and did not again go on
duty till 3 A.M., 9th, when, for the prolongation of this
parallel, with Captain Longdon, 10th Foot, as Acting
Engineer, I had some native workmen (Native Regiments I mean). The Perdasees performed their little
with bad grace and much grumbling, swearing that
such was not their employment. The fire burst so
heavily on us at 5, that we were unable to go on, and
the enemy running up to our very works, the working
party was taken out to drive them back; this they
succeeded in doing with three men wounded, but
sepoys are totally unfit for a night attack. They fire
at random with or without an object, with or without
an enemy.

"This indiscriminate work drew on us the fort's
heavy fire and prevented further operations. I was
not relieved till noon—the heat of the trenches who
shall describe—a burning sand and a vertical sun.
The thermometer under a Bengal tent 114°. Up to

* Afterwards Lord Napier of Magdala.

this time we had made no advance from the works
sketched out on the first day. The General's camp,
5000 or 6000 strong, lies to the E.S.E. side of
the fort, 2½ miles from Long Tom, who has occasionally dropt within the tents, and oft-times the
ground near the sentries is ploughed up by his
ravages. We have an 8-inch mortar battery at the
Ramtirat, the extreme right of our works; an 18-
pounder of 3 guns at the white well some 700 yards
to the left; Cortlandt's light 9 and 6-pounders are
again formed about the same distance to the left;
other temporary batteries have been put in position
along the parallel and removed again as circumstances have required.

"The Sikhs are beautiful shots, and scarce a yard
have we gained unpeppered or a shot have we fired
which has not been returned with wondrous precision. On the 9th, evening, it was resolved to attack
a little village, surrounded, or at any rate protected
as far as the eye can see, by a high wall. A square
building is the first thing that meets the eye. About
8 a storming party of Europeans, accompanied by
some of the 49th Native Infantry, moved out; the
position is about 600 yards in front of ours and en-
vironed by a jungle of lofty trees and brushwood, of
which it is at the very edge; when our party reached
it, they found the walls high, too much so to climb;
the light from the enemy's fire was like the mouth of
a volcano; the men, though falling fast, rushed in,
conceiving the fire and the burning light came from
the top of the building. No, it was from the loopholes with which the walls were pierced, crowds of
armed men firing their camel-guns and matchlocks
on the devoted party. Two light guns were now
brought up and two more companies of Europeans.
Three times they rushed to the walls and three times
were driven back shattered. Once the door was
burst open by an officer of the 69th (Richardson)
and a man of the 10th; the former was no sooner
in than his face and body were covered with sword-
cuts; severe wounds he received as he was dragged
away. Death's hand was so heavy that the place
could not be held, and the party was obliged to
etire, taking possession of an old building and demi-

fort-looking house about 300 yards in rear. Thus perished many a gallant fellow. The 10th lost 6 killed, 2 officers and 36 men wounded, 30 of the latter severely. I fancy our total casualties killed and wounded must have exceeded 150. I was not on duty during this attack, but went to the works at 4 A.M., the 10th, when by daylight the troops and guns were to move again on the same point. Accordingly Anderson's troop moved out, with a party of the 32nd, under shelter, to advance should the guns clear the way; scaling ladders were provided, but no need arose for their employment. Most heartily did the Sikhs return our fire, and after three hours of cannonade we saw them still rushing up, strengthening the building in rear of which they have thrown up entrenchments and made stockades, etc. About 8 A.M. all idea of assaulting the old place was relinquished, and we contented ourselves with pushing our troops into an advanced building some 100 yards ahead of that which we gained the previous night. I was present during this, which did not take place without some loss on our part: the brigadier was wounded, and many besides; fast and heavy the shots fell around. We succeeded in carrying out a battery which may be of use to-day. Thus, up to this time, we have gained nothing but a knowledge of their undaunted, resolute courage and coolness; to the very last they were advancing. A Gurkha regiment was brought to support, and ardently we hoped they purposed an attack on our camp. Europeans have been lost and the object for which the loss was incurred ungained! The General was down about the works yesterday, but not an order did he issue. I made a most ludicrous blunder: I had never before seen the General; during the attack I pointed out to Major Napier the enemy moving down in strength and completely under our fire, if that was opened, which I earnestly suggested should be done, and that we should forthwith send out skirmishers to take possession of some rough ground to the left. An old gent in a white jacket, with a plain staff-surgeon look, came up; Napier turned to him while I was speaking, and the old gent addressed some question to me, which deeming irrevelant, or at any rate of no importance compared with Napier's attention, I answered curtly and abruptly. Lo! Gordon, who was behind and listening to me, said to me, 'You treat the General coolly!' Lord! Lord! I thought he was either an old sapper sergeant or a deputy surgeon—the General!

"There's the want of a head palpable to the meanest observer. The General leaves much to the engineers, and yet fails to give them that support which such a legacy requires. Yesterday, when our affairs were certainly not brilliant to the eye, he stood about as though unconcerned as to the issue. Napier is cool, and, from all that is said, able. He is indefatigable, sparing himself neither exposure nor trouble. I had intended keeping a regular journal and dotting down events and the impressions as they arose; but the fatigue, the heat and excitement quite frustrated such views—after eight hours' duty in exposure to shot and sun alike dangerous, one returns totally incapacitated for even the light exertion of scribbling without thought or care, as I do this. Till to-day I have but sixteen hours between my eight hours' tour—now for once I have twenty.

"*11th*, 8 A.M. Nothing has occurred during the night; the enemy quiet, probably holding well in hand all their energies to resist our attack, which they may have anticipated.

"*13th*, 7 A.M. I came off a hot, well-sunned tour from 12 till 8 on the 11th, and was yesterday morning at 6 A.M. visited by the engineer brigade-major, with a paper, which I was to take to the advanced posts, containing directions for the sappers who were to accompany the advance and assault, of which, up to this hour, *no* one but the General and Napier were cognisant. He lent me his horse, and away I galloped. My brigade of sappers, with 100 Native Infantry as a working party to assist in throwing up works, was to accompany the stormers. I went down and found all there, except the 100 rank and file, which by some mistake were not forthcoming. However, we procured an excellent substitute in some sappers of Cortlandt's, fine, wiry, bold fellows.

"The advance began from two flanks, each headed by a company of Europeans—32nd and 10th—

supported by the remaining portion of their wings
with Native Infantry. The 10th Foot went up to
the post with admirable steadiness, the 8th Native
Infantry vying with them in coolness. The 32nd
were ordered to advance firing, so that their march
was not so steady to the eye. The reception given
at the building was most desperate. The place was
full of loopholes and swings for camel-guns; but so
gallant was the foe that on our approach they rushed
outside to charge us. The 32nd, on seeing this,
doubled in with a cheer. Now the struggle began:
the enemy got back, and every loophole was raging
death. The first man who ran up the scaling ladder
was Balfour of the 32nd—he was hacked fearfully
across the face, and before we could gain a position
on the top—which was to the best of my recollection
about 20 feet broad running all round, with a square
roof of some few feet higher in the centre—many of
the brave stormers knew the sleep which knows no
waking. While we were on the top of the building,
the enemy still were beneath in the central room,
from which they could command us above through
loops, and upon this the dying and the dead were
thickly strewn. Here it was that Colonel Pattoun
fell amongst many. He was calling for the ladders
which I was getting to go on to the next, a much
higher-walled and larger building than that we were
now in possession of. It was about 200 yards in
advance—so buried in trees that we were not aware
of its existence from our works.

"While we were on the top of the first place,
which was built of mud, the fire which had been
ignited at the bottom by some of the men, flamed
forth, and the centre, weakened by the loopholes
which we had made to command those inside, came
down with a great shudder. The flame caught their
ammunition, of which we knew not, and the interior
trembled fearfully, and the cry was raised, 'Mine.'
A fearful sight ensued, the dying and wounded so
thickly packed, friends and foes, though comparatively
few of the former at this place, were engulfed in
the flame, which burst out with renewed vigour,
having caught some of the dried grass which had
been their beds: poor wretches, their clothes were

on fire, the little they had! I got almost accustomed
to this during the day, for many, many did I see burning alive, their skins baked. Their matchlock lights,
burning when they were shot, set their clothes in a
flame, and their burnt skins were crackling as the
miserable creatures were weltering in the grilling sun.
The next place was not so desperately defended, though
larger. It seems to be a garden pleasure-house,
beautifully built. Yet, though I say not so desperately
defended, they resisted to the last, and fifty I suppose
were shot and bayoneted within it. In this some
spoil was found, and many carried away much who
were not there when we entered. Swords, percussion
pistols, were in a hole in the wall—silks, etc. In a
little cool place separate from the building, as we ran
through, I espied a bed which had not been long
quitted, evidently from its appearance belonging to
one of their chiefs. Peacock's plumes for brushing
away the flies from the sleeper lay at the head. I
seized one of these: all my plunder! The sepoys
plundered much, and there was none to stay them.
Napier was everywhere in the thick: if coolness and
command of his faculties merit anything, assuredly
does he *all* that can be bestowed. We took possession of a garden and the left front of the building;
the wall of this I got some sappers to make loops in
for the men to fire through; as your head above was
the signal that you were near 20 matchlocks and
zamburaks.

"Up to this time the fort and city guns had not
annoyed us, not knowing, I fancy, where to fire; but
now they began, and only by sticking close to the
wall could the men remain in safety. The H.A.
(Mackenzie) came up and took up an exposed position
to the left, and opened a heavy fire with their
6-pounders; but they lost many horses and men.
The enemy's entrenchments, fearfully deep and thick,
were scarcely 250 yards from the garden walls; with
the naked eye I could distinguish the men leaning
over to fire their long guns; of these we could quickly
have possessed ourselves, but, unless prepared to
advance and occupy the mound, about 700 yards
in advance, and bursting with metal, we could not
have held them. I suggested to put a couple of

6-pounders in the garden, which was acceded to;
after this I was employed in throwing up an entrench-
ment connecting Mackenzie's guns and the left of the
garden; this space was commanded by their heavy
guns from the parapet and by their zamburaks from
the trenches. A hot, biting fire was kept up on us
all day, to the cost of many; here I remained until
relieved, 6 P.M. I have no idea of our loss, the
amount I mean; it must have been severe. Bodies
were lying thick, and many I saw taken wounded to
the rear. A fine young officer, a great favourite,
Lloyd of the 8th Native Infantry, was cut down by
some villains whom he would not allow his men to
fire on. The party that cut him up represented
themselves as friends, and on approaching the sepoys
said, 'We have no quarrel with you, it's only with
the Sahib-log: leave them and come along, every man
shall have a gold necklace.' Letters were written to
the same effect and thrown amongst the sepoys, who
bayoneted the bearers.

"Braver men than Mulraj's never went out to
battle; they vie with the Europeans. When the
advance parties were outnumbered and cut up, the
rear were strengthening their works below and
sniping above from the parapet. 'Long Tom' has
been wondrously silent of late; the sepoys say he
is 'stiff.' I felt very strongly what poor Willie
(Anderson) said to me once, 'that it was quite an
experiment standing under fire.' I have seen this in
many, many instances — men whose names stand
higher than their merits. I feel quite grateful for the
coolness with which I can face a heavy fire without
dread. We are strange creatures of impulse and
emulation, and often, doubtless, I exposed myself
from seeing others hold back. The firing is a thing
one gets wondrously habituated to, and I can well
understand young soldiers flinching and unsteady,
though, perhaps, the old ones are apt to be cunning.
Europeans properly led will go anywhere—of that,
from observation, I am convinced.

"13*th*.—Nothing particular occurred during last
night or to-day; the enemy affected to make an
attack on our position, but a volley of musketry from
the trenches quickly drove them back home. We

were employed in throwing up batteries and
strengthening our works, to bear on the mound some
600 or 650, and the village to our left about 400 yards
distant. Their zamburaks gave us great annoyance,
and the heavy metal from the Khooni Burj soon
found us out. The workmen in the trenches were in
some cases wounded, and one or two Europeans
killed by round shot. Major Napier received a
severe contusion from the graze of a round-shot on
his knee. I was on duty from noon till 9 P.M.

"14th.—Preparing for duty this morning when
strange information was in circulation. Conferences
were being held, and the authorities congregated at
Major Napier's, the next tent—the General, etc.
Sher Singh had gone over during the night to the
enemy, with his guns, howitzers, and force. I know
not why this should cause great surprise, as his disaffection had been long mooted; nay more, his
followers were slain in arms against us on the 12th;
day by day reports were received that his men were
thronging to Mulraj; further than that even, on the
9th a man from the enemy's camp, whether an
escaped prisoner or spy I know not, stated that an
oath had been sworn on the 8th between the Dewan
and the Raja! This information came from a
Political the day following, yet were they not
'satisfied' of his treachery. He was allowed to
continue on the left of all with his guns, nearest the
fort gate and the point of temptation. Who will
believe such things? Even the night before (13th)
he was in Edwardes' camp; yet with all the suspicions
attached to his conduct, the certainty of his faithless-
ness in the mind of every individual in camp except
the Politicals, he was allowed to take his leave, which
he did by joining Mulraj forthwith.

"The strength of his army may be 5000, with 10
guns and 2 howitzers. From these we had never
derived the slightest aid; to us, therefore, there is no
loss, and it is a question whether such an increase in
aught save the guns can be a *gain* to Mulraj,
beleaguered in a small spot. Efficiency and union
are not promoted by crowds. It may be, nay it must
be, that this retirement is caused by other information
of which we are not yet in possession, the state of the

country alone must have had this effect on the Politicals; yet, if so, all experience tells us, in addition to the criminality of having suffered and sacrificed so much for no purpose, the greatest blunder we could commit in policy is allowing any difficulty time to get a head. If the country is inflammatory, much blood will be shed ere the ill-humour is eradicated; the first remedy would have cost many lives in our little force, but it would have brought honour to all—the fallen, the survivors, and Government; it would have crushed the serpent's head. Now we have kicked the stone, and it may roll far and wide. So much for the want of a leader: the force is weak doubtless, too much so for a systematic attack and to cope with difficulties which our books suggest to us; but not too weak considering the constitution, if led resolutely and wisely. We are weak in artillery officers, weak in guns; 1600 or 1700 Europeans though, and bolder and braver never seen. Nothing can surpass the 10th Foot. The saying runs in camp, with reference to the small force, the train, etc., the means against such a fort: 'A 1st class siege, a 2nd class train, a 3rd class army.' With a general, the army with all its weakness in engineers, is strong enough to have been now *within* the fort walls.

"The 15th was spent in peace till dusk, when silently all tents were struck; the Ramtirat being the only position on our old parallel still held. All night tents were being lowered and kits packed; much difficulty occurred in collecting carriage; no one *exactly knowing* much about it. I lay down amidst the row and confusion on the ground to get as much of a snooze as one could seize. Ritchie came up to join us, hoping to procure *some* slight aid in carriage, for none could he get. I was not a little amused at observing him about midnight putting on a clean shirt to start with, so that, if obliged to leave his traps behind, the dirty not the clean might remain. About 2 our anxieties were at an end, camels arrived: though I had given myself no uneasiness about the matter. I travelled with but two portmanteaus, and told my servants that under the worst they must contrive to remove *one* with clothes.

c

"At 3 A.M., finding that great numbers of camels had gone on, ours marched off. We closed up ourselves with poor Brown in a dooly, where he had been since 7 P.M., to the park: there Napier, Abercrombie, and several more were assembled, packing the few camels that remained with shot and sandbags, of which many were still on the ground. I had contrived to get a mount on an awkward brute—drayhorse stamp—designated by his owner an 'Arab,' and was sent off to the commissariat in search of conveyance for the ordnance. No officer was there—searching, I came upon an oldish fellow with a staff appearance whom I questioned: he told me he was not the man I wanted, but, instead of saying anything with reference to my business, he said—'By the bye, when you see Captain Lloyd (the commissariat officer), tell him the General has gone. I have withdrawn the artillery-guns and troop from the post held for the commissariat, as I don't consider it tenable.' Shortly after I met the commissariat officer, who could not give the carriage for the ordnance as the camels had not yet returned. I then delivered the message I had received from the unknown individual whose appearance I described. The officer forthwith withdrew from the post, leaving much grain and forage, thirty days' supply — thus were arrangements made and carried out. No order of march was given that I heard of, but parties moved off promiscuously as best suited them. Many 18-pounder and shot of larger and smaller size were carried off by Bhawal Khan's sowars in their hands! Thus we contrived to use our allies. As day broke, the enemy were seen in our old trenches, and moving out in some strength, horse and foot, to the S.E. These musters frightened the chivalrous brigadier (who had entrusted me with the order for the commissariat anent its withdrawal) whose force consisted of some 2000 cavalry, a European regiment—the gallant 10th—besides two or more native corps: and though aware that shot was still on the ground and other inferior supplies, he quickly left them to the enemy. Mulraj and Sher Singh were both capering in front with their light guns and some 5000 men; they drew within 800 yards of our flank! The sight of this induced Hervey to retire 'rather than risk! a general action'; these were the words of an officer commanding a brigade of British troops. A swoop might have been made which would have driven the enemy screeching back to their walls.

"After this I pressed on to the leading brigade, and passed through the camp of Cortlandt, Edwardes, and Lake, beyond which I found Europeans and natives, who had left with the baggage during the night, wandering about they knew not whither, without a guide or an officer to direct their march! Europeans thus singly and in files were moving about during the whole of the day. We halted at Cortlandt's tent, where we sat in the shade. Tea and biscuit were brought, and those who wished got a capital breakfast, for all alike were received with kindness. General Cortlandt is a fine-looking man, tall and stout, about thirty-five years old. His dress, like that of all the officers of the irregular troops, is loose, resembling the natives'. He is very dark, with fine features and dark eyes. The expression of his countenance pleasing. His manner particularly easy and conciliatory. His language in conversation good, and his ideas, as far as I have been able to form an opinion during the interviews I have had with him, sensible and clear. He is evidently more than popular with his men, whom he treats with great temper and kindness. His force consists of about 3000 men with several light guns, 12 perhaps. His artillery are remarkably soldierly men—capital shots. They are cool and determined fellows, who would accompany the guns anywhere, and stand by them to the last. Mulraj boasts that some were spared at Sobraon, these of Cortlandt's are of the same breed.

"Edwardes is an intelligent, fair-faced man between twenty-five and thirty years old. Nothing in his appearance to give the impression of daring—or remarkable in any way. I suspect he is a greatly over-rated man—one who had been made by circumstances, and thrust into a position which he lacks ability to fill. *Nous verrons.** My idea is that he has been a *dupe* throughout.

* See pages 122, 125-6, 135, 137, 189, and 231.

"Lake, an engineer officer at the head of Bhawal Khan's forces, is a different man from Edwardes in all respects. Sound without display — one whose *acts* will eventually raise him higher than all the others' flights, imaginary or real. He is very young, about twenty-five.

After the fighting of the 13th September, Multan lay within our grasp; but the defection of Sher Singh caused the siege to be raised on the 14th, and General Whish drew off a few miles to await reinforcements. The whole situation was indeed changed. In August, Chattar Singh had openly raised the standard of revolt, "devoting his head to God and his arms to the Khalsa." In September, with a force of 5000 infantry, 600 cavalry, and 16 guns, he moved towards Peshawar; Sher Singh, soon after rebelling at Multan, set off by forced marches to join him. The news of Sher Singh's defection was received on the 21st September at Peshawar, where the Darbar troops were already perilously excited. The courage, firmness, and energy of Colonel George Lawrence enabled him for a time to stave off the worst; but in the latter part of October the inevitable outbreak occurred, and Colonel Lawrence retired to Kohat, whither he had already sent his wife and family. There he was received by Sardar Sultan Muhammad Khan, Barakzai. Kohat was at that time an appendage of Kabul, and Sultan Muhammad had been the last Afghan governor of Peshawar before Ranjit Singh conquered the province in 1822. Chattar Singh entered Peshawar on the 31st October; he promised to make over the province to Sultan Muhammad, provided that the latter would surrender Colonel Lawrence, and the other British officers who were at Kohat. This Sultan Muhammad faithlessly did, and Colonel Lawrence found himself, with several other British officers, a prisoner in the hands of the Sikhs.

Directly the siege was raised, Daly hurried back to Karachi to rejoin his regiment, which formed part of the reinforcing column from Bombay. This column under Colonel the Honourable H. Dundas, C.B., 60th Rifles, had reached General Whish by the 22nd December, and the siege was resumed on the 27th December. Sir Henry Lawrence reached Multan from England on the 28th. The loss in General Whish's force up to this time had been 17 British officers and 238 of other ranks killed and wounded. The force at the renewed siege included the 10th and 32nd Regiments, the 60th Rifles, and 1st Bombay European Fusiliers, with five companies of European foot artillery : the total was over 15,500 men of all ranks; the irregular forces were, however, much weaker. Daly served through the final siege as Adjutant of the 1st Bombay Fusiliers, better known in those days by the soubriquet of the "Old Toughs." His work during the earlier period had elicited the following letter :—

"Camp before Multan, 17th September 1848.

"Sir,—I beg to convey to you this sense of my obligation for the zeal shown by you during the last few days' operations in the manner wherein you observed the enemy's position, and for your indefatigable observation of him, and recommendation of measures to counteract his designs.—I have, etc.,
R. Napier, *Major,*
Chief Engineer, Multan Field Force."

Daly's diary is continued :—

"*Camp Multan, Christmas Day,* 1848.—Orders were issued this day for the march of the Bombay

Column from its present position at Suruj-kund to Sital-ke-Mari, where the Bengal Column moved this morning. This is the position Whish occupied during the previous operations. Our camp was accordingly struck on the morning of the 26th, and every preparation made for a start; however, what with the delay in moving the commissariat, we did not quit our ground till near noon. Tents were down, and there we lay basking in the sun for the last camel to go, as we were to bring up the rear. On reaching Sital-ke-Mari I observed the General's tent in exactly the same spot as before, though the camp on this occasion fronted the fort, whereas formerly it showed a rear. We (the Bombay Column) were on the left. The first thing which struck me was the altered appearance of the face of the country between us and the fort. This latter formerly was scarcely visible at all; high as its towers are, these were almost screened by the numerous trees, thick and dark with foliage. Much of this change has, doubtless, been occasioned by the cold season withering the leaves and luxuriance; more by the hands of the Sikhs, who have been hewing and hacking the woods, and clearing the jungle of that which was a defence to them and the source of much annoyance to us. The fort and part of the town even are now clear to view; with the glass this afternoon I could see them working and entrenching themselves on the 'Mound,' which was to have been our prize on the 14th September, and beneath which we lay on the 12th September casting longing, anxious looks at its occupants. The orders of to-night are that the Bombay Force will parade in two columns at 11 A.M. to-morrow in front of the lines. The purpose for which this was to be was not known, it being merely said 'for service.'

"On the morning of the 27th, Colonel Dundas appeared, and then told us that our columns * would be under his own immediate command, as he intended being with us during the day, and that the object of the combined attack was that one column, composed

* Two squadrons cavalry, battering guns, two 9-pounder batteries, five companies 60th Rifles, 3rd Regiment Bombay Native Infantry, five companies Fusiliers, 4th Bombay Native Infantry (Rifles).

of 60th, 3rd, and under Colonel Capon, should attack, and, if possible, carry the 'Mound'; if any great resistance should be encountered, then to clear the places below. During this the Bengal Column was to attack the 'Idgah,' * and occupy a hill adjacent, and the possession of these were *the points* necessary for the effectual carrying on of the siege. Our column was to advance making a feint on *Sidi Lal ke Bede,* a high conical hill which the enemy held in some strength; our guns were to batter at this at a great pace, and should our attack assume a cheerful and successful aspect, the feint was to be made earnest and we were to go on.

"After this explanation of what was intended, we moved off: on arriving within about 200 yards of the trench made during last operations, two companies of the 4th Rifles were thrown out as skirmishers, we following in support of the Rifles. The enemy were now seen in some strength, retiring to high positions from which they commenced a distant fire. A couple of 9-pounders were brought up and opened on the hill and city walls, from which a few round shot began to drop; during this we took cover under the trench for a few moments. Colonel Dundas then ordered us to advance in line—this we continued to do for some distance, without firing a shot, the enemy slowly retiring before us, firing a good deal with but little effect up to this time. Thus we continued and the Sidi Lal ke Bede was crowned and won; on descending this the ground became broken and irregular, intersected with ravines. About 300 yards to our front and left were some buildings, from which a hottish fire was peppered down on us, and 3 or 4 men wounded, 1 killed. We cleared the front building and took cover under its walls and behind a mound as well as we could, the companies being formed up as the ground would admit of. During this a very annoying fire was opened on us by matchlock men, who occupied a row of buildings, houses, and gardens which ran along in front, leaving an open space of ground between us and them. The two supports of the Rifle skirmishers had halted to

* See page 17.

our right and rear. Finding many huts and walls to our left occupied, a sub-division was sent to clear them out; this was speedily done without loss to us.

"We had been here but a few minutes when the 4th skirmishers came clattering back closely and fiercely pursued by the enemy, who, with their long, sharp sabres were cutting at the riflemen until they threw themselves into the midst of us. Emboldened by this, the Sikhs began to throng the walls and gardens ahead, and many actually rushed up and sheltered themseves behind the very building on the opposite side of which we were! The wall to the left of our cover was low and broken; the rush was so sudden that much confusion ensued, and, as at this time there was no opportunity or space to form, I cried out to No. 10 (which was nearest) to 'Charge' —well they responded to the cry—Mules and I, Hitchcock, the lance-corporal, between us, and Nelson, a private of 10 company, were the first amongst the foe, who were crouched beneath the wall we sprang over! Up they jumped, and plied their bright sabres about their heads in gallant style, but the bayonet—that true weapon the bayonet, which never yet failed to bring success to the British soldier—was more than a match for the sword and matchlock. The first Sikh who bit the dust either bowed to my sword or Hitchcock's bayonet; this latter was borne through the chest of a tall, dark fellow, whose eye was glistening anxiously towards Mules, who, in rushing to meet the Sikh, stumbled, and so, by the bending of his body, escaped the blow aimed at his head. Poor Nelson, on my right hand, was fearfully, frightfully mauled and hacked by two slashing sword blows from a Sikh who never made a third.

"After this struggle hand-to-hand beneath the wall, they rushed back to their cover hotly pursued by No. 10, for when space was given, the other sub-division with King eagerly came to our aid. We charged across, and with our bayonets and cheers cleared the houses in front and then rejoined the main body. We had been back scarce five minutes when the dark faces and long matchlock barrels were seen amidst the same buildings from which we had just driven them. Without allowing them time to reassemble and occupy these places in great number (for shots already began to fall hotly), away we charged across the open space at them with Nos. 9 and 10, this time in our eagerness we drove them right through into the plain beyond, from which the city walls, distant perhaps 200 yards, were clear to view, nothing being between them and us but the Sikhs. This was the first idea we had of our position. A round shot or two from the ramparts quickly cleared our notions.

"Once again under shelter of the walls from behind which we had driven them, I sounded 'the Assembly,' for our little charging band amidst the narrow lanes chasing the enemy had become greatly scattered; twice the bugler blew his blast, and then we returned to the regiment. We were now able to explain our position, none of us being before aware that the town walls were so nigh. While debating on these points, orders were delivered by a staff officer for us to fall back and take cover under a garden wall. We imagined that this would not be effected without annoyance from the enemy, who had twice bearded us in our stronghold. The precautions we adopted were not called into play. The two bayonet charges and the slaughter we had then dealt gave them matter for deliberate reflection; not a Sikh pursued or was seen, and scarce was a matchlock turned toward us. Colonel Dundas, who was here, directed us to move on the right, sheltering ourselves under the high ground and irregular walls. The enemy soon began to pepper on us with their zamburaks and matchlocks, and the guns from the city walls dropped their messengers somewhat thick —the fire from the buildings and suburbs about we kept down tolerably well with our musketry, whenever an enemy was to be seen. The artillery from the Sidi Lal ke Bede (a high, coning hill about 150 paces to our rear) during this time opened a heavy cannonade over our heads on the city and fort, both of which were clearly discernible. The city walls could scarce have been more distant than 450 yards.

"Thus we remained till between 3 to 4 P.M., when to our surprise Leith marched down with the right wing (rather two companies) and took up a sheltered position to our left. At 4 a report was sent from the battery at Sidi Lal that the enemy were occupying the houses and walls to our right in strength, and apprehensions were expressed lest they should out-flank us, getting between the 60th left and ourselves. The Colonel then directed these places to be cleared, if necessary at the point of the bayonet, and an attempt made to open communication with the right of the 60th. Accordingly two companies were detached, 9 and 10, Woodward, May, Mules, King, Disbrowe, and myself. We marched off in sections, taking all the advantage the ground afforded, in a direct line to the right for about 400 yards, when, from some houses about 200 yards on our left, the enemy were seen in position in a nulla which ran along their front. The sections were wheeled round and a sharp fire immediately opened from the Sikhs.

"We continued to advance, and when within 100 yards the files were extended, orders given 'No man to fire,' but all forward at a steady double, leaving all to the bayonet. Many a red-coated Sikh was visible, but, after the first volley had been poured on us, the shots were irregular; the matchlock is not quickly loaded. Our cheer and double, despite the fall of two poor fellows in the leading section, evidently occasioned a sensation. We saw them dodging about the streets in numbers, firing, then bolting. So on we went; now a volley succeeded by a cheer and a charge. Every place was cleared. The doors were broken open, but no injury inflicted on those not bearing arms. Thus we went through what was almost a town in itself—random shots were fired on us from the corners, we 'doubled through,' and, on reaching the end of the street, to our amazement, the grim, fortified walls with their embrasures were gaping down on us! A clear square spot between us and them, a rendezvous it appeared for the townsmen in days of peace to ramble and breathe outside their fortification. We quickly withdrew under shelter of the building we had quitted, which protected us from the sight of the wall tenants. Our appearance outside was so sudden and unexpected that we met with no hail from their cannon.

"We pursued our course parallel to the wall, driving the Sikhs before us wherever they made a stand, still seeking the 60th left position. It was about here that a good many zamburak balls fell amongst us, one of which carried off the fleshy part of a man's heel in the midst of his section, and then with a ricochet struck my horse in the outer side of his chest, the ball passing out at the off side. He bled much, yet held his head up gallantly. Immediately after this escapade we espied some dark objects in a corner in our front; they were under cover of a building. We conjectured this must be the 60th detachment; the bugler sounded our call, which was quickly responded to, so our purpose was gained. We halted under a wall while with a couple of men I ran across to hail them. It was Clapcott of the 60th with his company, in a place not far distant from the 'Khooni Burj' Bastion. In the position they occupied they were secure from its fire. From him I heard of the success which had attended the 60th advance in the morning. They had carried the 'Mundee Awa' Mound, and Clapcott's post was now between it and the city wall. He told me of the gallant Major Gordon's fall. He was shot dead. A more chivalrous soldier and high-minded gentleman the British army never at any time numbered in its ranks. I had a peculiar opportunity of seeing his bearing during the operations of the 12th September, when he was here as an amateur, and amongst many brave and noble officers he was remarkable. Our small party of the *Napier* has lost its chosen; Brown by disease, Gordon in the field.

"Well—I rejoined my friends, and as darkness was drawing on and our object attained, we turned our steps back to the column, which we rejoined comfortably enough. Orders had been received for the regiment to fall back and occupy the Sidi Lal, protecting the guns and as much of the ground as we could between us and the 60th. Accordingly there we lay, Fusiliers, 19th, and Rifles; and a cold, raw bivouac it was, without coats or dinners. Success, however, had wondrously sweetened our tempers, and we were proof against all miseries. The behaviour of the men during these privations was beautiful, not a syllable of discontent was uttered. The contents of many haversacks were joyfully proffered to the officers, who had come unprovided. During the night, owing to the kindly arrangements of the commissariat, every man got his dram and his biscuit. The 19th and 4th were on our left. Colonel Dundas, no carpet leader, remained with us. We received a few shots, big and little, but no damage was done us.

"Daybreak was anxiously looked for by all. As it drew nigh, the cold for lightly clad men became piercing. The first order we received was to prepare to advance, as the town was to be stormed by escalade—another order, more pleasing under the circumstances, considering that we had been fighting all day previous, and suffering from cold, exposure, and hunger during the night, was to march the left wing to quarters. The whole of the right, having assembled at the hill during the night, was to stand fast, while we repaired back to our tents to refresh ourselves, and in no light estimation was this move held by us—our return of casualties since quitting on the previous morning, 3 killed and 29 wounded, being, I believe, far heavier than happened to any other corps engaged. The officers luckily escaped uninjured, Mules had his back scraped and I my hat cut off by a sword blow.

"29th.—Three companies marched down with the Major and myself to the mound Mundee Awa. These were distributed about, one being near the Delhi Gate, and a second near the Khooni Burj: in both places the batteries were in hard play at the walls, for the breaches were here to be made for the storming parties; during the afternoon the Major and I received orders to return to camp, as commanding officers and their staff were not to proceed to the works unless ordered to with their whole regiments."

The assault on the city was delivered on the afternoon of the 2nd January 1849. The attack on the main breach of the "Bloody Bastion" (Khooni Burj) was led by the Bombay Fusiliers.

THE 1ST BOMBAY EUROPEAN FUSILIERS STORMING THE BREACH AT THE KHOONI BURJ, MULTAN.

(Jan, 2nd, 1849, 3 P.M.)

[To face p. 44.

Daly wrote the following account :—

"On the morning of the 2nd January I was at Colonel Stalker's tent when Tapp galloped down with the order that the arrangements which had been made on the previous day for the storm of the city were to hold good for this day. Accordingly plans of the town were issued showing the streets the different columns of attack were to follow and positions which were to be occupied after the carrying and the passage of the breach. At 1 o'clock the regiment paraded in front of the camp. Every man was burning with eagerness for the assault, and many were seen in the ranks who should have been in hospital. Brigadier Stalker here joined us and we moved off, the 19th and 4th following us. On reaching the Mundee Awa mound a few round shot from the fort fell about us without doing much damage ; great indeed was our good fortune in reaching the place of formation preparatory to the storm without incurring any loss. I had not expected this. We were drawn up behind a large mound ; the road which led to the Khooni Burj and round the city was close to our right hand. The Fusiliers here formed in a column of sub-divisions right in front ; the 19th Native Infantry next, and the Rifles in rear. The engineer at the battery was to give the signal for the advance. At a few minutes before 3 a salvo was fired from the battery ; 'Forward' to the column was immediately given. The road to the breach was a winding one, broad enough for 18 men to march along. Leith, who commanded the right flank company, a fine, noble-looking soldier about 6 ft. 4 high, filed out into the highway and marched steadily off to the spot. No. 2 followed at about twenty paces interval ; 3, 4, 5 close on. Then again thirty paces and the left wing, with the colours of the old regiment flaunting in the wind. There was not so much firing down on us as we had expected.

"The breach was to our right of the Burj, a high tower and bastion on which formerly they had some heavy guns. The tower, though much shattered without, from being stockaded with thick timber and mud inside, was still a secure place of shelter for the enemy, and was occupied in strength. I can give you no accurate description of the breach we mounted. It was steep, and broken brick and mouldered dust gave beneath the feet, reminding me of the ascent of Vesuvius. We did not climb this unmolested; thick and hot the balls fell amongst us, but not a man was killed and strangely few wounded. When Leith crowned the height a volley from below was discharged, but they were too eager to fire and it passed overhead. Leith doubled down at the charge. On the town side of the breach they had dug a deep trench at the bottom; this was stockaded and covered over with planks and mattings. From this place they sprang up as Leith put his foot down to cross, and dozens of bright sabres were in the air. Few shots were fired on our side; both parties relied on the steel. Leith's long cavalry sword, such as no one but a stout man could wield, was smashed to pieces near the hilt. He himself received a couple of terrible sword cuts on his left arm and a ball through his right shoulder, and was taken to the rear.

"The regiment was now crowding forward under a heavy fire from the houses and Burj. On, on we poured, but for a quarter of an hour not 50 yards were won. Every narrow street was filled with matchlock men who, having discharged their pieces, resorted to the sword. Here many were wounded. A 9-pounder was taken in one of these narrow passages which was pointed down on us, though fortunately its too early discharge saved us from a terrible massacre. Here it became a hand-to-hand encounter. Tapp, who had come well to the front, about this time received wounds which disabled him for the day. Two other officers were also wounded here. The streets were so narrow and numerous and the resistance had been so determined, the enemy appearing on all sides, that it was found impossible to follow out the roads as detailed on the plan. Had the enemy taken the roads we wished, all would have been plain; no such feeling of sympathy did they display. I know these Sikhs well. I have had a good deal of experience of their mode of fighting. When they *do* turn, no breathing space should be allowed them. Any hesitation or pause on our side and again they rally, and forward they rush to the attack. The column which had been told off for the left was the headquarters of the corps, which the left wing and colours followed ; but all the companies were so broken up in the medley contest which had taken place, that amidst the din and smoke scarcely anything was discernible.

"When we came out to a somewhat clear space our party with the colours was indeed small. Joyful I felt at seeing Mules with a few others burst round the corner. I gave a cheer, which was gallantly taken up, and forward at the double we went, 120 men and about 8 officers. Now we pursued the best course I could remember from the plan ; but few of the enemy were to be seen except at angles and corners, where they occasionally frantically attacked us. The Brigadier was now with us. He in no way interfered, merely cheering us on by his voice and presence. On arriving at the centre of the town, a large square with a lofty masjid, the enemy were in strength, apparently resolved to make a stand. We fired a volley—a cheer, and our true friend the bayonet carried us triumphantly through. Here we halted for a few minutes, for the men were almost exhausted by their exertions. I blew the 'Advance' to deceive the enemy, and all of us pulled away at the contents of a few small canteens. Our little band then rushed forth, cheering as we advanced, and from one square building, occupied by a strong cavalry picquet, we drove them at the bayonet's point. I there cut down with my sword a couple of handsome standards, which we bore away with us. So we advanced towards the end of the city, not knowing whither. Our guides had been either killed or separated from us during the confusion. At last I seized a tall fellow, drew him from a house to lead us to the Lahore Gate. To our surprise he said, 'You are very near now ; this is the road to it.'

"A few yards further the rampart and clear country beyond opened to our view. A great cheer we gave. Mules and I, followed by a few men, rushed to the rampart ; between the end of the street and the rampart, which circled round the foot wall, was a hollow space with nothing but a few stables in it. The rampart was wide, this was the main rampart, which ran round the city. Here were at least 500 with sword and matchlock; some occupied the buildings to the left of the street's end, but the main body were out towards the fort. At first they began to disappear over the walls. Mules and I, thinking to secure the gate on the opposite side, were quickly brought to a sense of our position. Some of them came dashing forward towards us, and two fell on the bayonets of men at our side. The fort walls were alive with matchlocks, and their heavy guns had but to be depressed to command the spot. They were not long in observing this. One large-mouthed cannon blustered forth, but happily fell between us without doing any ill. Mules and I got back under cover, a sharp fire of matchlocks opened on us from the rampart, but generally too high; 3 of our little party were wounded and 1 shot dead.

"After a consultation with the Colonel, it was decided to leave 2 officers and 50 men to hold this passage, while we, in obedience to instructions, were to possess ourselves of the rampart and the Bohur and Pak Hurrun Gates. This done, we returned on our course, but that road which was so clear on the plan we found intricate. Passages and streets so narrow as not to admit of more than 3 or 4 men abreast. The fire as we approached the ramparts and from walls and loopholes was very annoying, and in one spot, midway between the Bohur and Lahore Gates, the resistance was such that we were obliged to take shelter in a temple to allow the men to recruit themselves. When we became a little refreshed, I took them out by another door from that we had entered and so contrived to outflank them. I seized two guides and made them march on, under threat of my sword bearing down on doubts of treachery. They led us on, but scarcely had we proceeded 200 yards, when again from what we afterwards found to be a barrack the fire was heavy. Both guides were shot and fell in front of me, one I think we left on the spot; but I cried out to charge up the hill; bravely they answered, up we dashed and gained the rampart above the gate. A 9-pounder was placed commanding one street by which they had expected us to appear. We poured a volley on them standing by it, and then forward at the bayonet, captured and spiked the gun.

"Further up we observed them in some strength; we poured volleys from under cover of the rising ground. Had they been aware of the weakness of our little band, not so easily would they have quitted their position. We at once, as night was drawing in, past five and a half, began to look to our position for the night, and distributed our little party into three bands; the worst was our ammunition, which was almost expended. While making these arrangements, Colonel Cheyne, the chief engineer, came up and expressed great satisfaction on hearing we had traversed the city and left a party at the Lahore Gate. We learnt from him that the regiment was about the city in companies, and now the great point was to hold these gates, the Bohur and the Lahore. Major Horner, 4th Rifles, with a large body of his men, joined about 6—and glad we were to see them; they had followed us. So strengthened, we sent a guard for ammunition, coats, and grog to the breach, about a mile distant, but there was no apprehension of any enemy between us and that Burj; we had well cleared this interval. Soon after dark the quarter-master sergeant, with arrack and coats for the men, appeared to our joy. I got a coat. By and by came the messman's servant with eatables. The night was passing in peace up to midnight and we were congratulating ourselves on our rest after the day's work; the poor wounded were well covered from the cold, but no opportunity occurred to remove them before daylight.

"About 1 A.M. a most fearful event occurred. While we were lying down near the wall, a trembling of the earth, followed instantaneously by flames and fire all round. Bricks falling, houses tottering, roofs off. All was darkness, save where lurid flames were rising amongst us. We cried out to the men to stand to their arms, and remain as steady as the convulsed state of the ground would permit them. Long, awfully long, it appeared ere even the worst passed away. When it had done so, the cries of many sufferers arose on every side. We could not in the

D

darkness see the havoc which had been committed, but in many places the fire which had caught pieces of wood still burned, and by its light a part of the ruin could be seen ; 60 Sappers (native) had been employed at the time of the outburst in opening the Gate, which had been stockaded and closed up with heavy timber beneath the archway ; 35 of these were buried alive, many others escaped with their lives indeed, but with limbs desperately damaged. The 4th Rifles also were among the unfortunates ; 10 of these poor fellows were killed and some 30 or more wounded. A few of the 19th Native Infantry with us were also among the victims. Strange that every officer escaped with no more serious damage than a blow from falling stone. Much of our ammunition, which was in boxes, continued to explode at various times. Close by the place, the next house, we knew to be a magazine well filled with powder ; and great were our apprehensions lest this catch a spark. It did not. The cause no one of us to this hour knows, whether a mine or powder (much of which was about in all places) ignited accidentally by the light and fires made by our sepoys. Many fancy a mine. I incline to the opinion that it was something of the kind ; probably a magazine accidentally fired by us.

"At 7 A.M. we marched off towards the Lahore Gate, and made perambulations through the town, which we found to be entirely our own. The coldest time I ever spent was in the bastion at the Bohur Gate. How our poor fellows so escaped was miraculous. The wounded too were just without its influence. The time we passed till daybreak was fearful, in momentary expectation of the great magazine, yet not daring to quit our position. As we marched to the Gate in the morning we saw some of the wretched sappers with their heads just visible above the ruins. We were relieved at 2, and marched into our tents. The Brigadier came with us. Before breaking off, he said one word of thanks to the men for their devoted gallantry,* to which they responded

---

* The colours were planted on the breach by Colour-Sergeant J. Bennett, of the "Old Toughs" (1st Bombay Fusiliers), who was thus mentioned in despatches by General Whish : " I would also bring to

with three cheers for the Brigadier, three cheers for the Commanding Officer, and three cheers for the Adjutant [Daly]. So ended the day which Sir Charles Napier prophesied would come 'when you will renovate your ancient fame.' In all, of the regi-

notice the conduct of Colour-Sergeant J. Bennett, 1st Fusiliers, who volunteered to accompany the storming party, and, rushing up the breach, planted the Union Jack on its crest, standing beside it until the whole Brigade had passed. The column and staff are riddled with balls." Sergeant Bennett subsequently received the following characteristic letter :—

"CALCUTTA, 20th May 1849.

"SERGEANT-MAJOR BENNETT,

"When in 1847 I presented the Fusiliers with their new colours, I said that the men of our days were as good as those of former days. I was right ; and Multan has proved every word! In former times Sergeant-Major Graham (if my memory serves me correctly) of the 1st Europeans, planted the old colours on the breach of Ahmedabad. He did a gallant action, and when you planted the British Standard on the breach of Multan, your deed was as brave as his, and is as renowned !

"The officers, non-commissioned officers, and privates of the 1st Europeans in both Presidencies have sustained, and even, if possible, surpassed by their valour in the present days, the glories of the past. Tell your comrades that I rejoiced when I heard the fame which you have all gained for those new colours that I had the honour of present-ing to the regiment in Scinde.

"I remain your sincere friend and well-wisher,

"C. J. NAPIER,
"Commander-in-Chief."

"P.S.—I should have written to you long ago, but delayed till my arrival in India."

In publishing this letter the Bombay Times wrote (16th August 1849) :—"It was the breach at Seringapatam, not Ahmedabad, that Sergeant Graham was the first to mount, though it was a Sergeant of the 'Old Toughs' who planted the colours on the walls of Ahmedabad. The coincidence is striking enough assuredly, but Sir C. Napier seems only aware of one half of it. Major Mignon, who led the Fusiliers up the breach at Multan, is the son of Colonel Mignon, who, exactly half a century ago, led the flank companies of the Bombay Army at the storming of Seringapatam." In January 1850, Sir Charles Napier met the regiment on the march at Pakka Serai, and made them another stirring speech :—"Soldiers of the 1st Bombay European Fusiliers ! When I last addressed you some three years since in pre-senting to you these splendid colours at Karachi," etc.

ment 6 were killed, 66 wounded, many never to rise again, and 5 officers, since marching out on the previous day."

The citadel still held out, and was on the point of being stormed when, on the 22nd, Mulraj, whose force was still from 3000 to 4000 men, surrendered unconditionally. The final siege thus lasted twenty-seven days; the British loss was 210 killed and 982 wounded: upwards of 13,000 shot and 26,000 shell had been fired into the city and fort. Daly was mentioned in despatches as "conspicuous for gallantry" both in the fighting of the 27th December and in the storm.

"The besieging army * did not march away to other fields without performing its last melancholy duty to the memory of Agnew and Anderson. The bodies of these officers were carefully—I may say affectionately—removed from the careless grave where they lay side by side, and, wrapped in Cashmere shawls (with a vain but natural desire to obliterate all traces of neglect), were borne by the soldiers of the 1st Bombay Fusiliers (Anderson's own regiment) to an honoured resting-place on the summit of Mulraj's citadel. By what way borne? Through the gate where they had been first assaulted! Oh, no! Through the broad and sloping breach which had been made by the British guns in the walls of the rebellious fortress of Multan."

* From *A Year on the Punjab Frontier in* 1848-49, by Herbert Edwardes, vol. ii., p. 708.

CHAPTER III

GUJERAT AND PESHAWAR

General course of the campaign ; battle of Gujerat ; pursuit of the Sikhs ; their surrender ; pursuit of the Afghans and occupation of Peshawar. Appointment of Sir C. Napier as Commander-in-Chief ; offers of staff employ in Bombay and the Punjab ; decision for the latter.

IN the meantime a great British army had been assembled at Ferozpur to put down the insurrection, which had now spread to the whole of the Punjab. This force entered Lahore shortly before the middle of November 1848, and was joined on the 21st November by Lord Gough, the Commander-in-Chief. On the 22nd November he gained the indecisive victory of Ramnugger. On the 10th January 1849, he was joined by Sir Henry Lawrence, who, hurrying out from England, had reached Multan just after Christmas, and had pressed on to join the main army directly after the successful assault of the 2nd January. On the 13th January 1849, was fought the bloody battle of Chillianwallah, in which Lord Gough's losses were terribly severe.

Immediately after Mulraj had surrendered, reinforcements were pushed forward to the field army. On the 19th February the 60th Rifles, 1st Bombay Fusiliers, and the 32nd Bombay Infantry reached

Gujerat. In the crowning victory of the 21st they formed the extreme left of our line. On the 22nd the Bombay troops accompanied General Gilbert's division in his pursuit of the Sikhs and Afghans, and marched 25 miles "in appalling heat and with no water." On the 28th February they were over the Jhelum. On the 8th March George Lawrence, with his wife and children, and the other prisoners were brought in, safe and sound, to Gilbert's camp. Negotiations followed for a general surrender of the Sikhs. Daly gives the following account of the event :—

"*9th March* (1849).—The Sher came himself, but Gilbert told him he must go back and make his people lay down their arms and deliver up their guns. The Sher went back to his camp last night with this message. They are close here, so the fighting, I fancy, is over. I had a long talk with a fine, soldierly-looking old man who had been a colonel in Ranjit Singh's time. He was one of the many Sikhs who went over to Sher Singh and forsook our people at Attock. He was particularly intelligent, very friendly and frank ; deplored the state of the country and their own impoverished condition, contrasting it with what they held in the Maharaja's day. He at once admitted having joined Sher Singh in the hope of restoring the falling time. Nobody knows (amongst us) what our destination is to be. Marching *day by day* is our present occupation.

"*12th, near Rawal Pindi.*—The events of yester-day and to-day are bringing the campaign to a close. Our march yesterday to this place was through a mountainous tract and ravines, which made the moving of guns and infantry a work of time and difficulty. Our ground here is in a lovely valley, smiling with green cornfields ; villages are sprinkled about by the sides of the hills. In front of our camp (we, the Bombay troops, are on the left) is a brawling river, now shallow ; from its opposite bank a mountain abruptly rises. Shortly after our arrival yesterday, we observed a number of horsemen on its brow. About an hour elapsed when a body of our irregular cavalry moved down to the left and mouth of the *debouché* from the mountain, and in a few minutes returned accompanied by several native horsemen. These were Sher Singh and his father with some of the chiefs. Father and son rode side by side. The Sher's face is of an oval form; his eyes dark and deep-set; a black beard surrounds all. The countenance is expressive of determination and devilry, for there's something peculiarly sinister about it. There's but little of dignity in his appearance, nothing of the Sikh; yet there is much about his general look which an ordinary man lacks. There's nothing of the ease-loving, luxurious Eastern. The father's features are fine; he looks a noble. He appeared sorrowful and worn, his head was almost concealed. Not so the son, who keenly eyed the soldiers who thronged the banks to see them pass. The Sher even tapped his forehead and salaamed to them. They were both well-mounted. By nightfall 17 guns had been brought into camp. Their horse artillery were well turned out. Some had as many as eight horses, others six in each gun; every horse a rider. The harness appointments bore traces of having been good. The artillerymen were well dressed too, although somewhat worn. Two of our guns which were lost at Chillianwallah were amongst those given up. These surrender days are days of storms. I told you of the wetting we all got when Mulraj surrendered. Well, yesterday, during the march the rain fell at various times, but towards night a fearful storm burst forth. Lightning so vivid that the whole camp was enveloped in a sheet of flame; thunder resounded through the mountains, and the rain fell in great torrents. I have witnessed some strange events during the last two months. Not the least seeing two armies lay down their arms, and this last came back from a distance to submit. This must be a blow to them; the feeling which brought them to such an act is utter helplessness. They say, 'What could we do? Dost Muhammad, now that disaster has befallen us, would give us up!'

"15th.—As we marched to this spot, Rawal

Pindi, yesterday, we saw the Sikh guns placed in regular order at the top of the pass. They were 32 in number, with 3 mortars and a howitzer. Many of the pieces were far larger in calibre than we had anticipated, several beautiful brass 18-pounders being among them. Two of our lost guns paraded with them. On our arrival here we found, I should say, 10,000 Sikh horsemen. They formed up and rode by by twos and threes, every man depositing his arms as he passed. Before night a mass of matchlocks, firelocks, swords, shields, and spears was collected, covering 20 square yards, and rising 8 or 10 feet high. A similar deposit took place at our yesterday's ground. Every fellow after thus laying down his arms is allowed to go free; poor devils, they seem starved. I must tell you that we pay every one a rupee. They are allowed to carry off their horses. These they will sell for anything. Mares, and very fine ones, I've seen; not many good nags for our purposes. I think we have made a great mistake in allowing this. Doubtless many of these horses were stolen from villages and towns. Moreover, we give them the means of moving off too easily; though they are abject and broken even to starvation, still I incline to the opinion that dismounting them would have been wise. What to do with the cattle would puzzle us perhaps.

"16*th* (*March* 1849).—We marched 14 miles this morning, moving parallel with the range of mountains, which are only 4 or 5 miles on our right. There was snow on their tops a few days since; they are scarcely higher than 1200 or 1300 feet. The climate is deliciously fresh and pleasant; the ground we passed over to-day was covered with dandelions and a kind of heath, bearing a purple flower, which perfumed the air with its sweetness. The flowers and plants are European; the wild geranium I picked; a few days more and we shall be in the land of violets. The peach and apple trees at Rawal Pindi were in blossom. Many Grecian coins, copper and silver, were in the bazaar. Hercules shone on most of them under divers representations. We are now but four marches from Attcok and some eight from Peshawar."

It was on Peshawar that the Afghans * were retiring, and strenuous efforts were made to come up with them.   Starting again on the night of the 16th, the column did 36 miles more without a halt. Another forced march of 31 miles brought them to the bridge of boats over the Indus.   The rear of the Afghans was in the act of crossing when Gilbert's cavalry arrived.   The Afghans at once broke the bridge, but sufficient boats were secured to restore communication.   On the 19th the force crossed the Indus, and on the 21st they marched 28 miles into Peshawar, whence the Afghans, two days before, had hurriedly withdrawn.   This ended the campaign. On the 30th March was issued the Proclamation which incorporated the Punjab in British India.

On the 23rd April 1849, Daly wrote from Peshawar :—

" The express announcing the appointment of Sir Charles Napier by *the nation en masse* reached us yesterday.   Verily the people at home seem panic-struck.   Some reason, doubtless, for change in the Chief there was, but it was as strong before as after Chillian.   Every battle in which the brave old lord has been the leader has been a scene of carnage†

---

* 1500 Afghan horse, under Akram Khan, son of the Amir Dost Muhammad Khan, had fought against us at Gujerat.

† Compare what Sir Henry Lawrence wrote in 1847, after the first Sikh War, in his essay on Lord Hardinge's Indian Administration :—" Too much has been said of the casualties during these battles, and we have only to look to the returns of the Peninsular War, or to those of Assaye, Argaum, Laswari, Delhi, Mehidpur, and Maharajpur, to find that the loss in former campaigns averaged at least as much as that of the Sikh battles, and generally—indeed in India always—from the same cause, the enemy's artillery.   It must ever be so.   Assaults are not to be made on positions bristling with heavy guns without loss ; and if more cautious measures, involving delay, might, in the first instance save some lives, it must also be borne in mind that such delays tend to give confidence to the enemy,

and slaughter from China to India; read of his victories won by his troops in spite of his blunders. Yet one feels for the sorrow which this act of Government will entail upon him. It will carry him down with grief and shame to his grave. Those who left him in such a position as to assemble and lead the Grand Army of the Punjab, on them be the blood of his confused battles. Sir Charles's arrival I hail, you may be assured, with delight.

"Now I will explain to you the position in which I am placed. A few days since I received a short note from Major Napier, dated Lahore, to this effect :—'How should you like to be second in command of one of the Contingent Corps to be raised in the Punjab? I have mentioned your name to the Resident (Sir H. Lawrence), and you are nominated to the appointment, which I hope will meet your views. The corps will be stationed at Peshawar.' Now only once have I seen Napier since we left Multan, and that but for a moment as we crossed the Jhelum. I never spoke to him of appointment or expected such from him, so you may be assured such a kindly remembrance was most pleasing. I replied thanking him, and, as he evinced so much interest in me, I mentioned plainly that I accepted the appointment gratefully as an opening to some position whereby one might eventually rise. That a second in command, though a proud position, was not what I looked to as a finale.

"Well, now comes the puzzle. The day before yesterday came the letter from the Adjutant-General,

who, on the other hand, promptly confronted and well beaten in a hand-to-hand fight, seldom renews the conflict,—deeds which at first sight may appear brutal and sanguinary, in the end may actually save life.

.   .   .   .

Our tale is that of the Governor-General, and our narrative must constantly keep him in sight ; but we should not for a moment imply that the Commander-in-Chief did not throughout the day (Ferozeshah) do all that a soldier could do.

Never, indeed, on India's fertile field of glory fought a braver spirit than Lord Gough, and we believe that no British general in the East ever won so many battles." (Page 298 of *Essays, Military and Political*, by Sir H. M. Lawrence.)

of which I send a copy. Now the advantages of
this latter are these. Young in the service and
placed on the door of the Adjutant-General's department unsolicited for service, so that one's rise in the
line would be certain, and in time to come I might
aspire to be Adjutant-General. Honours always
await him. Conferred on me in the manner the
appointment is, it would almost ensure active employment should an opportunity occur. Service is,
however, not likely to occur for many a year, so far
as one can judge.

"Now for the other; this morning I called on
Major George Lawrence (the brother of Sir Henry)
who had been prepared for an interview on the subject
by my friend Major Blood, an old schoolfellow and
Kabul ally of his. The Major said, 'I know what
you are come about. Speak freely your views and
wishes.' I did most plainly. I told him that the
advantages of both were so thoroughly appreciated
by me that the difficulties were rendered heavier by
this feeling—that I was choosing *my way in life.*
Once here, I must turn my soul to the one grand
object 'Advancement.' After a most kind discussion
of the pros and cons, he said, 'My brother knows no
such thing as interest. He has *carte blanche* from
the Governor-General to fill up the appointments,
military and civil, from the three Presidencies. He
asked Major Napier, a man in whom he has much
confidence, if he knew of any efficient men (Bombay).
Napier mentioned you in flattering terms. I hardly
remember for which you were marked off, whether
cavalry or infantry; but there was some talk between
them, Napier observing that he hardly thought you
would accept infantry. On that point be satisfied,
if that be any inducement. I guarantee you cavalry,
and you may be assured this is a field not lightly to
be estimated.'

"After much more in this way, I showed him
Hancock's letter. He said, 'I'll take a copy of this;
it's handsome indeed, and does and ought to give
you a high appreciation of the Bombay appointment.'
I laughingly said, 'Why, you see, with that in hand,
I would not dive empty-handed into the water without knowing the prizes at the bottom.' He replied,

'Yes. You are in a position to drive a bargain. I'll write to my brother John, who will have more leisure to attend to it than Henry, and ask what he can hold out to you.' So I quitted his house. The answer cannot be here for fourteen days. It makes no difference. I am in orders for the Brigade Majority. These are tempting things. In Bombay the best opening from a professional point of view in the army. Youth and service; near the Chief and Governor; at a good station; for the pleasurabilities, Poona has weight. Here, what but a few months since I would have given my right hand for, second in command of an irregular cavalry regiment, the favour of the Lawrences, and the door of preferment open. Many would cry out 'cavalry'; enough for the day is the good thereof. The command would in the course of a few years assuredly be mine, but I think I may look high; at any rate, we are told lofty aspirations raise the standard of the mind. Well, there is an honest pride mingling with the feelings raised by the position in which I now stand, which is, that it is won solely and entirely by my own exertions. I feel that much of this is owing to circumstances of favour which perhaps always accompany and aid fortune's children, yet none of it is to be attributed to outdoor interest. That is more than satisfactory. Vanity I have not about such things. Pride I may too much coax perhaps."

The Adjutant-General's demi-official letter to the officer commanding the 1st Bombay Fusiliers ran as follows :—

"*3rd April* (1849).—'The Commander-in-Chief has instructed me to acquaint you, that he has nominated Lieutenant Daly of the Fusiliers to the appointment of Brigade Major on the Establishment in succession to Captain Stiles, appointed a Deputy Assistant Adjutant-General, and that it has afforded His Excellency much gratification thus to mark his approbation of Lieutenant Daly's conspicuous gallantry at Multan, both on 27th December and on the 2nd January last, as specially reported by you and Brigadier Stalker, which the Commander-in-Chief begs that you will do him the favour to communicate to Lieutenant Daly.'"

Unofficially also came the information that he would be posted to Poona, and at this period he wrote home :—

"Probably after all I shall decide for Poona, though not until I see Lawrence's letter shall I make up my decision.   In giving up the Punjab, I resign the political line into which I could *easily* get, and once there, as Lawrence said, 'All India is open to you.'   However, 'annexed Punjab' differs from 'protected Punjab' materially."

The matter was decided at the end of May, when Daly received his first communication from Sir Henry Lawrence :—

"My dear Sir,—You are nominated to the command of the 1st Cavalry Regiment, to be raised at Peshawar.—Yours truly, H. M. Lawrence.   Simla, 24th May."

At the same time he received a similar intimation from the Board of Administration at Lahore, with instructions to join and assume command of the regiment at his earliest convenience.   The other officers were Lieutenant H. R. Nuttall, Madras Infantry, second in command, and Cornet H. Forbes, 1st Bengal Cavalry, adjutant.

CHAPTER IV

RAISING OF THE IST PUNJAB CAVALRY. (1849-52.)

Account of the Corps; sketch of some of the Native Officers; expedition through the Kohat Pass under Sir C. Napier; praise from the latter; life at Peshawar; friendship with Sir Colin Campbell; return to Kohat; inspection of the regiment; visit to Murree; Colonel Mansfield; Miranzai Expedition; Frontier affairs; invalided.

"THE 1st Regiment of Cavalry * was raised at Peshawar, under the direction of Colonel George Lawrence, by Lieutenant Daly, a distinguished and excellent officer of the Bombay service. The men mostly belong to the fine race of Eusafzai Pathans and several of the native officers are men of good family. Within a year the corps was brought to a high state of discipline. It was employed against the Afridis, the Swatis in Ranizai, and in the Kohat Pass, where its discipline and appearance attracted Sir Charles Napier's favourable notice. It is now stationed at Kohat, with a detachment at Bahadur Khel. The regiment is armed, dressed, and equipped in a style equal to the best irregular cavalry; all have carbines; the horses are strong and hardy, they are purchased from a subscription fund." Thus ran the first Administration Report of the Punjab.

* Now styled "21st Prince Albert Victor's Own Cavalry (Frontier Force), Daly's Horse."

The regiment was to consist of 588 natives of all ranks, with 4 British officers; the cost was Rs. 16,059 a month; the troopers received Rs. 20 a month. In July 1850, Daly himself sent home the following sketch :—

"My regiment consists of 4 British officers and 6 troops, each with its complement of native officers nearly 100 men, so that the corps is almost 600 strong. In India there are three distinct armies—Bengal, Madras, Bombay—each presidency has its separate military as well as civil government, but all under one Governor-General. In the Bengal army are 18 regiments of irregular cavalry, which have been raised from time to time during the wars as our dominions have extended. In Bombay there are 4 of these regiments; officered in each presidency from the line, either from a cavalry or infantry regiment as merit or interest may prevail. After the last campaign, on the annexation of the Punjab, the Governor-General decided, on the advice of Sir Henry Lawrence, to raise 5 regiments of cavalry and 5 of infantry. The Punjab having been conquered by a united force from the Bengal and Bombay armies, the Governor-General in handing over the patronage of these new regiments to Sir Henry Lawrence (who was appointed President of a Board for the Government of Punjab affairs) authorised him to select officers indiscriminately from Bengal, Madras, or Bombay, as he might see fit. The designations of the European officers are, commandant, 2nd in command, adjutant, and assistant surgeon. In my regiment each presidency has furnished an officer. A strange combination. A lieutenant, Bombay Army, commandant; a captain, Madras Army, 2nd in command; and a cornet of Bengal Cavalry, adjutant.

"In years past these regiments were embodied with a view to induce men of birth and position, too proud to enter the ordinary service, to embrace our employment. The system pursued was altogether different from that in the regular cavalry. Here a native of good birth and character was to command his troop, in which, of course, a number of his own dependents and followers would be. His pay is nearly £300. He is allowed to mount a certain number of his friends and followers on his own horses, otherwise the horse must be the property of the rider, who draws pay from Government for the service and support of himself and horse. The men arm, dress, and mount themselves, under the orders and responsibility of their commandants. Government provide *nothing* but pay and ammunition.

"The drill and discipline are the same as in the line. In almost every one of these corps are men of noble birth, whose fathers in former times were chiefs and rulers. I have several, and more gallant soldiers no army contains. They embrace the service with great delight, and the conduct of these regiments during the late wars was so excellent as to cause much desire among European officers to enter them. A native gentleman of birth and position can scarcely be excelled in the dignity of his deportment. Personally he is devotedly brave, and, as a body, with a British officer or two at their head in whom they have confidence, no troops could be finer. You may be assured that the 1st Punjab Cavalry, in the opinion of its commandant, lacks none of the qualifications which a gallant regiment should possess! The raising of a regiment gives one a great advantage in this respect; I know every man personally, who he is, and whence he came. Seeing that I have enlisted the corps, they look to me and not beyond, and so invest their commandant with all power. The pay of each officer is *consolidated* (lucky for the race of subalterns!)—commandant, Rs. 1080, or about £108 a month; second in command, Rs. 500; adjutant, Rs. 500; doctor, Rs. 530."

A more detailed account is embodied in the regimental records, taken from a memorandum which Daly drew up for his successor, immediately before his departure on sick leave in April 1852 :—

"I received my appointment to the command of the regiment to be raised at Peshawar,'

His army amounted but to 30,000 men, commanded and partially supplied by the brave Prince Christian of Anhalt. The Elector of Saxony, jealous of Frederick's acceptance of the crown and the leadership of the Lutheran party, seeing that he himself was Calvinist, cut off all hope of succour from Lusatia or Silesia. Austria had submitted, and even the Bohemians were disunited and without courage. The Bavarian army pressed on, since the season was advanced, and they hoped to effect a surprise which would bring about a victory. Frederick did his utmost to rally his dispirited troops by himself appearing in the camp, and reviving the courage of his nobles. The Bohemians, who had decided to act on the defensive, had begun to entrench themselves on the White Mountain near Prague—so excellent a position strategically, that the Duke and Boucquoi hesitated before giving battle ; this, however, they finally did, and in less than an hour this decisive action was over. At first it had seemed doubtful how the battle would end, but the Bavarian charge was invincible, and the victory was gained with a loss to the Bohemians of 4000 men. Frederick was summoned from Prague to hear of the disaster ; he asked for a cessation of hostilities, and was given eight hours, during which he, with his wife and family and chief officers, made his escape under cover of the night. The retreat was, to say the least, pusillanimous, for something might yet have been accomplished with the remaining forces ; but Frederick had little confidence in his supporters. He fled to Breslau, but soon removed from thence to the court of the Elector of Brandenburg, and finally to Holland, where he resided at the Hague under the protection of Prince Maurice. It is strange to think that of those who precipitately fled was the little Princess Elisabeth, just four years old, who was destined to be the friend and correspondent of Descartes in after years. She and her brother Charles Louis were left at Brandenburg, under their grandmother's care, while their parents made their way to Holland.

As for the Bavarians, they entered the town of

E

Prague, and sang the Te Deum; the estates did homage without conditions, and Silesia and Moravia followed in their steps. Three months' grace was given, and then followed the punishment of the offenders. Immense numbers of Calvinists suffered on the gallows, and their estates were confiscated. Protestant preachers were banished, and in time the Protestant religion was no more tolerated. Ferdinand had gained his end, and for a moment it seemed as though peace were in view. Tilly was left to govern Prague, and the Duke of Bavaria left the town on the 18th of December, to pass the rest of the winter at Munich.

Whether Descartes fought at the battle of Prague or not we do not know, but the six weeks during which the army was in the town afforded a valuable opportunity to him—six weeks which were occupied by the officers and soldiers very differently. So completely did the young man appear to be able to dissociate himself from his surroundings, that we can almost believe that this really was the date alluded to in his notes as being that on which he began to understand his *inventum mirabile* —a statement which has been discredited owing to the time being one when all men's minds, one would suppose, must have been occupied very differently than in speculation. Prague, to Descartes, was famous as the place where Tycho Brahe had spent his latter days, and where, after being forced to quit his famous observatory in the island on the Sound by the persecution of the nobles, he found a haven of rest under Rudolf II. He had died in 1601, nineteen years before, but his memory had been kept green through Kepler, his pupil and assistant. We cannot wonder that Descartes was keenly interested in the life of the great astronomer who migrated from Denmark with his family. We should like to believe that he had an opportunity of talking with his relations and descendants, as has been said by some of his biographers. But Baillet tells us that, from investigations made, this is most unlikely. Tycho had brought his many valuable instruments from Denmark to within a few miles of

Prague, where a new Uranienburg was to have been built; then they were taken to the Imperial palace, and finally bought from his heirs by Rudolf, who allowed no one of any sort to see them—not even Kepler, the astronomer royal, who complained bitterly of the restriction. Then came the troubles, and the Elector's army, knowing they were private property, broke and destroyed the collection. This occurred just a year before Descartes' arrival. The only thing that was saved was the great brass celestial globe, but that was not discovered till later; after many wanderings it was finally deposited at Copenhagen.

We have followed the fortunes of our philosopher-soldier, or, as we should rather say, soldier-philosopher, so far as regards his outward actions, and we may judge from his own account of it, what he was thinking and writing about during these eventful years which represented the critical period in his life. Descartes, as he tells us in the *Method*—that most wonderful auto-biography which relates to us so little of the "facts" of its writer's life, but so much of its actual events—was learning all this time the science of sciences, the know-ledge of himself, which is all to which the wisest man can, after all, attain. It was perhaps hardly true that he had abandoned the study of letters in favour of the "book of the world," but he had done his best to throw himself into practical affairs, so that by this means he might escape the pit-fall into which men of letters too often fell, of allowing their speculations to carry them beyond the limits of common-sense, and of giving free scope to vanity. If Truth were to be found in mixing with the world, Descartes was bent on finding it; but, as he himself realised, he was a stranger in the world into which he had entered—a stranger in a mask which concealed his true expression. He learned, what all men learn in time, that there is no sphere of life in which the contradictions of mankind can be got rid of; every-where alike is there error and deception : if we accept what is set before us by custom and example, we shall certainly go wrong. Truth must be sought for from the beginning: the Book of the World but sends us back to ourselves. Descartes' first reflections that winter at Neuberg, when free from cares and passions he remained the whole day in his well-warmed room, gave the colour to the remainder of his life. The student, undistracted by society that interested him, devoted his whole attention to his thoughts, and his thoughts directed the course of his later speculations. What, then, was the lesson learned? The first conclusion the young man came to was this: that seldom does a work on which many persons have been employed attain to the same perfection as that which has been carried out by one single directing mind: this we see clearly in buildings, or in cities which have grown from villages. And with nations the case is similar: civilisation is a growth which has largely come about through the necessity bred of suffering, while the direction of some wise legislation or the ordinances of God must be incomparably superior. Learning has suffered in this way; the sciences have gradually been drawn far from the truth which a sensible man, using his natural and unprejudiced judgment, would gather from his own experience. In childhood we are guided by those whose instructions are conflicting and not always for the best; and how can they be as correct as those which would have proceeded from our Reason had it been from the beginning mature, and had we allowed ourselves to be guided by it. As in the modern view of education, we do not seek so much to "put into" the brain of the child, as to "draw out" what is already there, though in a latent state.

But Descartes does not propose to adopt so revolutionary an idea as that a clean sweep should be made of all that our inherited learning and civilisation have brought to us, declaring that the world must make a new commencement. He takes the simile of a town which is not built afresh, but in which each private individual sees to his own house being renewed. So, he adds, "as for the opinions which, up to that time, I had embraced, I thought I could not do better than resolve at once to sweep them wholly away, that I might afterwards be in a position to admit either others more correct, or even perhaps the same when they had undergone the scrutiny of Reason. I firmly believed that in this way I should much better succeed in the conduct of my life, than if I built only upon old foundations, and leant upon principles which in my youth I had taken on trust."* Large bodies, if overthrown, are with difficulty set up again : with them it is dangerous to meddle, but with the individual it is different : "I have never contemplated anything higher than the reformation of my own opinions, basing them on a foundation wholly my own." And the attempt is, above all, not to be made indiscriminately by everyone. "The single design to strip oneself of all past beliefs is one that ought not to be taken by everyone. The majority of men is composed of two classes, for neither of which would this be at all a befitting resolution : in the *first* place, of those who, with more than a due confidence in their own powers, are precipitate in their judgments, and want the patience requisite for orderly and circumspect thinking ; whence it happens, that if men of this class once take the liberty to doubt of their accustomed opinions, and quit the beaten highway, they will never be able to tread the bye-way that would lead them by a shorter course, and will lose themselves and continue to wander for life : in the *second* place, of those who, possessed of sufficient sense or modesty to determine that there are others who excel them in the power of discriminating between truth and error, and by whom they may be instructed, ought rather to content themselves with the opinions of such, than trust to their own Reason for something better."† Then Descartes tells us the benefit which has come to him from learning, not from one school or master, but from the world. He would probably have placed himself with the latter of these classes had he not seen the world, and even in college life, learned that there is no opinion, however

* *Method*, pp. 13, 14.   † *Ibid.*, p. 15 ; (Veitch, p. 16).

absurd, that has not been maintained by some philosopher, and that those who hold these strange opinions are as rational as we. Our opinions are dependent largely on the customs of our country, and even an opinion on any matter of difficulty which is almost unanimously held, is not necessarily true, for the truth is more likely to be found by one individual than by many. He himself felt that there was no one on whom he could pin his faith with confidence, therefore he was constrained to use his reason. Then carefully and deliberately, "like one walking alone and in the dark," he set about his difficult task, not dismissing summarily any of the opinions that had crept into his belief without having been introduced by Reason, but carefully satisfying himself of the general nature of the task he was undertaking "to ascertain the true method by which to arrive at the knowledge of whatever lay within the compass of my powers." *

This bit of autobiography, so famous in French Literature, is perhaps more interesting than any other portion of Descartes' writings. It presents him to us grown to the stature of a man, and fully conscious of himself and of his powers, ready to grasp the world as his own, and yet having already learned the lesson of caution in his actual conclusions. All his philosophy seems to centre round the antithesis, present to all who think of such things at all, between "Opinion" on the one hand, and "Truth" upon the other. Where does the one end, or the other begin, if indeed it does begin at all? Is there, then, a Method that can help us in that all-important discovery, or must we remain of the mind of Xenophanes the Eleatic, that—

"No man at any time knew clearly . . .
For what he thinks to speak most perfectly
He knows that not at all; his own opinion cleaves to all."

Descartes held that this was not so; he believed that there was a Truth which might be reached, did we but

* *Method*, p. 17.

look for her aright, and clear our minds from the
prejudices that had accumulated in ages past.   Perhaps
others, if not he, might find that the task was not so
simple as he assumed ; but at least he made a new and
vigorous start upon the way which so many before and
since have followed—none of them entirely succeeding
in their quest, yet none of those who sought sincerely
being entirely disappointed.   Descartes' external life
was just his mental experiences in concrete form ; he
sought for truth in abstract study, in outward things,
in the world and all it teaches, and then finally by
study once more formulated his conclusions, and
reasoned out his experience.

Thus, in the beginning of his life, this scholar of the
Jesuits, who knew so well how to adapt the teaching of
his Method to the capacities of his scholars, and yet
who kept his end so faithfully before him, began with
the doctrines of his masters.   He studied Logic only
until he had become assured that Logic would teach
him nothing more than he already knew, and would
never add to knowledge.   We seem to hear the voice
of his successor Pascal, in his Provincial Letters, in the
words, "On examination I found that, as for Logic, its
syllogisms and the majority of its other precepts are of
avail rather in the communication of what we already
know, or even as the Art of Lully, in speaking without
judgment of things of which we are ignorant, than in
the investigation of the unknown ; and although this
science contains, indeed, a number of correct and very
excellent precepts, there are, nevertheless, so many
others, and these either injurious or superfluous,
mingled with the former, that it is almost quite as
difficult to effect a severance of the true from the false,
as it is to extract a Diana or a Minerva from a rough
block of marble."*   This meant that a great break had
been already made with the teaching of his childhood ;
it meant that, instead of inquiring into the way in
which knowledge is communicated, we try to extend
our knowledge, to learn to distinguish Truth from

* *Method*, p. 17 ; (Veitch, p. 18).

Falsehood as the Jesuits never did. To them, Truth was fixed and immovable; there was no question of discovering something fresh in what could only be revealed through some authoritative means. The Logic of the schools should in their view teach us all we want to know.

But now we must return to the events in Descartes' life. We left him after the battle of Prague in 1620. He remained in Prague until December, and then took up his winter quarters with a portion of the Duke of Bavaria's troops left in the extreme south of Bohemia. At this time a new and strange influence had come within his life. In that wonderfully productive winter spent with the Bavarian troops, while active operations were impossible, Descartes heard much of what was going on in the literary and scientific world. Amongst other things, he heard of that strange brotherhood of which we have so often read and yet of which we know so little—the Order of the Rosicrucians. They, it was said, taught a new wisdom, the hitherto undiscovered science. This was enough to excite Descartes' interest : Germany was thoroughly aroused; something had been discovered which was to be kept to the few initiated ones. The same Descartes who was in the habit of disdaining the work of others, began to think he had been precipitate in his judgments. Here was he searching for the Truth patiently and with difficulty, and there were men who declared the way had been opened to them. If these were simple imposters, then it was the duty of any honest man to expose their imposition ; but if on the issue which to him was all-important, they had found any light, then, as he told his friend, how despicable would it be in him to disdain to be taught anything out of which he might obtain new knowledge. He made it his duty to discover a member of this learned body, in order to discuss the matter with him and subsequently settle his own conclusions.*

* The treatise which Descartes specially dedicates to the Order, is that which was written in 1619-20 and never published, the *Polybii*

JAI SINGH.   ABED ALI KHAN.

NATIVE OFFICERS OF THE 1ST PUNJAB CAVALRY.

[To face p. 72.

Descartes' efforts to lay hold of this ever-vanishing society were in vain.   He was doubtless keenly interested and excited about what might be an interesting development of the doctrines of Paracelsus ; but it was, of course, quite contrary to his newly-formed principles to accept what he could not put clearly before his mind, and really experience.   Later on, as we shall see, he was somewhat ashamed of his youthful enthusiasm, and declared that, far from having belonged to the mysterious Order, he knew nothing of it, but possibly Père Mersenne may have influenced his judgment.   At any rate, having made up his mind that nothing was to be gained from this society, he found his difficulties as great as ever, and, as we have seen, he threw himself into active life in order to take refuge from himself.

After the battle of Prague, he once more shouldered his musket, or perhaps his pike, and decided again to join the Bavarian army—not the first soldier of his day who had become such to drive away the more persistent troubles of the mind.   It was not long before he joined the troops of Boucquoi in Hungary.   Frederick's cause was not as yet entirely lost.   Mansfeld fought bravely for him, and his father-in-law, who had been so cold when the Bohemian cause was at stake, aroused himself when he saw that the empire was threatening the Electorate as well, and sent supplies.   Transylvania and Hungary gave most important help to the outcast king.   The cessation of hostilities between Bethlem Gabor and the Emperor was followed by this old enemy of Austria over-

---

cosmopolitani Thesaurus mathematicus, which "sets forth the true means of solving this science, and in which it is demonstrated that nothing further can be supplied by the human mind"; "it is specially designed to relieve the pains of those who, entangled in the Gordian knot of the sciences, uselessly waste the oil of their genius." It is dedicated to all learned men, and more especially to the illustrious Brethren of the Rosicrucian Order in Germany. This may have been the treatise that in his journal he promises, if he can obtain sufficient books, and if it seems worthy of publication, on 23rd September 1620, though why the date should be thus fixed we do not know. Probably when the time came he did not consider it "worthy," and now all is lost excepting the simple title.

running Hungary once more, and calling himself its
king. Boucquoi was forced to evacuate Bohemia and
make his way to Hungary. Descartes had heard much
of Hungary and its troubles, and had met Hungarians
with the Imperial troops, therefore he was anxious to
visit the country and take his place in the Imperial
army. He joined Count Boucquoi in Moravia (where
he was occupied in reducing the towns which were
favourable to Frederick), offering himself to him as a
volunteer at the end of March 1621, while the general
was awaiting the results of negotiations between Gabor
and the estates of Hungary and the Emperor. Gabor
had taken the oath of fidelity to the Imperial House,
but, being in league with Frederick's party in Bohemia,
he entered Hungary with a large army, carrying all
before him. Pressburg soon capitulated, Gabor was
declared king, and religious toleration was established.
War had been resumed, but it was during some
temporary negotiations which ended in nothing that
Descartes appeared upon the scene. He accompanied,
Baillet tells us, the army of 22,000 men to the siege of
Pressburg, where Gabor had left a garrison, having
himself retired in possession of his crown. The town
held out till May; and after it submitted, other towns in
turn were successfully attacked.*

The town of Neuhaüsel, however, was not to be so
easily captured: it had an opening upon a river, and
large forces came to its succour from Bethlem Gabor
and others; still, things were favourable to the
Imperialists, until an engagement took place with a
party of Hungarian horsemen, when the brave Count
Boucquoi, deserted by his men, lost his life after
defending himself, almost single-handed, to the last.
The Imperial forces remained a few days longer for
appearance' sake, and then, completely dispirited at the
loss of their leader, retired during the night of 27th July
upon Pressburg once more.

This unaccustomed defeat seems to have completed
the dislike which Descartes had formed for the pro-

* Baillet, vol. i., p. 95.

fession that he had temporarily adopted. No doubt his experiences in this campaign must have been trying, and its inglorious close must have tried him most of all. It has been asserted that the young philosopher distinguished himself in his capacity as soldier, but Baillet characteristically discredits the tale. In his view, Descartes' mind was set on higher things than military distinction, and he considers that he would himself have told us had any such distinction been acquired. He relinquished the military service at this time, and never in serious warfare carried a musket more: the four years of experience had taught him much: he had grown into a man, and a man who had knowledge of the world and of his fellow-men: he had learned much of the motives which actuate these men in their relations with one another—much that he could not learn in a Jesuit school, nor in the solitude of his study. And now the "heat of youth" being, in his view, passed, he decides that the time has come for a new and very different line of life.

CHAPTER III

ALTHOUGH Descartes had once and for all abandoned the military profession, he had no idea of returning immediately to his country. War was being waged with the Huguenots—a war with which he may have had but little sympathy—the plague had been and was still desolating Paris; but, besides all this, his desire for travel was still far from satisfied. He had seen men, and he now desired to see countries; he would no longer follow the camp, but start forth by himself to make his discoveries. By so doing, he possibly laid himself open to censure; long after this, his enemy, Voetius, the Dutch theologian, under an assumed name, made a virulent attack upon him, accusing him, among other things, of quitting the army in disgust, because he saw no prospect of rising to a post of honour. The absurdity of this accusation is manifest, since Descartes was but a volunteer, with no ambition after a commission, nor, if we may judge by his later utterances, much enthusiasm for his profession. But the accusation seems to have stung none the less. He was seeking now for what so far he had not succeeded in finding. He had thought that what the philosophers, with their various systems and contradictory opinions, had failed to reach, might be at last discovered in the active life of the field, where, instead of giving themselves over to meditation, men set themselves to act. Surely, in that way, must they obtain a more definite and certain standard of truth and falsehood; shams must be shown up and reality revealed, when the false veneering of conventional life is removed. But here, too, he found that the same uncertainty and wavering were discovered. Men were guided by a hundred motives rather than the simple intentions of honest hearts. Varieties amongst men in active life were as great as amongst those books which had once been so deeply conned ; and who is to say which will direct us most surely? The World's Book is a great one, and it tells us many things which puzzle us. We can but spell out little bits here and there, even those of us who can read it best.

Descartes started off on his new task of seeking to know something of men and places, fresh from the turmoil and distraction of war, and he did so with one lesson, at least, well learned. For he had learned, as he tells us, to believe nothing simply on the evidence of those by whom it was commonly received, and thus to get rid of much real hindrance in taking to heart the lessons Reason has to teach.

He left Hungary in July 1621, probably with a carriage, and accompanied by servants, and made his way through Moravia to Silesia, where he seems to have remained at Breslau. The country must have been desolated by the Elector's war, and probably presented a depressing spectacle. Baillet thinks Descartes must have been present at the assembly of the States at Breslau, and soon after that (in November), the ceremony of administering the oath of allegiance to the Emperor there took place. He wished to see something of North Germany, and skirting Poland, he entered Pomerania. Here he arrived in autumn, and having visited the shores of the Baltic, he passed from Stettin to Brandenburg, whose Elector had just returned from receiving homage as King of Poland. Then he went on to the Duchy of Mecklenburg and into Holstein, from which some of his biographers erroneously think he went to Denmark—in reality, this was a later expedition.*

* Baillet, vol. i., p. 102.

Having made up his mind to go to Holland by water, Descartes dismissed his horses and servants, retaining only a single valet. He embarked somewhere on the Elbe, on a vessel which was chartered to take him to Eastern Friesland, since he had rather a strange desire to visit at leisure the sea-coasts of Germany—a dreary enough expedition, one would say, in a small boat in winter. Having investigated the Eastern Friesland, he was anxious to see the Western, and in order to be more free, he took a small boat for himself, meaning to make the short journey across the isthmus of the Ems from Emden. The expedition, however, proved very nearly fatal to him. His boatmen were sailors of the most barbarous description possible, and, being once well on his way, he discovered them to be unprincipled scoundrels. As he talked French with his valet, the sailors took him to be a foreign merchant, probably voyaging for trade purposes, and possessing large sums of money. They judged that, being a stranger not known in the country, he would not be missed if thrown overboard, and, on the old principle that dead men tell no tales, they decided on this step, especially as he seemed an inexperienced quiet young man, who would make but little resistance. Their plans were freely discussed, for they considered that their passenger would not understand their language.

Suddenly, however, the young man rose; his countenance assumed an aspect of severity, he drew his sword from its scabbard, spoke to the men in their own tongue, and threatened to stab them on the slightest provocation. The effect was instantaneous and marvellous: the courage of their would-be victim cowed them altogether, and the miserable men willingly submitted to conducting Descartes where he would. The incident was striking, and proved, if we wanted proof, that much had been learnt during these years of wandering and warfare: the art of managing men is not the least important art a young man can learn, and in pure physical courage he certainly cannot have been lacking

How he was acquainted with the dialect of the country, probably spoken by the men, we do not know : we may, however, believe that he had a talent for picking up languages and *patois* as he went.

Descartes did not stay long in Frisia, where there was not much to be seen but cultivated lands and marshes ; he soon passed on to Holland—the country that was going to be for so long a time his home—and here he passed a good part of the winter. Curiously enough, at the Hague there were three little courts being carried on at once—that of the States-General, where the affairs of the Republic were dealt with ; that of the Prince of Orange, under whom Descartes had served ; and finally, that of the exiled and attractive Queen of Bohemia, the Electress Palatine, who was surrounded by sympathetic friends endeavouring to console her for her past glories and present poverty. Descartes' life became, as we shall see, strangely bound up with the exiled royal family, the same family which not long before he had assisted in de-throning.

At this time the twelve years' truce made between the States and Spain in 1609, had but a few months expired, and war had once more been declared. Spinola, with his forces, was actually besieging the town of Juliers. L'Ecluse was attacked by Borgia, the governor of the citadel of Antwerp. Descartes, who had wished to avoid warfare, awaited at the Hague the issue of these sieges until January 1622. Spinola took the town and castle of Juliers, but Borgia was forced to raise that of l'Ecluse, after losing the greater part of his army. Early in February, Descartes felt at liberty to quit Holland, from which he made his way to the Spanish Netherlands, and there felt curious to see something of another court—that of the Infanta Isabella at Brussels. This court must have been one of the strangest Descartes ever visited ; for Isabella, who had become the widow of the Archduke Albert the previous year, governed her country as a Nun of the Order of St Clare, and though gentle and humane

to her own subjects, she carried on the war against the
Netherlands with the greatest vigour, under the
title of "Governess." She was much respected by
friends and enemies alike for her combination of
firmness and amiability, and deeply regretted on her
death, which took place in 1632.

Descartes' visit was but of a few days' duration : he
wished once more to return to France. Hearing,
however, that the plague, which for the two past years
had been desolating Paris, was not yet passed, and as
it was his father whom he specially wished to visit, he
journeyed across France to Rouen, from which place
he went on to Rennes in Brittany, arriving there about
the middle of March 1622. Nine years of absence had
changed the lad of seventeen into a man of six-and-
twenty — a man of experience and knowledge of
mankind, to whom the little world of Rennes might
seem dull and quiet enough. His father had become
a man of some importance in the local parlement. He
was already one of the leading senior members, and
next year was to become its "Doyen." Possibly these
matters did not seem of the same importance to the son
as to the father, or possibly the home life with a
stepmother and half-brother and sister whom he
hardly knew, did not present the interest it might have
done. His elder brother had been made a councillor
by his father's efforts, and his full sister was already
married. At anyrate, a few weeks after his arrival, his
father deemed it right to put René in possession of his
property, so far as it had come to him from his mother,
thus making him feel free to follow out his bent. The
brother and sister had already received the two-thirds
which fell to their share. René's part consisted of
three small properties, viz., those of Perron, Grand-
Maison and Le Marchais, besides a house in the town
of Poitiers, and some acres of arable land. The whole
of the property was situated in Poitou, and its new
owner was naturally anxious to see it before settling
what to do with it. In May he left for Poitou, and he
spent most of the summer partly at Châtellerault and

partly at Poitiers. Then he once more joined his father, who, during the parliamentary recess, spent much of his time at the property of his second wife, Chavagnes near Nantes.*

It does not appear that the young man obtained much assistance from his relatives as regards his future life. Very likely the advice offered might be that of living on his little property, or obtaining some safe berth in connection with the parlement, like his brother, and such suggestions would not appeal to one who meditated doing great things in the world. But life in his father's house without occupation was not to be borne ; therefore, when Lent of the following year came round, the young man made his way to Paris. The restricted interests and narrow life of the provinces must have chafed him, and he desired to see his friends in the great world once again, and learn the last political news and what was being said and done in the world of letters. At this time we must recollect that Brittany was far removed from Paris, and Paris was the centre of a literary life which seldom has been equalled. A glorious age was opening—the age of Corneille, Molière of the Précieux and the Précieuses, of Balzac and Voiture, of Mme. de Rambouillet and Mlle. de Scudéry—the age of Richelieu and the Academy so soon to be inaugurated. After the Treaty of Angoulême, which made peace in 1620 between Louis XIII. and his mother and the nobles, the Huguenots arose and made a bold effort after independence. But this rising, which threw France into a blaze, seemed to have roused in the young king all the best qualities he possessed. He confirmed the Edict of Nantes, marched against the enemy, and although the Huguenots held out stoutly, and seemed practically invincible, they at length were forced to come to terms, thus accepting the inevitable. By the Peace of Montpellier, signed on 19th October 1622, civil order was restored, and although religious toleration was accorded, a step was taken towards destroy-

* The first communication extant from René Descartes is one to his eldest brother, on business matters, dated 3rd April 1622.

F

ing the political influence of the Huguenots. The king and his mother had also come to terms, and what was more important than all, the great Richelieu was taken into the royal council. Descartes made his appearance in Paris on the dawn of a new era for France.

The events which had been taking place in Germany were naturally of excessive interest in France, which had not so far decided on the policy to be pursued. The transference of the Palatine Electorate from Frederick to Maximilian of Bavaria, which had taken place in February 1623, meant a transference of power from Protestantism to Catholicism, which was likely to be fraught with the most important consequences, and France would soon have to decide as to whether she was to interfere in the struggle that was inevitable, and, if so, at what point. Now all were curious for information, and therefore Descartes, fresh from his experiences in Germany and Holland, was naturally a *persona grata*, especially as he could formulate his views upon the origin of the troubles, as well as simply recount his personal experiences. But just when his popularity would have been at the highest, he was informed that, incredible as it seemed to them, a report had spread abroad amongst his friends that he had become a member of the secret Order of the Rosicrucians which had just become the subject of talk in Paris. His interest in it we have seen, but how far he had become actually involved with the Order, of course, we cannot tell: his biographer is very certain that he never was a member, and there is nothing in his writings to make one think he was. So far as we can say, at no time did his interest carry him beyond the bounds of reason. Descartes himself was inclined to think that the report was circulated by some enemy, who had known through his letters from Germany of his connection with the Order, and had exaggerated this connection in order that his reputation might suffer. Secret societies at that time had an evil reputation, and this society had first been heard of under another name from that by

which it had been known in Germany, where it had not
been ill thought of.   Unfortunately for those who were
supposed to support it, it came to be known in France
at the same time as a Spanish society, the Alumbrados
or Illuminati.   This entirely prejudged the Order in the
eyes of the critical Parisians : the members were turned
into ridicule, and called the Invisibles ; they were
introduced into the novels of the time, and farces were
acted in which they played a leading *rôle*. · When
Descartes arrived in Paris, he was greeted on the Pont
Neuf by songs concerning the supposed brotherhood.
A wonderful bill was posted on the street by some joker
more daring than the rest, to this effect : " We, the
deputies of the supreme college of the Brethren of the
Rose-cross, inhabit this town in visible form and
invisible form. . . . We teach and demonstrate with
neither books nor signs every language in the countries
which we inhabit."   It was really believed that a great
body of these " Invisibles " had taken up their abode in
Paris ; it was said that of thirty-six deputies who had
been sent from the head of the society to every part of
Europe, six had come to France, and that, having
advertised their arrival, they were lodged in the Marais
du Temple.   Yet another placard soon appeared, saying
that if any person wished to see them from mere curiosity, the wish would not be gratified.   But if they
really wished to join the confraternity, they who could
read the thought would show them the truth of their
promises.*

* The origin of this strange Order is as obscure as that of most
secret societies.   The society ascribed to itself immense antiquity,
although its origin, and even its name, seems wrapped in mystery.
Whether it owed its commencement to a certain Christian Rosencreutz
who appears to have been mythical, or to the symbolical signification of
its name, Ros or Rosa and Crux, it is impossible to say.   What we do
feel sure of is, that it was a development from the mysticism which
prevailed in Germany at the close of the sixteenth century.   A great
body of alchemists, magicians, and what not, followed upon the great
Paracelsus, seeking, after what they took to be his principles, to discover
the secret of the transmutation of metals, and the mystery of the universal
medicine and the philosopher's stone.   Some adopted less material views

We can imagine how Paris, relieved to be at rest from war and pestilence, and once more gaining its wonted light-heartedness, would excite itself over this imaginary invasion. We can picture how, in those ever-celebrated *salons*, the arguments for and against the brotherhood would be discussed by brilliant women and witty men. The opportunity was too good a one to be lost, and any unfortunate stranger coming to Paris from the country of its origin would at once be hailed as an imaginary apostle. Of course, in Descartes' case, there was circumstantial evidence, for was he not learned in strange and curious knowledge, and had he not confessed in letters written to friends how he had been attracted by this mysterious society? We may also add, was he not a striking-looking youth of good family and interesting history? All the necessary conditions were present for causing a *furore*, and it soon arose at the unfortunate René Descartes' expense. Most serious of all, his good friend Father Mersenne of the Minims had been distressed by the news concerning him. It was a real relief to him to see this friend once more: they had been separated for nine years, three of which the Father passed at the convent of Nevers, teaching philosophy and theology. In 1619, he was, however, summoned to Paris, in order to be Conventuel in the convent near the Palais Royal, where he remained till death. It was here that Descartes found him preparing the first volume of the commentaries on Genesis which he dedicated to the first and newly-made Archbishop of Paris. The connection between Genesis and the Rosicrucians might seem remote, but for Mersenne it existed, and Descartes appeared upon the scene just in

and a more exalted aim; differences of opinions occurred, and associations were formed for the discussion of the secret sciences. The Rosicrucians, so far as we can tell that they existed, were a theosophical sect, having no connection with Templars or Freemasons. They claimed to be a Christian Order, and at the same time a learned sect. This is how they attracted men such as Thomas Vaughan and Robert Fludd in England (the latter was on this account attacked by Père Mersenne), and Descartes himself in France.

time to give the writer the information he required;
although he declared his ignorance of the Order, it was
clear that at the least he knew as much as could be
known. Mersenne's indignation with the new doctrines
was unbounded. If his writings give a true account
of Rosicrucianism, we cannot cease to wonder that
Descartes should have been attracted by it, for, instead
of the clear and distinct views that he craved for, we have
what seem to us strange and incomprehensible signs and
symbols, literal interpretations of poetic imagery, and a
theosophy of a most confused description. Probably,
however, his interpretation of the Order was very
different from its earlier expositions, and probably, also,
the secret societies that sprang up at this time were
just so many protests against the grossness and
materialism of the life then carried on. Society in
France was as coarse as we should have expected it to
be under the influence of Henry IV., and a Spanish
regency : it was also, on the whole, an irreligious society
as well. We can, therefore, understand how the idea
of a body of reforming tendency might have struck
the imaginations of the Parisians, and ensured a
temporary interest.

Even after he had cleared himself of the strange
suspicions that had fallen upon him, the great world of
Paris did not satisfy the young philosopher any more
than it had done years before. It was a "great world"
that he had stepped into—and one into which a man of
wit and genius could obtain admission even without the
added qualification possessed by Descartes, of social
standing. It might, indeed, have carried away many a
man more mature in years than he, and we almost
wonder that, considering the life he had been leading,
he was not more entranced of it. He felt, however, the
longing for a vocation which would satisfy his ambitions,
and he still possessed that passionate desire to find the
Truth, which could not be satisfied in a Parisian *salon*,
however brilliant. The précieuses talked about what he
was trying to discover; they sought points of view,
while he was aiming at the substance. He saw his

friends all settled in some profession, or more often in some post or sinecure, which would give them occupation and remuneration for the remainder of their lives. But this was no inducement to young Descartes to follow suit; he felt he must have quietude, and, above all, the opportunity for thinking and not alone for acting. He appears at this time to have taken a dislike to mathematics, studied as an abstract science for itself, and without any view to its utility in the solution of other problems. He had ceased to study arithmetic for the last three years, and he had to refresh his knowledge when he wished to work out some problems. We have seen how, during his travels, he made a study of geometry, but already he was finding it also unprofitable. The fact appeared to be that, in studying both arithmetic and geometry (in his mind the key to all the other sciences), he had been dissatisfied with the books from which he studied. He found, as many who have been unintelligently instructed find in the present day, that he had only got mechanical methods of arriving at results, instead of reasons. He could not wonder at those who put aside these studies in disgust, either as puerile and vain, or else as difficult and obscure. He considered it vain to apply oneself to imaginary numbers and figures, as if that were sufficient in itself: new difficulties could with the greatest difficulty be resolved by them. The old mathematics, regarded as a necessary preliminary to philosophic study, must have been a very different science, however insufficient. It was based on certain elementary truths imposed by nature on the human mind, though later on overlaid with error. The writings of Pappus and Diophantes, though of less antiquity, Descartes believed bore traces of this lost science, and he considered that men have tried to revive it under the "barbaric name" of algebra, which, by clearing away the multitude of forms and figures, brings about that clearness and facility which ought to characterise true mathematics. This last Descartes takes to be Science as a whole—not arithmetic and geometry alone, but also astronomy, music, optics, and mechanics, and all the sciences which seek to investigate, and comprehend order and measure wherever they appear. Hence, in his *Rules for the Direction of the Mind*, Descartes urges men to study this science, which embraces all the objects to which the other sciences apply themselves, and which, though despised by many, is in reality most worthy of study.

Thus, for the time being, Descartes turned from the geometry and arithmetic of the day in disappointment. In the century preceding, the study of mathematics had been introduced into Italy, and numerous treatises, translations of the works of ancient geometers and commentaries on those works, appeared. Vieta made immense improvements in algebra by introducing the use of letters of the alphabet to stand for known quantities, and he also advanced the theory of equation, as did Harriot, an Englishman, while the Scottish Napier invented logarithms. But though great activity was being manifested on mathematical lines, it was left to Descartes himself to make the greatest stride of all, by allowing the mathematician to pass beyond the few regular curved lines, whose properties were known, and by the application of algebra to geometry, to overleap the narrow bounds within which it had hitherto been confined. But this is to anticipate.

In the meantime, geometry and physics were alike abandoned as unprofitable, and another line of study—that of morals—was adopted, as being the most practical and important to which the young man could possibly apply himself. The phase, as a phase, does not appear to have been of long duration : it was not long before Descartes returned to his first love, and throughout his life man in his moral relationship is not so often the object of his solicitude, as in his relationship to the world. Clerselier, who should have known, states that morals were constantly the object of his thought : to us, Descartes sometimes seems to look at ethics as a branch of physics which, as he tells Chanut, was most useful in giving a basis for morality.

The young man's stay in Paris was not of long

duration : after a two months' visit, he decided to return to his relatives in Brittany. At Rennes he obtained permission of his father to sell some of his property in Poitou, and then he made his way to Poitiers first, and then to Châtellerault.

June and part of July of 1623 were employed in business arrangements. The estate of Perron, which had come to him from his mother, Descartes sold, as also two small properties or farms and the house at Poitiers. Perron was held in fief from the duchy of Châtellerault. The estate of Perron thus passed from Descartes' hands, but in order to satisfy his relatives, he continued, in his family at least, to call himself by its name. He was now fairly rich, and able to direct his life as he would, independently of the opinions of his friends ; as we shall see, he had no idea of vegetating in the provinces, or even of spending a life of gaiety in the metropolis : his views, so far as they were formulated at all, were very different.

CHAPTER IV

ITALY AND PARIS, 1623-1628

YOUNG Descartes was by no means satisfied with the amount of travel he had succeeded in accomplishing. The *Wanderlust* was still upon him, and so early as March 1623, when in Paris, he appears to have written to his brother suggesting a journey to the neighbourhood of the Alps, where the husband of his godmother, who had charge of the commissariat of the troops, had died. Being anxious to depart, he made it a pretext for his journey that he was going to set the affairs of his relative in order, and, if possible, obtain the post of Intendant of the army. All preparations were made, and he was to leave by postchaise, having assured his friends that a voyage of the kind would be of the greatest use in teaching him the management of affairs, giving him further experience of the world, and helping him to form useful habits, adding that "if he did not return richer, at least he would return more capable." [*] However, either owing to his anxiety to sell his property, or for some other reasons unexplained, he had to delay his journey.

It was thus September 1623 when he really started and made his way to Basle and Switzerland, in order to see something of the country. On this journey, the traveller made a point of seeing as much of nature as he could, paying special attention to animal life, and to the conformation of the land : and this was at a time when such regions of inquiry were unusual. He

[*] Baillet, vol. i., p. 118.

directed his way to the Grisons, and there became
detained while the question of the Valtelline was under
debate.   The Spaniards, who garrisoned the Milanese,
had, in 1622, seized upon the valley of the Valtelline, and
obliged Chur, the chief town of the League of the
Grisons, to receive an imperial garrison, on the pretext
that they wished to protect the Catholics, and secure
communications with the Empire, by establishing
means of passing troops and stores from the Empire
to Milan.   The route from the south is through a pass,
half-way up the Valtelline, a broad valley which leads
into the other valley of the Adige, by which it was
easy to pass on by the Brenner into Germany.   The
possession of the valley was essential to the maintenance of the power of the Hapsburgs in Italy, but it
was subject to the League of the Grisons, which had
long been under the protection of France, and therefore,
when it was interfered with, France had every right to
intervene.   It was not, however, until two years later,
that Richelieu actually took this step, and drove the
imperial troops from Chur, and the papal army from
the Valtelline.

From the Valtelline the traveller made his way to
Tyrol, and then to Venice, after visiting the courts
of the Archduke Leopold, brother of the Emperor
Ferdinand II., at Innsbrück.   Descartes had purposely
arranged his plans so that he should reach Venice on
Ascension Day, and witness the well-known ceremony
of the Espousal of Venice to the Adriatic Sea.
Whether the wish to witness another interesting
ceremony of a kind entirely new to him, and the
natural desire to see the famous republic, attracted him
to Venice, or whether it was his old vow of four years
ago, after his season of enthusiasm, that lay upon his
mind, we do not know; but the fact is clear that now, at
last, he made the pilgrimage to Loretto.   Baillet merely
tells us that doubtless the circumstances under which
it was undertaken were "most edifying."*   Having,
as we suppose, attended to his spiritual affairs, he

* Baillet, vol. i., p. 120.

turned his attention to the temporal, which had been the excuse for his making so long and expensive a journey, but his efforts to procure a post in connection with the army, if ever made in good faith at all, did not succeed. Descartes' next interest was to make his way to Rome, which place he wished to reach after All Saints' Day. Pope Urban VIII. had announced, by a Bull in April 1624, a Jubilee which was to commence on Christmas Eve 1624, and end with the year 1625. The great basilicas of S. John Lateran, S. Peter, S. Paul, and Santa Maria Maggiore, were to be visited by the faithful for thirty consecutive days, and all indulgences were temporarily suspended in order to attract every good churchman, as far as possible, to Rome. Hardly anyone can be present at these great festivals of the church in that city of churches, where the outward acts of religion seem to be the only thought and occupation of thousands of men and women, without a deep impression being left. And if that is so now, when the spiritual power is no longer also a temporal power, and when the great spiritual hierarchy has been shorn of the greater part of its magnificence, and lives in great measure on the memory of glories passed away, what must it have been when Urban of the Barberini, that spiritual prince who never forgot that he was also a temporal prince, and who fortified Rome with ramparts, reigned in uncontrolled power? Descartes, coming as a young man from scenes of a very different kind, accustomed to rude camp life, and naturally susceptible to outside influence, was, for the time being, deeply moved. He had come through motives of curiosity, and he found a population drawn from every part of Catholic Europe, so to speak, upon its knees. Even the rumours of pestilence in and round the then unhealthy town, and the war which raged to the north, did not act as a deterrent to the true sons of the Church. Amongst the pilgrims was Ladislas, Prince and afterwards King of Poland, who had come from Breda and the Spanish Netherlands to

Rome, to be present at the procession of the Pope and Cardinals on Christmas Eve, in the great and hardly completed new basilica of S. Peter's. This was the prince who was the rejected suitor of Princess Elisabeth of Palatine, Descartes' future friend. There were other Catholic princes who had also found their way to the Holy City with motives probably of different sorts, but ostensibly to perform their religious duties. We have seen Descartes' passion for learning something of human nature in all its phases; here was his opportunity all ready to his hand. To him the study of these living men was far more than the sculptures, pictures, and ancient relics of every sort, which form the overpowering interest of Rome to the ordinary traveller. Such things never really had much fascination for Descartes, excepting as they bore upon his present work and thought. His knowledge of the classics was probably but slight; there is no evidence in his writings of a true interest in literature for its own sake. What did interest him, however, was nowhere to be found on a larger scale and in greater variety of character than at a great festival of the Church such as this, in a city crowded with pilgrims of every nationality and class. It is little wonder that he thought that his education in the knowledge of mankind could be carried on better under present conditions than in journeying, as he had some idea of doing, to Sicily and Spain. Just a year before this, Galileo had visited Rome for the third time, after the accession of Urban VIII. to the pontifical chair. The latter was one of the few cardinals who had opposed the decree of 1616, condemning the doctrine of the motion of the earth and ordering Galileo to renounce his opinions. Doubtless the great philosopher expected much from the enlightened Cardinal Barberini, who, indeed, received him most affably and warmly. But it was the same Pope who, nine years later, summoned the old man back to Rome, and forced him, through the Court of the Inquisition, to renounce the truths he had spent his life in learning. Descartes did not see Galileo, although it seems strange that he did not do so. He might easily have turned aside, like so many other travellers, to visit the famous man who then had reached the zenith of his reputation. In a letter to Mersenne in 1638, Descartes specifically states not only that he never saw Galileo, but also that he had no communication with him, desired nothing from him, and, so far as music goes, had forestalled him.* Baillet thinks that he had actually confused him with his father, who was learned in mathematics and wrote on music. It seems quite incredible that he really took the father for the son, and, so far as his condemnation by the Inquisition was concerned, Descartes was well acquainted with the facts, for, as we shall see, they prevented his publication of his treatise on "the World"; still, he evidently thought that the father's writings on music were the compositions of the son. There seems to have been a strange element in Descartes' character of something not far removed from jealousy, which prevented him from appreciating as they deserved, the writings of other scientific men whom he regarded as his rivals. His criticisms of them are carping and ungenerous, and he seems often to be afraid that the credit due to himself might not be fully or sufficiently awarded.

It was early in spring that Descartes left Rome for France by Tuscany, where he may have visited the court of Duke Ferdinand II. About the time he left, the Pope was sending his cardinal nephew to the court of France, to endeavour to arrange matters as regards the Valtelline. This nephew was interested in the sciences, and when Descartes paid his respects to him, he reciprocated his attention, and a friendship thus arose which was afterwards carried on by presents of books, and other expressions of esteem. Descartes did not wish to travel by sea with the *savants* who accompanied their chief, but preferred to make his way to France by land. When he reached Tuscany he learned that war had been declared between the Republic of

* *Corr.*, vol. ii., pp. 388, 389.

Genoa and the Duke of Savoy, Charles Emmanuel, who was being supported by a French force under the leadership of Lesdiguières. When Descartes reached his camp, Gavi, the Spanish party had been thrown back, and between Tortona and Genoa, was being besieged. It was situated in a place difficult of access, and excellently defended; in spite, however, of almost insuperable difficulties, under the able leadership of the aged Lesdiguières, the place at length capitulated. After this event, Descartes, with his soldier's spirit still burning within him, longed to witness the marvellous progress of the Duke of Savoy's army, which was reducing the whole country to submission. The Genoese and Spaniards afterwards took courage, and once more gathered together their forces. Without waiting to see the final issue, Descartes left the army to go straight to Turin, where, according to his wont, he investigated the system of government which obtained, and visited the court, which was now, however, deserted, owing to the war: he nevertheless succeeded in seeing Christine of France, daughter of Henry IV., and Princess of Piedmont, who had married a few years earlier.

In May the traveller made his way out of Italy by Susa, three years later to be the scene of Louis' and Richelieu's triumph. Here, after all his manifold and very various interests in Italy, and his recent military experiences, the old love of scientific investigation came back to him, and after crossing Mont Cenis, he turned aside to make observations on the height of the surrounding mountains. He likewise tried to discover the cause of thunder, and why it thundered more in summer than in winter. His theory, which is worked out in his book on Meteors, is based on his observations on avalanches, the sound of whose falling reminded him of thunder. He conjectured that the higher clouds, being surrounded by a heated atmosphere, fell upon those beneath, just as did the snow heated by the sun's rays, a theory which at the time, and before thunder was associated with electricity,

seemed probable enough. Other observations were also
made by Descartes at this time, more especially those
concerning lightning, whirlwinds, etc., and he also seems
to have made an endeavour to measure the height of
Mont Cenis from two points on the plains of Piedmont
by geometric methods.   At least, he describes these
methods to Mersenne, when the latter was thinking of
travelling to Italy, although he does not actually say he
adopted them himself. He also warns Mersenne against
the climate, from which he must have suffered, for he calls
it specially unhealthy for Frenchmen, and states that if
one wishes to keep well, one must eat little, although, as
he acknowledges, the temptation to exceed would not
be so great to one of Père Mersenne's calling as to
another.   Had it not been for the richness of the food
and the warmth, Descartes declares, in 1639, he would
have established himself in Italy rather than in Holland,
although he believes, in such a case, he would not have
been so healthy.*
On quitting Italy, Descartes posted to Poitou in
order to hear about certain property which he could not
sell before he left, and to tell his godmother of the affairs
of her late husband, respecting which he had made it
his business to inquire.   At Châtellerault, he was urged
to purchase the office of Lieutenant-General of the
place, but he rejected the suggestion on the ground that
he had not sufficient ready money to make the purchase.
Friends, however, were eager to assist in helping him
to secure a competency, and, as no interest was
demanded, he felt obliged to write to his father and consult him while he was at Poitiers. Considering, however,
that his father, then in Paris, would think him incapable
of fulfilling the duties of the office, since he had hitherto
had no profession but that of arms, and seeing that he
was now twenty-nine years of age and somewhat old to
begin his studies, he decided to follow him to Paris with
the object of informing him that he would study with a
procureur, in order to acquire the necessary knowledge. He started before receiving a reply, and arrived

* *Corr.*, vol. ii., pp. 623, 624.

in Paris early in July, just after his father had left for
Brittany. His mission was probably somewhat of a
fictitious one; but in any case, on reaching Paris he was
easily persuaded to remain, and to leave in abeyance the
Lieutenant-Generalship and provincial occupation in
any other form.

Parisian life was much more to his mind than that
of a provincial official or administrator. The legate
sent by the Pope to the King of France had arrived a
month before, and Descartes was glad to renew his
acquaintance with the cardinal, whom he had known in
Rome, and with whom he maintained a friendly intercourse. At this time he must also have heard with
some emotion of the fall of Breda, after a nine months'
siege undertaken by Spinola, and just two months after
Prince Maurice had been succeeded by his brother,
Frederick Henry.

Descartes took up his abode with a distant relative
and family friend, M. le Vasseur d'Etioles by name,
whose son was living when Baillet wrote, and from
whom he appears to have heard some details of his life.
We are told that Descartes' aims at this time were to
avoid affectation and irregularity so far as might be,
to hold the most moderate and unexaggerated opinions,
and to live simply and without superfluity. His table
was sufficient but plain, his servants few, and he was
unattended in the streets: his dress was of a "simple
green taffeta" such as then was worn, and he carried
plumes and sword, merely as "marks of quality with
which a gentleman of that day could not dispense." *

But the too long delayed decision as to a future
mode of life must now be made, and yet the young man
felt he could not make it. He had given much thought
to the subject, balanced the various advantages and
disadvantages of different callings, and, of course, if
poverty had been pressing, or if he had had a wife and
family to support, he must finally have made up his
mind to submit himself to the demands of the inevitable
in making a selection. But as it was, he was free, and

* Baillet, vol. i., p. 131.

and sun, and then more sun.   Water all brackish—
soda-water all dead—tea not drinkable—grapes not
ripe—African boys peeping in at every corner craving
and whining."

Daly wrote a sketch of the journey to a friend in
1855 :—

"Memoranda for the assistance of a Punjabi
invalid, carrying a shattered frame homewards over
the Alps, down the Rhine, and by Cologne, Malines,
and Calais, seeking rest and restoration of health in
England.

"The invalid is in Bombay : here he has to provide himself with other coinage than rupees.   In the
first place he may *pay down* to Alexandria, even to
Trieste—the first I think certainly advisable — it
saves carrying gold, or circular notes to be exchanged
by extortioners.   Pay then to Alexandria ; if the
invalid shall have resolved to follow the Trieste route,
he might pay even thus far in Bombay.   The fare
from Alexandria to Trieste by the Austrian Lloyds
is £16.

"A day will suffice for Trieste.   Steamers run
across to Venice three or four times weekly.   The
passage occupies about six hours.   The approach to
Venice cannot be described.   Rogers in his *Italy*
beautifully depicts the golden glistening beams
thrown afar by the glorious St Marks.   A London
tailor who was with us exclaimed, as the steamer
shot into the lagoon, 'For all the world like Battersea Reach.'   Yet the tailor had not seen the Battersea
view for three years.   Not even the Himalayas had
so much surprised him.

"At Venice the invalid must halt.   Venice,
wonderful Venice, Child of the Sea, nothing need
be said of you!   From Venice by rail to Verona.
There was an interval here of rail, which, I think,
has since been completed and now runs to Milan.
At Milan the invalid must repose — its curious
picture galleries, its heavenly cathedral, which spoils
the eye of its pleasures in viewing afterwards the
Gothic structures *en route*.   Wait for a clear day to

G

ascend the tower of the cathedral: the view thence cannot be surpassed. Italy at your feet—beautiful cities, rich plains, and minature cathedrals right up to the Alps; then Monte Rosa, with its never-melting snows; and, if the atmosphere be clear, the chamois may be distinguished by the sportsman!

"From Milan the invalid seeks Como by rail. We slept the night at the little town, and the next day took the steamer to Bellagio, where we landed, ran and climbed up mountains with convents and vineyards hanging on their sides—returned across the lake, were nearly upset in a storm in the passage—sat down to an epicurean dinner in the comfortable inn. After our feast, got into the steamer returning from the head of the lake, were overtaken by a storm and landed drenched with rain. The weather cleared towards evening, and we (who had engaged a carriage at Milan to carry us to Lucerne) started for St Gothard.

"Now this is a difficulty—Lucerne with Lugano, St Gothard, and the Devil's Bridge — or Lago Maggiore, the Splügen, and Geneva. We chose the former, being the quicker, I think. Lugano differed essentially from Como. I was more struck with its grandeur than with anything I had seen before. Stop at St Gothard. It is sorely cold. Taylor and I ran *up* a considerable part of the last stage playing at snowballs. We drank some sulphurous wine from the Hospice, and being hungry ate some black bread and mouldy cheese — visited some honoured and revered bones inside, saintly bones of men and dogs—saw two or three living canines, large and sagacious. The descent is steep and rapid—arrived at the stage below the Hospice, very frozen, we were treated with great kindness — well-fed and little charged. On again the following morning to Albergo, and this was the first time I realised the glory of the Alps. Ascending, I was disappointed—looking back from Albergo and the Devil's Bridge the *mighty* Alps appear. Across by steam to Lucerne. The lake will describe itself. Guide books will tell you every stone on its banks. From this we travelled by diligence to Basle. Here your Murray is of use. It points out battle-fields of old time. Fields of ancient fame whose stories have been sung by Schiller.

"From Basle routes are various. We went by rail to Strasburg—the cathedral and a large French army were seen—thence down the Rhine to Cologne; above Strasburg the Rhine banks are dull and dreary —flat and uninteresting. Even within the beautiful spots, there is much that requires a pleasant fancy and a happy temperament. From Cologne even an invalid may run by rail to Calais, although a pause about Malines would well repay. I mention Malines, but I would rest a day among the old Belgian cities."

After visiting the Isle of Wight, Daly crossed over to Ireland, where his father had established himself at the old family place of Daly's Grove, 9 miles from Ballinasloe, "a big house dropped down on the edge of a marsh." He found his father "right well and merry; devoted to gunnery—surrounded by colts and horses—knows the character of every horse within a circuit of 20 miles round." Here Daly received with great interest accounts of the Ranizai expedition, and his "heart ached to have been absent." He wrote to one of his closest friends at Kohat :—

"Well, even in the little I have seen of England, bright and beautiful as it is—and nothing one can conceive or remember of beauty can equal the reality of its hedgerows, fields, and forests—I rejoice that fortune led me to follow an energetic profession in a land of trial. Sorrow not that fate has made you a labourer in the world—rejoice rather."

Returning to the Isle of Wight, he was married in October 1852, to Susan Kirkpatrick, whom he had known from boyhood; she belonged to that branch *

* Of another branch of this family came Colonel William Kirk-patrick, who was the first British envoy to Nepal (1793), and was also Resident at the court of Scindia and at Hyderabad; a most distin-

of the Kirkpatricks of Closeburn, whose ancestor (a son of the first baronet) left Scotland and settled in the Isle of Wight towards the end of the 17th century; her mother, a Miss Hughes, came of an old Welsh family.

Shortly after his marriage, Daly settled down at Shanklin, and devoted himself to hunting. During trips to town he constantly went to hear debates in the House of Commons, and was "enchanted with Dizzie's ready wit and humour—his aptitude for repartee. I heard him shake Cobden's jacket most effectually in a rejoinder; his retort was so ready, so pliant, so plausible. Cobden possesses so much vulgarity of manner, such an arrogant tone, that nothing but the sterling talent of the man could bear him up."

On the news of Sir Henry Lawrence's withdrawal from the Punjab, Daly wrote to India: "My sympathy is with you all in the departure of Sir Henry from the land of his own winning. He deserves and has the love and respect of all who have served under him."

Daly was deeply stirred by the outbreak of war with Russia. In March 1854, he saw "the glorious fleet sail for the Baltic. We were on board a steamer, and had a clear view of the glorious scene which thousands had congregated from every part to witness. The weather suited the event—bright and hopeful. The Queen received the old Admiral and his

guished officer—see Introduction to Vol. III. of the *Wellesley Despatches*, p. 10. His brother James, who succeeded him at Hyderabad, was also very highly commended by Lord Wellesley. Yet a third brother, Achilles, was also President at Hyderabad, where he contracted a romantic marriage with the daughter of one of the Hyderabad nobles. From this marriage sprang the Kitty Kirkpatrick who is mentioned in Carlyle's *Reminiscences*.

captains on board the *Fairy*, and when they had paid
their duty, signal was made by the Admiral, 'Sail'—
so in her presence the canvas was unfurled, and ship
by ship they moved off. The *Fairy* remained
stationary near the Nab, and each noble vessel, as
she marched past the Sovereign, manned her yards
and sent forth a royal cheer, which was given back
from every boat crowding the water. The last to
pass was the *Wellington*, that stupendous ship—her
rigging was darkened with 1200 men, whose voices
resounded far and wide. The Queen thus sent forth
her fleet. Worthy of us all, was it not?"

In May 1854, Daly went to Woolwich to witness
the launch of the *Royal Albert*, and there met many
friends with whom the chances of service in the
Crimea were eagerly discussed. Taylor had applied
some time previously to Lord Hardinge for employment; the answer was that it did not lie in Lord
Hardinge's power to employ him. Since that,
however, Beatson, formerly of the Nizam's army, had
been employed with Greene, of the Sind Horse, under
him, but as yet no rank in the Queen's service had
been assigned to them. Daly had already endeavoured, without success, to ascertain whether or
not the Government had intentions of employing
officers from India. At the India House, Melvill,*
the secretary, said that the Company had no view of
sending forces, nor did they contemplate employing
officers as reported :—"If you wish to go to Turkey,
your course is to lay your services before Lord
Clarendon. I should think your experience is what
is required. Lord Clarendon will probably apply to

* Afterwards Sir James C. Melvill, K.C.B.; he was secretary from
1836 to 1858.

us for your services, which will be readily accorded."
Daly replied: "I should be happy to go if I could be
sent in an authorised manner. I have no wish to be
an amateur." There matters rested, and his thoughts
were soon turned back to India. Amongst others
who stayed with him at this period, and on whose
advice he much relied, was Colonel Mansfield, who
was expecting to return to India unless he could
obtain employment in Turkey. Under the rules then
in force, Daly had lost his staff appointment on taking
leave, and he was anxious as to his future. In
September, however, he received reassuring letters
from Henry and John Lawrence. Sir Henry offered
to receive his wife on their arrival in India until Daly
was settled; and sent him an extract from a letter in
which Lord Dalhousie said he would be glad to put
Daly back in the Punjab Frontier Force. Uncertain
though Daly's destination was, his wife accompanied
him to India. They journeyed by Trieste; were
delayed a week in Egypt waiting for the mail steamer
from Southampton; and their own steamer then took
ten days on the journey from Suez to Aden, and
twelve days from Aden to Bombay.

Arriving in Bombay at Christmas, 1854, Daly
was met with the news that proposals were before
Government for the formation of an irregular force,
to be styled "The Jehazpur Legion," in Rajputana,
and that Sir Henry Lawrence had recommended him
for the command as "one of the fittest men in India."
Disappointment was, however, in store. The scheme
for the "Legion" hung fire, and the rule as to the
number of absentees from the Company's European
regiments was in future to be rigidly enforced. The
maximum admissible number of absentees was

twelve per battalion. The Bombay Fusiliers had already thirteen absentees, of whom twelve held substantive extra-regimental appointments. Sir Henry Lawrence sent on to Daly a letter from Lord Dalhousie—"Final orders have not yet been passed as regards the Jehazpur proposal, and I doubt whether it can be done without reference to the Court. As regards Captain Daly, I need not repeat the assurance of my good opinion of him and my wish to serve him. But I fear that at present the number of absentees from his corps makes him ineligible for detached employment." To Sir John Lawrence also Lord Dalhousie wrote, on 22nd November 1854: "I have received your letter. Your brother is well aware of my willingness to serve Captain Daly, for I agreed to put him back in the Punjab Force some time ago. But Captain Daly did not return. According to the last Bombay Army List he is not returned yet, and at any rate there are thirteen officers absent from his regiment; so that for the present it is wholly impossible to appoint him to the Jehazpur Legion, even if that force should be embodied." With a sad heart, therefore, and regrets at not having delayed his return, Daly established himself at Colaba, in a bungalow "almost washed by the waves," and resumed regimental duty.

His thoughts and hopes were now again turned towards the Crimea, with the expectation that Indian officers and perhaps Indian troops might yet be sent. He wrote to Ross, who was still in the 1st Punjab Cavalry :—

"Lord Derby, you see, urges the employment of irregular cavalry from India. My deliberate opinion is that the irregular cavalry are in every way capacitated for such employment. With some exceptions they possess the physique and morale to bear them up, and I, for one, would proudly and gladly throw in my fate with an irregular cavalry regiment in a campaign against the Russians. I pray this may befall me, and that, should the Government decide on accepting volunteer regiments, I may be sent to our old corps with an announcement that, if they volunteer, we shall go. They would volunteer to a man. A little selection would be required, and then we could go with a regiment which would make one's blood glow. Neville Chamberlain * to command the brigade! Does not the unequal strife in the Crimea stir our hearts and make us long to stand by them, overburdened, overborne by toil and numbers."

To another friend he said :—

"To be doing nothing in these days is an affliction. I question whether a good appointment in India would satisfy me, and certainly no employment has not a soothing effect. When I left England, Company's officers were discouraged from going— now immediate promotion and the prospect of further is painted up to tickle their fancy. It is possible Lord Panmure, in his desire to do that something which the people so shout loudly for, may ask Lord Dalhousie to detach officers from India. I resolved to meet the possibility, and on the arrival of the last mail I wrote to Courtenay, the Private Secretary, begging him in such an event to name me as ready and proud to serve either with or without Indian troops."

The reply from Courtenay was that Lord Dalhousie had as yet received no requisition, but would bear in mind that Daly was a volunteer for the Crimea. To his old friend, General Vivian, Daly also wrote that he was ready to join him at the shortest notice, and had some hopes of success. "I

* The late Field-Marshal Sir Neville Chamberlain, G.C.B., etc. —afterwards a close friend of Daly's.

would rather go there for service than fill the best appointment here now."

In April 1855, the Fusiliers moved to Karachi. In May Sir Henry Lawrence wrote to Daly :—

"As far back as August last, I wrote to Lord Hardinge recommending a Turkish contingent, and mentioned your, Taylor, and Lumsden's names. Some months ago I told him and Lord Dalhousie too to consider *me* a volunteer!"

In August, on seeing Colonel Mansfield's appointment to the mission at Constantinople, Daly sought his advice :—

"I *long* and long to be where men are working and where work is followed by honour." "Mansfield," Daly gratefully tells, "wrote to me on the day my letter reached him—kindly and fully—counselling my remaining in India—he thinks the field was great had I come at first, and writes kindly touching his help should I pitch his advice over and cast my bread on the waters—*and very tempted* did I feel to do this. Had I been alone, there would have been no hesitation, no delay."

This was in early January 1856. He was in better spirits. The acting appointment of Brigade-Major at Karachi had given him "lots of little employment" for a couple of months; and he felt "the tide was swelling towards him," and should reach him before Lord Dalhousie's departure. As to absentees from his corps the ground was at last clear, and he wrote this to Sir Henry Lawrence. "His reply came by return of post—kind and curt as usual: 'By this day's dâk I have written sending extracts of your note, and shall be as glad as ever to get the legion and you too.'" The answer to Sir Henry was, "He is provided for." Meanwhile Daly had received two

telegrams from the Viceroy's Private Secretary : " Go
to Agra " ; and, " You are to command Oudh Cavalry."
The quickest route to Agra was by sea to Calcutta,
and Daly set out at once, leaving his wife at Karachi,
where a few days later was born her second son, to
whom Sir Henry Lawrence was godfather.

CHAPTER VI

RAISING OF THE 1st OUDH IRREGULAR CAVALRY, 1856-1857

Lucknow ; Mrs Daly's journey there ; formation of the Corps ; Sekrora ; the Persian War ; Gaieties at Sekrora and retrospect on the fate of some of those present ; the outlaw Fazl Ali ; appointment to the Guides ; visit to Sir Henry Lawrence at Lucknow ; Agra.

IT was at the beginning of February 1856 that the Proclamation was issued which declared that Oudh was henceforth to be incorporated in British India. Sir James Outram, who was at the time the Resident* at the Court of the King of Oudh, thereupon became Chief Commissioner of the new Province, and among the measures ordered for the administration was the enrolment of an Irregular Force. It was to share in the raising of this Force that Daly had been summoned from Karachi. He reached Lucknow just as the Annexation was announced, and was very kindly received by Outram, who told him his was the first name that Lord Dalhousie had put down for the Force, and that, when Outram asked for a Brigadier of Cavalry, Lord Dalhousie said, " No, I mean Daly to have the organisation and command of three regiments with his own." This intention was not carried out, as Lord Dalhousie laid down the Governor-Generalship on the last day of February 1856, and

* He succeeded Colonel Sleeman in the appointment in 1854.
107

unforeseen difficulties * arose on the score of Daly's
want of seniority. He was, therefore, left with the
command of the 1st Regiment only. He had with
him as second in command Captain W. T. Johnson,
who had served in the Crimea with the 20th Regiment, and had fought at the Alma and Inkerman ; and
as Adjutant Lieutenant Hope-Johnstone, who, however, was invalided in May ; Surgeon Greenhow, from
the Mhairwarra Battalion, was the medical officer.

Mrs Daly left Karachi on the 18th February
1856, made a short stay with friends at Bombay,
sailed thence on the 5th March, and arrived at Calcutta on the 18th. On the 21st she left Howrah by
train, reaching the terminus, Raneegunge, the next
morning. The onward journey, which was by dâk
carriage, she thus described :—

"A dâk ghari is a long wooden carriage, with
venetians all round for windows and awnings, which
stretch out beyond them. A small trunk and hamper
of necessaries are packed on the roof; there too the
khitmatgar or butler travels. Inside, two people lay
at length on the bed, which is put on the board seats ;
propped up by pillows, one can be very comfortable ;
there is a well beneath, and a cupboard with shelves
at one's feet, and a net from the top in which one
stows away all one's things. From the first, such
battles with the horses took place, that had I not been
pretty well drilled to a quiet sort of faith that 'it will
all come right' with a vicious horse at last, I know
not what I should have done. One horse at a time is
put in the ghari ; he goes 4 miles, then is changed.
Every fresh horse resists to the uttermost making

* As soon as Daly had obtained his Captaincy (1854), he was
recommended for a Brevet Majority on account of his services at
Multan, and Lord Dalhousie specially interested himself in the case.
Some technical difficulty arose, and the step was not granted. A
further reference home was then made on the subject, and the matter
was still undecided when the Mutiny broke out.

a start. The coachman whips and swears (I have no doubt) in his language; men seize the horse by the head calling him every imaginable bad name; others bind ropes round his legs to pull; half a dozen seize the wheels to force the carriage on. At last, after a long battle, the horse almost always yields and canters off at a good pace for 4 miles. Then the same scene occurs again. It is tiresome to people who want to sleep, and every stoppage brings a crowd of applicants for *bakhshish*. Then every night there is an hour or two lost in stopping to grease the wheels; the coachman never will manage to get this done at the place where one stops for the day. I usually travelled from 5 o'clock in the evening to 9 or 10 the following morning. There was always great difficulty in persuading the horses to go up hill; to make amends, they galloped *down* the steep roads, with no protection to prevent our going over the steep banks into the ravines below, at a pace that would astonish people at home.

"Some time in the second night we passed a river, then a shallow stream, but which in the rainy season becomes a powerful flood; the horse was taken out and the ghari dragged through by men. It was a picturesque scene, two round mud towers stood on the banks of the river, one on each side. A number of natives were collected at the ford, bullock carts, ekkas, and men on horseback; the hills were dimly visible, closing in the scene; a young moon scarcely gave a light, though she cast a long line of silver on the water; on the opposite bank a fire was burning, with natives grouped around it. Towards morning we reached the Saone; the horse was taken out, and the carriage dragged through the dry sandy banks and bed of the river and across the bridge of boats by bullocks. A long, wearisome business this. The sun was high when we reached Sasseram.

"The next night brought us to Benares; we reached the holy city so very early that it was too dark to see anything. We left on a hot, dusty afternoon about 5 o'clock; reached the shores of Jumna before daybreak; dawn came on as we laboured over the bridge of boats. The aspect of Allahabad in the early, hazy dawn was very pleasing;

the mud walls looked quite imposing; the little temples by the water's edge, the groups of cattle on their way to the jungle, and the boats floating lazily out for their day's work were very picturesque. We drove to a large, good, European hotel, intending to have an early breakfast and then go on for a stage or two. While at the hotel, I sketched from the balcony a view of the Jumna, with a distant glimpse of the Ganges at the junction of the two rivers; the fort, grey with the morning fog, and some of the curious boats, which I sketched carefully—little houses with thatched roofs built in them, with the most extraordinary arrangement of masts and poles—made a good subject. We started again soon, and stopped for the day at a bungalow in a grove of beautiful acacia trees, which looked most green and pleasant through the sultry day. In the evening we were off again; by starting early and staying out late, we managed to reach Cawnpore about 11 on the 29th."

Daly met his wife at Cawnpore, whence one more stage of dâk ghari brought them to Lucknow. She thus concluded her description of the journey:—

"We reached Lucknow early, passing innumerable mosques and temples with tall minarets, crowded bazaars, etc. As we drove out of the city into the open country I was charmed with the aspect of the Dilkusha Park through which we passed; the road, wide and good, ran through beautiful trees; we passed the Dilkusha Palace, a handsome house resembling a French château, approached by long flights of steps with pillars and balustrades and strange looking little pepper-box turrets and grotesque statues; a very favourite resort of the king, whose private property it has still continued. About a quarter of a mile further on we passed through a handsome but dilapidated gateway, with a broken statue of a man and a stag on the top of great iron gates well rusted on their hinges, into the Bebiapur Park. Here the park was more like a forest. Magnificent mango trees, pipul, acacia, banian, many of which I knew not the names, grew here in strength and beauty. We soon reached the encamp-

LUCKNOW.

[To face p. 110.

ment, for as yet the men have no huts—their tents pitched about under the trees, horses picqueted near, the sowars in white with scarlet turbans and cummer-bunds (sashes), the camp followers with coats and scarves of every hue, the little fires on the ground with women cooking chupatties, naked children rolling and playing beside them.   All this had a wonderfully bright and pleasant effect.   We passed another gate-way, where the guard house is, and drove up a slight hill to the Bebiapur Kothi or house.   I was charmed with the aspect of the large, comfortable mansion.

"From the flat roof of the house there is a very extensive view * for miles around in every direction over the flat but beautifully wooded scenery.   The domes and minarets of Lucknow rise above the *waves* of foliage formed by the trees of the Dilkusha Park.   Dilkusha Palace, nearer to us, is distinctly visible, so are the Martinière (a college founded by General Claude Martine, a French soldier of fortune who rose to be a general in the late King of Oudh's service), and a garden called the Vilaiti Bagh (foreign garden), a very favourite place of resort with the king.   The Goomti winds away into the distant plains, sometimes spreading out into wide sheets, where it flows close by Bebiapur, a narrow but deep stream.   Little villages with flat-roofed mud hovels are dotted about among the mango topes (clumps), herds of cattle graze on the plains, whilst already the patches of cultivation show where the harvest will be."

It was in Oudh as it had been in the Punjab : commandants had to make their own arrangements for arms, uniforms, and accoutrements.   Daly had his previous experience to guide him.   He wrote off at once to Ross, his great ally in the 1st Punjab Cavalry, who was then at home :—

"Now you must help in a business matter.   First the leathern accoutrements.   Ridgeway shall supply them as before, and I want them begun without

* This description is of interest as the Bebiapur House was Sir Colin Campbell's headquarters during the final attack on Lucknow exactly two years later : see page 191.

delay. Will you see whether patent leather would not be better. The pouches were too large before ; we had to cut them down. Put this afloat at once. About carbines I will write more fully next mail. I *incline* to think Sam Browne's method of slinging preferable. There are two great advantages arising therefrom : the barrel *up* and the length increased without inconvenience in carrying, and with much advantage to the weapon. I would go to Westley Richards. He has a wider repute, and can afford to turn them out cheaper than Greener." In July he sent another letter :—"I wrote you a line about carbines in March. Subsequently Outram told me to wait until the matter had been referred to the Government as to whether they would provide them. Of course the Government expressed astonishment, and now I have drawn up a paper for you which I think will enable you to form an opinion what you should do, as I leave all with yourself! This Pritchett rifle-carbine is a beautiful weapon, and would enable us to go anywhere and hold any post ; 10 a troop, the best shots in the corps. Look at the belts ; there must be a small *cap* bag, which I have not ordered, and which before we were obliged to get from Cawnpore." Lengthy was the correspondence with England on this and similar details.

Concerning the enlistment, Mrs Daly wrote :—

"Every morning men and horses come to be selected for the regiment ; they assemble on the open space before our house. The horses, wild-looking creatures, neighing and prancing, covered with all sorts of bright-coloured saddle-cloths and scarves from their noses to their saddle-girths ; men from all parts of India : Afghans and Pathans, with their large loose trousers, loose white linen coats, and curious erections and scarves on their heads : fine-looking Sikhs : Hindus and Muhammadans. Many of the men of Henry's old regiment have come down seeking service. He would like to raise his regiment of north country men, but the order is to enlist men of the King of Oudh's regiments. An hour or two is occupied by Henry in inspecting these candidates,

THE NEW REGIMENT   113

making them put their horses through all manner of
evolutions to prove that they can ride; listening to
their tales, reading their papers, etc."

As to the progress made, Daly wrote to Ross on
the 31st May 1856 :—

"When first I came here, Outram restricted us
to men of the old cavalry of the Government; a
miserable lot.   At my intercession he opened the
door a little to allow half a dozen non-commissioned
officers to be brought from other cavalry.   I have
Ghulam Mohi-ud-din, Ram Singh,* and two or three
old friends now on their journey.   Sundil Khan†
wishes much to come, and I will gladly take him, if he
can get leave.   I have about 300 men now; some
very fine: they move tolerably well even now.   I
have parade every morning at daybreak, drilling and
parading them *en masse* directly they have learnt
right from left.   Burnett is selecting Sikhs for me.   I
will have a troop of them.

"*16th July* 1856.—The regiment is now nearly
full.   Sundil Khan is to be transferred; Ghulam
Mohi-ud-din‡ and three or four others are here.   I have
made our old friend Ghulam Mohi-ud-din a jemadar.
Salar Bakhsh,§ from the Guide Corps, comes as
2nd resaldar.   I tried to get him in 1849 with
Sobhan Ali, but Lumsden would not let him go.   He
is a fine, handsome-looking, soldierly fellow, up to his
work.   All the native officers I have here command
troops *well*.   The regiment begins to move in
excellent order; 3 strong squadrons.   I shall make a
good corps.   I have the same uniform as before.
Scarcely any alterations worthy of remark.   The
clothing is now being made up in Bombay; it will be
shipped to Calcutta for about Rs. 30, and in addition
to being superior in quality will be cheaper than
anything I could get here.

"The climate of Oudh is very much that of

* See page 118 (note).   † See pages 66 and 151.
‡ Mrs Daly noted in 1859, "This man was faithful when all around
were false, and died of wounds, fighting on our side, at Lucknow." See
also page 175 (7th Sept.).
§ See page 241.

H

Bengal, I should think. Moist, very moist. It *must* be salubrious: the race of people one sees about look so stout and robust; so different from the fever-smitten inhabitants of the Punjab during August and September. The rains have not been violent hitherto; ever longer than twenty-four hours at a bout."

"*23rd September* 1856.—The regiment will be first-rate: it is finer as a whole than the 1st Punjab Cavalry. The men I have taken by single files, and all have passed the ordeal. Horses good. I mean it to be the finest irregular cavalry in India, and so it will be."

In the autumn the regiment was sent to an out-station. Daly was offered the choice of Sekrora or Pertabgarh, and chose the former, which is about 50 miles from Lucknow. He relieved the 5th Irregular Cavalry, under Macdonald, who had built good lines, for which Government gave funds. The 73rd Native Infantry had just left, and the garrison was for the future to consist of a regiment of cavalry, one of infantry, and a battery, all from the Oudh Irregular Force. The march was made early in October 1856:—

"The roads are but tracks," wrote Daly, "and these have been carried away by the heavy rains. We remained encamped in a pretty spot on the banks of the Gogra three days while the regiment passed over in boats; this was a slow process, as at the Ghât the river is a couple of miles in width. From the Gogra to Sekrora is but 16 miles, but a meandering river, the Surjoo, runs between; this and the Gogra would delight the heart of any fisherman; fish of every kind and of all sizes. Shortly before leaving Lucknow there was an inspection of my regiment. A thunderstorm came on just as we were mounting. When that had cleared off, there was not much daylight left. However, the Brigadier and his staff had come, also a friend of mine, a cavalry Brigadier, who had courteously ridden over 10 or 12 miles to be present. All went off *very* successfully; the regiment gave great satisfaction, even to me! The old Brigadier expressed much surprise and many congratulations, and concluded by saying he would make a special report to Government of the manner in which I had brought the corps into an effective state."

In *November* 1856, Daly wrote :—

"I am in an incipient trepidation about this Persian affair. I have written to the Lawrences to keep me informed should there be aught to move from the north-west. I should strive hard to find a place should any force move up to Kabul; and, if it be intended to afford the Dost the help of arms, there it will be applied; but I cannot see how such things can be, and peace reign in Europe with Russia. Persia must have Russia's aid or she will not move her smallest puppet. I see Mansfield in the Gazette, rank of Major-General while employed on particular service in *Poland*. What means this?"

"*7th December* 1856.—I see Mansfield is widening his footing at home; Consul-General at Warsaw. He has ability for any position, and that which is of more use in many cases than even talent itself (though in fact it is one of the greatest of talents), *tact*. Whether his ambition is for soldiership or diplomacy I know not; possibly he has chosen the latter. He is an excellent linguist, familiar with German and French, and I rather fancy has some knowledge of Italian. His mind is quickly applied to any point; then he has cultivated penmanship, and can express his ideas (and those of others too) clearly and pointedly. Mansfield may *choose* his course now; rise he certainly will.

"We have war on our hands here without being aware of it. Dost Muhammad is now at Peshawar at a conference with John Lawrence. John, George writes me, is as much opposed as the other two brothers to the aid of money and supplies which has been sent to Kabul. Lakhs of everything—rupees, muskets, ammunition—have been forwarded, and by and by, if actual warfare with Persia be the result, a force will go to the shoulders of our ally. Should that be, may I be there to see.

"*23rd January* 1857.—Since last writing, Johnson the second in command, has started for Bombay. He telegraphed Outram for employment, and got it, 'under Jacob with Arab levies.' I would have offered to join Outram, and I have reason to believe that my offer would have been accepted, but I could not do so without knowing the result of my Punjab attempt. At first, in common with everyone in India, I thought the Bushire attempt must end there, or, as before in '38, at Kharak.* Now it is evidently otherwise. The work will be there, but still I am inclined to believe that the Dost is to be supplied with officers as well as money wherewith to play our game. In such event my chances are good. My corps is a *very fine* one, and should no card turn up trumps to get me away, I shall volunteer with the regiment and plead hard. Here I cannot abide while the great game is played out almost within hearing.

"*7th February.*—Lumsden tells me the resolution, after endless darbars, is that neither officers nor troops are to advance, merely money and a mission to Kandahar, with a vakil at Kabul. He and his brother, with Cox the doctor, compose the mission, and their duty will be to see that the Dost keeps up an effective force with the 12 lakhs which he is to get annually while the war lasts; rather than that should cease, the old fellow and his adherents could afford to pay Persia half. A few days since came a letter from George Lawrence to the effect that Sir Henry, instead of starting for England according to his leave, had, at Lord Canning's urgent request, laid his dâk for *Lucknow*, where he will be in a few days. Sir Henry's advent is, of course, a matter of rejoicing; for me, however well inclined, he can do nothing in Oudh, and in Oudh I want nothing except to be helped out of it, and that help I shall ask of him. Since my last we have had the kind, gentlemanly, old Brigadier here reviewing us; he was very warm in his admiration of the corps, which is indeed a fine one."

---

* Kharak Island was occupied by an Anglo-Indian force in June 1838, evacuated in March 1842, reoccupied in December 1856, and again evacuated in March 1857, on the conclusion of hostilities with Persia. See Lord Curzon's *Persia*, vol. ii., p. 405.

On the 30*th January* 1857, Mrs Daly wrote :—

"Mr Jackson, the acting Chief Commissioner, is coming here in a few days with his two pretty nieces; there are five ladies in this station and two at Gonda, 15 miles off; it is decided that there are enough to get up a dance, and we are all highly busy now planning how it shall be." Two years later, after her return to England, she noted :—"I remember well how gay and merry we were preparing for that party! The kutcherry, or court-room, which was to be the ball-room, being whitewashed and decorated; the stands of arms, banners, and garlands of flowers that adorned the walls, the tents to be pitched, and the supper devised and cooked. Before many months were over how many of that little party had died a violent and dreadful death. The two fair girls for whom it was got up, encountered a fate * one shudders to think of. The bright, joyous Madeline indeed was spared after months of intolerable captivity and hardship; but Georgina, the gentle, lovely, elder sister, it is believed was murdered, together with poor Mrs Greene, after escaping from Sitapur. Mr Charles Boileau, the clever, agreeable, young civilian, who was believed to be the favoured lover of poor Georgina, murdered in a few weeks only by Fazl Ali; the first of the awful scenes of horror of that dreadful year. Mr Longueville Clark,† Mr Bax, both dancing so gaily that night, soon to meet a bloody death, with many others then present. But then we knew nothing of coming horrors. All was gay and everyone cheerful, and the little ball, got up in a rude out-station, gave more pleasure than many a grand entertainment.

"Next night we were all asked to dine with the Chief Commissioner in his tents : then came the first shock. News was brought that Fazl Ali, a noted outlaw, had plundered some Government thanas (police posts), murdered some villagers, etc. I was puzzled at the consultations of the gentlemen. Next morning I learnt that a 'daur,' or chase, had been

* See p. 209.
† Killed at Byram Ghat in June 1857, when endeavouring to escape.

decided on, and that Henry was going with a party of thirty or forty sowars to join a detachment of Captain Miles's regiment which had marched from Gonda. Next day was spent in selecting men and making arrangements; in the night he started off in pursuit."

On his return, Daly wrote the following account of his proceedings :—

"*9th March* 1857.—I rode in from Nanparah, about 70 miles distant, by moonlight on the night of the 5th. The pursuit was vain to effect capture; it proved to the people, a quiet race beaten by fever, that troops were never far from them; their awe of Fazl Ali is such that no one would reveal a word of his movements, though he is as well known throughout the district as was Rob Roy on his heather.

"*10th March.*—Thus far I wrote yesterday. A tragedy most grievous this desperado has now effected. Boileau the civilian (Deputy Commissioner of the District), with whom I went to Tulsipur, was murdered on the 7th or 8th; the particulars of the occurrence have not yet reached us. Yesterday I received a note from Boileau, dated 6th, telling me that the outlaw had again evaded the pursuit, and had made his escape into Nepal. Boileau left a body of men, and with an escort of six and a jemadar moved along the forest side to Tulsipur. What took place I have not yet ascertained.* Boileau was not thirty years of age, of a sweet and engaging disposition, of a most kindly, generous temperament,

---

* On the 19th March Mrs Daly wrote :—"Every day brings fresh accounts of the terrible affair. Poor fellow, he was brave and rash, and rushed on his death as it were. He came suddenly on Fazl Ali's party; he had but half a dozen men with him, these he separated and placed as sentries round the little village in which Fazl Ali was. Ram Singh, whose portrait hangs at home, alone remained with him. Whether he meant to wait till Lieutenant Clarke, known to be near, came up with his party, or what, none knew. He was discovered; suddenly a volley was fired from behind some buildings. Mr Boileau fell from his mare exclaiming, 'Oh Ram Singh! I am killed.' Another Sikh, Bhugwan Singh, came up; together they lifted the Sahib's body on to his horse; it fell off. Bhugwan Singh appears to have gone

RAM SINGH, AS A DAFADAR IN THE 1ST PUNJAB CAVALRY.

[To face p. 118.

possessed of excellent talents and of great perseverance. He was active and gallant, confiding and unsuspicious. Such was the fine English gentleman cut off by this fellow. Many a tale of bold, reckless ruffianism is told of Fazl Ali. His headquarters for years have been along the Tulsipur and Nandparah forest, and when pressed he has taken to Nepal. The Rani of Nandparah was constantly at war with the Raja of Tulsipur. Fazl Ali was occasionally on one side, occasionally on the other; but, wherever he was, that side had the prestige of success. After the annexation he went into Nepal, but of late has returned to our territory, and some *horridly* bloody murders have been committed by him.

"On our arrival at the scene of his depredations scarcely a word of information could we procure. However, with some sixty sowars I made a forced march to the end of the first ridge of hills where the Raptee jerks round the Valley of Nepal to flow into our territory. Here the hills sink into the plain, which is a dense forest. Goolerie, marked in the map, is a small space cut in the woods where the cow-herds bring their cattle to graze; here we found clear and recent traces of the fugitive, but the same silence amongst the people; not from disaffection to me, but from the awe of him and the fear of his revenge. This was his old haunt; here there was no food for man or beast, but what we had brought with us. I attempted to cut him off. I dismounted thirty Sikhs and Hillmen, and sent them up the pass which leads us into Nepal. These men took with them their swords and carbines, and a little flour; their trip was vain. We marched to the Nepal border, and had a

away. Ram Singh went in search of the other sowars to endeavour to persuade them to bring off poor Boileau's body; he could not induce them to venture. The firing was close and heavy, the Sahib dead, and they had but their swords. Still Henry is angry, and says they shall leave the regiment for deserting the body. Ram Singh returned alone and stood by the Sahib's body till he had four bullets in himself and his clothes; one in the wrist disabled him, but he made his escape. He went to Ghulam Mohi-ud-din, a resaldar who was at a village with a detachment not far off; they returned, but could not find the body, and Fazl Ali had gone off. Afterwards the body was found and sent into Lucknow for burial."

(head servant) comes to him every day for orders for dinner. I don't consider housekeeping his forte; we have very bad dinners often, but Sir Henry cares nothing about this, and the servants soon find it out. Then there is never any knowing how many guests will be present. One day I had sent out cards for a small dinner of fifteen; about two hours before dinner George Lawrence came up to tell me his uncle had forgotten to mention that he had invited about twenty others in addition.

"Henry is evidently a great favourite with Sir Henry, and this is very gratifying to know. He sends his bearer to call him at daybreak to go out riding. Sir Henry is most carefully inspecting the city and making various alterations and arrangements. When they come in, Sir Henry has his easy chair, books, and a cup of tea in the verandah, into which our rooms open. Our little one has already grown quite familiar with his godfather. Always good-natured and kind to children, Sir Henry takes a great deal of notice of him; the child runs up to him without hesitation, pulling his coat, touching his book; I rush out to fetch him in and apologise; but Sir Henry laughs, and says, 'I have had little children of my own.' In the afternoon we usually drive out with Sir Henry, and return to dress in a scramble for dinner.

"*6th April.*—Colonel Edwardes * is here. I am rather disappointed in him, having always looked upon him as a great hero. He may have been handsome once, but is stout and rather coarse now with a very Jewish cast of countenance; but I do not perceive what other people complain of—great vanity and contempt of other people's opinion. I was at church, and stopped with Sir Henry and Colonel Edwardes for the Sacrament. It is a long time since I had the comfort of receiving that, or of being at church at all. When we came in, I found Henry had returned from Sekrora, where he had gone for a day or two.

"Mr and Mrs Christian † are here; he is very

* The Commissioner of Peshawar, afterwards Sir Herbert Edwardes.

† Both killed at Sitapur, 3rd June 1857.

clever, his conversation very interesting. She is a delicate, gentle, young woman, pretty and pleasing, and beautifully dressed. Dr Ogilvie and his wife are also here. The breakfast is the agreeable party here; a meal that lasts from 10 till 12 o'clock. Gentlemen constantly dropping in; the conversation animated and pleasant, a great contrast to the usually vapid discourse one hears. Sir Henry himself so spirited, so agreeable in discourse; Colonel Edwardes, Mr Christian, Dr Ogilvie, my Henry, all clever men and quick in conversation. Major Banks * is often here. Colonel Goldney,† the Commissioner, is staying here; Captain Hayes‡ and many others constantly coming.

"One night there was a performance of amateur theatricals, with a ball afterwards, at the Residency in cantonments. Soon afterwards Sir Henry gave a fête to the men, women, and children of the 32nd Regiment. Henry had all the arrangements to make with Colonel Inglis. The entertainment was given in the Dilkusha Park, near the Martinière. There was dinner for the men and their wives, and a collation, iced champagne, etc., for the *élite*, who were all invited to be present; afterwards games, races, feats of horsemanship exhibited by the men of Major Gale's § regiment. In the evening a dance by moonlight out of doors. One evening Sir Henry drove us out to see the dear old house at Bebiapur. Another evening we went to the Martinière. Each day was fully occupied. Sir Henry hates state, and does not even like driving with four horses and being attended by horsemen and flags; but this is necessary for the Chief Commissioner's dignity. I had no time for fresh sketches of the picturesque city. The view from the top of the Residency is more beautiful than I can describe. Countless mosques and minarets on all sides; the bright green trees which intersperse them; the winding Goomtee; the vast expanse of

* Killed in Lucknow, 21st July 1857.
† Killed on the Gogra below Fyzabad, 9th June 1857 : see Kaye's *Sepoy War*, vol. iii., pp. 460-467.
‡ Killed on the Mynpoorie Road, 31st May 1857.
§ Killed at Rai Bareilly early in June 1857.

richly wooded plains; even the city looks beautiful when one is far above the dirt. In the fresh early morning or by the sweet calm moonlight it was inexpressibly lovely. One day I spent with the Gubbins; Mrs Gubbins is a very nice person; I like her and the Ommaneys * very much.

"12th April.—Still at Lucknow. We have been rather doubtful about undertaking the long, expensive journey, now that the Persian War coming to a close makes Major Lumsden's return probable; but Sir Henry advises Harry to go, saying, 'the Guide Corps is the most honourable appointment a man of your standing can hold, and if you lose a little money now, you will find the advantage by and by.' Fazl Ali is killed; at least so it is hoped and believed.

"A native gentleman here takes photographic likenesses, and has done several of Henry and me and baby. Whilst he was trying baby, Sir Henry came up to inspect. We persuaded him to sit for his likeness † (he had always a great dislike to being taken); the darogha was very successful.

"Sir Henry had a most romantic attachment for his wife, who has been dead about four years. She was, I believe, a talented and accomplished woman, well worthy of the love her noble husband bore her. One day Sir Henry's bearer called Eliza (maid) into his master's room, while he was out for his morning ride, and showed her a portrait which Sir Henry always wore round his neck; by some chance he had taken it off that morning and left it on his dressing-table; it was a miniature of Lady Lawrence taken when she was a girl, a pretty fair girl with long curls; the bearer said he had never known his master leave it off him before. Henry, who knew him before her death, says that, cheerful as he is, there is a great change in him. He certainly, more than anyone I ever knew, gives one the feeling of *living for another world;* he is perfectly cheerful, active, and interested in this, yet every now and then some little observation falls

---

* Mr Ommaney was killed early in the siege of Lucknow.

† The well-known portrait of Sir Henry, seated, in a black coat with the Star of the Bath, and wearing a cloth cap, was probably taken on this occasion.

from his lips which proves how fully he is *imbued* with the feeling of the transitory nature of our present existence, how *perfect* is his faith that *the real life is to come*. A deeply religious man, attached himself to all the ordinances of the church, he is towards others most tolerant and charitable in thought and deed. A noble Christian hero in every sense of the word. His munificence in all charitable institutions is the wonder and admiration of all who know him; yet he himself never seems to think he has done more than his *duty*. He is economical in his personal habits, yet most liberal to others, exercising an almost boundless hospitality, fond especially of collecting young people about him and not despising any of their amusements. I shall leave Lucknow with regret, for I have many pleasant acquaintances here, and many with whom I am sure I should soon be very friendly.

"*16th April, Agra.*—We left Lucknow on the night of the 13th-14th. Very sorry to depart, both of us, and I believe Sir Henry was sorry we should go; he came out to see us off, and seemed quite affected at parting with Harry."*

At the same period Daly wrote:—

"Colonel Edwardes is palpably a man above the mark in talent; makes good *hits* and points in conversation; he is subdued and somewhat grave; has somewhat the affectation of dignity. He has grown stout. He has a fine head and features like a Jew. In early youth he was frolicsome, gay, and witty; he seems now to have a puritanical conviction that such things are unbecoming. He is a religious man, careful of forms, and inclined somewhat to give out his opinion on controversial matters. He is friendly and polite

* That Sir Henry appreciated Daly is indicated by his mention of him in his essay on "The Indian Army," written in 1855-56, where, in speaking of the training of the native cavalry, he says, "An inspector is wanted; not an old Royal Dragoon officer, but a first-rate irregular officer—a Jacob, a Chamberlain, an Anderson, a Daly, or a Malcolm. A man, in short, who will go on common-sense principles, keep the men out of debt, insist on rational reform and rational treatment." (See *Essays, Military and Political*, by Sir H. M. Lawrence, p. 412.)

to me, yet I do not *warm* to him. He is somewhat diplomatic, and less straightforward than is pleasant. Unlike our noble, high-minded host, whose heart is full of true religion, whose mind is cultivated and generous; who is conversant with the history of the world, and the nature of men; keen in observation; quick in temper; a rare creature, made for love and honour."

On leaving Lucknow, Daly and his wife proceeded by Cawnpore and Mynpoorie to Agra. On the 16th April Mrs Daly wrote:—

"This evening we drove out to see the Taj, with which we were indeed delighted; well worth the détour of 70 miles to see it. Grand and solemn the vast fabric of white marble looks rising up amidst the dark foliage. Our first glimpse from the road as we approached Agra did not give one an idea of half its beauties, its *solemnity*. Seen by twilight the grand, pure, massive structure impresses one with awe as well as with admiration. All seems so chaste, so pure, and so mighty; so separate from the dust and turmoil of the busy world around. Two hundred years have passed over this unequalled monument raised by love, and still the tomb of Shah Jehan and his beloved wife rises in unsullied splendour with a grandeur and solemnity all its own.

"We reached the outer gate just as twilight was coming on, the moon shining above the dome. The view up the long avenue of yews, with the marble tank and marble paths on either side, to the Taj itself was impressive to the utmost. We walked up these marble roads; on either side marble paths branch off, and one has glimpses of gardens and bright flowers carefully kept beneath the shade of the mango groves. At the end of the avenue we ascended a flight of *such* steep steps and came on the spacious marble platform on which the Taj itself stands. From each corner of this platform rises a marble minaret. It is all marble; marble everywhere; the purest and whitest being reserved for the tomb, with its smooth, vast dome. I cannot tell you how this uniform, grand simplicity of material adds to the solemnity of the whole. Opposite the avenue by which we approach, the platform rises from the river. On either side of it, at some little distance, are handsome buildings in red stone, with white domes; but one's attention is riveted on the pure white tomb itself. We enter it; a vast domed apartment, with the most wonderful musical echo in it I ever heard. All beautiful white marble above, around, and under one's feet, except where chapters of the Koran, in Arabic, are inlaid in letters of black, and the ornamental inlaying of gold and jewels and precious stones on the tombs themselves and the screen which encloses them. The tomb of the Empress occupies the centre; that of Shah Jehan is by her side. The screen around the tombs is the most wonderful specimen of open-work carving in marble that I ever beheld. After all, the real tombs are in a vault exactly beneath those one sees on entering, and exact facsimiles of them, inlaid jewel-flowers and all.

"*17th.*—Early this morning we were up to pay the Taj a second visit. Beautiful as it is by daylight, I think one does not feel the same awe and reverence as by moonlight. Afterwards we visited the fort, a place of great strength, and the famous Moti Musjid (Pearl Mosque), also built by Shah Jehan; very beautiful, but not comparable to the Taj. In the fort we saw the 'Gates of Somnauth'; old worm-eaten things, not worth the fuss made about them."

Delhi was reached on the 18th April. Here they halted but a day, meeting an old home acquaintance who "talked a good deal of the disaffection of the troops, etc.," though it does not appear that the matter was regarded as of immediate importance. The 20th saw the little party at Umballa, whence, on the 21st, Daly started for Lahore. His wife and child left the same evening for Simla; by mid-day on the 22nd they reached Kasauli, of which Mrs Daly wrote :—

"We stopped to dine at the dâk bungalow, where I took a sketch of the Lawrence Asylum, about

vated, has not that generous delicacy, the great characteristic of his brother. Sir John is doubtless an
excellent Government servant—energetic, bold, and
vigilant—with his command is none of the love and
reverence which bear so much sway in Sir Henry's
case.

"*24th April.*—Edwardes arrived. He is more
familiar with Sir John than with Sir Henry—he
seems to suit his manners and his affection to the
distinct characters. His influence with both is great.
Great with Sir Henry, because Sir Henry believes
him a man of great ability, ruled by the highest and
purest principles; whereas with Sir John it is the
energy and adaptability of Edwardes which win
their way—the common-sense, active commission
John works to.

"*25th.*—Started for Jhelum at noon; crossed the
Chenab with two very intelligent men 'on the
Telegraph,' who had come down from Lahore to see
the cause of a stoppage in the communication. I
was much struck with these grammar-indifferent but
clear-headed fellows, possessed of a knowledge and
wielding it with an ease most enviable. Road bone-
breaking. Crossed the bridge of boats at a rattling
pace, recognised the Field of Gujerat and refreshed
my memory. Jhelum 106 miles; entered the
melancholy Doon about midnight.

"*26th.*—Reach Pindi, about 60 miles, at 8 P.M.
Kindly welcomed by Miller.

"*27th.*—Remained chatting with Miller and his
pleasant, cheerful wife till 6 P.M. Started on a horse
of his and rode the sixteen miles, and then to my
doolie den.

"*28th.*—Reached Attock at 8 A.M.; morning air
cool, atmosphere clear; felt quite touched at crossing
the old river and saluting again the old familiar hills,
with the light so clear on them that every fissure was
bare to view; reached Nowshera in two hours;
found Holmes-Scott,* boisterously pleased to see me
—had long chats. Reached Mardan about sunset."

* Of the 55th Native Infantry, which relieved the Guides at
Mardan on 13th May, and mutinied just afterwards; all the officers
were saved except the colonel, who committed suicide.

G. Lawrence

Colonel H. Edwardes   Sir Henry Lawrence

G. Lawrence
Colonel H. Edwardes   Sir Henry Lawrence

The officers present with the Guides were Battye, second in command; Kennedy, Commandant of Cavalry; Hawes, Adjutant; and Stewart, Assistant Surgeon.

The news of trouble at Meerut reached Edwardes at Peshawar on the night of the 11th May; next morn he heard of the Delhi outbreak. He telegraphed to John Lawrence proposing to form a movable column of Her Majesty's 24th and 27th, the Guides and some irregular cavalry. On the morning of the 13th, a bare fortnight after he first joined the corps, Daly received the news of the mutiny. He wrote in his diary for that day :—

"Heard at 8 this morning that the 55th Native Infantry had marched from Nowshera at gunfire to relieve the Guides at Mardan. About an hour afterwards received an order from Colonel Edwardes to move without delay with the corps into Nowshera. A private note * explained: open mutiny at Meerut

* "*Private.*—From Edwardes.

"PESHAWAR, 12*th May* 1857.

"That you may better know how to act on the enclosed instructions to move to Nowshera, I write privately to tell you that telegraphic news of open mutiny among the native troops at Meerut having reached us here to-day, we think a movable column should be assembled in the Punjab to get between the stations that *have* gone wrong and those that have *not;* and put down further disaffection by *force.* It is obviously necessary to constitute such a column of *reliable* troops, and therefore it has been proposed to get the Guides and Her Majesty's 27th together without delay as a part of the scheme, and, if these plans be matured, you will probably have to close upon Her Majesty's 24th and the Kumaon Battalion at Pindi, and there be joined by an irregular regiment from Kohat or Bannu, and perhaps more of that good quality. The 55th Native Infantry have therefore orders to receive charge of Mardan from you.

"If these arrangements take effect, you will have the most important service before you, and though painful, one that you will, I feel sure, find usefulness and honour in. The disaffection seems to have gone too far to be *talked* down; and Government must look now to men who can and will *put* it down."

and elsewhere; reliable troops to be collected and moved off towards Jhelum. No more scotching the snake. No more concessions and sympathetic speeches, drawing tears and fanning the flame, but treason and mutiny to be met by sternness and force. Handed over the fort, and marched at 6 P.M. with about 150 cavalry and 350 infantry. Reached Nowshera at midnight. Two hours after received an 'urgent' to proceed forthwith to Attock to relieve the three line companies in charge of the fort, and hold it until the arrival of a detachment from Kohat. Marched accordingly at daybreak. The men had had nothing to eat (the Ramzan) during the previous day, and were much distressed during this burning march: ere we reached Attock the heat was trying. We crossed the Indus soon after 10 A.M.

"15th.—Chamberlain cantered into Attock this morning. The General of the division was passing through, and it was settled that we should move on without assuming charge of the fort at all. I was pleasantly disappointed in Chamberlain; found him neither punctilious nor pedantic; a resolute, thoughtful *soldier;* neither brilliant nor cultivated, but sensible, grave, and solid, much impressed with the state of affairs, but looking at them manfully. The General, whom we went to see, a poor, weak, old gentleman in H.M.S., of a very different temper and style; frivolous in all points, petty, with no grasp, no knowledge; writing little notes to subordinates with much care and little grammar. Swam the Indus last night and again to-night; the current was strong, and I found I had no spare strength on my return.

"16th.—Boran, 32 miles from Attock. Marched at 2 A.M. in the midst of a sweeping, violent dust-storm, after which the air grew cool. Many of the men very sore-footed from that hot, long march from Mardan to Attock, but all cheerful and making light of their work. The Punjab is paying back to India all she cost her by sending troops stout and firm to her aid. Bugle at midnight, move off at 1 A.M.

"17th.—Jani-ki-Sang, 32 miles; a pleasant march, reaching our ground about 8 A.M. My own opinion of the present state of affairs is this. Many fine fellows may fall victims; but, *without* some terrible blow, Government would never set about the radical reform necessary. But for the belief that revolution was impending, no Reform Bill would have been carried in England; but for Lord Howe, the Mutiny of the Nore would have destroyed our fleet; but for Sir Charles Napier, England, in the north at least, would have seen a bloody civil war in 1839. Now the danger is faced and, however much it may spread, it will be put *down*, to the benefit of the army, in this way that it is well, even at the expense of pain and suffering, to eradicate a spreading ulcer. This is our case in India, and has been for many a long day. The day has come when we have strength, and peace without.

"18*th*.—Started at 1 A.M. Overtaken within 4 or 5 miles of Pindi by Edwardes, travelling down in a buggy to consult Sir John. I jumped into the buggy and went with him to Sir John's—reached at 5 A.M. Chamberlain in bed at the door. Sir John, in bed within, called us and began conversing on affairs with his old frankness and cordiality. Affairs are bad. The Punjab Ruler full of pluck and energy, and but little different in demeanour. The telegraphic messages from all quarters were detailed. Those from the Chief read the worst. He is evidently embarrassed and not buckling to with the mighty emergency. Destruction at Delhi most ruthless, most horrible. Meerut, strong in British troops, shows the worst front. If a cantonment with English infantry, dragoons, and artillerymen — in all at least 1600 strong—is unable to make play and break through the contemptible network, what can be expected where no English troops are? India holds not 28,000 of our countrymen in all.

"Sir John Lawrence made me stay with them— the two rooms in common—Sir John, Edwardes, Chamberlain, James, and myself. Heard the arrangement at Peshawar by which General Reed was impounded to the chief command in the Punjab. Edwardes and Nicholson, feeling they could best guide in the storm, and that the military disposition could not be theirs without a plan, resolved on calling a council — the General, Brigadier Cotton, and Chamberlain (in the secret). When they were assembled at the old General's table, Edwardes stated the case: the broad mutiny, the necessity for immediate action, and the cordial co-operation of all in authority: that to give this authority a point— proposed that the General should assume the chief command in the Punjab. The old General, in his sleeping drawers and slippers, looked puzzled and, almost before he knew what had taken place, the proceedings were on paper; orders out for the movement and collection of troops at various positions. Native troops suspected of disaffection at Peshawar were then and there directed to proceed to hold forts underneath the hills; the Guides to start forthwith, the European corps to be in hand. Even at the last, the old General looked bewildered and puzzled, with a doubting pride, which, however, found no vent in language. The Chief sat presiding in silence while these efforts to save India were manfully and nobly made.

"Sir John Lawrence's messages to the Commander-in-Chief pass beyond frank advice or even entreaty—'Act at once, march with any body of European troops to the spot, and the danger will disappear. Give it time, and it will flame through the land.' The Chief is in a strange land—ignorant of the troops, unaccustomed to military action in times of emergency, and consequently he hangs fire. Hence troops not disloyal become sulky and ready to burst forth and join their for the nonce companions triumphing in mutiny. No news from below Delhi for days; but five corps of European troops between Meerut and Calcutta. The strength in the Punjab is with us; a large body, some 12,000 British soldiers; no finger will be raised, no shot fired while their shadow is on the land; the disaffection which influences the native soldiery here is but the echo from below—the smoke of the fire below. It is on this ground where we are strong that we must be careful of throwing away our strength, or of so using it as to show our weakness where no British troops are. Hence I strongly counsel that no native troops in the Punjab should be disarmed unless an overt act of treason has been committed; to disband a whole corps on suspicion of bad faith, or even on conviction of its existence though not displayed, would be to turn the whole army against us. Many there must be from various causes and failings who are wishing to join in the outburst—to disband would thrust these into the flames and, when no controlling European power is in the Cantonment, the native powers will act in open sedition, seeing the fate those in our power have met with. Chamberlain felt this, and remarked that we must act in our strong places for our comrades in weak positions. We should not, unless *compelled*, do where we are strong what they can't do—for *us* to put out our strength may and would bring vengeance and destruction on them.

"All these matters were freely discussed, and perhaps this feeling at last influenced us in not seizing the artillery (native troops) guns this evening as it was intended I should do with the Guides. The Guides to go on as fast as possible towards the scene, preceding the columns. The Chief informed of our advance. Even amidst all the grave affairs Edwardes' wit and humour sparkle. He has named the old General 'the Dictator.' In the sort of Council of Discussion at Sir John's, the line of operations was fixed on, papers actually written by Edwardes, and then the remark—'Now let us send for the Dictator.' Thus, cut-and-dried affairs are put affirmatively to the General. Dreary these look to-day. Disaffection threatening among the troops in the districts. Sulky obedience at Sialkot; open insurrection at Ferozpur. Communications cut off from Meerut—no posts or telegraph from below—the Commander-in-Chief hesitating and nervous, without plan or purpose. All will go right by and by. The struggle will not swamp us, but open our eyes.

"19*th*.—Matters are brighter to-day. Nicholson with two squadrons arrived. Chamberlain to command the Movable Column over several seniors; he did not covet the appointment, which was, in fact, Edwardes' suggestion to 'the Dictator.' Sir John saw the corps this morning; most kind about all matters connected with the march and comfort of the men; even the smallest things were thought of; spoke very kindly on all matters. The Guides to be augmented should I retain the command; it will now become one of the finest in the country. Mighty must be the changes after this in the organisation of the force. God see Sir Henry through, then my hopes for India and for us all will run high.

"News less gloomy from below, though increasing anxiety over the Indus; the troops there are power-less for ill; they without their officers would be cut up on an announcement being made that the hill tribes were at liberty to plunder them. Agra safe—this is a mighty matter. I could not hope this. The fort was in the hands of native troops and the only European corps distant from it. However, the saviour of India, the telegraph, brought us word, 'Agra safe,' 'Moradabad safe,' 'Bareilly safe.' Now my anxiety is for Lucknow—there the burden of trouble and woe may be great. Sir John, full of pluck, fearing no responsibility; without com-munication or means of communication with the Governor - General, he has raised and is raising large bodies of troops, passing all the best corps of the Punjab Irregular Force towards India, urging and entreating the Commander-in-Chief to move. Affairs are brightening. All the old Sikh Sardars have come forward proffering their swords for us—not one noble, not one cultivator of the land has joined the rebels. There is no feeling in the country as yet, nor will any be roused, provided a single blow be struck and quickly struck. Matters may be bad for us, but with good European trooos and noble artillery, even if all the native army fell off, we could hold our own till succour should reach from home. Nothing but a disaster could effect that reform in our army which is so urgent—which has been so often and often forced on Government. The letters and messages which come in to Sir John prove how many are the gallant and noble sons England has in this grand land. Weakness and folly are abundant, but it makes one's heart gladden to feel how stout and high the minds of many.

"I am much struck with Chamberlain; lofty, high-minded, bold as a lion, no fire-eater, but with calm, resolute views, knowing the occasion and the trial.

"*Great is Edwardes'* tact, great his ability, powerful in language, fertile in resource, willing and humorous, able to throw fun and give life to the heaviest and darkest matter.   He is very witty in his observations about the Commander - in - Chief (General Anson)—'John, send a message thus :— "From Chief Commissioner, Punjab, to the Commander - in - Chief, wherever he may be hiding. Major A. See Rule 16.* When in doubt play a trump. Carry out your principles.   We, the council, headed by the Dictator, do hereby depose General A. from command of the army, and place in his position Lieutenant MacAndrew (who went near Delhi to reconnoitre), with the rank of Archbishop."'

"Edwardes is very plucky, clever with temper ; bending people to his views without appearing to care about it; very lively; different in every respect almost from the man we saw at Lucknow.   Now he is natural.

"I see Sir John, though throwing himself aside in a hundred trivial points, leaving their decision altogether when Edwardes and Chamberlain, yet *fixes himself* on certain points with a manly and gallant heart, most kind, most cordial, courting debate, open to conviction, and willing to concede or change, when this latter weakens not the whole ; rather than risk this, he would stick to a small error.

"*20th.*— Reached Mandra, 20 miles, at 5 A.M., having marched at 10 P.M. last night. Great difficulty in keeping awake; obliged to get off and walk, that succeeded in making me hot; mounted again, nearly off, eyes closed of themselves.   Halt for ten minutes, Battye and Hawes on the ground (rocks) asleep before stretched out.   We shall get over this in a day or two.   Night marching is less trying to the cattle.   Men very cheerful and ready to go anywhere ; none admit themselves too knocked up or too stiff to proceed.

"*21st.*—Sohawah, 24 miles, crossing the Bakrialla ; ravines and roads broken and intricate ; spent a burning day : marched at 8 P.M., wind scalding.

* A treatise on whist by " Major A." was popularly ascribed to General Anson.

"*22nd.*—Jhelum at 5 A.M. ; encamping ground by the river, delightfully fresh after 28 miles. First trumpet at dark ; crossed the river at 9. Great storm of dust and rain made the road difficult to follow.

"*23rd.*—Koria, 15 miles from the Chenab and 10 from Gujerat ; 21 miles from Jhelum. Roads heavy from the storm, air delicious and fresh ; so tired all night that I was compelled to walk to keep myself awake ; even that remedy failed, constantly found myself abreast of a sowar's horse. Some of the sowars in the rear troop, asleep, kept passing right up through the column : found excellent quarters. Resolved to take advantage of the cool day and push off to the Chenab. Cavalry first, infantry in evening. Marched cavalry at 3 P.M., reached the Chenab at 8 and commenced the crossing. All safe at Wazirabad at 7 A.M., 24th.

"*25th.*—Marched to Kamokee this morning by 7 A.M., 32 miles. Started for Lahore at 5 P.M., distance 30 miles.

"*26th.*—Reached Lahore at 6 A.M. Was met by the Commissioner and military secretary—difficulty about selecting recruits.

"*27th.*—Recruiting ; but terribly overcome with the report of the sufferings and exposure at Simla.

"*28th.*—Overtook the corps at Powindiah at 7 A.M.

"*29th.*—Reached the banks of the Sutlej close to Sobraon battlefield by 6 A.M., commenced the crossing at once. Here it was that the river ran red with Sikh blood. Determined to follow the Umballa road.

"*30th.*—Reached Mihna, 32 miles, about 7 A.M. The cross-country road sent many straggling ; some did not reach till dark ; there was baggage still missing and 3 men when four o'clock struck. Resolved on a short march and to leave at the usual time, so as to enable them to make a *night's* rest. Marched at 6 P.M. to Ingraon, 14 miles ; reached before midnight.

"*31st.*—Had a delightful sleep. Men much refreshed. Letter from Commissioner at Ludhiana, inviting us all to him. Marched at 7 P.M.

" 1st *June.*—Reached Ludhiana, 24 miles, at 3 A.M., and at once composed ourselves to sleep till daybreak at the foot of the Kutcherry steps, the lowest step serving as a pillow. Awoke by Nicolas standing over us and announcing Ricketts' house was a mile distant. Greatly comforted, we went to Ricketts'; a thoroughly warm and hearty welcome; splendid quarters, large grand house, books, reviews, rods, guns, all strewed about; the temperature enjoyable, tatties, cold water, iced ginger-beer, *cold* sheets to lie on; it was like the first day on the hills to a man who has galloped through the sun from the plains. Ricketts,* a pleasant, bold fellow, looking the difficulties of the times in the face like a man. Ludhiana would explode if a spark were to go up elsewhere; small chance for Ricketts and his few friends, with their jagirdar horse, should this be the case. Marched on Alawi-ke-Serai at 7.30 P.M., distance 28 miles.

" *2nd.*—Got a sight of the Serai soon after daybreak. Had two hours' sleep off the reel, and was much refreshed. The men very cheery. The plan of getting a cup of tea at our halt at midnight is a great break. Officers and men fall to sleep on the ground for an hour, and the difficulty is, who shall remain awake to sound the trumpet. Off to Rajpoora, distance 28 miles, at 7 this evening.

" *3rd.*—Reached the old Serai with the cavalry at dawn, just as the light was breaking; to sleep at once under a wall so as to prevent the sun's early interference. He rises full of fire and heat now. Comfortable quarters in the old Serai. The men sleeping and eating about. Started for Umballa at 6 P.M.; marched through the Cantonment at 1 A.M., every house deserted—chowkidar alert in each compound. Patrols of the Patiala Raja's sowars going 'rounds' with lighted matches—a large encampment of these fellows about. Our guide took us down to the 'Boobial Tope.' *Magnificent* trees, under which a score of horses can stand free from the sun, and a large tank; altogether a beautiful spot. We all laid

* For an account of Ricketts' gallant and resourceful proceedings, see Kaye's *Sepoy War*, vol. ii., p. 506 *et seq.* He received the C.B.

down to rest by the trunk of an old banyan tree. A few weeks ago how hard and strange we should have thought thus sleeping in the open without any other pillow than a stone; now our great object is to get down, sleep is never far from us. When daylight came, we saw houses around us outside the park. Soon I was disturbed by a gentleman on horseback come to give help in moving the corps and carriages for the men.

"*4th.*—Marched to Pipli, 26 miles, by 4.30 this morning. Road very heavy. Heard last evening from Barnes, the Commissioner, of the affair with the Meerut Force. The last attack made on them was as much as they could manage to beat off. Succour needed by them, as they could not and would not give an inch, though pressed by numbers, in want of ammunition, and exhausted by fatigue and heat.

"*5th.*—Pipli. Arrived at dawn. Road heavy. Spent the day in the tahsil, and marched for Karnal, 24 miles, at sunset. Joined by Khan Singh Rosa.*

"*6th.*—Reached Karnal at 3 A.M. Cholera appeared amongst us this evening and attacked three Gurkhas; 1 cook died, 7 or 8 men under its pressure by sunset; obliged to leave 5 men behind. A requisition from the magistrate to burn and destroy three villages by way of keeping the road open; told him I would engage that the doing so would close it to-morrow, unless troops should remain; they would be irritated and desperate. The magistrate, however, pressing, and, as I learnt that open outrages had been committed by one village, I moved off with less compunction."

The requisition of the magistrate, Mr Le Bas, was strongly backed by Sir Theophilus Metcalfe. A day was occupied in punishing the villages; the Guides had 1 man killed and 3 wounded. The delay made the Guides miss the action of Badli-ki-Serai. On the morning of the 8th June, they had reached

---

* Khan Singh Rosa had fought against us at Chillianwalla in command of a cavalry regiment, see pages 69 and 146.

Larsauli, 32 miles; "cholera lighter." Edwardes, writing on that day, said :—

"We are all delighted at the march the Guides have been making. It is the talk of the border. I hope the men will fill their pockets in the sack of Delhi. Herewith some more chits from Kandahar. We are reorganising the native army! The Supreme Government seems to have disappeared. Bring back some standards from the palace—especially Bahadur Shah's trousers."

On the *9th June* the Guides joined the Delhi Force. "Their stately height and martial bearing *made all who saw them proud to have such aid. They came in as firm and light as if they had marched but a mile." The orders of the day by Major-General Sir H. Barnard, in announcing the arrival of the Guides, said that the corps had "marched from Marden to Delhi, a distance of 580 miles, in twenty-two days—a march to which Sir H. Barnard believes there is no parallel on record." The march, which was made at the hottest time of the year, has, in fact, always been regarded as one of the most notable achievements of the war.

As the Guides approached the Ridge after a march of 30 miles, a staff officer galloped up—"How soon can you be ready to go into action?" "In half an hour." Edwardes wrote :—

"The Guides made surprising efforts. They started six hours after the receipt of orders, fully equipped for service, and marched 580 miles, fifty marches, in twenty-two days with three halts made by order. Three hours after their arrival at Delhi they were engaged hand-to-hand with the enemy, and every single British officer was more or less wounded."

* From *The Siege of Delhi, by One who Served There*, p. 89.

Daly wrote to his wife :—

"*9th June.*—Camp before Delhi. We marched in this morning, getting a hearty welcome from the camp. The fire of the enemy is very light; very different from Multan. The affair yesterday was brilliant enough; we should have been in time for it but for the village campaign! The men are in great spirits."

His diary entry for the day was: "The regiment hotly engaged. Battye * mortally wounded—noble Battye, ever in front; Khan Singh Rosa hard hit; Hawes clipt across the face with a sword, and many good men down. Men behaved heroically, *impetuously.*" Daly had his horse killed under him, and was struck in the leg by a spent bullet. Kennedy also was slightly hurt. In a letter to Daly, Edwardes said :—

"Amidst all our joy at the march and brave deeds of the Guides, we are greatly grieved to hear of poor young Battye's death. He was full of hope and promise, and is indeed a flower fallen from the chaplet of our Indian Army."

"Poor gallant Battye!" wrote Daly to his wife. "There was some slight hope on the morning of the 10th, though none on the evening, of his wound. I never saw a bolder or truer soldier. He was shot by a fellow within a couple of yards of him, right through the lower part of the stomach. I believe he had two or three wounds. I did not see it occur; he was on my right. The last time I saw him in the fight I shouted to him, 'Gallant Battye, well done, brave Battye.' He was buried the day after our arrival, and at about the time we marched past the burial ground the day before."

The general facts connected with the "siege" of Delhi are well known. On the death of the Commander-in-Chief, General Anson, at Kurnal on the

* See p. 366.

THE GUIDE BURJ PESHAWAR.

(From a drawing by Lieut. H. Hawes, Guide Corps, 1861.)

[To face p. 142.

Tooleram. A Gourka in the Guide Corps.

[To face p. 142.

27th May 1857, General Sir H. Barnard succeeded
to the command.   He continued the advance on
Delhi ; was joined at Alipore on the 7th June by the
Meerut Force under Brigadier Wilson; fought the
successful action of Badli-ki-Serai on the 8th, and
on the same day took up his position on the
celebrated "Ridge" before Delhi.   His force consisted of about 3000 European troops, Reid's
Gurkhas (the Sirmoor battalion), the Guides (who
joined on the 9th), and a few other native troops.
The first considerable reinforcement to arrive was a
contingent sent by the Maharaja of Jaipur; then
followed a small column from the Punjab of 850 men,
chiefly natives, with 4 European horse artillery guns,
on the 23rd June.   Four days later came the first
substantial aid from the Punjab, 2700 men, of whom
about half Europeans.   The total of effectives before
Delhi on the 8th July was returned as 6600 men.

On the 5th July Sir H. Barnard died, and was
succeeded by General Reed, who, however, was
invalided on the 17th July, the command then
passing to Brigadier-General Archdale Wilson.

During a considerable portion of June and July
the condition of the British force more nearly
resembled that of a besieged than of a besieging
army.   Of the numbers of the enemy it is impossible
to form any reliable estimate, but they were continu-
ally receiving additions to their strength, and from
first to last the total of trained sepoys who
entered Delhi must have been at least 40,000 men.
Throughout the early weeks of the siege the difficulties and anxieties of the British were greatly
enhanced by the absence of any reliable intelligence
as to what was proceeding down country, and by the

terrible tales of the outrages committed at Cawnpore and elsewhere. The tide turned in the middle of August with the arrival of the Punjab Column under Nicholson, who, on the 26th August, achieved a brilliant success at Najafgarh. The heavy siege guns reached the Ridge on the 4th September; the last troops from Meerut on the 6th; the Kashmir contingent on the 8th. The assault was delivered on the 13th September, and the Palace was in our hands and resistance at an end on the 20th September.

Throughout these months, mainly owing to the loyal and active assistance of the Sikh chiefs of Pataila, Nabha, and Jhind, there was practically no interruption in communications between the Delhi Force and Upper India. To and from Simla the post plied with great irregularity, and the subjoined comments on the progress of events are mainly taken from Daly's letters * to his wife.

The Guides were posted on the right of the Ridge, where, besides taking their share in the general operations, they held with the Gurkhas the position and outposts in and round Hindu Rao's house. During the siege the enemy delivered twenty-six separate attacks on this part of our line. One attack on the 1st-2nd August lasted the whole night and day. From the 6th to the 13th August there was "constant worrying night and day."

On hearing of the fighting on the 9th June, Sir John Lawrence at once wrote to Daly :—

"I was glad to get your letter of the 10th, and rejoiced to hear how admirably the Guides have

---

* Daly's letters and diaries were placed at the disposal of Kaye, when writing his *History of the Sepoy War*, which contains many quotations from Daly's writings.

behaved. Poor Battye, we all grieve for him greatly. We are sending you every man we can muster— Rothney's Sikhs, Coke's regiment, and some Punjab cavalry—also a regiment and a half of Europeans and some 200 artillerymen. We are getting Hughes' cavalry also up, and will push it on also, I hope. I have seen from the first that native troops would be greatly wanted at Delhi: but for General Johnstone's * folly, Rothney's Sikhs and Nicholson's† cavalry would have been with you by this. I have offered to send either Chamberlain or Nicholson to headquarters, whichever General Reed likes. The one who remains to command the Movable Column. Both are first-rate soldiers, good in council, and strong in fight. I wish we had a few others like them.

"Pray tell the Guides how delighted I am with their good conduct. If I can do anything for you in any way, pray command me.

"We are all quiet here, but Peshawar has given us, and must give us, great anxiety. We are obliged to place troops there, which would be of the highest value down below. We have three European regiments, 24 guns, Wilde's and Vaughan's regiments of infantry;—not one of the native infantry or Hindustani corps of cavalry are to be trusted.

"You will have heard of the Jullundhur mutiny. The rebels started for Loodhianah, a distance of but 25 miles, General Johnstone in pursuit and a river in front of the mutineers. He allowed every man to escape across, though they were more than thirty hours doing this. And this is the man whom you will probably see commanding a division at Delhi before long.

"On hearing of this, I sent off an express to disarm the 62nd and 69th at Multan, who had been giving signs of being about to show their teeth. It was effected by Crawford Chamberlain with his own corps, Green's, and Hughes', without the aid of a European soldier. These are the kind of men we want in command of our troops. When I see some

* See Kaye's *Sepoy War*, vol. ii., p. 507.

† Charles Nicholson, brother of John, to whom is the reference immediately below.

K

of the men we entrust with our troops, I almost think that a curse from the Almighty is on us."

The following day (16th June) Lawrence wrote :—

"Many thanks for your notes. You are a capital correspondent. We are all greatly grieved to hear of poor Quintin Battye's death; but from the moment we found he was shot in the stomach, we feared he was gone. I enclose a letter from Sirdar Nehal Singh to Khan Singh Rosa. I wrote yesterday to Khan Singh myself, praising him for his good conduct, and promising to provide for his family in the event of his death. I also have given him 1000 rupees for his expenses. What pay does he get? or does he get any? Let me know how this is managed. We are sending all the reinforcements we can muster. They should be fully equal to 1000 European infantry, 200 artillery, 1000 native infantry, and 400 or 500 horse. And all ought to be at Delhi in a fortnight, say by the 1st of July, and some earlier. The Punjab Infantry is so tied by having to look after the frontier, including Peshawar and all the Poorbeah regiments, that it is not easy to send many more.
"I shall recommend to Government that Kennedy succeed Battye; get him put in orders. Look out for some smart young fellow to join the corps and act as adjutant. If there be any one in camp you fancy, General Reed will let you have him, I expect. If he is elsewhere, let me know.
"We are all well on the Peshawar frontier, and indeed elsewhere. But we have to look sharp, and rule with an iron hand.
"About 50 Guides, horse and foot, start from this for Delhi this evening."

By the mid-day post on the 19th June, Daly wrote to his wife :—

"We are making advances and have batteries in an advanced position nearly ready to open. I hope much from these. The walls are brittle, so are the hearts of the defenders. If our reinforcements would appear, the blow would not, could not, be distant. I feel sure that the defence will be poor. I have just been with Sir Harry Barnard, who sent for me to consult about cutting off the Jullundhur mutineers, of which I fear there is but a slight chance. We are very quiet, nothing but the occasional boom of an 18-pounder or the smash of a shell. We have considerable reinforcements from a native prince, the Raja of Jaipur. They are Rajputs, adepts in looting, but I suspect not favourably inclined to close fighting. There are 3000 infantry and a large body of cavalry; this will help us in investing the place at any rate."

The same evening Daly was very severely wounded. It was at Nawabgunge, and there was not during the siege a more perilous hour. Daly himself afterwards gave this description of the action :—

"At a time when every available British bayonet was engaged in the front, the enemy, under cover of the thick foliage, a large body of all arms, moved round to our right and rear. The move was a surprise which almost overwhelmed us. We had nothing at first but a portion of the 9th Lancers, the Guide Cavalry, and 4 guns, wherewith to meet and repel the attack. Sir Hope Grant, who was in command, divided his small body (for the ground was broken and thick with gardens and trees) and detached me to the left with 2 of Major Tombs' guns under Lieutenant Hills, a troop 9th Lancers, and the Guides Cavalry. I quickly found myself in the presence of a powerful force, with 6 or 8 guns in position immediately to my front, and a mass of infantry and cavalry. Knowing that there was nothing to fall back on, I directed Lieutenant Hills at once to get his guns into action, and detached all but a handful of Guides, which I left with the guns, to clear the left flank already threatened by the enemy's cavalry. We were thus barely holding our own, Sir Hope hotly engaged on my right, when Major Tombs came up with the remainder of his guns.

The enemy, observing our weakness and the absence of infantry, were now closing on us in such numbers that Major Tombs said to me, 'I fear I must ask you to charge to save my guns.' I was the only British officer with the cavalry, a few Guides only; with these I broke through the infantry and reached the enemy's guns. This diversion cleared our front, and gave time for the arrival of reinforcements."

Daly received a bullet through his left shoulder, and that arm was crippled for life, though he retained the use of the hand. As he lay on the ground in the rapidly gathering dusk, his men at first failed to find him, but his whereabouts was pointed out to them by one of the enemy who who had served in the 1st Oudh Irregular Cavalry.* He was thus more fortunate than Yule, commanding the 9th Lancers, of whom Daly observed a few days later—"Poor Yule! I knew him well; he came up after I was down; He trotted by me as I lay on the ground. It was quite dusk. He *ought* not to have been killed. The darkness did it. I fear he was left but wounded. The enemy prowled about the field during the night and found him there." About the same time Becher, the Quarter-Master-General, was wounded, and Sir Hope Grant escaped only by holding on to the tail of his orderly's horse. The guns served against us

* This was a man of whom Mrs Daly had written in November 1856 :—"There is a young Shahzadah (prince) in this regiment (the 1st Oudh I. C.) a grandson or nephew of Shuja-ul-Mulk. A handsome, elegant boy of eighteen, pale and delicate, with beautiful eyes, a very interesting-looking lad. Henry took him from great poverty. The grandson of a king, he is thankful to be a jemadar (cornet) in a regiment with £40 a year. Henry has taken quite a fancy to him, has him into the house to talk to him, gives him quinine, etc." In 1859, she added a marginal note in her diary—"This poor boy had a sad fate ; he joined the rebels, almost from compulsion. At Delhi, when Henry was wounded, he told some of the Guides where the Sahib lay. He was afterwards hanged, I fear on the taking of Delhi."

included those of Abbott's battery, which had formed part of the "illustrious garrison" of Jalalabad, and which bore the mural crown. Daly wrote: "It was *pitch* dark when we retired from the field; otherwise we should have taken every gun they brought out. One gun and two carriages were taken the following morning, when, at my suggestion, the General sent out a party to sweep the ground."

It was generally felt that Daly had fully earned the V.C., and that same evening General Barnard, when visiting him, personally expressed regret that the V.C. was not open to officers in the East India Company's Service. Early in 1859, when the V.C. had been thrown open to the Company's officers, Sir Hope Grant strongly recommended Daly to Lord Clyde for the decoration. Tombs wrote to Daly:—

"I have a very vivid remembrance of the occurrences of the 19th June 1857, in which you were severely wounded. Two of my guns were in action on the road leading through the Sabzi Mandi, and were supported by the late Major Yule's troops of 9th Lancers and some of your men. The enemy had possession of the ground to our right front, gardens and high mud-banks; and taking advantage of these latter, gradually crept closer and closer to the guns—so close, indeed, as to be able to pick off my gunners as they worked the guns, and rendering it almost impossible to serve them. I recollect perfectly asking you to charge, and at the time I felt the guns must be lost unless you did so, for it was impossible for me to retire without compromising our troops, who were, as I supposed, advancing on my right on the other side of the Ochterlony Garden. I did not actually witness your charge, but I saw you brought back severely wounded a few minutes afterwards, and I have no hesitation in saying that in all human probability that charge saved the guns

from falling into the hands of the enemy for the time ;
I had so many casualties that I could not have
moved my guns without assistance."

Hills wrote :—

"We were in a very nasty position, and the
enemy were very close to the guns and doing us great
damage with their sharpshooters. Daly's charge
was a desperate one, right up to the enemy's guns.
It was a most perilous and bold movement, but
necessary to save the guns."

Sir Hope Grant wrote to Daly :—

"I trust the Victoria Cross may be bestowed
upon you. No one has deserved it better. The
charge you made on the 19th June was of the most
serious importance, as there was no time during the
whole siege that we had such difficulties to contend
with, or were so nearly annihilated."

The reply to Sir Hope was :—

"His Excellency has been obliged to decline for-
warding claims of this sort made so long after the
occurrence for which the claim is preferred."

Hope Grant then informed Daly privately :—

"I know Lord Clyde thinks an officer who is
eligible for the Bath—which you have got—ought
not to get the Victoria Cross. He thinks it ought
not to be given to a higher rank than captain." *

When Daly was disabled, the active command of
the Guides was at first entrusted to Hodson, who had
previously served with the corps and was known to
the men. Hodson held the acting command for about
five weeks, and was then succeeded by Shebbearne.
Daly, though unable to move, still regulated all regi-

* In 1859, when this was written, Daly was a brevet lieut.-colonel.

mental matters and was able to maintain a regular correspondence. He wrote to his wife :—

"*24th June*.—The Sikh corps which arrived yesterday have already given the enemy a taste of their quality. Yesterday, firing continued throughout the day; the enemy came out in great force, sniping and occupying gardens and suburbs; their loss was immense. The consequence is not a shot has been fired to-day as yet. They get a sickener of fighting if they attack, and take to looting till the arrival of fresh troops. It is the mighty arsenal and the prestige of the place which gives them strength. I have a native officer in the city now. He was in for four days and came out. He gives a lamentable account of the state of the city. Dissension and mutiny among themselves; robbing and fighting, and everything that is bad. Sundil Khan was on leave, and came to join me here.

"*25th*.—Chamberlain * arrived yesterday with my old friend Walker.

"The Raja of Jhind's men do well; they had little fighting where I was, though.

"*28th June*.—We had our first fall of rain yesterday; a heavy storm ushering in the rains; to-day it is cloudy, with the sun beaming through upon us. More reinforcements marched in this morning—guns and Europeans. A meeting of the engineers and leaders has been held, and I have no doubt soon we shall strike our blow. Coke must be within a day or two. He is 700 strong; men inured to fighting, and better up to this work than most Europeans, who are beaten by the sun, and who expose themselves in their white shirt sleeves in a cruel way.

"*1st July*.—Good news from below. An officer rode in from Agra to-day. All well there. General Wheeler marching with European corps to its aid; from this we infer that all must be well at Lucknow, as he would not otherwise leave Cawnpore."

Daly's wound, of which he endeavoured to make

* Colonel (afterwards Sir Neville) Chamberlain joined as Adjutant-General.

light, had called forth many anxious inquiries, and about this time he received the two following letters :—

From Edwardes, Peshawar, 30th June 1857 :—

"We all hope you are getting—or got—well.

"These are not times in which (with Lord Brougham's dedication to the Marquess of Wellesley) we can apostrophise—'The rare felicity of England; so rich in talent and capacity for affairs that she can spare from her service such men as '—you.

"Is that 'Lieutenant Chalmers of the Guides' who got wounded on 27th June, young Chalmers of 51st Native Infantry? If so, he is a good fellow. I only sent him to Pindi, and didn't expect he would turn up so soon at Delhi."

From Sir John Lawrence, 4th July 1857 :—

"Ever since I heard you were not in danger I have been entirely satisfied. I am much afraid that the poor Guides have suffered greatly. What with the enemy and cholera their ranks must have been fearfully thinned. I have sent you down some 200 picked Punjabis, mounted on horses of the 6th and 8th Cavalry, under Lieutenant Bayley. This will be a grand reinforcement for your cavalry.

"We are keeping all quiet in the Punjab, and exerting ourselves to get up a decent force by the cold weather. But I do not like to overdo the thing. For we have barely 5000 Europeans in the Punjab; and it is just possible that we may have the Punjabis even against us, if this style of thing goes on much longer. We have not heard a word from below, I mean from Calcutta, later than the 9th of June. There should, by this time, be ten European regiments below Meerut. This is a goodly array, and had we got them at the beginning of the affair, it would have altered its present aspect most considerably. I hope that in another fifteen days we shall hear of the arrival of the China troops. If you cannot write, get some one to do so for you, and let us know what force the Guides muster. Upwards of a hundred furlough men must have joined since you marched. Try and get the Guides to keep themselves clean and dry. These precautions are great safeguards against cholera."

In the latter part of June the difficulties of the force before Delhi were at their height, and it was decided to attempt no offensive move until reinforcements arrived. Edwardes wrote to Lawrence on the 26th June: "The Empire's reconquest hangs on the Punjab." On the 28th June, General Barnard wrote to Sir John Lawrence: "So far, we have not silenced a single gun, and they return us to this day at least four to one." Lawrence was then seriously considering a withdrawal from Peshawar in order to free for the field the troops which were in garrison there. The decision was, however, to retain Peshawar, and this was fully endorsed by the first message which came through from Lord Canning (15th July): "Hold on to Peshawar to the last."

With the commencement of July a more confident spirit prevailed at Delhi, as is shown by Daly's letters and diary :—

"*3rd July.*—Our force here is now a splendid one. Delhi should have been ours this morning! Everything was arranged; plans drawn; regiments told off (they did not know it); when information was brought that the Bareilly Force, which is encamped outside, would do their initiative fighting * this morning, and this upset the scheme!

"Rain fell last night; it was cloudy and would have enabled our troops to approach all unseen, and

* Elsewhere Daly explained: "The fights which occur outside are with new arrivals of mutineers; they are not allowed to enter the city till they have shown their pluck. It is said that out of the large body we met on the night of the 19th, not one hundred found their way in; they were so beaten and dispersed."

there was dissension amongst the mutineers. No attack has been made on us, though Delhi was spared (!) to enable them to do so.

"The attack would have been made just before daylight. Now the moon and the day meet, so the difficulty of creeping up is increased.

"Few in camp know what was intended.

"*4th July.*—Last night late, we got information that a large party, 4000 or 5000 cavalry and infantry with some guns, had marched out in the direction of Alipore, 8 miles on the Karnal road, with a view to cutting up a little post of ours there. Well, they went: they had not the pluck so to attack the small detachment there as to get at them. Coke, with his own corps, 350 Europeans, and Charlie Blunt's troop, marched off at 3 this morning to endeavour to cut them off returning. The cowardly loons would not stand for a moment. Coke opened his guns on them, but, despite their strength, no sooner did he get within 500 or 600 yards of them than they bolted, pitching away shoes, belts, etc. They were in red. Little honour do they do us in fighting. They *never stand*.

"The new engineer, Colonel Baird Smith, has arrived, very tired. Until he has made himself acquainted with the place nothing will be done. He is said to be a very able man. Rest assured of this, whenever the assault shall occur, the enemy will not stand.

"*5th July.*—General Barnard has an attack of cholera from which it is feared the brave, kindly, old man cannot rally; this will be a general grief, for, however wavering and undecided as an officer, there never was a man so made to win people's hearts by kindness and unselfishness.

"*6th July.*—Poor General Barnard died yesterday. No doubt, on him, like General Anson, worry and anxiety laid the seeds of the destroyer. He was the very gamest, kindest, and kindliest gentleman I ever met. He had no mind, no resolution save what he got from others. General Reed assumes the command himself *nominally*. He has no health, no anything, to enable him to do of himself. Poor General Barnard's advisers were all who spoke to him.   I think Chamberlain is likely to lead and to be trusted by General Reed.   So far, it may be a great improvement.

"There was a terrific storm which lasted nearly throughout the night.   The sun is now shining, and lights up the camp picturesquely; it is a pretty sight to see the soldiers of the various corps in front of their tents amusing themselves, chatting in groups, jumping, and throwing round-shot, as though nothing serious was going on, nor has it ever occurred to them that there was anything doubtful in the conflict. Scarcely a shot has been fired to-day.   There was a good deal of disturbance in the city, rowing amongst themselves.   You must not allude to it, but the king is trying to make terms, and has asked, 'would his pension be guaranteed, etc.'   Him away, the prestige of the matter is smashed; still I would grant him *never* a promise till his submission shall be full.

"*7th.*—Three engineers concocted the scheme* which was to have come off on the 12th June, the first of which I told you, a few days after my arrival. Greathed was the prime mover in what was as desperate and wild a plan as was ever concocted; the other engineer, a very clever fellow, although he signed the paper, said afterwards he could not possibly see his way through it.

"The plan concocted the other night will eventually be adopted.   It is by Taylor and Walker.   The moon is the great obstacle now.   From all we can gather, the country is certainly quieter, and my own belief is that the fall of Delhi would soon smash

* This refers to the proposal for a *coup-de-main* immediately after the force arrived before Delhi.   A copy of the scheme, in what appears to be rough draft form, is among Daly's papers.   It is headed "Project of attack on the City of Delhi, prepared for submission to Major-General Sir H. Barnard, K.C.B.," and is dated "Camp Delhi Cantonment, 11th June 1857."   The scheme is quoted, almost *in extenso*, at pages 526-7 of the *History of the Sepoy War*, vol. ii., where Kaye tells that it was signed by four subalterns—Wilberforce Greathed, Maunsell and Chesney of the Engineers, and Hodson.   Barnard accepted the scheme.   The troops were warned and the attempt was to be made.   But when the selected force was assembling soon after midnight on the 11th, it was found that some of the troops had not arrived and the venture was necessarily postponed.

the whole outbreak. The arsenal has been their stronghold; without it they are little powerful, for they would never stand, even at 10 to 1, against our troops in the field.

"*9th July.*—We have had a lively morning.* About 10 this morning, just as the rain had commenced to drizzle, a party of cavalry was seen near our out battery. The cavalry was not fired at, though the artilleryman had a lighted portfire; he deemed them our own; they moved round to our rear and there again were thought to be ours, and unmolested. At last fifteen or twenty rushed over the Canal Bridge into our camp and shouted to some native artillerymen then horsing their guns to join them. The cavalry men began to cut away at the horses' ropes in the lines. Our men rushed out of their tents, but had a difficulty in firing because *our* native horse artillery (who had been shouted to by these fellows) were between our fire. The artillerymen called out to our men, 'Never mind us, don't spare them, fire away.' They were soon polished off. A large force of cavalry was out, but a small portion only made the rush.

"They have been quiet for days and we were quite prepared for a row to-day, and but for the rain, doubtless they would have come out, for they were outside the gate in the morning with guns and elephants. I had quite calculated on seizing some of their guns to-day, though they are 'mighty' careful of 'em, as old Pepys would have written, and keep them at a great distance from us.

"I had a letter from Sir Colin (Campbell) yesterday; he says ten European corps are below Agra, viz.: 10th, 43rd, 35th, 84th, Madras Fusiliers, 64th, 78th, one Ceylon regiment, 53rd, 32nd; in another fifteen days we should hear of the China troops, which, with marines, ought to give us 5000 men more.

"*10th July.*—The affair of yesterday was much more serious and much more successful than I anticipated. The loss of the enemy, killed and

* It was in the scrimmage of the 9th July that Tombs and Hills won the Victoria Cross.—Kaye's *Sepoy War*, vol. ii., p. 575 *et seq.*

wounded, could not be less than 1000; this estimate, from what we can gather, is far from exaggerated. Outside one little post, held by a company of the Guides, between 80 and 90 of the enemy's bodies were counted. I have no doubt this has been a heavy lesson to them. Still Chamberlain is a queer fellow, and very likely will make no assault till he learns of troops closing up from below. He argues that their dissensions increase and their strength fades away; that except in the vicinity of Delhi things are quieting down, and that by delay we shall have less loss.

"11th July.—We are looking out to hear something certain of movements below. There must now be several corps in the vicinity of Cawnpore, and may be we shall hear of a couple of them at least marching up to make a diversion for us. Whether they will find us outside or inside is a problem. My own opinion, which is that of every engineer officer, is that the assault should have taken place, *as was arranged*, on the morning following the arrival of Coke and the fresh troops (the 61st and 8th). *Numbers* are of no service in a city; 500 disciplined men are more likely to do good work in a street than 5000. 'Them's my sentiments,' and they are not singular in the camp. We have lots of good men and true, though heaps and heaps of muffs and old women, and not a few of these unfortunately in places of responsibility. Scarcely a shot has been fired to-day. The enemy were employed for hours in carrying off their dead and wounded, yet *many, many* of the former remained on the field.

"14th July.—A Sikh of my Oudh corps came in yesterday bearing letters from Agra. He confirms the report of corps having reached Cawnpore. It is said six regiments have arrived there. At any rate the Delhi people, who know the news down to Calcutta, have it that 'the British have re-established their rule at Cawnpore and Futtehgarh, and that troops are moving up.' Chamberlain has resolved on making no assault till troops arrive, and no doubt troops will be here soon. He is in capital spirits, and convinced that he is adopting the wisest course. It *may* be wise now, but it was a gross blunder deferring the assault after the arrival of Coke, 61st, and 8th.

It is not merely this place but it would have smashed *Rebellion.* The fall of this place, if not too long deferred, will effect *wonders.* Ferozepore, Phillour, Agra, Allahabad, and Delhi are our magazines; three of these have strong forts; these magazines and Loodianah contain all our reserve artillery, ammunition, and arms. At first our fears were strong that Agra, Phillour, and Allahabad had fallen into their hands. All these places would stand sieges, and we should be without the means of firing a round at them! We found that by *wondrous fortune* these forts were saved to us; yet the mutineers had attempted all of them! Phillour,* whence our supplies for this siege are brought, was saved by an hour and a night's march; Agra by stratagem; Allahabad in the presence of the rebels. Fortune and Providence befriended us, not our own foresight or wisdom. When news of their safety reached us, I felt the worst was over. Without these arsenals we should have been in sore difficulties. Cantonments are destroyed—no great matter. The treacherous brutal murders, the lives of gallant and good men, of women fair and dear—these are *terrible* things; but the light is visible through the darkness. There is little beyond Delhi which will cause us trouble and loss. Delhi is discomforted with the news of the fights and defeats at Cawnpore, and at the utter failure of their own thousands against our tens.

"15*th July.*—Yesterday I told you firing was going on. Well, the enemy having expended thousands of cartridges, at 3 P.M. our loss was three or four wounded; the enemy began retreating. A force went out and, in the rush in driving the enemy in, got under the fire of the city walls. Chamberlain, who remained in camp till 4 P.M., now went out. He is a heroic, dashing fellow; he pursued. He was hit; arm broken. Walker, my friend, got a flesh wound through the thigh, and is not much damaged; not so Chamberlain, but his arm will be saved, we hope. Tell Mrs Norman her husband† possesses

* See Kaye's *Sepoy War*, vol. ii., p. 445.

† The late Field-Marshal Sir Henry Norman, G.C.B., etc.; Viceroy-designate of India in 1839.

the respect and goodwill, *hearty* goodwill, of every man in the camp, and the camp holds no better or more cheery soldier. He always does what is best at the time, and does it with a cheerful soldier's heart.

"*17th July*.—Poor General Reed leaves to-night. He never ought to have come here. Brigadier Wilson gets the command with the rank of Brigadier-General. He is an artillery officer; just a stout, gallant Englishman. I should not expect anything very distinguished from him, but always firmness and gallantry. He is decidedly the best we have. Chamberlain's tent is next to mine, and I see him often; he is of *heroic* mould, gallant, and forward to a fault; he is doing *capitally;* he has always been a most temperate man. He has a fine, gallant-looking person; tall, with a soldierly gait; head well put on; fine principles, and an *honest* heart; most conscientious. His education and reading had been narrow; his views are more limited than they should be, and adhered to with an obstinate tenacity which neither reason nor justice can change.

"*18th July*.—All well with Sir Henry (Lawrence) on the 2nd at Lucknow. A portion of the 84th Foot was with him in addition to the 32nd, and he was well able to hold out. I have just had a visit from Jai Singh, 1st P. C., who marched in this evening; not a little pleased he was. The Sikhs have been thoroughly staunch and firm throughout the country. At Jhelum they severed ithemselves from their *comrades* in the 14th, joined us, and attacked them. Men of the Oudh Cavalry on leave in the Punjab come in by single files.

There are several buggies * about the camp, which may be seen every night in display up the main street, one palki ghari also. A buggy was sold the other day by auction, but a pot of jam nearly fetched as much. Some epicures bought tins of bacon at the rate of 4 rupees a mouthful, I believe. With all ordinary things we are well supplied; at one time fowls were unknown, but lately they have appeared. Grain is very cheap. When I want books I send to the lines and tell the men. Various descriptions turn up; amongst others, I have Scott's Poetry and the third volume of Macaulay's History. The health of

* A sort of covered dogcart.

the troops is *excellent*, much better than in quarters. All well at Agra a few days ago.

"*23rd July.*—We have had a fight in a new direction to-day, opposite the Cashmere Gate and towards Metcalfe's house. The enemy brought out guns and infantry, and opened a heavy fire on our battery. A detachment from Metcalfe's house made an attempt to get round to their rear, while engaged with firing on us, and so cut off their guns; the detachment reached within 300 yards unperceived, and a column which moved down in front got within a lesser distance, but to no purpose. Pandy no sooner saw that he was to be closed with than he put to his horses and fled helter-skelter across the glacis. I fancy our troops were too easy in the pursuit; however, luckily our loss was slight; killed and wounded estimated about twenty. Two officers who should not have been there, were hit; one an excellent officer, whose services are most valuable, is *hors de combat* for some time, Colonel Seaton.

"The weather is cool and pleasant; we have had two or three light showers; extraordinary weather for the rains. Gulab Singh * has lent Sir John 10 lakhs, money being scarce; this is good, and shows how well the cunning old fox sees the game.

"*24th July.*—Tell Mrs Norman that it has been *generally* resolved (by the General, too) that her husband's life is too valuable to the army to be subject to chance shots, and therefore it has been ordered, and *he too* has been ordered, that he is not to go to the advanced posts during operations. The other head-quarter people take care of themselves without orders!"

"*25th July.*—The Punjab will send a large con-

* Gulab Singh, "the Talleyrand of the East," was a Dogra Rajput; he was raised to high office by Ranjit Singh, who conferred on him the Principality of Jamu. In the stormy times which followed Ranjit Singh's death, Gulab Singh took a leading part in Punjab politics, and, in connection with the arrangements made under the Treaty of Lahore in 1846 (after our defeat of the Sikhs at Sobraon), Kashmir was made over to him by the British for a payment of a crore and a half of rupees (one and a half millions sterling), and he was recognised as a Ruling Chief. He died in the latter part of 1857, and was succeeded by his son, Ranbir Singh. See also vol. ii., pp. 75-76, of Sir H. Lawrence's *Adventures of an Officer, etc.*

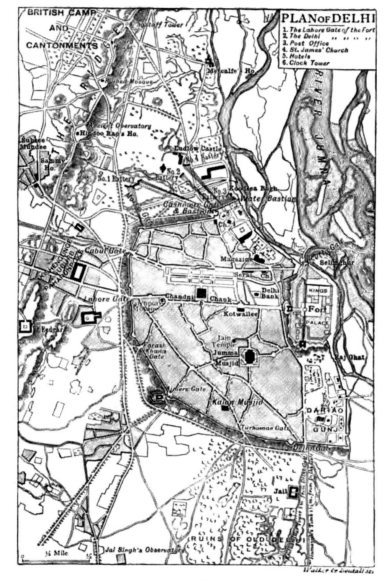

PLAN OF DELHI.

[To face p. 160.

tribution to us, a force larger than our present. Nicholson is already on the march. These troops may reach before those from below, and these latter may have to act elsewhere.

"*27th July.*—There is no doubt we have won a great victory at Fattehpur, just below Cawnpore, in beating the representative (adopted son) of the Peshwa; we took 12 guns and 7 lakhs of treasure. This has come with authority from Agra, and Scindia, the Ruler of Gwalior, has sent his congratulations. I feared more from him than from anybody, but he is behaving *nobly*. He has kept his mutinous troops (*our Contingent!* which we gave him to have drilled and disciplined!) in check. All the *Independent States* have behaved well towards us. Light is breaking everywhere.

"*28th July.*—I had a long cheery letter from Sir John last evening. All is well with Sir Henry; his front was so stout and his preparations so vigorous, that I doubt if he was ever pressed. Reinforcements have gone to him.

"*29th July.*—The dark days are gone. I can scarce give you a better illustration of the change which is influencing the country than in the supplies which reach our camp; on our first arrival the feeling that our rule was *doomed* and at *an end* was so widespread and so thoroughly believed that nobody brought in anything for sale; sheep, poor and thin, could be had only at the commissariat, and at rupees 5 each! Grain 10 seers the rupee! Fowls unknown. Now sheep are as common as were jackals at Sekrora; grain is 45 to 50 seers; poultry of all kinds abundant; boots, shoes, even macassar oil! These are strong symptoms. The servants in camp have behaved marvellously well. I never knew them better. The mutineers are at loggerheads, and much dispirited at their failures so oft incurred in attack, and at the knowledge of our troops advancing from below. We know for certain that Lord Elgin has consented to the coming of the China troops. The steamers were off the coast of Malabar in the first week in June. They would be turned from Singapore, and I should think might be looked for in Calcutta about the *last* week in June.

L

"30th July.—You see with this mutiny how long it has been working up. What warnings we have had. Remember our conversations at Lucknow: Sir Henry's opinion: my opinion of General Hearsay's [*] proceedings (vaunted and praised at home):—our belief then that the *whole* army was rotten; that no efforts were being made to stem it. Remember Sir Henry's views the last day or two at Lucknow."

About this time Daly received the following letters :—

From Edwardes, Peshawar, 21st July :—

"Yes. I daresay the assault would have succeeded when your reinforcements first reached; but like Sevastopol, it is possible that we may find that the protracted struggle and delay have been in our favour. The mutineers, instead of scattering over the country, have concentrated there and thrown themselves, in fight after fight, upon their fate. Depend upon it your army, though not taking Delhi, is performing no ignoble duty in destroying the battalions which possessed our discipline and betrayed it! The mischief, which delay would cause, *has* been caused. There seems less necessity for a *coup-de-main* every week. I should be inclined now to take the other line, and spend the rains in killing mutineers —leaving the fortress for the opening of the winter campaign.

"Here we have been most providentially quiet. When the Sepoy army mutinies, the frontier seems to take to peace. We have our little troubles, rumours, anxieties, and even fights, but as a mass the tribes seem to stand aloof and gape.

"James and Vaughan are this morning attacking Narinji.[†]

---

[*] See Kaye's *Sepoy War*, vol. i., p. 524 *et seq.*

[†] A good deal of trouble was at this time caused by the Hindustani fanatics under Maulavi Inayat Ali Khan. This culminated in a punitive expedition in April 1858, under the command of Sir Sydney Cotton. For an account of the Hindustani fanatics, see page 80 *et seq.* of the *Record of Expeditions against the North-West Frontier Tribes of India*, by Paget and Mason (1885).

"I hope by your writing you are nearly recovered. I do all I can for your men's families here. I have given severe wiggings to two or three fellows of yours who have come down lately from Kabul and Tirah, and they have gone off hot foot to Delhi swearing they are 'murids' (disciples: *i.e.*, eagerly loyal)."

From Sir John Lawrence, 25th July 1857:—

"You will see that we are sending down upwards of 4000 good and reliable troops, and not a Poorbeah among them. We hope that 1200 or 1300 will be Europeans. We have no more Europeans to give you unless we evacuate Peshawar. We have not more than 2200 this side of the Indus, of whom many are weakly men, and 300 of them not even arrived from Karachi.

"We may gradually send you more natives, but no Europeans. I should hope, however, that these reinforcements will suffice until troops arrive from below. We hear that Cawnpore has been reoccupied and Lucknow probably relieved. This should enable our troops to move on to Agra. From thence it is but a short spell to Aligarh and Shahdarrah. We might and should send some guns to effect a junction, and then advance and batter the Palace and river-side of Delhi, and effect a diversion at the moment of assault. A few heavy guns would soon make the Palace too hot for His Imperial Majesty, and create a great sensation.

"If things go wrong at Delhi, and it be a question of more Europeans from this or a retreat, I am for evacuating Peshawar and Kohat, and sending the whole down. If we are beaten at Delhi and have to retreat, our army will be destroyed. Neither Peshawar nor even the Punjab will then be of much good—both will go. Whereas the Peshawar and Kohat Force would give Europeans 3000, Punjab Regiments 5000, Multani Horse 1000—9000—besides some 30 guns. Now in my mind such a force, brought into the field in time, will turn the tide, or at anyrate stem it until the cold weather. But such a force when the army before Delhi is gone, and the Punjab in insurrection will be swallowed up in the general whirlwind. I hope and expect that there will be no occasion for this sacrifice. But no man can say what is in store for us. And it is necessary that we take a statesmanlike view of the subject, and decide on the line of policy to be followed; otherwise when the time comes we shall be unable to act.

"Read this to Chamberlain, and let me know his views. I am for holding Lahore and Multan to extremity and no more, sending the women and children down to Karachi, if things go wrong at Delhi. Nicholson with H.M.'s 52nd must be across the Beas to-day."

From Edwardes, 27th July 1857 :—

"So Sir P. G. [Patrick Grant] has 'hove in sight' at last; and announced himself at Cawnpore on 11th July with six European regiments for Delhi! And our Fancy Man, Nicholson, has gone down from this side with his shirt sleeves up; and so I hope this is the beginning of the end, and Delhi will be surrounded at last, and assailed and squashed. Let me know if you wish me to do anything in the recruiting line for you."

From Edwardes, Peshawar, 29th July 1857 :—

"*Are* you getting any *certain* news of *any* reinforcements from below, or not?

"We have heard publicly that Sir Patrick Grant with six European regiments was at Cawnpore directed 'to Delhi — with care,' on 11th July. Privately we hear it is a false report. Truth probably midway.

"Vaughan and James are again invited by Molvee Inayat Ali to keep the Eed at Narinji with him on Saturday—and we have sent out knives and forks and cold soirée. The Akhund * of Swat turns up his nose at these Hindustani Ghazis, and behaves himself like a gentleman.

* The Badshah (King) of Swat, who had been set by the Akhund (religious leader), had died the very day (11th May) of the mutiny at Meerut, and the Swatis were too much occupied with their own affairs to give trouble. (See also footnote at p. 80.)

"We are intensely anxious about your force, and hope there really are succours coming to you from below, for *we* can do little more; unless we abandon the frontier—which I believe would be fatal.

"All well at Kandahar on 13th July.

"Your soldiers never write to their fathers, mothers, or sweethearts—and a precious row I have at my house about it. If you would only send up some captured trophy you would do good."

From Sir John Lawrence, 2nd August 1857 :—

"I see the Kumaonis joined you this morning, and if you can only keep well, our other reinforcements will soon be up. Nicholson, with the 52nd and 61st and Green's regiment and the new Punjab levy, will bring up more than 2000 men. He is now moving towards Umballa from Loodhiana. It has struck me that if you were to write to one of our Punjabis he might be raising men for the Guides. I see by the last return from Norman that you are very weak in infantry, though pretty well off in cavalry. By the way, did 50 sowars whom Lake sent down ever join you? It was intended that they should do so. You will have heard of the flight of the greater part of the 26th from Meean Meer. They marched straight away in the middle of the day, and no one made any effort in cantonments to stop them. The country people and police, however, intercepted and killed many of them; some were drowned, and the rest taken and executed. Not above 100 can have escaped.

"It is very odd our hearing no authentic intelligence from Cawnpore. By this time Havelock should be at Aligarh. I am afraid that Lucknow affairs have claimed his presence. The mail is in; but on the 26th June the good folks in England do not seem to have realised our danger, or to have stirred their stumps to aid us effectually."

The extracts from Daly's letters are resumed :—

"*2nd August.*—We have been employed lately in making the defences perfect, so that our men may hold them unexposed, yet well able to open on the meney a she approaches. The result of it was shown last night. The fire was continued without interruption, and is in fact still going on in a mild way; but during the night the peals of musketry were *very heavy;* the enemy must have fired tens of thousands of rounds, besides round shot from the wall. Bugles were sounding all night in the city, and outside voices and shouting for the *advance*, but Pandy (this is the universal name for the mutineers: Mangal Pandy was the first man tried and executed for mutiny)—Pandy has not increased his courage as the moon fell. I have not heard that we lost any *one* during the night, and since their firing has commenced our killed and wounded does not exceed a dozen. We have had one sad loss; Travers * was peeping over a work and got shot in the forehead. He is not dead, but there is no hope of recovery. During the last twenty-four hours, despite the rounds and rounds by thousands which have been expended, but two others besides him have been mortally hit. I consider this the most successful and scientific drubbing we have shown Pandy. His loss has been great; his ammunition has been expended by cartloads; he has never seen our men. These are the lessons we should teach when acting on the defensive. Pursuing brings us loss when we have to return.

"*4th August.*—Yesterday the Sikh Jewan Singh and Jowahir Singh (whom I had sent to Cawnpore to ascertain matters and carry letters) arrived. They left this on 16th July, reached Cawnpore 22nd. They found General Havelock there with the 78th Highlanders, 1st Madras Fusiliers, and Sikh corps with guns. Havelock's letter was as follows: 'I regret to say Sir Hugh Wheeler was basely betrayed and destroyed, 27th ultimo, by Nana Sahib. Thank God, I have met with great and complete success. I have encountered the rebels in three engagements, and on each occasion took every gun from them, and defeated them with great slaughter. I have destroyed Bitore (the residence of the Nana, who headed the rebels), and am now marching to Lucknow, which holds out stoutly and well. My orders are strict to

* Of the 1st Punjab Infantry. He had served with Daly at Kohat.

relieve Lucknow. I have sent a copy of your letter to Sir Patrick Grant. Reinforcements are on the march in strength, including the China Force, and Sir Patrick Grant himself will soon be here.'

"Jewan Singh said notes were passing to and fro between Havelock and Lucknow. While they were seated with General Havelock, a messenger came with a note from the 'Bara Sahib' (Chief Authority). Jowahir Singh questioned him about the Sahib Log (English); he said the ladies and children were all comfortable in the Taikhana (underground rooms), and the Sahibs safe and unassailable; that all was well with them. This gave us comfort; the letter was dated from that bridge where toll is levied between Cawnpore and Lucknow, one march from the former, 25th July. Well, an hour after the receipt of the above, a note was brought from Agra, in which was given a copy of a letter from Havelock, dated Cawnpore, 18th July, and sent from Agra, 31st. In this he writes: 'Sir Henry Lawrence was wounded on the 2nd July, and died 4th July.' This caused great consternation and grief. I questioned Jewan Singh long as to whether he had heard any talk of Sir Henry's having been wounded, or sick; he persists that Sir Henry is well, that the messenger said he—Sir Henry—had given him the letter. Moreover, when I explained what was the report, the Sikh and Jowahir Singh both exclaimed: 'People go to and fro from Lucknow; all talk of Sir Henry's stoutness, and speak of him just as we speak of you in the regiment' (meaning men were familiar with his name); they said everybody speaks of Sir H. Wheeler's murder, therefore it is not likely such a death as Sir Henry's would be unknown. I am comforted by this. Havelock does not allude to it in his letter, 26th, and on arrival at Cawnpore reports, etc., may have reached him not to be relied on. I have been sorely upset about this. Better have lost Lucknow than Sir Henry. Lucknow can be retaken, but he cannot be replaced; at this season there is no man in India whose character and peculiar knowledge would be so useful to the Government. God grant it may not be true!

"*5th August.*—Colonel Nicholson is here, but

goes back to meet his column; there is doubtless a good deal of jealousy about the supercession, but put all the Queen's colonels together who are in camp (Greathed inclusive), and you could not extract a *man* who would be *willing* even to incur the responsibility of commanding this force. *All* here rejoiced at Chamberlain's arrival, and not one would have attempted to urge a word which would throw the command on himself. Colonel Campbell is, I believe, an *excellent* regimental officer, but there is a vast difference between such a man and one who is able to head and manage a force in the field. Moreover, Colonel Campbell had no experience of actual service, good as he is—and there is no doubt there is no commanding officer here half as good.

"I thought at one time that there would be a *sudden* and a great fall in Government Paper (India), and wrote to Bombay to buy a lot in such event. It has fallen but 1 and 1½ per cent. in Bombay.

"*6th August.*—The news of Cawnpore was flitting about the camp early last month, but without confirmation; one could not credit such brutality. Even now, what puzzles us all is that so resolute and experienced a soldier as Wheeler should have dreamt of terms, or of faith. We shall hear more by and by of the cause which led him to this, but of the massacre there is no doubt.

"*9th August.*—The news in the *Lahore Chronicle* about poor Sir Henry is from the same source I mentioned. I have yet hope, and God grant there may be ground for it. *Calamity, indeed, for India it would be.*

"*11th August.*—I fear the report of Sir Henry. We now learn a round shot struck his shoulder; if so—and there are details, sad details—death would follow; few, few survive the shock of a round shot. I seemed to have some close tie to him. He rests in peace and would not be sorry, personally, to quit the world his loved wife no longer held a place in.

"*12th August.*—You will have learnt of Sir Henry. I clung to hope for many a day, in fact *until yesterday.* In these days of battle and death there is so much to excite the mind that one is not long by possibility in one vein of thought; but I felt beaten down when this sad tale reached me. Reflection brings home to one the great public loss which his death occasions. At any time India would mourn his fall, but *now*, when she so much needed his guidance and his wisdom, the death of the soldier statesman fills all with grief. The public calamity overpowers the consideration and thought of private and personal bereavement. I do indeed feel that I have lost a prop in the world. He was a rare specimen of God's handiwork.

"This morning we made a capital *coup*. The enemy has been bringing his guns out into the open and has annoyed our picquets. We have somewhat tempted him to this by making no rush to get them. Yesterday it was resolved to seize those in the vicinity of the Metcalfe picquet, and accordingly a force was told off to attack this morning. It was kept a profound secret. I was one of the half-dozen who were aware of it. As the bugles announced the dawn I anxiously awaited the sound of musketry; quickly it fell on the ear, and, as I *wished* to hear, in one clear volley *at first*, and that before the light would enable the enemy to discern from the walls what was going on; no desultory fire, but a quick, sharp volley. This denoted success, that our column had been able to approach near without detection. All the guns (4, including a howitzer) were captured, and the enemy sorely mauled, for he was completely surprised. The very horses were taken with the guns. Our loss was not heavy considering; one officer only mortally wounded. The Brigadier (Showers) was hit twice, —on the top of his finger, and by a bullet glancing round underneath his arm. Coke got a flesh wound, nothing bad, just as he seized the leading horses by the head. The troops were in *high glee*, and this has given delight to every one. We had taken no heavy guns since the night I was wounded."

On the same date he wrote to England :—

"We are well here, though still without the walls of Delhi; our position has much strengthened; we await but reinforcements to stake *the* blow. The enemy is cowed, and makes not the ventures he formerly did. Colonel Nicholson's column comes in to-morrow or the 14th; 3000—1000 being Europeans. *Then I hope* nothing will delay the capture of Delhi, unless we should hear of the advance of troops from below.

"The country, wherever our troops approach, relapses into its old habits, and scarcely can a spectator believe in the bloody revolution which has torn up the old associations. Deserters from Delhi are numerous; they are not allowed to bear away arms, so the deserting mutineers are plundered by the villagers. It is estimated that there have been 35,000 or 40,000 fighting men within the walls; perhaps now 15,000 could not be mustered. They *may* have had 10,000 killed and wounded. There are always in every camp croakers, but I have never observed anything but the most cheerful spirit amongst the soldiery. The Europeans near my tent, whenever the evening is cool and Pandy quiet, play away at their games as though there was no more serious occupation. Of an evening till Tattoo they walk up and down the road (my tent is at the corner) neatly dressed, laughing and chatting in merry style. I have never heard amongst them at any time, even when we were weak in numbers, and the work was even more *harassing* than now, I have never heard a desponding word; of the result they never doubted. The same with the Guides and Ghurkhas. The Europeans have sometimes fought badly, but they have never talked despondingly; now all look cheerful and hopeful. Pandy, we know, is in much distress; he knows not what to do; to fly home, there he will be followed; to remain here, he will be slain. The 60th Rifles are *beyond value;* the old men of the corps. I consider, and I expect it is the general opinion, that 100 Riflemen equal 200 of any of the British infantry we have. I wish you could see the *spirit* which actuates the Guides; how cheerful they are amidst wounds and death; with what heroic devotion they rush forward.

"*13th August.*—Good news from Lucknow last evening. General Havelock had encountered all the Oudh force, a few miles the Cawnpore side of Lucknow; the fight lasted long; he utterly defeated them, and took 20 guns.   No mention of Sir Henry, and my hope died three days ago.

"*14th August.*—The Punjab column came in this evening.   The siege train is far behind.   I don't think that would delay us, but with it are two corps, and a portion of one will relieve the 60th Rifles at Meerut—nearly 400 good soldiers, who will then join us.   We are strong enough for the assault now, I have no doubt, but probably it will not be made.

"*16th August.*—The siege train will be at Umballa about 19th or 20th.   This was not required under the circumstances of the first propositions for attack; blowing in the gates and escalading were the ideas then.   Now a breach will be made; probably breaches in two places.

"*18th August.*—Nothing certain of an advance from Cawnpore, though *certain* troops in numbers are gathering.   I put no faith in the paper reports because I can always trace their origin.   We know all that is known and can be known.   The information respecting Sir Henry's wound was from two quarters, both *native;* but I have *no* hope—none.

"*19th August.*—News from General Havelock that, having received reinforcements, he was about to march (next morning) on Lucknow; that he had thoroughly discomfited the enemy, and had taken between 40 and 50 guns; after settling Lucknow he should proceed to Agra, and thence to Delhi.   All this is well, and, what I believe is better, there is no intention of awaiting his advent.   The camp looks very picturesque; the sun shining on the tents, which are pitched about in all directions, and are on every hillock.   One of the bands plays within the Staff Square every evening, and people ride round, laugh, chat, and gather together as though nothing of unusual importance was going on.

"*26th August.*—The large siege train from Ferozpur is now near at hand, escorted by a Punjab corps, and 3500 Dogras (a hill tribe), a contingent offered by Gulab Singh before his death, and subsequently despatched by his son and successor, are at Umballa *en route*.   The day of reckoning is near. Two days ago we received information that the enemy had moved out of the city with 5000 or 6000 men and 18 guns, attempting to get by a circuitous route to our rear. General Cortlandt, of Edwardes' renown, is at-Hansi, holding that country with a body of newly raised irregulars. A force marched from this yesterday at 6 A.M. to cut off the enemy. Rain fell in torrents at midday, and greatly did we fear that it would impede and prevent the passage of our guns across the heavy ground. Happily, however, thanks to the good pluck of the men and the energy of the commander—a fine fellow, an old Punjab friend of mine, Colonel Nicholson—the force crossed the swampy ground. They marched on 18 miles, attacked and thoroughly routed the enemy, taking 12 guns—all that had crossed the canal. Our loss was slight in number, but it included young Lumsden of Coke's corps, brother of Major Lumsden,* and well worthy to be so; a fine, gallant young soldier, shot through the heart: but two other officers were touched; one, a doctor, killed, and one wounded."

To England Daly wrote at this time :—

"There is one difficulty which was known to no one perhaps, save the engineer of the place—the walls have been lately repaired and rebuilt †; the ditch outside is so deep, and the counterscarp of the glacis so raised, that unless guns are *on* the very counterscarp it would be impossible to *raze* the wall. A breach bringing down the upper portion and leaving perhaps 8 feet or 10 of the thick, *can* be made at 400 yards, and this will be done immediately the train arrives.

"In the assault I think the flight and rush will be great. Some buildings and places will, I fear, be held with tenacity, and loss, heavy loss, will be ours. Nevertheless it must be undertaken, and the sooner the better; while Delhi remains with them, India is said, amidst a nation of liars, to be in the possession of the mutineers. With Delhi will pass the great struggle, and the guerilla war which will ensue will be more of punishment than opposition.

* Major Lumsden was the substantive Commandant of the Guides. He was at this time employed with the Kandahar Mission.

† By Lieut. Robert Napier (afterwards Field-Marshal Lord Napier of Magdala): see *Forty-One Years in India*, by Field-Marshal Lord Roberts, vol. i., pp. 162-3.

"Death and misery have run wild in many a happy home, many a noble, many a cherished spirit has fled ; but it is evident that the blow was to fall some time. It is no mere mutiny, but the struggle, the revolt, of the army we have disciplined and trained. My opinion for the future in India is that the native *regular* army will cease ; it will not be re-established in Bengal. The regular army should consist entirely of Europeans ; railways pushed on ; the Europeans garrisoned in the best climates ; * 60,000 European troops for the Punjab, North-West, and Bengal.

"India should be the nursery of the British army ; they would be available for service in any part of the world—the bulk of them trained troops. John Bull does not relish being behindhand when a war breaks forth ; yet it must be so, as the profession of arms is unpopular at home, and John loves not the sight of 'idling Red Coats.' God help them, poor fellows ! they have little idling here ; we have had upwards of 120 officers killed and wounded, and at least 1500 men ; in proportion to strength engaged, Sevastopol casualties were not so high ! To hark back to the army. The native portion to be reduced half at least, and kept in the irregular form : *i.e.*, 4 officers to each corps, and officers of selection ; then the 3rd body of the army to be *police* for general duty. Never again would there be an army in the land to contest the supremacy with its rulers.

"*29th August.*—I forgot to mention yesterday about Sir Colin Campbell. General Anson's death was telegraphed, and reached London on the 12th July. Sir Colin was offered, and more I suppose in these days, the command of the army, and started the next day and overtook the mails. He sent a telegram to Mansfield at Warsaw, offering him 'the chief of the staff' ; accepted, and Mansfield will be out by the next steamer. You know my opinion of Sir Colin.

---

* Sir H. Lawrence, in his *Adventures of an Officer, etc.* (1845), had written :—"Considerations of finance, as well as of humanity, might open the eyes of those in authority to the advantages of locating the European troops in the hill stations, with such facilities for communication as might enable the men to be brought down speedily on any emergency."

I know he has not capacity sufficient for the position and work such as now there will be. Mansfield, on whom he leans *entirely*, has the capacity, but his intellect is subtle, and his character inspires no man with confidence. I like him, but I question whether anybody else in camp does; but even with my feelings towards him and knowledge of his ability, I cannot bring myself to say that I should confide in him. Both have no affection for the Company's service; in fact I have no doubt it will cease to exist. How the army will be reconstituted it is hard to say, but I lean very much to a letter published in the *Times*, and signed 'M.P.' India will be in future the garrison for British troops : hill stations, good roads (rail), rapid communication.

"*30th August.*—News from Cawnpore, 13th and 17th. Havelock had gone out again to Bhitoor, and had punished and *mauled* the mutinous 42nd, which was marching across from Saugor. This is the last of the mutinous corps on foot.

"All well at Lucknow. Reinforcements will soon be with Havelock in strength; there is no mention from Cawnpore of Lucknow being in trouble.

"*1st September.*—Everything is in readiness to commence close operations immediately on the siege train's appearance. The Rifles and artillery at Meerut have moved. 'General' Nicholson is in the tent talking. The siege train will be here on the 5th. Captain Wilde's Punjab Corps has passed Umballa, so have the Dogras; therefore our strength is being collected at Najatgarh. Nicholson accomplished what I believe *no other man* here would have done, and this is the impression of every man with whom I have spoken. So many guns were not taken even on the 8th June. Nicholson is *able*, *vigorous*, and brave as a lion. You remember dear Sir Henry's kindly, affectionate feeling towards him; it was not without sound cause.

"General Havelock's force was but 1400 or 1500, without cavalry; *heaps of guns*, but few gunners.

"*4th September.*—The siege train is in, and in a few days everything will be ready for work. Sir T. Metcalfe was in here just now, and gave me an account of his miraculous escape (from Delhi).

"*6th September.*—The following is the plan of

operations. It is known to none but the engineers and three others. We shall erect two batteries to-morrow night, and hope to have them in readiness for breaching the *following* morning. They will pound the whole of the 8th, during the early morning of which another battery will be prepared at a spot which affords shelter, and is within 200 or 250 yards of the Cashmere Gate. The breaching batteries with the heavy guns will be 600 yards from the walls ; on the 9th, should all be ready, the assault will be made. Should matters go well, should the fire of our batteries be as successful as anticipated, the assault will come off in two places ; the Guides will not assault. Should the fire not be so effective, we must delay a little.

"*7th September*. — 10-gun battery commenced within 600 yards, after heavy firing from the Moree (grape) and musketry on the working party, about 9 P.M. Happily the enemy's fire was diverted to the ridge, and the work at 11 P.M. was proceeding satis-factorily. Jowahir Singh returned from Cawnpore 10 P.M.—good account. General Havelock awaits but the arrival of the 5th and 90th—God willing —to relieve Lucknow. Jowahir Singh affirms that he saw Forbes, the doctor, Hardinge, etc., all well at Lucknow. Ghulam Mohi-ud-din killed in a sally from the Muchee Bhawan, which we had been obliged to relinquish, with stores.

"Saw my father's death, 15th July, in the *Extra* : re-read all the letters in which his state was men-tioned.—God rest him.

"*8th.*—Battery (divided in two at 150 yards dis-tant) completed before daylight—3 guns in position. The enemy apparently astonished when morning dis-closed the battery so close to the walls. Bugles sounded the 'Assembly,' and great was the cry to go forth to the attack ; however, no great advance took place ; some cavalry galloped as though meaning the battery, but a shower of grape quelled them ; our loss, 2 officers, and about 20 men killed and wounded. The erection of the battery cost us no life. Parties at work at nightfall to make mortar batteries in the Kudsia Bagh and prepare the breaching battery. Went up to the Mosque battery with the Brigadier at evening to observe the fire ; the Moree (bastion) still alive.

"*9th.*—The breaching battery worked up to the embrasures during the night.   Mortar batteries finished : 10 heavy guns well at work tearing down the defences.   Baird Smith full of life, but the spirit and energy of Taylor * are on the ground and do the work ; Baird Smith fitfully wanders about ; heavy complaints of the General's vacillation and want of reliance.   Pandy did little damage during the night ; his guns from Kishengunge do most and heaviest damage.   Our loss severe : evening 7th, 2 officers and 18 men killed, 57 wounded.

"*10th September.*—The operations are progressing satisfactorily and successfully, though, from the nature of the ground, the works have been slower than was anticipated.   Heavy firing last night on the working parties.   However, it is now but a question of hours.   In all sieges the last operations cannot be looked to within a few hours of certainty ; at Multan we paraded three times for the storm.   Went to the Ridge with Chamberlain.

"*11th September.*—Taylor called, telling us all his work was over.   All the batteries needed have been erected ; one will not open fire till to-morrow morning or at midnight, otherwise all is in readiness.   To-morrow *should* suffice for the pounding of the works, but it is not possible to say until the effect of the fire has been seen for some hours.   We have one battery which has got to open 160 yards from the wall ; this will astonish our friend Pandy.

"*12th September.*—Meeting at the General's to hear plan of assault — 3 columns, Nicholson 1st, Campbell 3rd, Jones 2nd.   Campbell's for the Jama Masjid—the most trying work in my mind, but he is resolute and good.   Nicholson leads, no lesser man could lead.   Longfield reserve, Denny camp and convalescents.   Reid to attack Paharipur with Guides and Gurkhas, and contingent.   Fagan, an officer who has universal respect—whose name was in everyone's mouth, so cheerful, so hardy, so heroic, was shot dead or nearly so, as he sat on the trail of his gun watching the effect of the shot for which he had just laid.   Great regret throughout the camp. Storm to-morrow!"

* Afterwards General Sir Alexander Taylor, G.C.B.

Daly's wound still incapacitated him from active duty; with Chamberlain, he watched the assault from the top of Hindu Rao's house, "able neither to ride nor run," though he descended, and took charge of the picquet when things looked black through the check to Reid's column.*

Next day he wrote :—

"*14th September.*—The assault came off at daybreak. I was not near the breach and therefore cannot describe the sight, which must have been glorious ; our troops there behaved with all their rightful valour. The troops had to escalade ; the Gate (Cashmere) was blown in ; but few survived who performed the deed. We hold the walls and bastions which formerly so worried us, and have established ourselves well in the city. The enemy fought stoutly in several places. They have bolted in numbers, and have rushed out of the city.

"The attack from here (Hindu Rao's house) on a party outside in great strength and numbers, in which Guides, Ghurkhas, and some Europeans, with the contingent from Cashmere, suffered heavy loss, failed in capturing the guns on which they made the assault ; however, everybody is as well as we could expect. Colonel Campbell has a slight wound ; he has done, and is doing, his work heroically. I came up here last night thinking I might be of use, and I found it was so.

"*15th September.*—Loss we encountered, but the success was great. But for this failure on the right in an *outside* attack, all would have been glorious. We are now shelling the Palace and battering old Selim Ghar. *Hundreds* have quitted Delhi. Animals laden with all sorts of spoil we can observe moving away. There was not much resistance at the breach, but the firing on our advancing column was heavy, and our loss was heavy. Afterwards the troops

* The check was mainly ascribed to Reid receiving a severe and disabling wound just as he was completing his dispositions for the attack. The position after the check was one of great danger. (See Kaye's *Sepoy War*, vol. iii., p. 611.)

advanced along the ramparts at a great pace, capturing guns and driving the mutineers away without difficulty, until we came to a halt at one bastion for supports and ammunition. Here for the first time the opposition became stiff; 10 officers, I think, of the Fusiliers were killed and wounded. Nicholson, exhorting the men to make a manful rush, got his bad wound. Welby Greathed wounded; arm broken, but not badly. It looks so singular to observe our people quietly moving along the front of the walls where death was so busy but a few days ago. Pandy is sorely disheartened, but still holds out desperately in some places. Nearly every heavy gun has been captured.

"*16th September.*—We have been doing well and making progress since yesterday. Kishengunge has been evacuated; they have left guns and have evaporated. The Magazine was assaulted at dawn, after having been breached; 125 guns, with munitions of war, etc. We lost nothing; 3 or 4 men wounded. To-day matters are going very *well;* the roads full of bolters. Nicholson, *the* General, and a great officer he will be if saved, is but a trifle better.

"*17th September.*—Our operations are doing well; no lives, or few, lost yesterday. I have not been in the city, but am in command of this position (Hindu Rao's house, etc.), which I can manage though unable to run a stride, and I am glad to be of any use. I have the Guide Infantry, Ghurkhas, and some of the 61st Foot, Bengal Fusiliers, and artillery. I have had no sleep for two nights.

"*18th September.*—The blow has been a heavy one, and Delhi will long carry with it many tearful memories. We are progressing. Chamberlain is in the city and doing all he can. From poor Nicholson we may not look for aid again : I fear he is very bad. All feeling about supersession had passed. I think his valour and perception were such that all felt he was born for command.

"*19th September.*—General Nicholson is dangerously ill; I fear much for him; he will be a *heavy loss* indeed. Murray of the Guides: he was wounded a bit on the 25th June, and again in July, never seriously, but his health was bad, and he was sent to

Kasauli and recovered, and returned looking strong
and well about the 6th of this month. I had got him,
a month ago, an adjutancy of one of the new regiments. As I mentioned, the Guides were not in the
assault of the city, but in the action on the right.
The Guide officers, with a few men and a few
Europeans, made a rush across a terrible fire attempting to gain a breast cover. Murray, one of the foremost, brave lad, was shot through the chest and fell
dead. Captain M'Barnett fell at the same moment,
or nearly so. The loss was heavy amongst 60th,
Fusiliers, 61st, Guides, and Ghurkhas.

"We lost nobody yesterday. It would be possible
to clear the place with a rush, but to save life we are
adopting the plan of steady advance.

"*22nd*.—The old king is in our hands, and had
our information been worth anything, his sons *
also would be prisoners. Some Sikh sowars of
Hodson's came on them; not knowing who they were,
plundered the sons, and took no heed of their capture.
We shall get them yet, I hope; that Mirza Mogul
Beg must be hanged as high as possible. Our
terrible loss is Nicholson; his services we have no
longer, and I fear his life can hardly be looked for.
He is so ill and worn. Everybody else among the
wounded is doing well."

It was to Daly's tent that Nicholson was borne
when wounded. After his death, which occurred on
the 23rd September, Chamberlain and Daly formed
the committee of adjustment on his affairs. Daly
now heard from Sir John Lawrence, dated 19th
September :—

"I have to thank you for your letter giving an
account of the assault; almost the only one any of
my friends have sent me. It strikes me very forcibly
that, as you say, it was a mistake attacking
Kishengunge at all. It could hardly fail to fall, if
we were successful in the town. And the men
expended in this erratic attack would have done good

* Afterwards captured and shot by Hodson.

service elsewhere. But it was unreasonable to suppose that the Cashmere troops could face 18-pounders. I would have been for leaving 400 or 500 of these well posted to mask Kishengunge.

"It seems to me, moreover, that we made a mistake in attempting too much on the morning of the 14th, and perhaps might have done better had we been less ambitious. I did not get any plan of the attack, but I hear that it embraced the expulsion of the mutineers from the whole of the city. If this was true, surely it was too great a task for the means at our disposal. Perhaps I may be wrong in my criticisms, but I do not make them after the affair. This I thought from the time that matters assumed their present gravity.

"I feel very much vexed that I have no reinforcements to send to Delhi; we are barely holding the country and no more. And had I not some good men about me, we should not do this. At Murree we had a petty affair which showed we were not over-secure. At Peshawar the slightest spark would cause a general conflagration. Even while I write we have a disaffection among the wild tribes in the jungles, half-way between this and Multan, which may give us trouble. They have intercepted the post, and seem bent on mischief.

"This delay in sending troops from England, or rather in not sending some of them inland, may breed great misfortunes. God grant us success. It is very terrible to think how much will depend on the next few days. I trust that the troops will be kept well in hand, and full time taken in mastering each point. We cannot afford to lose many men. We have no reserve to give you. I am hunting up all the officers I can lay hands on. General Cotton is sending some 19, and some more will go down from this division. I trust, therefore, that full 40 will be available after clearing out Simla and Mussooree. I hope the Guides did not suffer much. How is Khan Singh Rosa?"

On the 27th, Daly wrote from the Jama Masjid :—

"I have come down here to pay Major Coke a visit. He is quartered in this magnificent pile with

his corps.   The city is a wondrous sight; doors and
windows broken open, here and there a cat peering.
Bottles, boxes, bedding, furniture, and articles
beggaring description cast about.   Men of all colours
(soldiers) searching and plundering.   The inhabitants
roaming about helpless and hungry in every direction.   Nobles and delicate women, still carrying
jewels and wealth, without food and almost without
covering.   The desolation no language can paint.
The retribution will be palpable.   The Guides will
march back as soon as English troops arrive.   Had
we to depend on home succour, what would our hold
on India have been worth?   The fall of Delhi has
been the fall of the rebel cause.   Walking about the
streets of Delhi one could only wonder how we had
acquired it.   The rebels in some places were ready
for a stiff resistance.   Sand bags in piles, guns loaded
to the muzzle and placed in position, all betokened
that which they had no leadership or heart to carry
out.   We have struggled and reeled through our
trials."

At the beginning of October Daly, who was still
crippled with his wound, was granted a few weeks'
leave to Simla, whence he wrote on the 12th October
to England :—

"The relief of Lucknow has taken place.   I grieve
for the death of General Neill.   We had many *rolled*
pieces of paper from him during our struggle at Delhi.
His heart and courage were always high; he seemed
to be the Nicholson of that force.   Our column, which
has marched by Aligarh to Agra, is pursuing its
course with little molestation or opposition.   The
mutineers evacuate each place and throw away their
arms as we approach.   We have sustained *terrible*
blows in the fall of our best men.   Colonel Greathed,
who commands that force, was sent, not on account
of his capacity, but because the men of capacity were
either killed or wounded.   It was to have been
Nicholson's post, and there neither is nor was any
man who could so thoroughly have filled it.   One can
feel the blunders of the Crimean War, for truly few

of the Queen's officers have had any experience of any service beyond mess management, and their views are narrow and regimental. They are altogether ignorant of the broader duties, and *know nothing* of the interests at stake.

"Lord Canning has to answer for the delay at Lucknow. Had Sir John Lawrence pursued the same policy, we should have been overwhelmed at Delhi, and the north-west would have been swamped. Lord Canning seems to have had thought and care for nothing but Calcutta and Bengal, whereas the latter (for Calcutta had ships and sailors, citizens and volunteers) did but faintly through the Sepoy corps, and they were few, reflect the tone above. Lord Canning at first was plucky; as the troubles gained strength he lost it. It is melancholy to read the debates on our affairs; the 'weighing of suggestions' by Lord Palmerston as to the passage of troops through Egypt. De Lacy Evans dwells on this in a great deal of twaddle, 20th August, and Lord Palmerston replies with thanks. We who looked for aid in July learn that in August and September the near road was thought worthy of consideration. Had Government but sent 500 men to Bombay, the effect would have been substantial; it was heartrending to read the flummery that was spoken about the strong arm of England, and to learn that steamers were leaving every fortnight, which might each time have brought 500 soldiers, with nothing but debates and promises.

"I know not just at present whether my connection with the Guides will continue or not. I wrote to ask Sir John; he replied: 'Something satisfactory will assuredly turn up; how I cannot say, for I do not know. Lumsden will not return till December, therefore all that will be necessary is to provide for you or him then.' I should have liked, what Susie so much wished, to be military secretary to Sir Henry. *He* would have been pleased also, I think and feel. Now I have no fancy for the appointment. Sir John is *most kind, most cordial*, we have kept up an intimate correspondence during the war, and it has happened in several instances that I have asked for appointments for those who have distin-

guished themselves and for men of whom I have
thought well. In no case has he ever replied by
letter, but the Gazette has *at once* announced the
appointment, and this even to commands of corps.
Nevertheless he is not to me what Sir Henry was.
I had a *love* for him exceeding even the admiration
and reverence in which I held his lofty character,
his great attainments; as Lumsden said, in writing
of his death from Candahar, 'it is much, Daly, to
have known one such man.' I have a sort of
melancholy satisfaction in the knowledge that Susan
saw him and learnt to appreciate him."

The Guides left Delhi to return to Mardan on
the 18th December 1857. They first marched to
Peshawar, where they arrived on the 2nd February
1858, and were given a great reception. A division
order of that date by Major-General Sir Sydney
Cotton, commanding the Peshawar Division,
began :—

"Major-General Cotton makes known throughout
the division under his orders that the troops of the
Peshawar cantonment were paraded under his
personal command to-day to receive and welcome
the corps of Guides on its arrival in cantonment from
the siege of Delhi. A royal salute was fired in
honour of the Guides on their approaching the
parade-ground, and the troops saluted when the
General delivered addresses to the troops and to
the Peshawar force."

Four combatant British officers marched to Delhi
with the Guides: 15 others were attached to the
corps for various periods during the siege. Of these
19, 3 were killed, 1 died, and 8 were wounded;
one of the latter was wounded six times, one four
times, at least two others were wounded more than
once. Edwardes said in a speech at a banquet:
"There was not one officer of the Guides who was

on their return to Peshawar not wounded at least once. Sometimes every officer was laid up with wounds, and an entirely new set of officers had to be appointed." Of native ranks the strength on reaching Delhi was 218 cavalry and 423 infantry, the reinforcements subsequently received at various times were 205 cavalry and 241 infantry, making a grand total of 1107. The losses were, in the cavalry, 28 killed and 49 wounded, or over 18 per cent.; and in the infantry, 99 killed and 173 wounded, or nearly 41 per cent. Even these percentages do not give an adequate idea of the loss,* because a considerable proportion of the reinforcements did not arrive till the struggle was virtually over.

Twenty-five native officers and men of the Guides received the Order of Merit for distinguished conduct before Delhi. Fifty-four men were specially mentioned in regimental orders, and promoted on

---

* These figures are taken from the regimental history of the corps of Guides: they do not tally, as regards initial strength, with those given by Norman, the Assistant Adjutant-General of the Army, who was on the spot and in a position to obtain accurate returns. In his *Narrative of the Campaign of the Delhi Army*, dated 28th October 1857, he writes thus (p. 47): "All behaved nobly, but it may be permitted to allude somewhat to those corps most constantly engaged from the beginning, the 60th Rifles, Sirmoor Battalion, and Guides. Probably not one day throughout the siege passed without a casualty in one of these corps; placed in the very front of our position, they were ever under fire. Their courage, their high qualifications as skirmishers, their cheerfulness, their steadiness, were beyond commendation. Their losses in action show the nature of the service.

"The Rifles commenced with 440 of all ranks; a few days before the storm they received a reinforcement of nearly 200 men: their total casualties were 389.

"The Sirmoor Battalion commenced 450 strong, and once was joined by a draft of 90 men. Its total casualties amounted to 319.

"The Guides commenced with about 550 (cavalry and infantry), and the casualties were 313."

the spot to the commissioned or non-commissioned ranks "for gallantry in the field."

The Court of Directors, in one of the last letters which they wrote (No. 50, dated the 30th August 1858), thus addressed the Government of India :—

"We cannot too strongly express our entire concurrence in the sentiments expressed by Major-General Cotton in his Division Order on the occasion of the return of the Guides to the Frontier.

"That corps, by the extraordinary alacrity with which they proceeded to Delhi, marching 580 miles in twenty-one days, and having during those twenty-one days turned off the road 12 miles one night to attack mutineers ; by their remarkable services before Delhi, where, for nearly four months, both officers and men were constantly in action, sometimes twice a day; by their singular fidelity, as shown by the fact that of 800 men not one man deserted to the enemy, whilst 350 of them were killed and wounded ; and by their heroic gallantry, having established for themselves the strongest claim to our approbation and favour. We desire that these our sentiments may be conveyed to them through their gallant commander, Major Daly."

CHAPTER VIII

LUCKNOW—1858

The general position; summons to Lucknow; capture of the city; death of Hodson; appointed to Hodson's Horse; memorandum on the Corps; Lucknow after the capture; Napier; operations at Moosabagh; hopes for Sir John Lawrence as Governor-General; Russell of the *Times*; Chamberlain and Mansfield; Hearsay's story.

AFTER the fall of Delhi, Daly spent his few weeks' leave with his wife at Simla. She had been in Simla throughout the anxious time at the commencement of the mutiny, when the station was entirely without defence or defenders and the rising of the Ghurkha regiment at Jutogh was for some days hourly expected. Daly returned to Delhi at the end of November, and immediately after this the Guides were ordered back to Mardan. Mrs Daly joined her husband at Umballa and marched with the corps to Lahore, whence he took his wife and children to Multan *en route* for England. They arrived at Multan on the 11th January 1858, after seven days' march. Mrs Daly wrote :—

"We accomplished the journey without danger or difficulty. The country looks deserted and bare; the rebels of the Gogaira * district are thoroughly

* A rising of the wild and wandering tribesmen of this tract occurred in September, the news reaching Sir John Lawrence the very day (14th September) that Delhi was assaulted. The disaffection at first seemed likely to spread, but was suppressed by Sir John's prompt and vigorous measures.

dispersed, it is said. Sowars are posted along the road, and they give you a guard from chauki to chauki, if you wish it. We usually had a few sowars if we were out late at night, but all appeared perfectly quiet, and Europeans are marching up the road constantly. There are 'Serais' about 12 miles apart along the road. These Serais, large walled enclosures for the protection of travellers, have each of them a room or two where one can sleep. There are four or five dâk bungalows on the road, but these have been plundered and all the furniture stolen. We had no adventures beyond an occasional break-down of luggage carts, or a pair of bullocks that would not stir."

After seeing his family on board a boat on the Indus, Daly returned by mail-cart to Lahore. The 210 miles occupied twenty-six hours :—

"The roads, broken up by constant traffic which has lately set in, are in a state indescribable." After a day at Lahore, he proceeded to Jhelum : "Here the road was better, and we did the 100 miles in nine hours. I often wish my head was towards the army and the camp for service. I must try to get down ; but just now, as the Guides have returned, this will not be easy. The infantry are almost annihilated : killed, wounded, and sick are so numerous that the corps must be renovated. Good men in the field are scarce. Great man there has not been since Henry Lawrence and Nicholson's spirits. They were of a separate class."

"The work in Oudh must now be going on. Sir Colin has a large force to wield ; how different from our advance on Delhi, 1500 infantry. He is strong in artillery, efficient in cavalry, and with the prestige of success in every struggle ; for, amidst the thousand fights, often with incapable leaders and insufficient parties, defeat has never dimmed us. The people of Oudh, *i.e.*, the soldiery, know full well the approach of the end ; whereas, in all the early days they fought not merely for victory,—they deemed that secure with such a handful of competitors as we were,—they fought for *extermination*. Now the tables are turned. I have little doubt hundreds would accept *any* terms they could get; thousands will bolt into the forests and deserts of Oudh. Nevertheless there must be a struggle under the great gateways, in the courtyards and palaces which Susan has painted; but as I have said, all things chime well for the attack, whereas, nobody at a distance can describe the feeling of dismay which smote us at Delhi in July and August, when, instead of the armed men who, in our fancy, were walking the decks of the steamers, we received debates, long heroic speeches of standing by us to the last, but an intimation that ships were quicker than steamers, that the Overland Route, which two dragoon corps, with all their paraphernalia, had taken the previous year for India, was tedious and impracticable. Yet the Bombay Government in *May* telegraphed to Calcutta for permission to despatch steamers and ships, which they had in abundance in the harbour (just returned from the Persian campaign) to Suez. So great was the need felt, that to my knowledge in May it was suggested to Lord Elphinstone to request the Governor of Malta to despatch two corps from Malta without awaiting the sanction from home, and Lord Elphinstone *all but did it*. Oh how we cheered the few allies we had by telling them of the speed with which English troops would quit England. Many of us, all of us, fancied that Lord Palmerston, with his *Civis Romanus sum* notions and with the experience of the Crimea at hand, would have met the moment. How *bitter* was our disappointment; how sad the day in camp when these things became known! Sir John wrote to me, 'the Government at home have a mind to leave us alone.' Had the Mauritius and Cape governors taken the same view, the Bombay army would have gone in numbers : *one* corps sufficed to stay it, and that corps landed from the Mauritius! 200 or 400 men *from England* in Bombay in July would have been the preservation of Central India. The villains *placarded* about, 'So many months and not a boasted Englishman has come to the rescue; they cannot come, for that good Muhammadan the Sultan has stopped the road.'"

The reception given to the Guides at Peshawar has already been related. Daly himself stayed some little time with Edwardes, of whom he wrote to his wife :—

"Edwardes is a charming companion; he has a rich mind, his knowledge is well in hand, and the method and style of expression are very happy; he speaks with great self-possession and readiness, is as apt in speaking as in conversation; his system is to put his whole strength into everything he does. You know my love for him was not *thorough;* that interview at Rawal Pindi, on our downward route warmed me somewhat to him, and certainly increased my admiration and respect for his capacity and courage. He is warm and cordial to me."

Daly was now offered the appointment of Deputy Commissioner of Kohat. He declined, remarking, "The pay and position are good, but it is in a corner, and I would rather be in the world in these days." The Guides reached Mardan on the 11th February 1858, when a great deal of work had to be done in settling accounts, returns, etc.

Daly's old friend Mansfield was now chief of the staff to Sir Colin Campbell, and while Daly was at Peshawar, Edwardes had received a telegram, "The Chief of the Staff enquires where is Captain Daly?" The reply was, "At Peshawar, ready for orders." Hearing nothing more, Daly wrote to Mansfield that he had for some days expected orders to start, but now imagined that there was no immediate opening, and that he regretted this, as he would like to have seen the Lucknow struggle. On the 23rd February, by the advice of the medical authorities at Peshawar, he underwent a painful operation in the hope that it would result in his recovering power in the left shoulder, which was stiff and the arm useless from the effects of his wound. Two days later came another telegram to Edwardes from Mansfield at Lucknow :—

"Will you kindly send an express to Captain Daly of the Guides to ask him to come down and live here with me. The Commander-in-Chief has given me leave to make this offer. For the present I can do nothing more, but he will understand it all as an answer to his note. I do not see why he should not be in time for the struggle, if he makes haste."

Sir John Lawrence readily accorded the necessary permission, and Daly, with his crippled shoulder, set off at once.

After arrival at Lucknow he wrote :—

"I reached Bebiapur on the 9th. The head-quarters were in our old quarters. The Commander-in-Chief, Mansfield, and all the swells were, on my arrival, at the Martinière, which had been attacked from the Dilkusha. I rode across, and met a most hearty reception; Sir Colin markedly cordial and jolly; Hope-Johnstone and many an old friend's face; Delhi companions and Oudh allies. I left Mardan at 7 A.M. on the 1st, in a cold, misty rain, the ground slippery and heavy. Kennedy drove me to Nowshera. I rode on and reached Rawal Pindi before 8 P.M.; 100 miles over. I was obliged to stop the night at Pindi, and to start off my bag for Jhelum, which I reached the following morning. I got into the mail-cart for Lahore about noon on the 3rd, and reached that night at 12; started again for Umballa at 7 A.M., 4th; stopped at Ludhiana for half an hour, very hungry and somewhat tired with shoulder pains, however a glass of beer and some cold meat refreshed me and on I went; entered Umballa about 7 A.M., 5th, breakfast and off again; got to Karnal at 7 P.M., was hospitably received and fed by the civilian; off again, and into Delhi about 7 A.M. on the 6th. I drove to Sir John's; he was in tents, most hearty and most kind: it was arranged that I should spend the day there, and off again in the evening. Chamberlain

LUCKNOW.

[To face p. 190

was written to of my arrival; he came down; about
an hour after a visitor called and told of my honours
(Brevet-Major and C.B.). Sir John was delighted.
  "I travelled from Delhi by palki ghari; delightful
rest after the mail-cart. I continued without a pause
till I reached Cawnpore, 4 P.M., 8th. 'Major-General
Sir John Inglis' was in command; he put me up for
the night. I sent a telegram to Lucknow announcing
my arrival, and received an order to be passed on,
riding irregular cavalry horses. It was my intention
to leave at daybreak, but Inglis had much to tell me
of the garrison and Lucknow and dear Sir Henry.
I remained chattering with him till 9 A.M. I passed
Charlie Blunt, now in command of a battery, had a
chat, rode his horse 30 miles, and made the gates of
Bebiapur at 3 P.M. I rode from Cawnpore to Lucknow without an escort. Troops and people were
passing to and fro. I found a large encampment at
Alumbagh. Bebiapur House is unaltered. Dilkusha
was occupied by our troops, and our guns from there
had pounded the Martinière, which had been wantonly
destroyed, i.e., the interior. Yesterday morning we
commenced the interior and real operations. Major
Banks' house is in our possession. Sir Colin,
Mansfield, and I were there all day. This is a
pleasant sort of warfare after Delhi; a large force
with all appliances. You will learn all particulars
from Russell of the *Times*, who has just been in this
tent.
  "12th March.—You will have heard ere this of
the complete success of the operations of yesterday.
The cordon is closing in on every side; the loss we
sustained yesterday was slight: poor Hodson was
badly wounded in the city, whither he had gone to
speak to Colonel Napier during the operations.
Mansfield wishes me to assume command of his
corps, which is stronger than any here. I have told
you how well and more than well disposed to me are
the Chief and Mansfield; the latter treats me altogether in the olden familiar style.
  "17th March.—I have been busy and absent on a
raid; we returned yesterday. Poor Hodson died the
day after his wound. He was brought in in a
dhoolie, from which he was not removed until after

death. It chanced I was at Banks' house when he was brought in. I spoke to him, fetched a doctor for him, and helped to attend on him: poor fellow, we had strong hopes for his life, but internal bleeding came on and soon swept him away; he was wounded about 5 P.M., and died the following day at noon. During the night he rallied *much*, and until 10 A.M. there was no immediate danger and much ground for hope. He was very calm. He was, as I always thought, a wondrous compound; ability high and strong; great capacity of mind; power and energy, physical and mental. His ability had received more culture than falls to the lot of most of us. He did not quit England till twenty-three years of age, when he was a B.A. and somewhat distinguished at Cambridge. He is a great loss to the service, for doubtless he had done great soldiership. He was attended during that evening by Dr Clifford, and afterwards by Dr Anderson, who remained with him till the end. We buried him on the evening of the 12th March, at the Martinière. Sir Colin and Mansfield were at his funeral.

"The corps is some 1200 strong, and will be the nucleus of two or three regiments, I believe. The kindness of Sir Colin and Mansfield makes my position here very pleasant. Mansfield is wise and wary; as cool and gentlemanly now that he manages the affairs of this army as when picking strawberries at Gatcombe. The deference and respect shown to him are great; with me he is as of old, and when we are alone asks and adopts my suggestions."

Daly left for his successor the following "Rough Notes and Memoranda respecting Hodson's Horse." Hodson, mortally wounded at the Begam Kothi on the evening of the 11th March 1858, died in the back room on the ground floor of Banks' house on the following morning.

"I assumed command of the corps at the Alumbagh on the following day. It numbered present about 750 sabres. The officers were the two Goughs (Hugh on his back wounded), Wise,

Mecham, Baker, Trench, and Anderson the assistant surgeon. The regiment, so much of it as was then present, had been paid by advances to 31st January 1858. In the treasure chest, which was counted by Captain Gough, was Rs. 16,000. No English muster roll or pay abstract had been framed. No English paper of any sort, record, receipt, account, or statement, was forthcoming. The only English paper known was the registry of a few names in Hugh Gough's handwriting, which is now, as then, in the muster roll book.

"The enrolment of men for the corps had begun in June 1857. Rs. 119,557/10/4 had been taken up, and all save the 16,000 had been disbursed. It was alarming to know that for the account* of this one was entirely in the hands of the munshis: the times were pressing; work and movement the lot of all, and in this vocation no man had been more active or more zealous that poor Hodson. He possessed a rarely clear head and keen memory, and on these and the munshis was his sole reliance. No European officer knew anything of the affairs of the regiment. Everything was done by himself. I made Mecham officiating second in command, and gave him charge of the treasure chest, with directions to take down from Dumichand and Gurdial, the two munshis, without delay a statement of the expenditure. Dumichand had been a khazanchi (treasurer) at Lahore; on him, on the faithfulness of his accounts, we were entirely dependent; though without experience of the pay rules, he is well versed in accounts. Speaking now on an intimate knowledge of Dumi-

---

* The elucidation and settlement of the corps' accounts proved a work of the utmost difficulty; but was eventually completed, early in 1859, to the entire satisfaction of Government, mainly through the zeal, energy, and application of Lieutenant R. B. Anderson, 1st Bombay Fusiliers, who was attached to the force, by Daly's request, as Brigade Major. This very promising young officer, a brother of Daly's old friend slain at Multan, met his death during the China campaign in distressing circumstances. Serving as Adjutant of Fane's Horse, he was taken prisoner, with his escort, on the 18th September 1860, when carrying a flag of truce, and succumbed about the end of that month to the barbarous treatment of his captors.

chand's conduct, I bear grateful testimony to his zeal
and honesty; had he played false, I cannot picture
the result. Gurdial is more conversant with the
rules of the service, for he had served as a pay
munshi in the Guides: he is clever and quick at
figures, but, being much addicted to opium, cannot
be relied on.

"Never before was corps raised as this has been
raised; troop by troop, detachment by detachment,
the Punjab supplied them and down they marched to
Delhi, not only without drill, but there were few
among them who had crossed even a khazi tat (a
common pony). They were now mounted on whatever horses could be procured; these were chiefly
stud, received from the dismounted cavalry corps:
thus they began to share in operations in the field, in
which they have been engaged without interruption
from that date to the present. Mr Montgomery,
then Judicial Commissioner at Lahore, liberally
aided the enrolment. One troop, Man Singh's, was
raised and inspected by him; Raja Tej Singh
embodied Bhal Singh's troop, and Sheikh Imamuddin
Atta-ullah Khan's. These three marched to Delhi
and there joined poor Hodson about the middle of
July 1857. Previous to their arrival, Hodson had
begun the regiment, taking as a nucleus a few of the
Raja of Jhind's men; these, however, were eventually resumed, and the first of the corps at Delhi were
the three troops just named.

"Macdowell, 2nd European Regiment, now joined
as second in command, and remained with the corps
till he was killed at Shamanow, 27th July 1858.
Hugh Gough came shortly afterwards, and acted as
adjutant till 26th February 1858, when a severe wound,
received in charging a battery near the Alumbagh, so
disabled him that he was compelled to go away.
Many of the men, hastily collected, caught at the
plough tail, cut a ludicrous figure mounted on the
big, obstinate stud horses, with English saddles,
bumping through the Delhi camp: the regiment then
acquired a nickname which it long retained, 'the
Plungers.' Jai Singh's and Sharif Ali Khan's troops
joined in August; the former raised by Shamshere
Singh, Sardar, and the latter by Sheikh Imamuddin;

later came Muhammad Raza * with the troop raised
by himself and his brother. Fateh Ali Shah, who
had formerly served with me in the Oudh Cavalry,
raised a troop in a few days; being a son of the
Afghan chief, Jan Fishan Khan, he had the command
of money. This was perhaps the worst troop the
corps had seen. Some 40 or 50 were his own
Bargheers, the scum of Meerut and the Delhi camp
in September 1857. Hugh Gough, with Baker and
about 230 sowars (Jai Singh and Bhal Singh),
formed part of Colonel Greathed's column, which
marched from Delhi 27th September. Baker, with
about 30 or 40 men, was dropped at Koel. Gough
came on with the remainder, and, joining the Chief's
corps, was of the Bailie Guard reserve force. After
the relief, Hugh Gough and his squadron were at the
Alumbagh with General Outram, until the Chief's
return for the final smash. Halket, who joined the
squadron at Agra, was mortally wounded at the
Secundra Bagh.

"Hodson, with the headquarters of the regiment,
paraded with the column of Brigadier-General
Showers through the Jaggar district, and on his
return, after the interval of a few weeks during which
the regiment was at Meerut, he again took the field
with Brigadier Seaton's column, which marched from
Delhi about the 7th December. The regiment took
its full share in the operations of that march, and

---

* Muhammad Raza's son has recently forwarded to me a copy of
a certificate granted to his father by my father, and bearing date
Camp, Bhinga, 11th February 1859. It runs :—"Muhammad Raza
Khan joined the Irregular Horse of the late Major Hodson at Delhi
a day or two before the storm (14th September 1857). He has served
throughout the war, and on all occasions has been conspicuous for
chivalric valour. Now that peace is restored, it is his wish to return
to his home at Lahore, whence he came to raise and command a
troop, chiefly of his own retainers, for service.

"Muhammad Raza's gallantry has won for him the first class of
the Order of Merit, and a representation has been submitted to
Government soliciting that the pension (Rs. 200), which he enjoys on
account of former services, may be increased. I commend Muhammad
Raza Khan to the kindly, courteous consideration of all British
officers. A braver soldier never took the field.—H. D."

subsequently joining the Commander-in-Chief, came
on to Lucknow.

"I have now run down to the period when I
assumed command. I lost no time in submitting to
the Commander-in-Chief that there were no English
records or accounts of any kind to be found, and
earnestly entreated that an officer might be specially
deputed to the clearing up of the past: there was a
disposition to accede to this suggestion, but at the
time there was no officer of business habits available
for the duty; the service was going on, and one
drifted on from day to day without the possibility of
pulling up; at this period there were some 400 men
dismounted at Meerut, and about 100 at headquarters
in the same condition; upwards of 1000 of those
with horses had no saddles. Plunder and the tales
of golden floods had enticed many of the relatives
and friends of the sowars from the Punjab; the lines
of the regiment were full of these amateurs; they
wore the uniform and have sometimes, in the absence
of the sowars, actually attended parades and taken
duty.

"In a skirmish I was at first surprised to see the
great array at the commencement; their occupation,
however, quickly thinned the gathering. I had much
difficulty in breaking through this combination. The
duties which fell to the corps during the siege were
harassing, but of fighting there was little. After the
evacuation of Lucknow, the regiment had little rest:
sometimes at Muhammad Bagh with constant gallops,
sometimes at the Chinhat Road. This state of
things continued till the strength and display of the
rebels at Nawabgunge forced us, for the preservation
of Lucknow, to march out and attack them. This
was done by Sir Hope Grant on the morning of the
13th June. Russell, in one of his letters, wrote: 'I
am told Hodson's Horse refused to charge at
Nawabgunge.' This was not so. On us fell the
brunt of that day's fight. A squadron of the 7th
Hussars charged the body of fanatics which severed
from the main gathering; but, with this exception,
all the cavalry work of the day fell to us, and our
casualties equalled, or very nearly so, those of the
whole force engaged; 2 officers and 30 men killed

or wounded and about 15 or 16 horses. The tale of misbehaviour arose from the presence of a detachment of Bruce's Police Sowars, dressed in khaki like the Horse, formed up in line with them; this detachment had never seen its officer till a day or two before—Lieutenant Hill, a very gallant and dashing fellow, who, full of excitement and disappointment, was sorely upset that the men did not follow him in the charge: they knew him not and heeded him not; yet many were good soldiers, and I have no doubt have since proved so.

"Baker, the adjutant, particularly distinguished himself, and by his conduct won my confidence. Mecham, with Fraser, led a squadron round to bear down on the flank of the rebels, while I charged their front. Mecham's conduct of the troops was admirable, and, though badly wounded, he did not quit his post till the day's work was over. Man Singh, Resaldar, received four wounds; Fatteh Ali Shah behaved right well; there was much single combat fighting.

"Just prior to marching for Nawabgunge, I had received authority to organise the mass into two corps of irregular cavalry, agreeably with a suggestion I made on assuming command. Finding, however, the numbers on the rolls in excess of two corps, and that, although there were scores unfit for the service (men who had been attracted by the hope of plunder) in the ranks, even after their discharge the troop officers would remain for 16 troops, I submitted for consideration to enrol a Pathan squadron for each corps, and so form three regiments instead of two. The Sikh and Punjabi-Musulman element was too strong. This proposition was acceded to, and three regiments have arisen. It was my wish that each regiment should possess a Pathan squadron, and with this view I detached an officer to recruit, and placed the matter in Lumsden's hands. Thus about 300 Pathans would have been entertained to complete the complement. All this was cut short by Sir John Lawrence, who felt that the Punjab and frontier had given enough to India*: 100 men or thereabouts came down, and these are chiefly with the third regiment. Amongst those sent by Edwardes is Ishmael Khan, son of Darria Khan, the outlaw of the border. Darria Khan's crumbling old fort is close under the Khyber Hills, and in this stronghold he bade defiance to the Sikhs. He came down and fought against us at Gujerat, and subsequently committed many a border raid ; is still an outlaw.

"It was the intention of the Commander-in-Chief that, at any rate for organisation and during the war, the three corps should be formed on the model of the Sind Horse in its early days : one commandant for the whole, and each corps with a second in command. This was the recommendation made to Government. Since Jacob became a Brigadier-General, the Sind Horse has changed its formation, and each corps has its separate commander, with Jacob commandant of the body. The Government have placed the corps of Hodson's Horse on the last footing. In each corps I have placed a Sikh Sardar of weight and character. They are men of the old regime. Bhal Singh and Jai Singh fought against us in the Punjab war, and none have been stouter for us in this struggle.

"The first regiment sorely needs rest and refitting. The troops of that corps have not yet been in quarters. After the action of Nawabgunge, the main body, first and second regiments, marched with General Grant to Daliabad and Fyzabad ; near the former place Palliser joined. From Fyzabad the first regiment marched with Brigadier Horsford to Sultanpur ; after its occupation much patrolling fell to the men. In September and October a strong detachment marched with General Grant to clear the

---

* On the 3rd August 1858 Lieutenant L. F. Wells, who had been in command of the depot of Hodson's Horse at Meerut since the 24th December 1857, reported :—"Since that period I have received from the Punjab nearly 700 recruits ; out of this number I have forwarded to Lucknow nearly 400 men and officers (natives), having first drilled them to the best of my ability during the short time I was allowed for that purpose. I have been the only officer with the depot since its formation."

Doab between the Gogra and the Goomtee to the eastwards. Returning to Sultanpur the whole force marched by the Khandoo Nadi, Jagdespur, Rampur, Kussiole, to Amethi, and thence back through Beiswallah again by Sultanpur to Fyzabad to cross the Gogra 25th November 1858. At the Khandoo Nadi Palliser was severely wounded; the rebels were here in strength. Gee, who had joined the corps in August, caught fever; Palliser and he were both so ill and weak in November that it was necessary to send them to Lucknow; there poor Gee, a man of great accomplishments and high character in his profession, died, and Palliser was obliged to quit for Europe. Sarel joined the second regiment at Fyzabad in September 1858; that corps was less harassed by patrols and quickly benefited by Sarel's kindly and skilful handling; his excellent temper and tact worked well. This corps joined the first and crossed the Gogra on the 25th November. The two remained together, engaged in the trans-Gogra service, till 1st February 1859, when the second marched for Lucknow, leaving the first at Bhingoh. The third regiment has been formed from the depot at Meerut; all of them had reached Lucknow by October 1858, about 80 per 100 still dismounted. Mecham, who was in command of the second regiment till Sarel's arrival, now proceeded to Lucknow to the third. This corps is well up in foot drill and mindful of discipline; they had been ten or twelve months daily at drill—the main body Sikhs.

"To meet the liabilities of the regimental chest I have put in all proceeds of captured property, bullocks, or elephants, for which Government rewards have been received; plunder found on the men or in the lines. The first benefit which thus arises clears the Government; after that it is with the regiment; for whatever balance there may be on adjustment should be paid to the Chanda or clothing funds of the first and second regiments. It is not desirable that the individual who plunders should derive any benefit from an action through which he has probably thrown his duty on others.

"A knowledge of the irregular cavalry system can only be attained by daily intimacy with its working : yet there are a few general principles which should be impressed on all. Much rough work falls to the irregular cavalry; long patrols; hard gallops; difficult reconnaissances; work which can only be accomplished by men satisfied with themselves, their condition, and their comrades. My experience of them leads me to say they will bear any hammering provided that they meet with kind treatment; that which has the most weight with them is personal knowledge; strive above all things to know the individual; the stroll through the lines should lead to a chat about the sowar and his nag; thus an influence is established, and the Sikh or Pathan bound to serve his officer. Cold formality and abuse as certainly bring discontent and carelessness in their train. I take it, where one officer has obtained more success with irregulars than another, it may be traced to his knowledge of his men; that he has not disregarded their little tales."

Immediately after the final occupation of Lucknow, Daly wrote to his wife, dating his letter "Martinière Park, where the 32nd banquet was held * :"—

"Lucknow is now as Delhi was—full of desolation. About that open court within the Roumi Darwaza is a troop of artillery encamped. In the Emambarah are the 79th Highlanders. The streets, courts, and narrow ways hold nothing but our camp followers plundering. Bodies of flying soldiers, shot in all sorts of grotesque attitudes, burning and putrid, carcasses of every animal clog and stop the passages; but the half million of inhabitants, where are they?

"The preparations for resistance were made with a skill and perseverance which no words can adequately describe : there is not a corner, an angle, a street, or a building without its defence :—either a buttress looped with holes or an abattis of timber and mud :—batteries and trenches intersecting each other : not a garden in the vicinity on which labour had not been spent. The one business of Secundra Bagh, where 2000 and odd were slain, and *not one*

---

* See p. 123, *supra.*

ENTRANCE TO THE KING'S PALACE IN THE CITY, LUCKNOW, 1856.

[To face p. 200.

permitted to escape, settled the defence of all isolated gardens and works, however skilfully prepared. They have held none since.*

"The Residency is a heap of ruins; the walls are either defaced or knocked down; the pillars broken and on the ground; the rooms half choked with the débris of the roof. The Kaisar Bagh and the gateways you sketched are immense mounds of earth; batteries fitted with guns. I went to the graveyard, to the spot where Sir Henry was laid. I sat for a long time under a tree in the old garden, looking at the wreck and allowing memory and fancy full play. The church is down to its very foundation; the marks of the buttresses alone remain. Of the verandah in the Residency, where we were wont to lounge with Sir Henry, and where he and I used to have our chats, scarce a sign remains. The once tall pillars, now none of them above two or three feet high, lean about. Destruction and desolation fill the place; the stairs by which we used to ascend returning from church have one or two steps remaining. One tall palm tree appears undamaged, and that is all that remains as in aforetime. Fayrer's house was less touched than any. The utter and complete annihilation took place during the rebel tenure, after Sir Colin relieved and withdrew the garrison.

"I have seen a good deal of my old friend Colonel Napier; he was the chief engineer here, and displayed the same chivalrous qualities I knew of old. His character is rare; pure and noble, with great ability; *boy-like* courage; a most lovable fellow; he and I are very cordial. I believe he has a tenderness for me, and I am so proud of his regard. I think I had an opportunity of paying him back some of the early debt of kindness by the way I could speak to Mansfield

* The Secundra Bagh was stormed on the 16th November 1857, when Sir Colin Campbell relieved Lucknow. At the end of November Sir Colin, with a large convoy of ladies, children, sick, and wounded, withdrew to Cawnpore. Sir James Outram, whose headquarters were at the Alumbagh about 2 miles from Lucknow, was left to threaten the city and hold the enemy. Lucknow was finally captured in March 1858, when the resistance offered by the mutineers was, for the most part, comparatively feeble

and Sir Colin of him. The testimony to him in the despatch is handsome, but I shall not be satisfied unless it results in his being K.C.B. What he is anxious for is a Major-Generalship. He wants to *soldier;* he is all a soldier and Chief.

"An officer of the 13th Native Infantry was actually left in the Residency when Sir Colin evacuated the place. Before quitting, people went about from room to room shouting out. The 13th man had fallen asleep in a dark corner, and heard nothing of the exodus; when he awoke, several hours after his companions had left, he was struck by the deep silence; finding out his loneliness, he jumped up and ran down the streets and through the palaces and courtyards, without encountering a person, till he reached the Secundra Bagh, where he found the rear guard of the Highlanders!

"*25th March.*—We had a pursuit the other day, and cut up a considerable number; less damage done though than should have been. The country was alive with armed men. Every field we entered, fellows started out of the long grass in which they had attempted to conceal themselves. Mansfield has lent me a tent; I have a carpet-bag, so am not much embarrassed with baggage. My difficulty is for a horse. Nothing good under £150; nothing *rideable* under £50.

"*27th March.*—Moosabagh. Our force was so much on the move for some days that I had no opportunity of writing. We marched from Alumbagh to get round between Bareilly and Lucknow. The object was to effect a surprise; that we should be in a position to cut the enemy off in their retreat on Rohilkhand after Outram had attacked the Moosabagh Palace. We marched away at 3 A.M., pitch dark. The ground was luckily clear during the early part, but about 7 A.M. we reached the ravines. The country is all alike; belts of trees and thick underwood; at this season, when the foliage is dense and dark and fields thick and high, it is almost impossible to move cavalry at all. We marched through a strong village, well looped with holes, and in every respect ready for us; luckily but a few shots were fired, and the infantry got through with but little opposition ; outside, the gardens were close to the walls, and the country all around strewed and streaming with people. Inhabitants who had fled from us, many sepoys who had taken refuge there ; many, too, were pouring out of Lucknow 10 miles distant. Here we had a little skirmishing and lost valuable time.

"The intention was that cavalry and infantry should also pass through the village, but the Brigadier, finding it narrow and intricate, took fright and ordered them to attempt to pass the canal and move round. The order was in a manner misunderstood, and the arms were severed till near 1 o'clock, by which time we ought to have been in full chase from Moosabagh. The heat at midday was trying : the infantry had been afoot since 3 A.M., and now had to go on. We moved along skirmishing in the corn and jungle with desperadoes, who got out of the ravines and deep ground like quail. After a time we reached within 2 miles of Moosabagh or less : here the country was thickly wooded, with villages and gardens. We gave the men a rest under the trees, and sent forward to know the result of the attack under General Outram. No messenger could reach ; armed men were all around. From one little fort, near a tank where our horses were being watered, a sharp fire was opened ; some men were wounded, and 2 or 3 horses actually captured. We moved up a couple of guns to shell the inmates. After two or three rounds some 50 or 60 fellows moved out quietly, and without noise or confusion steered straight to attack the guns. Some 30 of the 7th Hussars chanced to be on duty there ; they charged in amongst these fanatics, but, being men of war, they did not charge *through*, but pulled up and entered into single combats with the footmen, who were scarcely visible in the long grass and thick corn. Two officers were knocked down and one fine, gallant boy was actually hacked and cut before their eyes. Nobody could rescue him. Some of my men came up and went dashing in gallantly ; two of these (Sikhs), finding the ground not good for horses, dismounted and closed with sword and spear. At last every man was killed ; we had 3 or 4 officers wounded, but the British soldiers escaped with 2 or 3 wounded.

"We bivouacked for the night; the next morning we learnt that Outram's attack had been successful. We believed that the enemy had eluded us, for though we had cut up a considerable number, the bulk we had never seen; they had passed up near the banks of the river and amidst the woods and ravines, and would not have been visible even had we been nearer. The following morning about 10 I received a note from the Brigadier: 'Come up as quick as you can and order a squadron of your regiment to follow; the rebels are streaming out of the fort.' I galloped off, and from the top of the palace saw a large number of infantry and an elephant or two and some horsemen. The look-out reported that a large body had already passed across the open space, and were concealed behind the wood. My advice was asked and given thus *: 'Push the 1st Sikh Cavalry (close to us) and a squadron of the 7th Hussars along the trail, right on their rear; follow yourself with the remainder of the cavalry with infantry, and do what may be required.' The Brigadier meant to follow this, but *funked* and did it in part only; he ordered the 1st Sikh Cavalry to make a sweep, and followed himself with the remainder of the troops. Luckily for the success of the pursuit, the officer commanding the 1st Sikh Cavalry (Wale), a fine, gallant, cheery officer, pushed on and cut up a large number, throwing the whole of the rebels into confusion; in effecting this, however, the noble fellow lost his life; he was shot dead; nearly all the officers of the corps were slightly wounded. We chased for 6 miles, but the effect of the whole was lost by the Brigadier's hesitation at first.

"On our arrival at the Moosabagh (20th March), the fields had been deserted in the middle of the harvest, the sheaves of corn were on the ground; the bullocks were actually yoked to the well to revolve

---

* In a despatch dated the 26th March 1858, Sir Colin Campbell wrote of Daly: "This officer by his activity and zeal, added to his knowledge of Indian warfare, has been of great service to the Brigadier he served under."

the wheel to irrigate the soil. For months the sound
of cannon had not ceased, and during the few previous days the fighting of all kinds, the movements in
retreat from the city, had caused as much confusion
as it was possible to excite. Yet the husbandman,
uninterested as to who conquered, sowed his cucumber
seed, and went on gathering up the corn which our
camp followers and oxen quickly possessed themselves of.

"You will hear by this mail of the explosion at
Gwalior. I hope the telegraph may also announce
that Rose * was on the spot. Had this, or anything
like it, occurred while our little force was before Delhi,
what result could have happened? It was not willed
that we should be destroyed. These disturbances in
Central India I place on the shoulders of the late
Ministry; they wantonly and insolently left us to die,
and gave over Central India to revolution and civil
war. I think, with our great steam power, the Cape
must always be the grand high road for the relief and
support of our troops; but for an emergency such as
that which arose it was cruel to leave Bombay and
Central India to hap-hazard. I go as far as Sir
John Lawrence, who termed the neglect 'treasonable
ignorance.'

"John Lawrence as Governor-General† would be
better for India than 10,000 British troops. He
would strengthen Sir Colin in every way. Sir John's
experience in a military point is considerable, and for
the desiderata nowadays his views are more practical than the Chief's. There is a disposition to run a
tilt against Sir Colin—most unjustly in my opinion.
No doubt small errors he may have, he must have,
committed; he has been hampered by Government,
by the prosecution of many and distant operations;

---

* Sir Hugh Rose, afterwards Lord Strathnairn.

† In April 1858 Neville Chamberlain wrote to Daly:—"If Lord
Canning goes, and that quickly, I certainly hope that Sir John Lawrence may be his successor. India under his rule for two years
would rise like a giant refreshed. We should have a re-organised
army, re-organised systems of civil administrations, and all departments brought under control, which is far from being the case at
present."

and, above all, he has to guard against a single or
chance failure; and to do this he is obliged to send
larger bodies of troops for operations than perhaps
they need. Many of his lieutenants are untried; all
or nearly all the colonels of corps from home are,
despite Crimean experience, ignorant of their profession, and incapable of taking care of themselves; then,
too, the regiments are boys, hastily collected without
discipline.

"*7th April.*—I believe there is no part of our old
provinces wherein our rule will be received with so
much satisfaction as this troubled province. The
small and even considerable landholders and cultivators look to us for *Peace;* one district has been so
much and so long in contention with its neighbours
that there is not one ready or willing to continue the
struggle. A column will move from this to operate
in Rohilkhand, the last province in which Rebel Rule
is known. Matters are now in the course of settlement. No city of name or fame, when Bareilly shall
have fallen, will remain : nearly *all* our own guns
have been recaptured. The people are being everywhere disarmed. Sir Colin will not continue out here
longer than he can help, and Lord Canning must
resign; he cannot serve with Lord Derby. I incline
to think the latter, with a view of hitting the public,
may appoint John Lawrence Governor-General;
then Edwardes would rule in the Punjab. Lord
Canning wrote Sir Colin that he had wished to send
him to Oudh, but that his presence was necessary in
the Punjab; unless Edwardes can see the Government of the Punjab before him, he will not like being
made a necessity against his own advancement.

"Mansfield has made Russell (the *Times* correspondent) a portion of the army—a department.
He is supplied with *full* information on *all* points,
bound only neither to discuss nor reveal purposes and
intentions in this country : by the time such matters
can be published in England, the danger which might
result from our object being known is past. Russell is
full of humour, a keen, quick-eyed Irishman. He
is a great pen-painter. Mansfield has not so much
respect for the tact and knack of language as many
of the uninitiated.

" *30th April.*—I spoke to Mansfield of Chamberlain. I mentioned his great qualifications as a soldier, and pointed out somewhat earnestly the loss Sir Colin was inflicting on himself, and on the service at large, by not placing him in a prominent command. I reiterated this on hearing of Walpole's horrid disaster. I was moved to this, not merely by friendship for Chamberlain, but because I am jealous of the character of our service, and *often* pained to see men playing at war who are *totally* ignorant of the principles on which it should be conducted.

"Chamberlain *looks* what he truly is, a high and noble soldier. I have always held that he did wrong to resign the Adjutant-Generalship at the time he did, and on the ground he did so. The appointment is not in his line. He is not fond of penmanship and hates *office* work, but he could have rendered *great* service to *us all.* Mansfield is improved too ; he is a *broader* man for his European experience :—I have endeavoured to wipe out the feeling Chamberlain had of him."

Daly was in constant communication with Mansfield, who wrote to him on the 10th May 1858, from Fatteh Singh :—

"I have received your two notes. For the first I am very much obliged to you. I can assure you without affectation that to feel that our labours are appreciated by men, who, like yourself, know what work and responsibility mean, is a recompense greater than almost any other. I have communicated your letter recommending Nawabgunge as a station for a brigade during the summer to Sir Colin, and I support it strongly, not only because of the necessity of averting menace and panic from the city, but also because it is indispensable to keep a certain radius from Lucknow free from molestation to ensure the incoming of supplies. When Grant moved to the northward, it was my desire that the column to which you belong should have gone to the south-east—in short, have made the march in which Grant is now engaged. Thus it would have formed part of the general dissemination of columns, viz. : Walpole,

Grant, and Lugard, instead of being isolated, as it now is, and therefore *pro tanto* ineffective, although a few forts may be destroyed. However, it was deemed dangerous to denude the city so much, and you encamped at Dilkusha instead. I think an opportunity was then lost, and it appears the same thing has occurred to you.

"The ubiquitous Moulvi * is in person at Mohumdee, where he has been ever since our entry into Rohilkhand. Jones (6oth) relieved Shah-jehanpur on the 11th instant from the state of siege in which it was held by the Moulvi. The latter returned to the scratch, and attacked Jones with a great force of cavalry yesterday. The sowars galloped up to the guns and suffered a good deal, our loss being next to nothing. But this shows with what spirit the insurrection throughout the two provinces is animated, and how thoroughly we are put on the defensive in consequence of the government determination to operate over an extent which is out of all proportion with the means at our disposal.

"Our disposition in Rohilkhand is as follows :— Bijnour is held by a movable column ; ultimately, after the Mohumdee gathering is dispersed, Morada-bad by one Punjab infantry, one irregular cavalry regiment, wing of British infantry, and guns *à discrétion ;* Bareilly, by a strong brigade of all the arms ; Shahjehanpur, etc., and Budaon by a regiment of Punjab infantry and irregular cavalry. The Terai cannot be touched during the present season, there-fore, beyond Pitabad, the collector will not amass any revenue just now. All the Rohilkhand swells, the Nana, and the Moulvi are, it is said, together at Mohumdee. John Jones of the 6oth has done remark-ably well, whether by advice of his subordinates or by his own promptings, of course, I don't know. His march has been spirited and successful, while military precaution has not been forgotten. We hope to be with him at Shahjehanpur the day after to-morrow,

* This man proclaimed the restoration of the rule of the Emperor of Delhi, and succeeded, for a time, in establishing a sort of provisional government. See Kaye's *Sepoy War*, vol. ii., p. 261.

and then go to Fattehghur, where I hope I have induced the Chief to put up for two or three months.

"I intend to oppose any more movement in Oudh till we are prepared to move six or eight columns at the same time, and to drop garrisons sufficient for self-protection as we go along. What is now being done is of no use for permanent occupation; advantageous perhaps from a certain political point of view, but otherwise of little avail. I have got the whole scheme in my head of what should and eventually must be done, but in the meantime we must rest on our oars, give repose to the over-worked troops, and get a herd of native levies, police or military, to help us hold the country after our advances have been pushed. Pray write to me frequently. Your observations and experience are very valuable to Sir Colin, and I need not tell you he thoroughly appreciates the value of your information and your suggestions."

On the 9th June, Daly recorded the following melancholy tale * :—

"I have had Captain Hearsay here this morning. I had the opportunity to do him a service; on my representation of his usefulness and knowledge of Oudh and native character, the Chief took him with him to Bareilly; he has now returned. Hearsay had just reached Sitapur from wandering about the forests of Oudh at the beginning of the Mutiny. He was ignorant of the scenes at Meerut and Delhi, and quite unprepared for what almost immediately took place. When the horrors commenced at Sitapur, those of our country-fellows who escaped, did so in two small bodies. Burnes—poor, gallant, high-hearted boy—went across the river; the younger Miss Jackson † was with her brother and Burnes. Hearsay and his party, eleven I think, took, in the

---

* A more detailed story by Hearsay is given at p. 96 *et seq.* of the *Narrative of the Mutinies in Oudh*, by Captain G. Hutchinson, Military Secretary to the Chief Commissioner.

† The younger Miss Jackson was carried into Lucknow by the mutineers, and after enduring dreadful privations, was rescued in March 1858. Kaye's *Sepoy War*, vol. iii., p. 492.

O

confusion, another route. With the latter were Mrs Greene and Miss Jackson, and a sergeant-major's wife. They were for two days without any food save what they could *scrape* out of the villages, all empty and deserted, towards the Terai. Mrs Greene believed her husband to be murdered, her baby was with the wet-nurse! she had got off alone! She was broken and nervous; God knows there had been enough to try better strung nerves than hers. Miss Jackson—that fragile, delicate girl—bore hunger, distress, fatigue, and all the anguish of the situation, with a rare and beautiful fortitude. Hearsay thought to get them out of the country down to Goruckpore by decking them as a marriage procession. He is half a native, is familiar with every twig and footpath in Oudh. He obtained two palanquins and some bearers whom he could trust, and on they went, with success, through several considerable villages. The plan failed; how, I know not, but I imagine through treachery. Hearsay knew the Raja of Khyreeghur well and sent to him. The response was true and kind; however, after wandering about for some time, 600 sepoys were detached to bring them into Lucknow. This body came to them and treated them respectfully, and marched them off. After two or three days of this escort, the little party held a council; it was decided to attempt an escape. The ladies fully concurred. It was better to die there in the forest than to be reserved for a worse fate in Lucknow. I have said these sepoys were respectful and chatty. The fugitives contrived to get the main body, 600, to start on the march; a guard went with the tent, and 16 sepoys only remained. The plan was to put the ladies on the elephant, and for the gentlemen to ride. A drizzling rain favoured the project; they got off. After penetrating the forest for some distance the hue and cry commenced; the country was up. On the elephant were the two ladies, the sergeant's wife, and Mr Carthew of Shahjehanpore; the sergeant-major's son was on foot; in this raid they were severed from the gentlemen, and no reliable information has been obtained of them since! Some say they were brought to Lucknow. Some, that they are even yet alive.

"The gentlemen rode on to the banks of a river. The wild, coarse grass of the forest was high and dense; here they tried to conceal themselves, and remained for two days, hoping to hear of the ladies (my heart shudders even now for them). During this the sepoys came up and opened a fire on the grass where they believed them to be concealed. There was but one boat, and it was on the other side and not procurable; had they got this in time, all might have passed in safety. At last the gentlemen, leaving their horses tied to trees, swam across, and there they wandered without food or clothing for some days, until the same friendly Raja heard of them, and had them conveyed to a small hamlet in a distant valley. By and by, as time went on, he arranged a place of shelter for them in the first range of the Nepal Hills, and thither they went, and were wanderers for four months. Several died of the jungle fever; they had to conceal themselves to preserve their lives. At last Hearsay, with *one* companion, I think, about December reached Mussoorie! Once he dressed himself as a Muhammadan, and taking sword and shield from his friend the Raja, and a couple of coolies from a neighbouring village (the coolies did not know he was aught but what he appeared), he attempted to get through to Goruckpore; *en route* on one occasion he was met by a party of sowars, some of whom he knew! He sat down with them, smoked a pipe, etc., heard their news, and told a tale of himself. They said, 'There is not an Englishman left in the country except the few at the Bailie Guard,* and very likely they have been killed ere this'; they spoke of the times as being great for them; they considered themselves as rulers, the only subjects were the cultivators and Bunniahs! It was a Rule! no obedience. Hearsay was asked what he was seeking:—'Service as a sowar, he had been formerly in the Raja of Bulrampore's service.'"

---

* *I.e.*, the beleaguered garrison in Lucknow.

CHAPTER IX

SIR HOPE GRANT'S OPERATIONS IN OUDH, 1858-1859

Hope Grant ; action of Nawabgunge ; Sir Colin Campbell's peerage ;
   Outram and Oudh ; Mansfield ; march to Fyzabad ; question of
   army re-organisation and the future of the Company's officers ;
   passage of the Goomtee ; engagement on the Khandoo River ;
   the proclamation and amnesty ; Amethi ; passage of the Gogra ;
   Sekrora ; the Raja of Bulrampur ; the Naval Brigade ; pursuit in
   the Terai, capture of guns ; a scramble in Nepal ; fight near
   Tulsipur ; departure for England.

"On the 11th June I received an intimation from my
old Delhi friend, General Grant, that I was to
accompany him with all the men I could collect in an
attack he was about to make on a great gathering of
rebel Rajas, Zamindars, and sepoys at Nawabgunge.
The fact is, we had so long delayed doing anything
towards driving the rebels out of this, that they began
to dream dreams of conquest and recovery, and many
thousands were collected here ; for miles around in
every Tope (grove) was some Raja with his followers.
Men who are for us were compelled to join against
us, or submit to have their estates plundered and
themselves driven out.   There had been a good deal
of correspondence between Sir Colin and Sir Hope
Grant, who commands in Oudh.   The latter, not
knowing all the points, wished to make the site of
our column for the rains Chinhat, and this Sir Colin
was inclined to accede to.   For all purposes desired,
the brigade would have been useless.   I felt that if I
could see and talk with Hope Grant all would be
well : he did not know whence Mansfield got his
notions, nor would it suit his character that he should
do so. Yet he is the kindest, the noblest of soldiers,

so generous in his estimation of others, so *self-sacrificing*, always in the thick of the fight, always at work, *very pious*, *very* cheerful and jolly: nothing daunts him, for somehow he does not see the heavy matters, and perhaps, if he did, he would not understand them. I am *fond* of him. He was my daily visitor at Delhi when I was on my back.

"We marched to Chinhat on the morning of the 12th: 7th Hussars, a squadron of the Bays; 600 irregular horsemen under me; guns, two batteries and a troop; two battalions Rifle Brigade, 1200, chiefly boys; and Major Vaughan's Punjab corps. A force capable of going *anywhere*. Nawabgunge was known to hold 12,000 of the enemy of sorts, with 10 or 12 guns. At Chinhat it was ordered that we should march at 11 P.M., so as to reach the vicinity of Nawabgunge about daybreak. Grant sent for me in the evening at Chinhat to talk matters over. I suggested 'Strike and pack your camp now by daylight. Everybody sleeps in the open, and by thus doing, when we move five or six hours hence, the men will only have to jump up and shake themselves; and, above all, do not attempt to carry our baggage; the night will be dark; we are not going to follow the main road, and, if the baggage animals accompany us, they will stray all over the country; our troops will be embarrassed and occupied guarding them; the rebels with their numbers can afford to play a game they understand well, cutting up baggage.' After some discussion he concurred; the baggage to remain on the ground packed, with a guard, until sent for by us; fortunate, indeed, it was that this was done. We had on arrival to fight at all points at once; having no impediment, this we could do without difficulty. The enemy was all around us, and his first and only cavalry move was to get at our baggage which he found not. The fight began at about 4 A.M. on Sunday, 13th June, and was over at 8 A.M. The General said, 'But for your suggestions, Daly, we should not have met with this great success.' Not many men would so speak. I must attempt to describe the fight.

"We moved along the high road till within 3 miles of Nawabgunge, when we struck off to the left so as to sweep round. It was desired to reach a village 1½ miles distant about daybreak. No accident occurred; all came as intended; the halt sounded. The men had a tot of grog given out, and chewed whatever they had with them. Daylight now met us. The march had been a *very hot* one; very fatiguing despite the slowness of the pace; the wind was in our backs, and hot, driving the thick dust all over us. We had half an hour's rest for this grog process—up and off. The advance guard had scarcely gone 300 yards when a challenge was given, 'Who kum dar?' repeated, and then the pattering of muskets and matchlocks on us. I was 500 yards behind with the cavalry. On the firing I trotted forward alone, for the General had desired me to come to the front. As I moved along, the round shot began to fall unpleasantly about, and on a narrow bridge which we were compelled to cross, the range had evidently been carefully measured, for the practice was good. However, a few rounds from our artillery soon made them clear off, and we crossed with the loss of but one poor artilleryman.

"When I got over, I received an order to come forward with all the cavalry; just at this time I saw a body of rebel cavalry, 200 or 300, the only body seen during the morning, trotting round to our left and rear. I therefore halted my regiment and galloped forward to report. It was lucky that I did so, for, though I did nothing against them, the delay made me available to move in another direction where the fight eventually occurred. I was ordered to the right. The plain was beautifully open; a deep ravine or two and some trees near the village about three-quarter mile distant. The rebels were on our rear and on our right in force, with guns, but few cavalry. The sight was really picturesque. We had but two companies of infantry near, and I was not pleased. I chanced to see Major Carleton with his battery; I directed him to gallop round and bring his guns into action, and that I would support him; he complied. To make a handsome demonstration, I got into line; I had with me 200 police, so we had 600 cavalry deployed. My intention was to charge in line to the right as soon as they appeared shaken by our artillery. Their fire on us was good; the shot and shell fell thick among us, and the musketry reached us. As usual, we suffered much less than could have been expected. Grant came down and *joined* in two or three charges. We took * all the

* Daly furnished the following report :—

"To the Brigade Major,   Camp near Nawabgunge,
  "Cavalry Brigade.   14*th June* 1858.

"Sir,—Agreeably with the orders of Brigadier Hagart, I have the honour to report the operations of the regiment under my command, while not under his immediate observation yesterday.

"2. About 5 A.M. I received instructions from Major Hamilton, the Assistant Adjutant-General, to move with my corps and the squadron of Police under Lieut. Hill to a plain to the right, to meet the enemy who was showing in strength and threatening our right and rear. The enemy had 2 guns in position to our right rear, distant about 1000 yards; round them the rebels mustered in force, and, though severely handled by 4 guns of Major Carlton's battery, they still held very tenaciously. The length of their line, though broken in spots, was upwards of a mile circling round Nawabgunge, on the flanks of which at the commencement of the day were 2 guns and a large body of infantry.

"3. The ground between us and the enemy on the right is well adapted for cavalry, for, although there was a ravine within a few yards of their front, it was not sufficient to stop a horse; as I deployed prior to making the charge, I detached Lieut. Mecham with Lieut. the Hon. J. Fraser and 100 sabres to cross the ravine (which was deep higher up), and to bear down on their left flank. Finding the enemy in greater strength than could be observed from the front, this officer judiciously delayed the movement till the advance on the left took place. I much regret to state that in gallantly making this charge over broken ground Lieut. Mecham was severely wounded, his horse received a couple of bullets and two sword cuts. Lieut. Fraser was also slightly wounded, but the rebels were driven back in confusion.

"4. We made two charges on the enemy's line; the first, although we broke through, was but partially successful since we failed to capture the guns; the dust created by the advance was so thick and heavy that it was not until our return, when I rode with a handful of men close to the guns, that I was aware the bulk of the regiment had borne away too far to the left.

"5. In a subsequent charge by a portion of the regiment the guns were captured; many of the enemy stood to the last and received the charge with musket and sword; they were sabred or shot.

guns we saw but two, which from tne extent of the fight they got away. They were broken and so dispersed that there was no possibility of pursuit, and further, our troops were tired by the heat. The sun and fatigue took off many a fine lad; upwards of 30 died of sunstroke. I think many might have been spared, but officers just out from home are ignorant and sinfully careless of the effects of the direful sun. I had 4 men killed, 21 wounded, and a good many horses killed. This is the only successful coup we have made in Oudh since Lucknow fell, and the effect will be good. General Grant, now that he has been here, sees as clearly as I do the necessity of fixing a strong brigade here, to give security and to show that we mean to *hold* the Province.

"*26th June.*—Everything is on the mend. We want now a few men to lead divisions not bound down and cramped by the ancient laws and principles of war, which were in vogue in the Middle Ages and in defiance of which Napoleon, to the disgust of the old Austrian Generals in Italy, marched and moved without reference to seasons and camps, to lick them! We are beginning to find this out, and after a few more absurdities and considerable losses, no doubt we shall right ourselves. I am not saying this with reference to dear old Sir Colin. To my mind, knowing how terribly he is enveloped in ancient prejudices, it is wonderful to contemplate what he has done; and, further, the Chief of this army should run no risk or possibility of failure. Sir Colin would

In this charge Lieut. and Adjutant Baker and Resaldar Man Singh particularly distinguished themselves; they rode straight on the guns and closed with the desperate men defending them. The Resaldar had his horse cut in three places across the chest. Jamadar Hussain Ali, seeing Lieut. Baker hard pressed, dismounted and threw himself on the gunner.

"6. I would desire to bring to the notice of the Major-General the zealous and efficient services rendered on this and previous occasions by the Medical Officer, Dr Anderson. He was in the field sharing in every movement, and was thus enabled to render immediate aid to those requiring it. It is not too much to say that more than one owes limb and perhaps life to his ready attention.

"7. During the later period the Major-General came up, and the subsequent movements were made under his supervision."

have been happier in command of a brigade, and I think there is no man in the army who would command a brigade in difficulties with greater spirit. All in all, he has done well and more than well. He has had a hard game with many of his lieutenants, with Horse Guards and parliamentary interests, but utterly incapable; yet even the Commander-in-Chief dare not put them aside. The peerage will bring with it no satisfaction: he said to me one day very mournfully, 'I am wifeless and childless—a lone man. The rank and wealth and honours, which would have gladdened those dear to me, come to me when all who loved me in my youth are gone. Ah, Daly, I have suffered poverty and hardship. For years, for the want of a few hundred pounds, I was compelled to live in the West Indies, unable to purchase the promotion I *craved* for, and which younger men about me were getting as they wished: those were bitter days.' Did I tell you of the pretty letter *
which the Queen wrote Sir Colin? Womanly praise, touching in expression, with this finale: 'The Queen, however, has one reproof to make. Sir Colin Campbell too much exposes a life very precious to the nation.' Was not this beautiful? Such things make loyal and heroic soldiers.

"Sir James Outram, in his usual style, praises everybody, and not less than 200 officers possess notes (private) testifying to their heroism! some chance to be otherwise regarded amongst their comrades! You know I, in common with all the world, *like* Sir James Outram, and to me he is kinder and heartier even than to others; but I look on him as a thorough blunderer in war and politics; chivalrously brave, *physically* brave and stout-hearted. 'Go ahead—I lead' is his style of fighting; no construction, no order. In politics, unless when vastly excited, I have always seen him too indolent to be interested in anything; there is no man living in my estimation so answerable for all the mistakes in the annexation of Oudh as Outram. Sir Henry was first offered the appointment: seeing it was with a view to annexation, he, in his noble way, lucidly laid

* The full text of this letter is given in Shadwell's *Life of Lord Clyde*; the quotation is not quite exact.

before the Governor-General his opinions opposing
the *swoop*. After that Lord Dalhousie got Outram,
the non-annexationist, the friend of the Amirs, to do
his will. Had Sir Henry Lawrence come to Oudh
in those early days, it is useless to speculate on what
changes it would have made. There would have
been no heroic garrison at the Residency, with parapet
and ditches that a baby of three could pass. The
mutiny would have worked its way, and Oudh would
have been affected ; but it is more than doubtful if
the Talukdars, the Dukes of Bedford of Oudh, would
have joined against us. Sir Henry foresaw the
mutiny. Neither he nor any man on earth foresaw
the extent ; but I can remember in those days when
the news of the Barrackpore and Dinapore disaffec-
tions used to reach us, how fully his mind was
imbued with the depth and breadth of the crisis.

"Sir William Mansfield, K.C.B. ! this is but the
first link in his tether ; that man will rise. He has
nerve to *bear any responsibility*, the great bugbear in
public life. He has a keen, cultivated intellect, a
sharp temper well in hand and ready for *use ;* his
education is European, his knowledge European ; and
therefore, I think he will end as Ambassador at Con-
stantinople or St Petersburg, or as England's
General, should need be. He has the powers of combination ; whether he is a General actually in the
field I know not ; I have had no opportunity of judg-
ing ; but it is more than probable he is capable of
anything !"

"*22nd July.*—I am with a gallant force *en route*
for Fyzabad, which we are to occupy, and thence will
be the base of operations for the cold weather move
trans-Gogra. Usually at this season it would be
impossible to move artillery and carts across the
country, for the roads are mere tracks, with many
deep water-courses and streams intersecting them.
But during this year no rain has fallen in the ordinary
course. The marshy ground is slightly wet, and the
streams a little swollen, nothing more. The appearance of everything exquisitely fresh and green, for
the showers have been sufficiently frequent to keep
nature verdant. Our column consists of one troop
R.A., one battery R.A. with 4 heavy guns and their

complement of ammunition, 7th Hussars, 400 sabres of mine, one squadron 1st Sikh Cavalry, one battalion Rifle Brigade, Madras European Fusiliers, and 5th Punjab Infantry. Had poor Havelock had such a complete force his march would have been one of triumph. General Grant is with us; he is always ready, seizes every opportunity of work. Brigadier Horsford, C.B., will command at Fyzabad; the little I know of him I like; a straightforward man; but, as I have often said, all these new Queen's officers have to be taught their profession in the field. Whatever they may know of drills and dress, they know nothing of actual service. There is no doubt this move should have taken place long ago; that had we moved on Fyzabad after our victory of the 13th ultimo, it would have been a triumphal march and attended with great *éclat.* Now we are enabled to go by a fluke of weather, the like of which is unknown and unremembered by the oldest inhabitant. It is all right though, and therefore seems almost captious to complain. Matters are looking well, and, if good sense guides our civil and district rulers, India will do well, despite the many obstacles that oppose us, the greatest of which is the faction fight at home. With Sir John Lawrence Governor-General, many a sword might be hung up.

"*Camp, Durriabad, 25th July.*—We marched through the old city yesterday, and encamped on the site of our former cantonment. The streets were totally deserted and the doors of the houses barred; here and there on the roofs were seen a few figures. The rebels, many of them true Pandies, had been here for some time, but all levanted two days prior to our coming; the people cultivate their fields, guide their ploughs, and look up as we move along; now and then the headmen of the village come out with their offerings to welcome us, and declaim in great anguish against the tyranny and plunder they have undergone. No doubt this class will rejoice in the restoration of our Government, in a power to protect them. They *speak* of the year of annexation as their time of comfort, and probably never before had they known a season of such freedom and ease.

"*Fyzabad, 31st July.*—On the 29th, on approach-

ing the city, the force halted, and cavalry and artillery
formed up with the intention of trotting down to the
ferry, leaving infantry and heavy guns behind. We
passed through the main streets of Fyzabad; the
beauty of those avenues of tamarind must be seen
to be appreciated; I have never seen tree or
verdure such as Fyzabad presents. You remember
Macaulay's description of Fyzabad in his Warren
Hastings, when he speaks of the pressure put upon
the princes to make them supply our wants. The
city, from its position on the Gogra, and the extreme
fertility of the district, has always been highly
favoured by the Muhammadans, who once esteemed
it the capital of the province. To the Hindus its
temples are considered hardly less sacred than those
of Agra and Benares. The temples of Ajudhya are
some 4 or 5 miles beyond Fyzabad, rich by endow-
ment, and by the pilgrimages from all parts of India.
The sacred images are hung about with gold,
jewellery, and precious stones of every denomination.
The Priesthood are by thousands. We trotted
through the midst of these temples, the steps studded
over with the Fakirs. The people of the city seemed
friendly and even pleased to see us; their shops open.
This place will eventually become a very favourite
station. The Gogra is more easily navigable than
any river in India at this season.

"5th August.—The campaign is being trodden
out fast; the difficulties of Oudh will disappear; little
affairs there will be, but not many of these. A few
months, and order will rule."

The future of the officers of the East India Company's service was a question which was beginning
to trouble Daly's mind. He had received from
Mansfield the following letter, dated Allahabad, the
12th July 1858:—

"I should have answered your last letter long ago,
but you will excuse me for not writing notes of ceremony when I have nothing to tell and nothing to ask
about. I read your account of the action at Nawabgunge with the greatest interest, and I should much

like to have been an actor in the scene. We have started from here a small brigade of 1200 infantry, with light and heavy guns, to reduce the nest of forts at the south-east corner of Oudh. I expect that the first of these will be attacked in a day or two. It has been long necessary, but the troops to do it have only just been got here with infinite labour and paring in other quarters. In Behar we are very active, and I hope you will hear little more from that quarter. A small reinforcement has gone to Goruckpur, which, though not sufficient for any offensive movement will, I hope, suffice for the local wants of that district.

"I am turning my thoughts very seriously to the question of the reconstitution of the army, and I want your opinion on one point. It appears to me that we should learn an important lesson from the picture of loyalty afforded by the Bombay and Madras armies. It is idle to attribute that fact to a little improved system or discipline as compared with the army of Bengal. The loyalty of this or that section of the native troops, during the tremendous ordeal through which they have lately passed, is simply an affair of circumstance. In the two southern armies the fact of their being two separate bodies, with a strong jealousy and *esprit de corps* running through them, preserved them in the fiery trial. It seems to me, therefore, that we should enlarge on the idea therein conveyed, and have three or four distinct armies for this Presidency: say one for the Punjab, one for the North-West, and one for Bengal. While the troops would be thus localised in a great measure for ordinary times, I would entertain them on first enlistment for general service in case of war either beyond the frontier or in any part of the empire, precisely as before. But this foreign service should never be protracted, and it should not occur except for real war or active purposes. There should be a difference in uniform between the different armies, and only local enlistment should be permitted. Let me hear what you think of these notions. As yet they are quite crude in my head, and I should like to have a practical opinion from you on their feasibility."

In his reply Daly wrote :—

"I quite concur with you that we must look to other causes than the mere difference of drill and discipline for the staunchness of the armies of Madras and Bombay. It is ridiculous to impute their steadiness to more or less of supervision. No doubt, it is to be found, as in the Sikh, Pathan, and Gurkha, in the distinction of race. Observe in Bombay this was so strong that the Pandy element in each corps exploded without touching the Mahrattas and others in the same company; for instance, in the 12th Bombay Infantry, and in the Bombay Lancers at Mhow.

"The corps which have been disbanded in Bombay, the 21st and 27th, were composed of men of Hindustan; the former was filled with those grand-looking fellows of Oudh, and considered to be in the *highest* state of efficiency. This settles the question. Bombay and Madras may enrol their distinct armies, but with Bengal and the North-West it will not be easy to maintain the distinctions. Bombay has its Mahrattas, Bhils, Kulis, also men of the lower Concan, not legitimate Mahrattas, but a race much attracted to our service, which holds large numbers of them. The Revolution has occurred in time to save the Sikhs and us. But a few years, a short generation, and under the principles we had established the race would have disappeared. Subject to Brahminical influence in corps in which their numbers and position failed to make them independent, it was the opinion of the best of them, which I have often heard expressed with a mournful shake of the head, that the days of the Guru's followers were few. Had the Mutiny overtaken us at such a time, and after the Sikh had forgotten his war-calling and his contempt for Pandy, it is hard to say what amount of British troops could have reconquered India for us.

"I would not have every corps of a separate race. I would have a considerable proportion formed, as are the Guides and many of the Punjab corps :—the Pathan, the Dogra, the Gurkha, Sikh, and Punjabi. The company should be complete of its kind. The greatest harmony prevailed in the Guides, though the Gurkhas could not communicate with the Afridis. The Pathan advanced with more than his usual dash after he had learnt to know the stout, unflinching support which he would meet with under any circumstances from the Gurkha; and the Gurkha always speaks admiringly of the fiery Pathan.

"I should hope the bearing of the Punjabi corps during this war has fairly and fully established the advantages of the irregular system in an army like ours, when men in the usual course get a command about the age Sir Colin gets his peerage. No regiments have ever fought for us as the Guides, the Gurkhas, and the Punjab corps engaged in the war. Death and disease have changed their officers, but the gallantry and discipline of the corps remained."

Daly's views on the future of the Company's officers are expressed in a letter written from Fyzabad to Lord Stanley,* on the 19th August 1858 :—

"My Lord,
          "The tour of 1852 along our rugged frontier through Eusafzai by Peshawar, Kohat, and the Indus Border, and the associations connected with Sir Henry Lawrence, may recall to your lordship's memory the writer of this : remembering the frankness of your lordship in those days, I venture thus to write now.

"I have seen much of the troubles and trials from which we are now emerging. Within twelve hours of the Delhi massacre the 'Lightning Wire' had put me in motion; I was marching with the Guides bound for Delhi, 600 miles distant. I saw the first gun planted against its walls, was throughout the struggle and present at its conquest. I was in command of a large body of horse at the fall of Lucknow, since when I have been constantly in the field.

"On the annexation of Oudh, I came to the province to enrol irregular cavalry, and remained till within a few weeks of the Mutiny. During that year of annexation I was thrown much with the people;

* Lord Stanley had become President of the Board of Control (India) in Lord Derby's Administration.

the deed may have been a blunder; certainly the time and mode of execution were ill-chosen; but setting all such opinions aside, no impartial man could fail to observe that the result was highly popular with the cultivators and small proprietors, in proof of which tracts of land, miles in extent, which had been for years deserted and thrown out of cultivation, came again under the plough. An investigation will show, I suspect, that it was not the loss of territory which Talukdars, the Feudal Barons, the Warwicks, grieved over, but the loss of influence, the power over life and limb exercised in a way too wanton to bear description or obtain belief in England. General Sleeman, a non-annexationist, in his notes throws a light on the state of the country.

"It is probable, however, that by no line of conduct towards Oudh could the Mutiny have been staved off: the mighty army of India had felt its own power: from the day we were rolled back from Afghanistan, they viewed us in a new light; they saw we could submit to failure. In the terrible battles of the Sutlej and the Punjab, they learnt their strength and boastfully spoke of it. For years it has been the custom to concede everything asked or suggested to the sepoy, who was hedged with so much punctilio and respect that he rebuked his officer. We have gone on extending our territory over hundreds of square miles, till "the red line" is everywhere, without adding a British soldier; his presence was so rare that men journeyed for days without seeing one. Sepoys wrote to one another of the prevalence of black grain, and black cattle, and the rarity of white! So inflammable, so combustible was the mass, that a spark at any moment for years past would have exploded the whole, and that too without any particular conspiracy or combination.

"There are many at home to whom the future presents no difficulties, and who regard the past chiefly for the display of their powers and musings. They comfortably relieve themselves of all responsibility by thrusting the burden upon us. Mr Roebuck, for instance, evidently is convinced that the English mind is incapable of development out of Sheffield or the City; that Indian Englishmen are worth nothing

[Photo Hughes & Mullins.

SIR HENRY DALY.

[To face p. 224.

better than a sneer. Debates exhibiting every capacity; commissions of the most acute and thoughtful men in England, may go on ; but after all, India must be held by an army of British soldiers. It was not so held, hence the Mutiny. The sepoy was cheaper than the Englishman in the monthly balance sheet, and, as we acquired territory and desired economy, he was taken, and in such numbers, that at last he thought he was big.

"The horror of the Mutiny no man could foresee ; but all who have associated with Sir Henry Lawrence know how deeply he was impressed with the dangerous strength of the native army ; how much he depreciated extension of territory, without an adequate increase of European troops. He arrived at Lucknow 20th March 1857 : from the first day of his arrival he accepted the situation ; he predicted the storm. I was by his side from 20th March to 14th April, when I quitted for the Punjab. His labours were incessant ; every place was visited with a view to defence ; preparations of every kind were initiated, quietly but earnestly ; none but those in his confidence could suppose under his quiet tones lurked the suspicions, nay convictions, of danger, which he entertained. Darbars were held, and all the court nobles invited : his conciliatory influence, his great character, did stay the evil. Oudh did not rise till the North-West was gone, and our little force at Delhi was almost in its death throes. The storage of grain, ammunition, etc., was ridiculed by those about him, in whose eyes ho change was near, for the sepoy still did his guards and observed his duties ; but for Henry Lawrence, not one man of that garrison would have lived to tell the tale of glory. I have been tedious, but your lordship will be interested in the last accounts of that noble man.

"Mr Russell describes very beautifully the advance of our army in Rohilkhand : 'It moves on, but takes no hold of the country.' Take the facts— Rohilkhand is quiet ; the revenue regularly paid ; and scarcely a shot has been fired there for months. Again, our advance on Fyzabad—no doubt there was a great gathering of rebels of sorts here ; our force was not above 1500 infantry, 800 cavalry, with

P

guns; yet the gathering dispersed without firing a shot: between Fyzabad and Lucknow, 90 miles, we have two weak posts and two only; supplies and travellers move to and fro without hindrance. Had the people been hostile, this could be hardly so. There is much about Fyzabad to excite the enthusiasm of Muhammadans and Hindus. It is the ancient capital and many stately tombs and lofty minars tell the Muhammadan of the burial places of his early Nawabs. Here are the temples of Ajudhya, probably the most wealthy in India, and to the Hindus scarcely less sacred than those of Benares.

"I would not have it inferred that the people are particularly well inclined towards us; they are now, as in the Duke's days at the beginning of the century, 'Philosophers about their Rulers,' bending to the storm, plundering the weak. When we were in jeopardy, anarchy ensued; attacks were made on all who could not defend themselves. The sepoys, rich with the plunder of Delhi, feared to pass through the country in small parties because they were stripped by the villagers. The difficulties attending the settlement of Oudh have been enhanced by the hungry lawyers and fortune hunters who hang about the Oudh courtiers in London; every word which has a favourable sound is freely translated. A few weeks ago a man of wealth and position in Lucknow told a native officer of mine, 'We hear from London that matters are progressing most favourably for us. England is growing sick of the war. If we can keep up the game a little longer, your troops will be withdrawn and Oudh restored!' The result is that hundreds craving for order fear to cast in their lot with us, believing our rule to be temporary.

"Now, my Lord, let me ask what is to become of the Company's officers? Merely to change our name and leave us in other respects as before, less the privileges and honours of the service, thrown 'open' to our brothers of Her Majesty's army, who have superseded and are superseding us in rank and promotion, and must therefore do so in influence and position, will be, as Mr Gladstone observed, 'to deal hardly with us.' To say to us:—You belong to the army of the Queen; you are no longer the army of a

Company in Leadenhall Street, you retain all your privileges of pension (for which, by the way, you subscribe) and service, and are in no way to intermingle with the army of the Horse Guards. Your rank will be regulated as heretofore ; no interference with your becoming Captains after fifteen or twenty years' service and Lieut.-Colonels after thirty-five, your commissions in your respective grades will be allowed still!! to give you standing according to date with those officers of the Horse Guards who become Lieut.-Colonels before you have passed through the Lieutenants and Captains ere you have headed the list of ensigns. It is true we have thrown 'open' to the sister service the appointments and commands which have made so many of your officers eminent and distinguished, and which have been compensation to you for painful exile and slow promotion. The school which has brought forth Munro, Malcolm (the Duke wanted to get the latter * to Spain, and said he would give *any* two for him), Lawrence, Edwardes, Chamberlain, Lumsden, and a host of ready soldiers, who have preserved for the army of India a prestige and tone which almost every officer has individually enhanced during the present struggle. The inevitable result of this 'throwing open' all our advantages to those who come and go as they list, and leaving us but our banishment and gradation, must be to sink the service. How can officers, bound to India, contend with officers of the Horse Guards, who so readily attain promotion in such various ways : by passing for a month or two to the West Indies, by the Augmentation Battalion, by the 'substantive' rank, by the 'unattached,' and by God knows how many means and appliances ? These must bear

* The Duke of Wellington, then Colonel Wellesley, first met Sir John (then Captain) Malcolm on the march to Seringapatam. Kaye states (Preface to his *Life of Sir John Malcolm*), "There was no one to whom the Duke wrote more unreservedly than to Sir John Malcolm." Kaye also mentions (vol. ii. of the *Life*, page 90, footnote) the desire of the Duke to have Malcolm and Munro with him in Spain, and the Duke's strong opinion that the officers of the East India Company's army should be made available for service in Europe.

away all the higher appointments, and leave but a
few Police Adjutancies for the veteran subalterns of
India, who are thought to be so thankful for their
transfer to the Crown (Lord Ellenborough) that they
will pass their days in comfortable gratitude. If the
army of India is to preserve its character, it must not
be clipped of its only attractions and rewards. Few
men of education would come to India for service in
the army had they nothing to look to beyond a £200
pension after a quarter of a century residence and
constant supercession by officers flitting to and fro
from England: either these privileges must be
retained, or the army incorporated with the army
of England. It is for statesmen to weigh this linking
of England and India. Personally, I have but little
interest in the result. I have been fortunate, and
hold a position which is not likely to be affected by
any change; moreover, I am not bound to India for a
livelihood. Should I outlive this struggle, which is
now being fast trampled out, the probability is that my
residence in India will be short.

"I offer no apology for thus trespassing on your
lordship, for, should an apology be deemed necessary,
I could urge nothing."

To this Lord Stanley replied, thanking Daly for
his "most interesting letter," and adding a hope that
the Company's officers would in no way suffer from
the change of system.

The diary continues :—

"*26th August, Right bank of the Goomtee, Sultanpur.*—The passage of this river has been an interesting scene. Rafts placed across cranky dinghies
which require constant baling to prevent them from
sinking; charpoys (native bedsteads) on ghurrahs
(earthen pots), which bear our saddles, and every
contrivance to compel the obstinate horses to face
the stream, which runs with depth for about 90
yards and with a strong current. We had got over
about 200 by 7 P.M. The General wished all to
cross, so as to make way for the 7th Hussars, so the
process went on all night with noise and clamour.

We have come over in light trim. Tents to protect the Europeans; no other baggage; the food ready cooked. They got over very well on the rafts, and last evening the Madras Fusiliers and Vaughan's Punjabis moved up to clear out a village and some broken ground some 900 yards beyond the river. The rebels bolted without firing a musket. They threw a few round shot into our camp, without, however, doing any injury.

"30*th August*—After the passage we found ourselves on a neck of land, which the twisting, winding Goomtee flowed round, making us impregnable and unassailable. We might and ought to have advanced to the attack on the 29th. There is a rule in India which admits not of exception—'Whenever British troops confront an enemy, they *must* attack and without delay.' But the General was embarrassed by letters from headquarters, which led him to think that Colonel Berkeley's brigade at Soraon would move up simultaneously and therefore it was well not to hurry the attack. The rebels grew bold, seeing that we were cautious, and every evening their cavalry paraded in a vaunting way towards our camp; there was a good display of horsemen, who preserved some formation; they trotted along and formed line, and their leaders advanced some 300 or 400 yards beyond their picket, which held a mound with a deep nullah running round it, about 1200 yards from our post. It was not possible for us to make a dash straight down, on account of the intervening ravines. These parades took place 26th, 27th; on the 28th the General made up his mind to go at them on the following day. Everything was settled to advance on the morning of the 29th, 3 A.M. On the afternoon of 28th, about 4 P.M., the usual parade of rebels began, but with the addition of infantry and a gun. Sir William Russell sent word to the General that the enemy were about to attack us in force. The order for all to be in readiness was given, and shortly we all turned out. It was a very pretty sight when we got to the front. The Madras Fusiliers had rushed forward in skirmishing order, and were driving the rebels from every ravine; the firing was quick and wild; I galloped out with my cavalry, but there was nothing for cavalry to do. I joined the General, who, as usual, was forward, almost amidst the skirmishers. I am on very familiar terms with him; I said, 'Now that you have come out, although there is but little of daylight left, don't stop. The enemy is on the move, the cantonments can now be gained without even a shot; on, on.' The General saw there was truth in this and, late as it was, was almost giving the order; but a cautious old fellow near him turned the tables against me, and there we stood. The rebels, finding we did not advance, began to gather courage to stand and throw in a good deal of wild firing, without, however, doing us any damage, as we had but 3 or 4 men wounded. A few shells from our guns checked their ardour, and darkness almost overtook us on the ground. I feared that in our retirement we should suffer loss. However, whether damaged by our fire or panic-stricken by the display of troops we made, the rebels fell back. We were up by 3 A.M. yesterday morning, and moved off by the moon, which was high and clear. Our advance was picturesque; a long line of skirmishers; 4 guns on each side of the road, with a troop of hussars and a troop of mine; then the remainder of infantry and cavalry, etc. A force which, well-handled, nothing in Oudh could resist. Our march was bloodless. Every rebel had bolted during the night, taking with them their guns.

"*Sultanpur, 30th September.*—We have had *the rain of Oudh* during the last few days. The season which has not hitherto received its quantity is now being paid up in full. We have had nothing to do here, but we have had two or three little affairs, affairs which plainly indicate the state of Pandy's mind. Losses to him of hundreds without 20 casualties on our side; his fighting is reduced to the worst. After all, Delhi was the field which in more ways than one decided the fate of India. The rebels fought there in all their pride of power and numbers, and the failure has tainted their arms ever since. Had the enemy won *confidence* in those struggles, not all the troops England has sent forth would have sufficed to win back half of Bengal even.

11*th* "*October.*—We made our first march this

morning. Fresh and pleasant is the country through which we passed, rich in foliage and beauty. Our force is not large; 200 hussars, 100 of mine, the Rifle Brigade, 2 H.A. guns, with a considerable portion of that weighty and grievous siege train. The object of our coming is to aid Colonel Kelly, who is moving with a column from Azimgarh to Atrowlea; there are some two or three forts on the right bank of the Gogra, which it will be necessary to reduce should there be any attempt to hold them. Colonel Kelly has reached Atrowlea, and in two days we may hear that the country along the bank is deserted. We then return to Sultanpur.

"I cannot understand Edwardes going, as it is said he will do soon. True it is that he has been harassed by work and responsibility, and that his exertions have not been duly acknowledged, and not at all rewarded. Sir John Lawrence's departure would have put him in a foremost place. He would have been sent to Oudh as Chief Commissioner, but that John Lawrence said the frontier could not spare him. I cannot think Edwardes huffed: he is too high-minded for that: I suspect his domesticities bear down his ambition; to nothing else can I attribute his policy; he is ambitious, vastly ambitious; it may be that ambition tempts him home; but he is too high in India, too successful, too young and too old to do *very* well at home.

"We shall know something ere long of the destination of the army. My notion is that though the officers of the Army of India will, of course, suffer in the transaction, that the tone and character of the Army of England—a great matter—will vastly improve. In India, men of H.M.'s corps are without occupation; they become mess presidents, tiffin eaters, grumblers, and billiard players; the field which yields so much honour, develops so much character, is closed to them. Hence it is that a Queen's corps in India is usually a narrow, ignorant circle. Now should India be thrown open to the Army of England (*i.e.*, all made *the army*), all in turn pass through India, as the corps pass through the West Indies, very great will be the improvement in soldiership and education. If, on the other hand, the E.I.C. army is simply transferred to the Crown, and kept up as an Indian army, the men composing it will still keep the loaves and fishes, for a time at any rate, but will eventually sink into an inferior service, whereas this is not now felt. The army of the country is distinct: its officers fill all the positions of the ruling power; they win distinction as diplomatists, surveyors, engineers, captains. Amongst them are men like Edwardes, Chamberlain, Outram, and in looking back the train of heroes and statesmen is so long the eye can hardly reach it: from Clive to Henry Lawrence, what wondrous men has not India produced and brought out!

"30*th October*.—We marched back to Sultanpur on the 23rd, and marched again on the 25th. On the 27th we marched to Doalpur, so as to be within a morning's distance of the Khandoo, a small river which runs into the Goomtee. The banks of this are steep and dry; ravines and nullahs intersect the ground about; dense forests and topes of trees everywhere abound. It was there the troops of rebels who quitted Sultanpur pulled up, and better cover could not have been chosen. Across the Khandoo is a strong stone bridge; a bridge of olden days; this was the only spot at which to cross. Beyond and behind the rebels had thrown up earthworks with embrasures for 4 guns, prettily revetted, and finished in the most artistic style. The batteries beyond swept the road of approach—the battery behind covered the bridge.

"My advance guard of 10 sowars, about 600 yards in front of the column, carefully reconnoitred; a few figures were seen about the first battery, which was empty; I doubt if a gun had ever been in it. The General and I went forward and reconnoitred, and saw that the second battery was also empty. The ground now became raviny and wild. I cantered on a few hundred yards to see the state of things, believing all to have gone. I observed a line of men moving in broken order through the jungle; here and there were open patches through which could be seen the long, tall sepoys in white clothing with their sloped muskets. It was now decided to gallop forward with a troop of mine, a troop of the hussars, and 2 guns. On we went; we could observe dust of moving bodies in many directions. It was difficult work for cavalry: trees of size; ravines, patches of woods; everywhere impossible ground for cavalry. Had the rebels quietly held their own, we should never have driven them out, and we must have suffered; but they were harassed and without metal. Why they remained so long to fall back at last is a problem never to be solved. They do things beyond computation.

"In my mind there is no work so unsatisfactory for cavalry, so dangerous to life, as a pursuit of this kind—following up on broken ground sullen, sulky, desperate men, who walk with a bent gait, here and there doubling, till the horsemen are on them, then turn and discharge their muskets, sometimes wildly, more frequently right on the attacker, and then stand and die like heroes. The same men who have left works and positions admirably adapted for defence, when they think death has come, meet it in a manner to win admiration. A few sepoys had got into a bit of close ground, surrounded and encased with thick prickly-pear hedges; we were looking for a place to penetrate when a sepoy took a shot at me, missed within 3 yards, but hit the sowar who was following in the breast. Palliser was riding up on the other side, near the corner, when he was shot, and toppled off his horse; a gallant Pathan sprang from his horse right down on the fellow who had fired at Palliser; a desperate struggle ensued for a few minutes, and then the Pathan cleft the sepoy to pieces. Palliser, who is a truly gallant, fine fellow, is doing well. After this I turned and pursued a gun track to the river 7 miles; it had not crossed, but I never saw it.

"On the 29th a portion of the force under Brigadier Horsford moved out to attack a fort about 7 miles distant. We found it deserted, but the wheel tracks of the guns were so recent that it was resolved to pursue. Brigadier Horsford made over to me 4 guns, the 7th Hussars, and 100 of my men for the purpose; an exciting gallop it was; each mile seemed to strengthen our hopes of closing on the fugitives, 4 guns and a great rebel, 'Mendee Hussan.' We had no made roads, but went across fields, through woods, following the wheels. After about 8 miles we saw a few footmen. and horsemen scattered about, and the villagers told us the guns were not far ahead. We increased the pace, so much so that with my men and a troop of the hussars I had outridden the others. There was nothing, however, for it but speed, so I pressed on fancying the tracks ensured success. We ran to the bank of the Goomtee, and as we reached the bank about 100 rebels sprang into the water and swam to the other side: they had been taken completely by surprise. To this spot the guns were clearly tracked ; the fact we found to be that the guns were brought down with a view to being crossed over, but finding that delay would ensue in preparing the platform to cross them from the boats, they were taken back on the morning of our arrival. They had gone to the west, to a small fort owned by Mendee Hussan, some 12 or 14 miles up the Goomtee. Thus our attempt failed. I got one small gun which they had left, and we had to return to our encampment 17 miles distant.

"We have reached the destination assigned to us, 10 miles north-west of Amethi, while the fort is to be attacked from the south. My belief is that it will be relinquished. I cannot think that the Raja, with 3000 men, will attempt a defence. However, one can reason on none of their acts.

"The Proclamation and Amnesty will be published this afternoon. The former the people and troops will have difficulty in comprehending. In their eyes and in the eyes of their fathers before them, the government was 'Koompanie Bahadoor' (the East India Company), and what Badhshaie (Queen) can be greater will be a puzzle. The Amnesty I rejoice at : without it I can see no *end*. Many will take exception to its broadness, and many will regret that so much villainy should get away unpunished. Probably the greatest scoundrels will do so ; but to drag on the guerilla warfare is to throw good and valuable lives, and our very supremacy, order, and power into jeopardy. I have just heard from Neville Chamberlain, who wrote on the 3rd November from Dera Ismael Khan—'We proclaimed Her Majesty here this morning. Lots of gunpowder fired on the occasion. I am glad we had Europeans on the ground, though few in numbers. They are the first in these parts since Alexander's days. I watch your progress on the map, and shall be glad when you have *all* cleared up to the left bank of the Gogra.'

"*Jagdespur*, 19*th November.*—The force I am with separates to-morrow morning. All the infantry, 7th Hussars, and artillery go Lucknow-wards. I with 300 of my horse trot to Sultanpur, where we cross the Gogra by bridge; a large force will be assembled there, and we shall sweep up by Gonda, Sekrora, and Baraitch.

"We gathered in great strength around the jungle fort of Amethi—three armies, with guns enough to carry Oudh at a sweep. The Raja at the last moment sent in his submission, but during the night his followers, sepoys, and matchlock men, broke through, as it was easy for them to do in such a country, and bolted. Thus we got possession of an empty fort, and 13 instead of, at least, 25 or 30 guns; the remainder we suppose have been buried. We marched away with the view of cutting off the fugitives and closing round the great fort of Beni Madhu at Sharkipur. We found Amethi like all the forts we have seen in this part of Oudh. The outer ditch is 4 or 5 miles in circumference, deep and narrow; the enclosure a deep jungle through which roads have been cut. The corundah bush, bearing a prickly thorn which covers the ground like the bramble, fills the space; even an elephant could scarcely penetrate. There are two ditches and two walls within the outer circumference: at points are bastions of mud, with embrasures commanding the approaches. At one corner is a village, within which the immediate followers of the Raja live. Within the interior wall are the house and courtyards for the Zenanah and the Raja, and in all these places more space is required for the lady portion than for aught else. There were two mines sunk near the gate, but altogether the strength of the place was in its position. Such was its extent, and so concealed among the trees and bushes, that shells might fall for six months without reaching the point desired.

"So much for Amethi. We moved on and on until we came to the fort of Beni Madhu on the 16th. The fort is some 14 miles from Delama, and 10 miles from Rai Bareilly. We moved round to the north-east side; the Chief and his force within 3 miles of us to the south-west. As we approached we observed small bodies of cavalry moving about, footmen with bundles, etc., and amongst them doubtless some sepoys. We encircled the place as fast as we could in such a jungle; an investment with even 40,000 men would be quite impossible. There are four ghurras, or forts, and villages within one ditch or wall, 8 miles in circumference. Terms had been offered to Beni Madhu, and he had sent to know what his reception would be. Therefore there was no doubt about holding out. I felt sure the bolting had been going on for days. So it proved; the following morning, although our pickets and vedettes had been placed according to military principles, the forts were deserted. I have a strong conviction that nobody was left on our arrival but the few cavalry for display whom we saw caracoling.

"The order to march came: Rai Bareilly for us. We had moved out but a few miles, when cheery old Sir Colin, with General Mansfield, came galloping to our front. There was a wild report that the enemy were in strength before us. This soon subsided, and the Chief went back to his troops. Biswarrah, as this province is called, is the heart of the sepoy kingdom. You will observe the actual war is at an end. They fly everywhere and fight nowhere, even about their own homesteads. Insurrection will gradually die out; there will be no grand smash. Rai Bareilly is a powerful place, and has been of great importance. A large and ancient fort of brick and stone with lofty walls frowning over the city; and there is many a mark of strife and shot about it; it was here poor Major Gale was killed. We moved to Nolan Gange, and so to this place (Jagdespur) yesterday afternoon. To-morrow the General and his staff and I trot away for Fyzabad, and there the last chapter of the Oudh War will be worked. My old 1st Punjab Cavalry will be brigaded with me.

"*28th November, opposite Fyzabad.*—We galloped

into Sultanpur, about 30 miles; waited there a day, then on in two marches to Fyzabad. The bridge for crossing was in readiness: the brigade of infantry, 1st Punjab Cavalry, wing 9th Lancers, one and a half troops H.A., a battery of guns of size, were assembled. The rebels had small batteries along the banks, from which occasionally light guns fired; a few matchlocks and muskets were visible lining the bank; instead of the width of waters we had left in August there was a good mile of sand or bog. The General resolved to cross on the night of 24th and early morning 25th. We had already a battery at the head of the bridge trans-Gogra. A regiment of Sikh infantry was thrown over the river in boats higher up. They were to remain quiet and concealed until our battery opened, and this was to be with the first streak of dawn. The infantry and guns began the passage of the bridge at 3 A.M. The moon was bright and clear, and, as no baggage was to go, no confusion occurred. Over the bridgeway was strewed a thick layer of sand; all sound was deadened.

"By 5 A.M. the cavalry were over the bridge, and formed in line on the side. With the first faint light of day our guns opened. The Sikh regiment on our left gave a shrieking shout, and moved up the right flank of the rebel works; there was a good deal of wild firing as the enemy forsook their batteries. The bed of the Gogra is very wide: the cavalry followed the infantry, and by daylight we were close to the bank; here, for about 40 or 50 paces wide, was the remnant of the river. The soil was dark and quaggy; to our right was a gun with its horses sunk deep, and in the vicinity all was commotion. The bog was heaving with every effort of the horses, rising and falling with every tramp. In the leading troop of the 9th Lancers some of the horses sunk to the saddle flaps. I sought a place higher up and got over very well with 300 or 400 men, but those who followed found this ground like a jelly. Thus we had a great delay; had 50 *women* remained, our passage would have been a work of great loss. Once over, we pressed on the cavalry and guns, leaving the infantry. We pursued some 12 or 14 miles; the country was open, and admirably adapted for the movement of cavalry, the only ground I have seen in Oudh which is so.   After going 5 miles we picked up 2 guns and a carriage.   Fugitives were seen running in all directions.   The fields were high with dhall, like riding through a shrubbery.   Subsequently, we captured other 3 guns, among them an English 24-lb. howitzer. We charged in amongst them and cut up a number. The rout was complete and thorough, and all in all it was perhaps the most successful affair in a little way that I have seen.   The Raja of Gonda was the leader of the force here; a cowardly loon he is; 'tis said he mounted his elephant and bolted at the first discharge of our guns.   Some sepoys of Captain Boileau's regiment were amongst the rabble.

"The Gonda Raja has sent to know what terms will be granted him; he will be liberally treated, so I hope he will come in.   The answer to one and all now in arms against us should be, 'If you are out in arms on January 1st, restoration of property will be impossible.   Everything you have ever held will be confiscated, and you will be an outlaw.'   We blunder in *discussion*.   Our vacillation towards the Amethi man, the manner in which he was allowed to play with and alter our ultimatum, has done us no good. The only chance of anything good happening to them should be instant submission.   The sepoys even now cannot believe in the Amnesty.   A man who came in the other day said, 'We enlisted under the Articles of War.   What has the Proclamation to do with us?'

"*Bunkassia, 8th December.*—Here we are at the Gonda Raja's fort.   We marched through a dense jungle.   On our approaching the place, the sowars, who were 500 yards in advance, sent back to say that armed men had broken away from the villages near, and that horsemen had been seen; by the General's desire I cantered forward, and took a sweep round. I observed a good many running in a sort of broken line, and a gathering near the edge of the forest, which is thick along the banks of the Biswah, a small river.   I came round to Sir Hope, reporting that I had seen some fugitives; I did not think their number serious, but one of the captured said there were 2 guns in the wood.   The country was very close, many clumps of trees scattered about, but the line of unbroken wood ran along the banks of the stream. The main column of infantry had not yet arrived, but the encamping ground was being marked out. The pickets had been ordered out, when a sowar galloped in saying, 'The enemy is moving in large numbers along the wood; cavalry, infantry, and elephant.' On looking, a body was visible on the very road I had just passed. The truth was that some 4000 men of sorts—700 or 800 regular infantry, and about 300 cavalry of various corps, together with the Gonda Raja's own followers—occupied the side of the wood, and were encamped in the neighbouring topes. When I came up they were cooking; our arrival was totally unexpected; a surprise on both sides. I passed one body; they must have been all at food.

"Immediately on my moving round they got under arms, and those whom we now observed had formed a kind of line. One swell bedecked with red was conspicuous marshalling the ranks. We had with us 200 infantry and 2 guns, 40 of my men, and 100 9th Lancers. Behind them was the wood. We trotted down our guns, threw out the infantry to cover our left, and opened within 400 yards of them. We fired the first shot, but quickly their shots replied. Our guns rattled in and advanced farther. The enemy at this time were moving off in numbers, skirting the forest. At last, on the arrival of our infantry, we closed on the wood; 2 guns fell into our hands; their round shot smashed a fine fellow, an artilleryman, in the leg and killed a horse; we had no other casualties beyond a scratch or two. We advanced to the fort to find it empty. Gonda is about 10 or 12 miles distant.

"The Chief is, or will be in a day or two, at Bairam Ghât waiting for boats. He wishes to cross to give the final swoop. Probably before he can get over with his great array all will be broken up. However, despatches will be written and marches made in a delightful climate, so it doesn't much matter, provided that the rebels fail in getting away. My fear is lest they should get away now, and turn up again in the hot weather. Nothing can surpass the beauty and purity of the atmosphere now with those snowy peaks of the grand Nepal mountains sparkling in the sun.

"*Sekrora, 12th December.*—We arrived here yesterday. Our old house is a heap of ruins, the road which ran in front of it has been ploughed up and sown with barley. The houses were destroyed by Bala Rao, a brother of the Nana. The people of Sekrora came out in numbers to bring their supplies with more readiness than we have observed elsewhere. Our course is to Tulsipur, and thence to sweep up the left bank of the Raptee. My trip of 1857 after Fazl Ali now stands me in good stead."

There was no loss of life at Sekrora. Almost all the troops mutinied, but they treated their officers with respect, and permitted them to depart uninjured. Daly received the following account from his old corps :—

"The way in which we left Sekrora was, in short, this. After our 1st squadron mutinied (together with Major Gale's) on the road between Cawnpore and Mynpooree, and murdered 3 out of the 4 officers with them, viz., Captain Hayes, Mr Barbor, and young Mr Fayrer, we began to feel very *shaky* at Sekrora. Rumours had long been about among the men that *Europeans* were coming to take the guns of Mr Bonham's battery, etc., etc. We tried to reassure the men, of course, and they seemed satisfied. Two fires occurred in the lines of Captain Boileau's regiment, and great uneasiness was evidently going on. Captain Forbes had gone to Cawnpore; Mr Bax to visit his brother at Ghazipur; Captain Tulloch to the hills. We had but few of our men left; for all but about 130 or 140 had gone into Lucknow, etc. We talked of sending the ladies away, but Captain Boileau had it represented to him that it would not be safe to do so, as the men might mutiny. They therefore remained till the 7th June 1857, when, early in the morning, Captain Forbes arrived with 25 of our Sikhs with him, and orders from Sir Henry Lawrence to take the ladies to Lucknow."

Daly had written to his wife on the 10th June 1857, from before Delhi :—

"You will be sorry to hear that a squadron of my Oudh regiment went wrong:—One squadron of mine and a squadron of Gale's under poor Hayes; the worst man *they could have selected*, inasmuch as the old Oudh soldiers of the corps consider him the cause of all their trouble. I have not heard of them since. I *think* the regiment would not have broken hurriedly had I been present, and I have no doubt that many are firm yet."

Of the native officers, Sundil Khan, as already mentioned, joined Daly at Delhi, and Mohi-ud-din was killed fighting on our side in Lucknow. There were 75 Sikhs and Pathans in the regiment, and all these, or nearly all, remained staunch. Sir Henry Lawrence, writing on the 12th June 1857 to Mr Colvin, Lieutenant-Governor of the North-West, said— "All our irregular cavalry, except about 60 Sikhs of Daly's corps, are either very shaky or have deserted."

Of Salar Bakhsh, Daly wrote in 1857 :—

"There are a few pleasing traits of fidelity, and his is one of the best I know. He *ought* to have gone wrong, and there would be *little* blame attachable to him had he done so. He came to our officers after the outbreak—I mean officers at another station—and asked them what he should do; they gave him cold comfort; sent him off and told him to go down and join his regiment!! He went, was stripped and plundered by some mutineers of the 7th Cavalry; still he went on, and, I believe, joined Sir Henry in Lucknow."

In July 1858 Daly submitted the following official report regarding charges connected with carbines for the 1st Oudh Irregular Cavalry :—

"On the annexation of Oudh I was appointed to command the 1st Oudh Cavalry. Sir James Outram, the Chief Commissioner, through his military secretary, the late Captain Hayes, issued instructions to the

Q

commandants of cavalry that they should immediately make arrangements for arming their men with percussion carbines and appropriate appointments. This could only be done from Europe, as arms were not supplied by the State, nor were those carbines which were made available for purchase from the arsenal at all within the means of the sowar."

"Just prior to my departure from Oudh in April 1857, a portion of the carbines and belts which I had ordered from Europe had arrived and had been distributed to the regiment. The carbines for which compensation is now sought were, I am informed, taken within the Residency defences, and were used by the volunteers and others requiring arms. Since the second siege I myself have seen some of them in the hands of the volunteer cavalry."

To his wife he wrote on the 14th December 1858, from a camp near Bulrampur :—

"You remember my talking of the little Raja of Bulrampur. He has behaved with most steadfast loyalty to us throughout the struggle. His elephants were sent to Sekrora for the transport of the ladies and children to Lucknow, and with him took refuge all the officers and civilians who were saved. His position has been difficult during the past six months ; beset by rebels in all directions ; nevertheless he has maintained his ground. His chief town was plundered a few days ago by a host of fugitives. I wrote to him congratulating him on his loyalty and gallantry, reminding him of our previous intercourse, and saying what pleasure it will give me to introduce him to the General. I received a delighted reply. We shall meet him to-morrow. The fighting across the Raptee will be slight. I question our firing a shot. All the small Rajas creep to Bulrampur and seek the influence which he is proud to use in their behalf.

"31st December (Camp Puchpurwa, 14 miles North-East of Tulsipur).—We have made a detour by Heer towards Bansee, thence by the north along the borders of Nepal, concluding yesterday with a passage of the forest under the hills. The General took down a force without baggage of any kind to work the forest; he took me to command the cavalry which accompanied him; four troops 9th Lancers, and my own men, 13th Infantry (Sikhs), artillery, etc. We had nothing to do; a long march into the forest, skirting its edges, and then round the camp, which we reached just after sunset. Bala Rao, the Nana's brother, is in the forest within a few miles of us. There he cannot stay, for food is only procurable through plunder, and then it is mere rice and dhall. With him are many sepoys and ruffians whose deeds have put them out of the Proclamation. However, the great difficulty is in getting the Proclamation made known. The Nana, Bala Rao, and others, upon whose persons are rewards, prevent the publication of the Government Notification, and alter it for their own purposes.

"*2nd January* 1859 (*Camp near Tulsipur*).—I have just been down to the Naval Brigade to say farewell to Captain Sotheby; they go shipwards to-morrow; to Allahabad, thence to Calcutta. I could tell many laughable anecdotes of the sailors. They have small howitzers, drawn by small ponies, which the sailors ride horse-artillery fashion. On the march, if they encounter any obstacle, such as a ravine or a mound, they are off in a moment, and with one *great pull altogether*, out or over go gun-carriage and steeds. We rode down to see them march to join our camp the other day : Jacks, dressed in their straw hats and blue shirts and pants just as they would be at Portsmouth, *astride the ponies*. A halt is sounded; the leading tar near turned round to his near comrade in the saddle, 'I say, Bill, it's Heave to,' on which they shot off. A parade is required: shrilly sounds the boatswain's whistle and a gruff voice 'all hands,' on which they roll up. Colonel Payne of the 53rd told me that at the Tulsipur fight the other day he saw the sailors with their pony artillery skirmishing side by side with his men, dragging the guns and 'slewing' them about, as they call it, as though on deck.

"The rebels are confined to the forest; they must either pass through the first range into the broken valley which I entered in pursuit of Fazl Ali, or starve and disperse in the jungle. Life could not be sustained there after the first fall of rain by people unacclimatised. I fear we shall not now get the Nana or his brother. Individuals can so easily escape; and somehow war made formally and according to system against rebels beaten and discouraged does not bring telling results: they escape; they are driven now to the uttermost parts, and, if we can deprive them of their guns, our police are sufficiently numerous and organised to prevent their gathering for plunder during the hot season.

"*Chunderpur, left bank of the Raptee,* 11*th January* 1859.—I believe I may confirm what you already have read—that the campaign is at an end. The Chief, who was with an army 30 miles north-west of this, has hied away to Lucknow to meet Lord Canning. Thousands of the rebels have taken refuge in Nepal; within the same range of hills, and by the same routes as I chased Fazl Ali. Neither horses nor guns could pass over or through the mountains, so that lots of both have been left to their fate. On the 4th we made a grand haul of guns. We made a long march along the Terai on the 3rd. I had spies (herdsmen with cattle in the forest) on the *qui vive;* about 4 P.M. on the 3rd, as we were on the move, a good spy came running up, 'The rebels, with 18 guns, are within 4 miles of us, not expecting you, and such is the plundered state of the villages that no one will whisper your arrival.' I asked the man, pointing to the sun, whether he would be above or below the horizon when we reached the rebel camp; he replied, 'just dipping.' This fixed us for the night. We moved off at early dawn. About 3 miles further on, at the very edge of the forest, we espied a body of about 100 or 200 men, and 2 or 3 horsemen. We prepared for work; that morning we captured 15 guns in the forest, and that without losing a man; so broken in spirit, starving, and hopeless were they. The brother of the Nana (Bala Rao) was the chief, but he was not present at the so-called fight. Many of his followers knew nothing of the Amnesty. He and those like him, murderers and outlaws, conceal all they can from those about them. Jung Bahadur will have a difficult part to play; he has issued a proclamation refusing shelter to the rebels within the Nepalese territory. Many have given themselves up, and, unless implicated in deeds of murder, they are allowed to go free. The whole thing is gone. Central India still holds Tantia Topee; a few weeks and this will end.

"*Camp Bhinga, 17th January* 1859.—I have a good many officers here now; Sir Henry Havelock * amongst them; a fine young fellow, chivalric, frank, and dashing, about thirty years old; devoted to his profession, in which by his resolution and daring he has already won much distinction; his father's son in many respects.

"I have received the *Life of Mr Polehampton*. He was indeed of a healthy temperament, a man blessed in youth, with those near him to love and foster, a happy home, a sound education, training at old Eton and Cambridge. Brothers about the same age, of similar tastes, his friends and companions. Everything around him in his career calculated to strengthen and expand the good. I like the man, and I like his own view of his character. He was in the world and of the world. There was, till a few days ago, in the camp one of very much the same mould: a Scotch clergyman; a simple character with much less cultivation than the child of Eton; but I suspect not less endowed, or less good. He was attached to the 79th Highlanders; a Presbyterian, yet in the midday he read prayers and a sermon at the General's tent, and in the evening he read again to the soldiers (a parade) of the Church of England, and gave an extempore discourse. His accent is broad and uncouth; his language nervous and clear; fluency is natural to him, yet it never degenerated to verbosity. I have rarely listened to smoother eloquence. He was much liked by all, for he lived amongst us to talk, walk, work, and do good. He too, like poor Polehampton, is physically gifted, a handsome man of pleasant address, beaming with life and health.

"I remain out here in command some time longer. I shall have one regiment Hodson's Horse, Colonel Gordon's Sikhs, some Engineers, and Major Middle-

* The late Sir Henry Havelock-Allen, shot in the Khyber Pass, 30th December 1897.

ton's troop R.H.A. A nice command; but there is 'nothing in it,' work is over. You ask about Norman.* On the day of his captaincy he will be Major, Lieut.-Colonel, C.B., perhaps full Colonel. He deserves it all and more. His services and knowledge have been of the highest value. My regiment, the 1st Punjab Cavalry, has made many reputations in this war, and stands avowedly the first in character.

"*Camp Tulsipur,* 11*th March.*—Two days ago Brigadier Horsford and I, with two or three officers and a few men, had a scramble to look into Nepal. The path runs for the first 3 miles through a forest; then you follow the bed of a mountain stream in which there is but little water now, though wild and grand are the ravages of the torrent which sweeps down during the monsoon. Trees of stupendous size lie about, huge boulders tossed fantastically here and there, fanciful caves with lichens and creepers, chines, and scarped rocks, over which hang lofty trees and pines. We had to follow this course for 10 miles, then began the ascent, which was about 3 miles, ere the crown was reached. Suddenly the valley of the Raptee appeared. It was about 6 miles in width, forests and swamps, the river tortuous; from this ridge the other five ridges were visible which stand between us and the eternal snows. The ascent was so steep and rugged that a pony could with difficulty be led up. My little Pegu alone accomplished it, and he had to be picked up several times. Yet there were signs of an elephant having passed over, and the remains of a dead horse or two told us of the attempt of the rebels to move by that route.

"*Camp* 12 *miles north of Tulsipur, under the Nepal Hills,* 1*st April* 1859.—I little thought to see any more fighting, yet we have had a fight. It came about thus: the rebels, driven from Bootwal at the foot of the Nepalese mountains, marched up in strength by the forest to within 15 or 20 miles of this. Their object is to break away from the forest, where starvation and disease await its denizens. We were aware of their movements; on the evening of the 30th March, Brigadier Horsford and I concocted an advanced post at this place. The 1st Sikh Infantry

* The late Field-Marshal Sir Henry Norman.

marched some 8 miles from us with 30 sowars, to intercept stragglers and prevent the passage. The Sikh infantry reached the ground about 8 A.M. About 9 A.M. the pickets came galloping in, 'The rebels are advancing in strength.' A camel sowar of mine came back with the announcement that the enemy were in great strength, and that the Sikhs were beset and hard pressed. I ordered 'boots and saddles' and every man to be in readiness, and mounting my pony galloped to the Brigadier's tent, told him the news and what I had done. We chatted the matter over, and in less than five minutes I was back in the artillery lines with orders for them to turn out sharp, and carry as many of the 53rd on the gun carriages as possible. In twenty minutes we were on the road; a squadron was left to escort the guns, while the Brigadier accompanied me with some 200 sowars. We trotted and cantered the 7 or 8 miles, for as we approached the forest the musketry came quick on our ears.

"Soon our eyes fell on a wondrous gathering. The enemy all around. My advance guard, about 30 sowars under M'Gregor, a *very gallant* young officer, was already in the thick of it; passing the infantry, who were a good deal broken and fatigued, he dashed into the midst of the fight; the smash with them was great; on all sides they gave way, and seeing the dust I suppose they fancied a large army was at hand. Gordon's Sikhs suffered much. The second in command, a fine young fellow named Grant, was killed; a fresh English boy shot through the body; some 7 native officers and men killed, and 40 wounded. Out of my little party we had 1 killed and 9 wounded, 1 horse killed and 7 wounded. Had the Sikhs not been there, the rebels would have passed; indeed, a wing would have been overwhelmed, great as is the cowardice of the rebels as a body. I mean that 10,000 do not avail to overcome a single 1000 of Sikhs led by British officers; yet individually, when they know death is at hand, they struggle with a resolution and daring unknown to the European. Several times it occurred yesterday that a sepoy, finding himself alone and no escape, would, after discharging his musket at his pursuer, throw down his musket, draw his sword and stand at bay. No single horseman is a match for an active swordsman on foot. I have seen five British dragoons around one of these, and he defending himself and taunting them. Yesterday Anderson had something of this kind with a fanatic, in which Anderson behaved with great coolness and courage, and slew his opponent without any injury to himself. The rebels killed yesterday were all sepoys."

"*2nd April.*—This morning 150 sowars came in and delivered up their arms to me, amongst others Aman Beg and Amir Beg. Their condition is utterly wretched; rice, uncertain hours, have begun their work; scarcely could 100 of these sowars walk at noon! It is evident from their statements that the Pandies hold the Terai in greater horror than we do, and *coûte que coûte* they have resolved to quit the forest, and this, I hold, will be the beginning of the end; if pressed by us at all points, succumb they must. Fever in the afternoon.

"*4th April.*—Rode through the forest with the Brigadier this morning; the felled trees across the paths had effectually closed the paths for animals and baggage travelling. There are still parties hanging about; we heard dropping shots. The main body has doubtless gone on. Fever attacked me about 11 A.M., and I was under the blankets till 3 or 4 P.M.; very much knocked up by this bout; resolved to start for Lucknow to-morrow.

"*5th April.*—Homeward bound! Left Lerwah at 4 A.M. Just as I entered the dhooly, the Brigadier sent an express from Ramsay of the Kumaon battalion imploring immediate aid; that he was surrounded. Ramsay evidently panic-stricken. The Brigadier asked my advice, which was, 'The swell is westwards; move yourself with wing of the 53rd, 2 or 4 guns, a wing of the Sikhs, and 200 horse.' I got into Tulsipur about 8 A.M. Hughes followed me; the Brigadier had ordered him to take 200 horse and 2 guns westward, but begged Hughes to see me. I wrote to the Brigadier enforcing my opinion; this had its effect, and about 4 P.M. he came up and marched away. We discussed all the probabilities. I warned him to take heed; that the rebels had no settled plan, but would bolt in *any* direction which appeared open. Came in to Bulrampur; could hardly sit on my pony.

"*6th April.*—No news at Bulrampur, but as the country is unsettled, and the rebels may cross the Rapti at any point, I would not allow two Rifle Brigade officers to go straight to Baraitch. I quitted Bulrampur at 2 A.M. and marched to within 8 miles of Gonda. Hot wind, but a noble grove sheltered me from the sun. Started again at 5 P.M.; when within a few miles of Gonda, heard that the rebels had crossed and were but a few miles from our line; reached Gonda at 7 P.M. Sent a telegram to General Grant, suggesting that a wing 20th Foot, 2 guns, and 200 horse, should start *at once* along the Bulrampur road to prevent the rebels from breaking. Left Gonda at 8 P.M., passed through Sekrora during the night, reached Byram Ghât at 6 A.M. 7th April, very tired and feverish; sat under the trees. By and by a troop 3rd Horse Artillery came up from Durriabad, and *very well* they looked and moved. Mules brought up my tent 36 miles since evening; the old tent pole broke on this the last occasion required; got a native officer's pâl (small tent), and was comfortable enough; quitted Byram Ghât at 6 P.M.; met Mecham with 3rd Regiment, the Bays, and artillery, bound for Byram Ghât. Colonel Walker, a fresh man, in command.

"*8th April.*—Made Lucknow at 7 A.M.; found Sarel, and the General came up to talk over events; while here, we drew up and despatched an order for Walker to move straight on Sekrora and to direct Mecham on Gonda. I got the map and pointed out to the General the necessity for pressing troops, horse, and guns to the east of the Gonda and Bulrampur road, and suggested that a wing of 3rd Hodson's Horse should move without delay from Gonda. The General looked harassed and fagged; he seemed more cheery after our chat and arrangements; kindly wanted me to go to his house.

"*9th April.*—Went before the Committee; the superintending surgeon recommended me to see Ferguson and Symes at home about my arm; very kind about my going; thought it was well for me to start without delay as I am a good deal shaken.

Sarel and I dined with the General; while at dinner a telegram from the Chief directing the General to go to Fyzabad to be near the operations. The General a good deal cut up at affairs; his heart is bent on going home 30th April, and this will probably prevent him.

"*13th April.*—Spent a gossiping day with Wingfield, Chief Commissioner; frank and free as usual, not in the smallest degree touched by his elevation. We discussed the characters of all the military leaders during the war, and compared our various experiences."

The 3rd Regiment of Hodson's Horse was shortly afterwards engaged in the Gonda district, and on the 20th April Daly heard from one of the officers :—

"I was in a little affair with the enemy the other day at a place called Koel ka Jungal. The men of the 3rd Regiment behaved very well under fire and in action. Wade's Horse and ourselves polished off about 300 of the enemy together, *all Pandies*. My casualties were 8 men wounded, 5 horses wounded, and 1 horse killed. We had a tremendous *daur* (chase) in dense jungle yesterday, and captured the colours of a native infantry regiment, sky-blue facings; I suppose the 15th Native Infantry. Also the Queen's colour, a good beginning for the 3rd Regiment."

At the end of the month Daly handed over the command to Hughes, his old successor in the 1st Punjab Cavalry, who, on his suggestion, had been selected to succeed him in Hodson's Horse. Early in May Daly sailed from Calcutta for England. He observed, "I think I was the first commanding officer of the Punjab Force in motion during the war, and certainly I was the last."

Shortly before his departure, which was on sick certificate, he received the following letter from Mansfield :—

"I am grieved to hear of the cause of your return to England, although I am not by any means taken by surprise. I gather from your letter that you are not in a position to retain your appointment, though it is not stated positively. Supposing such to be the case, I cannot say what may be the ultimate construction of the corps you have brought into order, whether to keep it as it is now in the form of a brigade, or to have three separate regiments. I believe the latter to be the more convenient now, whereas it was impossible when the Augean task of reducing order into it was undertaken by you.

"I will have a note taken of the officers you recommend, but I must tell you candidly we have many claimants for irregular commands who cannot be put aside. Lieut. Mecham has a very strong claim. But there is immense inconvenience in appointing *lieutenants* to command irregular corps in these days when there are hundreds of captains afloat who, whatever their antecedents, must be employed somehow."

CHAPTER X

CENTRAL INDIA HORSE AND GWALIOR, 1861-1869

Return to India ; appointment to the Central India Horse ; death of
    Lord Clyde ; Napier's recommendation of Daly for the good
    service pension ; entry into regular political employ as Political
    Agent at Gwalior ; relations with Scindia ; Scindia's administra-
    tion ; Scindia's views on British rule. Appointment as Agent to
    the Governor-General in Central India.

AT the beginning of 1860, under medical advice,
Daly applied for an extension of his leave. In reply,
he was informed that the appointment of commandant of Hodson's Horse had been abolished from
the 12th December 1859, the three regiments * being
placed on the same footing as other regiments of
irregular cavalry. Shortly after this he heard from
the Viceroy's private secretary :—

"Lord Canning wishes me to tell you that the
abolition of your appointment was not in any way
connected with your compulsory absence from India.
The measure was one out of many reductions made
by Government for State reasons, and would not
have been otherwise had you remained on the spot."

Coupled with this was an assurance that his
"services and claims would never be forgotten by
Lord Canning."

* Two are now the 9th Hodson's Horse and the 10th Duke of
Cambridge's Own Lancers (Hodson's Horse) ; the third was disbanded about 1861.

288

In these circumstances Daly remained at home until the latter part of 1861, when, on his return to India, he was appointed to the command of the Central India Horse,* with whom he served for the next five years. The corps, which consisted of two regiments, each about 500 strong, was thus described in the first Administration Report of the Central India Agency (that for 1865-1866) :—

"The Central India Horse is a most useful and valuable force ; and it is not too much to say that the general security of the trunk road is chiefly owing to its services.   It has further done much towards suppressing crime, generally of a predatory character, throughout western Malwa, and in the states and districts around and to the south of Goona.   The force is well-mounted, and admirably equipped and drilled, and is in every respect in a thoroughly efficient condition ; and its able commandant, Colonel Daly, C.B., and his officers may be justly proud of it."

On his arrival in India, Daly was at first somewhat disposed to return to purely military duty on the Punjab frontier, but was strongly dissuaded by Mansfield, who wrote early in December 1861 :—

"The wild soldiering success of the last twenty years is, I believe, pretty nearly over for a long time

* Now the 38th Central India Horse and 39th Central India Horse.   The former was raised in 1858, by Captain H. O. Mayne, on a nucleus of the faithful remains of the cavalry of the Gwalior, Bhopal, and Malwa contingents, and was originally styled "Mayne's Horse." The force was augmented in 1860 to a corps of three regiments (Beatson's Horse being incorporated), and the first of these became, the same year, the 1st Regiment of Central India Horse.   Received the present designation in 1903.

The 39th Central India Horse was raised at Hyderabad in 1858 by Colonel W. F. Beatson, as the 1st Regiment of Beatson's Horse; became the 2nd Regiment of Mayne's Horse 1860 ; the 2nd Regiment Central India Horse the same year ; received the present designation in 1903.

to come; and the toga, or at least the Windsor uniform of the Political Agency, will henceforth bring a man more distinction than the sword, if, as I believe, we have fairly entered on a peace cycle in this country; the war cycle which commenced with the invasion of Afghanistan in the days of Lord Auckland, and the breaking up the foundation of our old Policy, having come to an end with the conclusive blow given to the native reaction in 1858-1859."

With these views Daly, in part at least, agreed, for a couple of months later he wrote home from Goona :—

"India at any rate, I think, has entered on a cycle of peace. The military service here is in a state of convulsion. The retirement scheme is now taking effect. The Gazette has already published the names of the field officers who have availed themselves of the bonus, and in a few days we shall know the captains who have sent in their decision. More field officers would have gone had they been able to go; but many of those of the period (twenty-five years army rank) had not, through furlough and sick certificate, *served* in India the pension time, and were thus precluded from availing themselves of the offer. The anxiety to go is great among the body. Sir C. Wood proposed to include in his scheme 300; 240 odd have accepted. It is said he will now bid lower; *i.e.*, twenty-two years or twenty; I doubt this. Some part of the retirement scheme may effect my promotion, therefore I look with interest to the *finale* of the plan.

"Goona is not tempting in appearance; it is but a wretched village, which supplies the very poorest of native produce. Mine is the only house in the cantonment; the sheds in which the officers live are coverings of bamboo and mud, under which tents were originally pitched. My house is of great prettiness; quaint it is; more like a musjid, or rather a temple, than the residence of an Englishman. There is a beautiful garden attached, immensely large, with wells and water-courses. All this was the

GOONA, C. I., RESIDENCE OF COMMANDANT, CENTRAL INDIA HORSE.

[To face p. 254.

work of an officer (English) in Scindia's service, who
resided here alone for many years prior to the Mutiny.
An officer of the Engineers told me the other day
that, in olden times, he had sat in the garden porch
of the Scindia officer and shot panthers. There are
some handsome trees just about the house, and here
alone; elsewhere the wild coarse grass, 2 or 3 feet
high, rank and yellow, extends far and wide, for the
inhabitants are few and cultivation limited; standing
up like sentinels at intervals are tall cocoa trees. The
country has very much the appearance of that in
which Mark Tapley's virtue of jollity was tried. It
is a great place for sport. Tigers have been killed,
even last year, within a mile of my house. In May
last, a party from Goona during a month bagged
sixteen tigers and as many bears. Despite the wild,
desolate appearance of this place, it is esteemed
healthy, and is certainly a pleasant climate for India;
now fires are very enjoyable. It was great good
luck falling so quickly on good pay and employment;
there is attached to the command a duty I value, the
political charge of the district; it belongs *ex officio* to
the commandant; it brings one into association with
all the Rajas and nobles around, and gives one an
interest. I hope by and by it may lead to my getting
into the political line altogether."

For this appointment he was, so he believed,
largely indebted to the spontaneous intervention of
his old friend Napier, who had held a command
during the final repression of the rebels in Central
India. In the following May, Napier wrote:—

"I will not wait to write you on all the Central
Indian points that I feel interest in, and which your
note has freshened up, as I might find it, like my last
letter, one of the stones of the eternal pavement—not
of paradise. But I write a line in reply at once
because I fear you may have thought me unkind or
lukewarm about your appointment, as I never wrote
to you then. It was the only application I ever made
to Lord Canning for an officer not having served immediately under my command. I, however, made my

application for you on the ground of public service entirely, and I believe the representation of your fitness for political employ carried the day against a dangerous competitor. In this, however, I acted entirely on public grounds, and Lord Canning knew well I neither did nor would ask any private favour. Bowie was a very valuable ally, and very warm in your favour, but you owe your appointment entirely to your own public character, and to no solicitation of your friends.

"I found the work in Central India best done by small parties under such men as Bradford,* Blair, Roome, honest old Rice (of the 'Tigers'), and constantly sent them against parties that my neighbours pushed in vain with brigades. I felt inclined to despair when I thought of Central India and its remote prospect of civilisation, and—I speak with deference now to a political—its political system. It is the object of politicals to keep matters smooth, but it was remarked to me happily by one of your native councillors, the completion of the railways will do more to civilise India than a thousand schools.

"I entirely agree with you as to the chiefs. I never found them difficult, nor forgetful of any kindness. I have the deepest regard for the natives generally, in spite of the Mutiny, and should rejoice in the opportunity of influencing the chiefs in the direction of civilisation. My first advice to all the Rajput chiefs was to educate their sons. There is a great virtue in the Rajputs—inconvenient to us—no price can induce them to betray a fugitive guest."

The Commandant of the Central India Horse then held political charge of the Western Malwa Agency, which included the States of Jaora, Ratlam, Sitamau, and Sailana, with the Malwa districts of Gwalior, Indore, Jhalawar, Dewas, and Tonk. The years which followed were a period of some anxiety; for, throughout Central India, the crops were generally below the average from 1861-1862 to 1864-1865,

* Now Colonel Sir Edward Bradford, Bart, G.C.B., G.C.V.O., K.C.S.I.

THE RESIDENCY, INDORE, 1870.

[To face p. 295]

stocks in Malwa had been depleted by the extraordinary demands received from Bombay, and at the commencement of the monsoon of 1865, a scarcity of food, amounting to actual famine in the western division, prevailed throughout Malwa. A peculiarly fatal type of fever, known as the "Guzerati sickness," was also prevalent. The conditions were therefore such as to call forth all Daly's energy and activity. At that period railways were unknown in Central India: the main line of communication through the Agency was the Grand Trunk Road from Agra to Bombay; the black cotton soil through which it passed cut up terribly during the rains, but experiments in metalling had only just been commenced, while the opening out of new roads had scarcely been attempted. The zeal which Daly devoted in later years to opening up the land-locked areas of Central India may doubtless be in part ascribed to the difficulties with which he had to contend in Malwa.

In 1863 Daly was much moved by the death of Lord Clyde, regarding which he received the following letter from Mansfield :—

"POONA, 11/10/63.

"MY DEAR DALY,
            "I am always glad to hear from you, but more especially on such a theme as that forming the subject of your last letter. In this world of graves and tombstones, it in general makes but little impression on us when one more is added to the latter, when one more familiar form subsides into the ever open mouth of the former. But I can truly say that the loss of our poor friend Sir Colin—he would never allow me to call him Clyde—has caused me a feeling of sadness of which I hardly deemed myself capable except in the case of the nearest blood relations. I suppose this strong feeling is not merely one of friendship and recollection of old kindness, but that

R

ance. He really *could not* turn people out ; in short, in this he sometimes failed. But he scolded much, and had a biting sarcasm. This procured him many enemies which a colder but dangerous severity would have saved him, while the latter would or might have ruined the individuals he always spared. I used to tell him his 'bark was worse than his bite,' and I have often made him bite.

"I sum up the whole, as you apparently do, that he was the beau idéal of a lieutenant who might command a Corps d'Armée, of which the initiative should come from such a Chief as Napoleon or the Duke. He was of the highest class of military executive, and there masterful. Such, I think, was his own view of his abilities, though there was such a modesty about the man that it was impossible to draw him with a view of self-appreciation.—Ever yours very sincerely,

"W. MANSFIELD."

In August 1864 Daly was promoted to full Colonel, and two years later Sir Robert Napier, now Commander-in-Chief, Bombay, recommended him for the good service pension (which was duly granted) in the following terms :—

"COMMANDER-IN-CHIEF'S OFFICE,
"HEADQUARTERS, BOMBAY, 20th *April* 1866.
"SIR,
"I have the honour to submit, for the consideration of His Excellency the Honourable the Governor, a statement of the services of Colonel Daly, C.B., Bombay Staff Corps, commanding the Central India Horse, an officer most distinguished in the field, whom I would earnestly recommend to His Excellency as specially deserving of the good service pension.

"Colonel Daly's commissions are dated Ensign, 1840 ; Lieutenant, 1843 ; Captain, 1854 ; Brevet-Major, 1858 ; Brevet - Lieutenant - Colonel, 1858 ; Colonel, 1864. And his field services are as follows :—

"Served as a Volunteer during the first siege of

Multan as Assistant Engineer; was Adjutant of the
1st Bombay Fusiliers at the final siege, and was
engaged in the storming of the suburbs, 27th December 1848 (especially mentioned in the despatch).
Storm of the city on the 2nd January 1849, and
named in the despatch 'conspicuous for gallantry.'

"Battle of Gujerat and the pursuit to the Khyber
Pass.

"Raised the 1st Punjab Cavalry, and commanded
the corps in the passage of the Kohat Pass under Sir
C. Napier.

"In command of the 1st Punjab Cavalry in the
first Miranzai expedition, and in several affairs on the
frontier during 1850, 1851, 1852.

"Raised the 1st Oudh Cavalry in 1856.

"In command of the Guides in 1857, and marched
them to Delhi: one of the most remarkable military
marches on record.

"Was present throughout the siege of Delhi, and
slightly wounded on the 9th June (horse killed), and
dangerously wounded 19th June, in charging the
enemy's guns (horse wounded); commanded the
Guides, etc., on the 14th September.

"Siege of Lucknow, March 1858, and commanded
'Hodson's Horse,' on Major Hodson's death, during
the siege.

"Formed Hodson's Horse into a brigade of three
regiments, and commanded the whole throughout the
operations in Oudh, 1858-1859, under Sir Hope
Grant, including the action of Nawabgunge, passage
of the Gumti, Pandu Nadi, etc.; passage of the
Gogra, affairs in the Terai, Jewrah Pass, etc.

"The intelligence and zeal displayed by Lieutenant
Daly as a Volunteer Assistant Field Engineer at the
siege of Multan led to my recommending him to the
late Sir Henry Lawrence for command of one of the
new regiments raised for the Punjab service in 1848,
and I have been familiar with the uniformly high
character which Colonel Daly has since maintained
in every duty, whether civil or military, in which he has
been engaged, and the very high estimation in which
his services have been held by the ruling authorities
in India.

"As Colonel Daly has not been serving in the

Bombay Presidency, I have thought it necessary to detail his services, though, I fear, imperfectly, but I have little doubt that his merits are known to His Excellency in Council, and that my solicitation for the good service pension for him will be fully supported by the Government of his own proper Presidency.—I have, etc.,

"R. NAPIER, *Lieut.-General,* "*Commander-in-Chief.*"

At this time also, Napier made enquiry from Daly as to his views regarding a brigade command in the Bombay Presidency, Aden being specially suggested; but Daly decided, not without some misgivings, to decline the offer and to fix his hopes on the political line. Shortly before this, Colonel Meade, the Agent to the Governor-General in Central India, had contemplated long furlough, and Daly, knowing that he could rely on Meade's support, had hopes of obtaining the acting vacancy. He wrote to a friend :—

"Touching my prospects in the event of Meade's going home—these are certainly not weakened by the personality of those in a position to be 'pushed up.' There are three possible competitors in the Agency, and in Rajputana there is nobody with any spring :—but as you say, success in this matter will rest on other grounds. I know Sir John* well, and he has known me with considerable intimacy for years, and, though this was chiefly due to his brothers, Sir Henry and George (both my true friends), he has a kindly feeling towards me. Sir Henry nominated me when quite a young subaltern (after the seige of Multan) to raise the 1st Punjab Cavalry, a frontier regiment, and my success won his cordial friendship. During my service on the Peshawar frontier I became associated with Nicholson, Edwardes, Lumsden, etc.; and then sprang up an acquaintance, and more, with

* Sir John Lawrence, who had now become Viceroy and Governor-General.

Colonel Mansfield* and *Sir Colin* Campbell. I was for years in intimate correspondence with Sir Henry— up to within a few days of his end; and at his instance Sir John (then ruling in the Punjab) appointed me (on Lumsden's Candahar expedition) to command Henry's own corps, the Guides, which I marched to Delhi and led there. That march from Mardan to Delhi, 590 miles in twenty-two days in the heats of May and June, with cavalry and infantry, has never been equalled in India. I have said that the Viceroy's knowledge of me was chiefly through his brothers; but it became confidential during the mutiny, and his letters to me during the Delhi struggle were numerous and full of his mind. Our position and the possible eventualities were discussed with the utmost freedom. Sir John's views were higher than the world is now inclined to believe, and he never in the darkest moment lost sight of the public service. He knew that Nicholson disliked him personally and evinced his feeling in contemptuous speech, or still more contemptuous silence, towards his chief; but this had not the slightest effect on Sir John's desire to put the best man of the situation in authority. (By the way, who is to write the article on Nicholson† in the *Calcutta Review?* He was a grander and more Plutarchian man than Kaye painted and rouged.) After Delhi and Hodson's death, I formed the body of horse which bore his name into three corps and commanded this brigade till the end of the war; and, but for this command and my desire to see the last of the military service, I should have passed into political employment in Rajputana, for which *Sir John* had commended me to Lord Canning.

"I have given these particulars of my own career

---

* At this time Lieutenant-General Sir William Mansfield, Commander-in-Chief in Bombay.

† On this subject, Daly subsequently wrote to the same correspondent:—"I will write to Major Malleson. I know him by name and character; he is brother-in-law to Quentin Battye of the Guides, the Knight of the White Plume who fell in his 'first fight' under my command at Delhi. I have often heard him allude to Malleson; M. will handle the grander points of Nicholson's character: Kaye cushions all his heroes in velvet."

that you may understand how I stand with the Governor-General. He has forgotten none of these things, though I believe his memory is much affected by his eyes and ears. He is warm to old allies near him, somewhat careless of those at a distance. I am sure the more you know of the Governor-General the more you will appreciate his rare common sense, always at hand : the grit too is palpable."

Of the political service generally, Daly had not at this time a high opinion. He wrote to the same friend :—

"With the exception of a few of the highest in the calling, the British Political Agents who spent their days and *nights* at native courts, cut off from association of their countrymen, have not been types of which we can be proud; nowadays something more is looked for than mere subserviency to the Chief; some familiarity with the public opinion of our own country and a general knowledge of the people of India are requisite in the representative of the Government of India. My charge in Western Malwa (Malcolm's own country) with the scores of thakurs and Chiefs receiving stipends from Holkar, Scindia, etc., under our guarantee—without which their incomes would be worth only what their swords and spears could plunder—includes Jaora, Ratlam, Sailana, besides provinces subject to Gwalior, Indore, Dewas, and Patan, and extends to Neemuch. So you see there are few Agencies with more varied interests."

In the end Meade postponed his leave, and it was not till early in 1867 that Daly obtained his first substantial advancement in the political service, when he was appointed to officiate as Political Agent at Gwalior. The Gwalior appointment was the most important of the seven political charges forming the Central India Agency, over which presided the Agent to the Governor-General in Central India, with headquarters at Indore.

Daly's old friend Crawford Chamberlain almost immediately afterwards took up the command of the troops at Gwalior, where the two worked in close accord. The situation at Gwalior was difficult, and the character and influence of the Maharaja Jayaji Rao Scindia made the political duties of special interest and delicacy. Daly had been for several years personally known to the Maharaja, and his work in Western Malwa had brought him into constant communication with the officials of the Gwalior Darbar. He had also learnt to appreciate the work and character of that great statesman Dinkar Rao (Raja Sir Dinkar Rao, K.C.S.I.), who had been Scindia's minister during the mutiny. "Dinkar Rao," wrote Daly, "is the *one* native whose purity nobody of any creed or colour questions: all mention his name with deference, even reverence."

There was thus nothing new to Daly in associations with Gwalior, and in March 1867 he wrote :—

"There is a great deal that is good in Scindia, and I think, had he been fairly handled in youth, the man would now be worthy his position; his ability developed wonderfully between 1854 and 1858, showing that the stuff was in him. It was Sir Dinkar Rao's calm wisdom which saved Gwalior, but undoubtedly Scindia deserves much for being capable of being saved by *one* man, when *all* else were for rebellion. He retains every string of office in his own hands; there is not a man about him with authority to spend a rupee, as he is entirely his own minister; without doubt there is nobody now in Scindia's court with anything like the Chief's ability; he knows this, and believes himself capable of anything. The prosperity of his State is due entirely to the settlements made by Dinkar Rao. It was he who carved out the paths, which, though now covered with briars, are still paths for use. *Nobody knows all this better than the Maharaja himself.* In conversation, though without education but that attained since manhood, he is intelligent and pleasant; seizes on points readily, and now can command the temper which years ago used to break forth in horrible violence; he is thoroughly alive to his status towards Government—no glamour there: 'I take wishes to be orders, tell me what is wanted and I will do it.'"

Within a few weeks of Daly's arrival at Gwalior a serious matter had to be dealt with—the dispersal of Scindia's police force and the distribution of his regular troops, hitherto massed at the capital. In a letter to the Maharaja the Viceroy had advised His Highness "to distribute from a half to a third" of his army in different parts of his territories, urging "that large bodies of troops, collected for long periods with little to occupy their minds, become difficult of control and dangerous to their own rulers."

The Agent to the Governor-General in Central India, Colonel Meade, visited Gwalior, and the views of Government were conveyed to Scindia orally and privately by Meade and Daly. Daly wrote :—

"The decision of the Government that the police should be disembodied was received by Scindia calmly, and apparently without much interest; whereas, despite the most painful efforts, his emotion respecting the dispersion of the regular troops could not be suppressed, though with a distinct admission that the wishes of the Viceroy were law to him, and that, whatever the sacrifice to himself, there would be no hesitation in obedience. Within a few days it was arranged that orders for the disembodiment of the police should be issued forthwith; with the sanction of the Viceroy, the distribution of the regular troops should be deferred till after the celebration of the Dasehra at Gwalior. Colonel Meade quitted Gwalior a few days after this arrangement had been come to, leaving Scindia grievously depressed: for weeks following he almost abstained from business, and, as in his own person he represents the Darbar and all authority, the deadlock was serious. I sought an opportunity of discussing with him alone the position which he had assumed; the conversation was long and painful; yet it seemed to give him relief; he promised to renew attention to general work, and very cordially invited me at any time to talk frankly with him on any subject. Since that conversation. there has been no reserve between us, and frequently he has alluded to his 'grief,' which still oppresses him, though less visibly than formerly. I have never avoided the subject, believing that the ventilation of it with me is calculated to work some good on one whose associates dare but echo his voice. The army was his idol; its discipline his constant occupation; the only books with which he has any acquaintance are those connected with drill and military pursuits. Therefore it was he pleaded sorely that his toy might be spared. With all this was the tone of direct subjugation to the will of Government, that he is 'as clay in the potter's hands.' Every effort was made to spare his feelings; not a line in the vernacular was penned to the Darbar on the subject. Scindia gave his own orders, and, at the time appointed by himself after the Dasehra, effect was quietly given to the Viceroy's advice.

" It is pleasant to turn to Scindia's personal bearing in his intercourse with the Political Agent. He is accessible at any time, and, even when brooding over the fancies which affect him most, he is never wanting in kindly courtesy. He will listen to anything urged; bear his part fairly in discussion and face to face in a pleasant way; not shrink from pressure for a decision. During these discussions and since, I have attempted to impress on Scindia the advisability of changing the *matériel* of his force; that he should no longer enlist men who have served in our army, or entertain recruits from British territory. Oudh and the neighbourhood of Cawnpore have hitherto been common recruiting fields, supplying not only our own regular contingents, but the need of Chiefs who maintain disciplined corps. Members of the same family serve the Queen at Morar, Scindia at the Lashkar, the Nizam at Hyderabad, and the Gaekwar at Baroda. Scindia's force should be entirely recruited from his own territories, and thus distinct from that of the Government of India. The change will not be easy, but the step is important and should be steadily kept in view."

In the same report Daly discussed the peculiar difficulties in the way of improving the administration in Gwalior :—

"There is an entire absence of individual responsibility in the heads of departments. There is neither council nor councillor : the Maharaja rules everything. He alone is the Government. In capacity and administrative ability there is no one about him to compare with him, but many things are hid from him. Information trickles to him through crooked and narrow channels, not likely to bear many truths of current life. The Court Newsman culls from the Native Press remarks upon Gwalior and its Chief. Several of his officials have a good knowledge of English, and similarly work the English papers (published in India), of which many are taken in. Thus the Maharaja is pretty sure to learn in one way or another what is written about him, and he is keen on this point. It was thus His Highness became acquainted with the publication of my confidential report on Gwalior * through the press quite as soon as I did. It is no light tribute to his good feeling to say that he did not allow this to mar the freedom of our intercourse. He was conscious of the truth of what was written, and that nothing was set down in malice.

"Scindia is desirous of improving his Government, but the question is beset with difficulties. In Native Governments the salaries of officials of all grades are inadequate to their position without illicit gains. They are not fixed high, in the expectation that men will resist temptation, but low, from the knowledge

* See Appendix A.

that they will yield to it. Dustoories (presents) and nazarana (fees), attach to every proceeding, and every step in each proceeding ; without such accompaniments, few officials would do anything, and no suitor would expect anything to be done. To compensate for these, a public servant must not only be well paid, and so removed from the need of other emoluments than the salary of his office, but he must be hedged about by laws and a fixed procedure, which have no existence in Native States. Scindia, with the prestige of his name and undoubted power—with his capacity and aptitude to master business—might so remodel his Government as to make it a blessing to the people ; for no man more thoroughly knows the weak points of the present system than he does, and he is not without ambition to win fame as an administrator ; but the apparent increase in the cost of administration, which the fair payment of State servants would entail, will, I fear, deter him from such a sustained effort as the circumstances demand.

"At this time, when public attention is attracted to the bearing in India of the British Government as a Paramount Power, special interest attaches to the expressed views of, perhaps, the richest and most powerful Chief in the country. I will, therefore, give the substance of conversations I have held with him. He invariably speaks of himself as the special ally of the British Government, as being, in fact, part of it, and considers that his unflinching fidelity places him in a nearer position to it than any other Chief. Scindia said :—'I fully appreciate the value of the British Government to us, the Chiefs of India. The feeling of order and security which pervades all classes is a substance—a silent working power never attained under any previous rule ; and, as natives of India still are, it would be impossible for any Native Government to attain it. I have watched it and thought of it long. It springs from causes, many of which are hidden from us, but to me the most striking is the careful way in which you husband your experience. Your records are so preserved, that in almost all the positions filled by your officers, the current of business is little affected by the men themselves. With a Native

Government it is entirely otherwise; its servants pay no deference to the records of their predecessors to follow them, rather the reverse. There are no such links of responsibility as you maintain; nor with natives would it be possible to bring about the unity of feeling and loyalty to one another which exists amongst you.

" 'Your prestige fills men's minds to an extent which, to men who know how things were carried on scarce fifty years ago, seems beyond belief. Within that period when Mahrattas went from time to time from Gwalior to the Deccan, small parties were not safe. The departure was an epoch in the year. Their friends parted from them knowing that they had set out on a journey of danger—perils through thugs, robbers, spoliation, and black-mail levied on them by the States through which they must pass; these things men, not old, still speak of. Now, all pass to and fro without danger and without hindrance —the poorest traveller feels as safe as the richest— for you make as much effort to protect the poor as the rich. I never put myself upon the mail-cart, unattended and perhaps unknown, without appreciating the strength of your rule. It is a substance— I leave Gwalior without apprehension, and my absence occasions no distrust. Then again, there is no doubt a general faith in your justice. Your Government, though often hard, curt, and inconsiderate in its treatment of the prejudices, or, if you like, weaknesses of the Chiefs, yet, on the whole, treats them with a liberality which they never show to one another. And, now that annexation is at an end, we breathe freely even when our failings are probed and our shortcomings discussed. Notwithstanding that your subjects are perhaps richer and more prosperous than the same classes in Native States, you are not popular. I speak as a friend. I travel a good deal about your territory, and hear much which never reaches your ears. The people are bewildered by your legislation; you coil "Act" upon "Act," "Code" upon "Code," with sections innumerable. You never leave them alone. I am told that your district officers have less intercourse with their ryots than formerly; there is more of system and less sympathy nowadays.

" ' In your desire to press on improvements, you overlook the vast difference between us and you. Some of your reforms have been excellent, such as the abolition of sati, child-murder, and many others. There are others again which seem meddlesome. Take, for instance, your attempt to interfere with and curtail marriage expenses. The people do not understand this, and there are not wanting many who point to these acts as showing your purpose to upset caste and custom. What good have you done? Such interference is vain, and gets you into bad odour. Now there is a circular canvassing the opinions of Chiefs with a view to decreasing pilgrimages and fairs at shrines during the hot season, on the ground that such gatherings cause and diffuse cholera, etc. Well, this may be so; but very few of the Chiefs whose advice you have asked will believe that your object is as set forth; and pilgrims and others, whose very existence depends upon their going at certain seasons to shrines, etc., will be troubled, and throng more and more, thinking that the end is at hand. Why raise the question? You might have contented yourselves with adopting on the spot every measure which seemed requisite for sanitation. This would have been gradually understood.'

" The wisdom of these remarks commands attention. Such criticisms from such a quarter are not only valuable in themselves, but mark a state of mind in Scindia which shows that the cause of progress is gathering strength by example. I break no confidence in thus dwelling on these conversations. It will cheer His Highness to know that the Government attaches value to the sentiments he has expressed, and gathers from them a renewed assurance of improving rule in Gwalior.

" On my arrival at Gwalior in February 1867, I found cases and references which had been dragging for years, important or unimportant. The transmission gave occupation and writing to men who had no power to dispose of them. I had many discussions with Scindia, whose accessibility and good humour admit of these being carried on with the utmost freedom. He acknowledged the waste of time caused by the many paper references, and expressed his willingness to meet my views. His Highness has thoroughly acted in this spirit, and the business relations between the Agency and the Darbar are now on a pleasant and satisfactory footing. There are no arrears, correspondence has decreased, and questions are discussed orally with the Maharaja and Dewan."

In acknowledging the above, which was embodied in the Administration Report for 1867-68, the Foreign Secretary wrote to Colonel Meade :—

"The confidential remarks of His Highness as to the relative merits of native and British rule, conveyed in the report of Colonel Daly as gathered from familiar conversations with the Maharaja, are such as every British official who is called on either to administer executive government directly, or to interpose with suggestions and advice to native rulers, would do well to bear in mind. The feeling of personal confidence and attachment to the British Government and its officers displayed by the Maharaja is a subject of real satisfaction, and it is one that reflects credit on the tact and good management of Colonel Daly and of General Chamberlain, commanding the Gwalior district, by whom, at a particular crisis, this result has been attained. His Excellency concurs with you in thinking, as already intimated, that Colonel Daly is especially entitled to the acknowledgments of the Government of India for the services rendered by him at the Gwalior Agency."

In England, at about this time, an unusual degree of attention was being directed towards the affairs of Native States in connection with the restoration of Mysore to native rule. Some extracts may be given from Daly's private letters of the period :—

"Rawlinson speaks of the *stir* in Native States by the quickening influence of European civilisation. He has never been in a *Native* State; his experience is of Afghanistan and Persia; neither he nor one of the Home agitators, except Hamilton, ever saw a Native

State. Here (Gwalior) such is the 'stir of civilisation' that not a rupee can be got for a road or work of utility, beyond the sum Scindia is squeezed into giving; no interior road or work is ever carried on. *Fakirs* are feasted, thousands spent on them and astrologers, in the Holi drunkenness ; but nothing o; the quickenings of progress, such as Europeans designate progress.

"You invite me to discuss Native States and their government. The theme is tempting at the first glance, and that only. I began it indeed, but to make the sketches of any value it would be necessary to describe the government as now conducted. I could not do this without giving offence, for the truth is ten times worse than anything which fancy could devise. Scindia's State is practically one of the best as far as we know, but *that knowledge is very slight ;* no servant or subject of his is allowed to visit or speak to British officers ; if one of his nobles were to pay me a visit without having obtained permission, he would be a marked man ; tyranny and oppression in many matters baffle belief, but no sign is made by us. If it were known that our aid would be given in any case of oppression, the road would be thronged with shrieking petitioners, but this sort of intercession would never become us ; it should be prophylactic to be of use, and in the large States the opportunity for this is past.

"Lord Cranborne says Sir George Clerke told him that he had never known of a migration from a Native State to the British ; but, bad taste though it was, the reverse is not uncommon. What twaddle is this? George Clerke of Umballa's experience of Native States is aged thirty or forty years. What are the facts? In Esagarh, a large and rich province, villages are depopulated, lands waste; in Scindia's and Holkar's districts in Malwa, it is the same. These tracts are now as Oudh was in 1855, as described by Sleeman and Outram. What is the condition in Oudh now? Where in British territory does land lie waste? Do you not remember in your passage from Indore to Gwalior, the bleak deserted vista which everywhere greeted you? Soil of the richest untouched : *that* is the condition of great States.

S

"It is a pretty thing to talk of 'a well-governed Native State.' Where is this to be found? In those States, small and dependent, which, but for our support, would be swallowed up. With them is much that suits the native tastes. British ideas worked by themselves. Wherever this is the case you will find prosperity and population. This should have been the case here with Scindia; but we wrecked ourselves and Dinkar Rao, and so left Scindia with his own fickle temper to guide him. Seeing all this I could not write the truth; harm would follow. It must be our rule to work out better things by winning the Chiefs to ourselves. Scindia is good in many points; sensitively desirous to win our approbation, and in this way we may find a way of winning him to good purposes. He is like a trout and wants tickling. Speak kindly of him and be careful to eschew satire of him. He should be dealt with *tenderly* and *gently;* praised for his good acts and so won over. I have written you this to give you a notion of the moody nature of one who ought to be better than he is. Yet, as he is, the difference between him and others is great. Of late years we have in no way helped him. Still I do not despair. I am sure with all these semi-educated Chiefs, we do not well to be angry; we must treat them with forbearance. Good is to be attained by personal influence only; for few indeed are they who value principles. There is but one Dinkar Rao. If it should happen that he be restored to position here, and stranger things have happened, Scindia would find immense relief and happiness, the country would rise in glee; even now, despite the knowledge that to name Dinkar Rao is disgrace, as he passes through towns and hamlets, all run out with clasped hands to bless him for his settlement, and that it is to which Scindia owes the order now existing despite the laches. The more I see of Dinkar Rao the more I esteem his rare purity. What a Governor of a province he would make! Calmly wise, honestly good. That man should be an Indian Councillor nobly paid. So should we recognise ability and *service.* We are beginning at the wrong end of the stick."

MAHARAJA SIR JAYAJI RAO SCINDIA, G.C.B.

[To face p. 274.

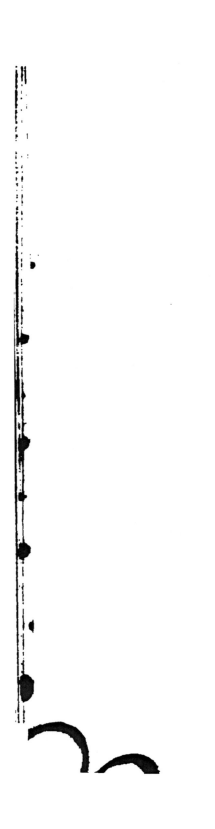

In one of the above quotations from his annual report, Daly refers to the publication of a confidential memorandum* in which he had dealt with the affairs of Gwalior. The memorandum was written in response to a circular which was issued by the Government of India, in consequence of some remarks made in the House of Commons by Lord Cranborne (the late Marquess of Salisbury), who, in the debate on the Mysore question, expressed a doubt whether, in the estimation of the natives, the British system of administration was superior to that in force in the Native States. The publication of his remarks took Daly entirely by surprise and greatly vexed him. He wrote privately to a friend :—

"An essay on British or Native rule might be as well cooked up in Oxford as Calcutta, in the way that recent travels in Abyssinia† are now under process at the British Museum. But it requires a man to be on the premises to know how sausages are made. I was asked *confidentially* for information on the working of the Government machinery in the State to which I am accredited. I drew up the curtain on the system, and in so doing, made personal allusions which I would have omitted had I known that publication was at hand. Mark the difference of tone of those who wrote for themselves in print! they paint Oliver without moles! I said as little as I could through fear of writing too much ; but to have left out the personal bearing would have been striking out Hamlet. Moreover, had I contemplated publication, I would have told Scindia, so that the blow should not fall from an outsider. He is an extraordinary compound and can bare frankness. There is much to like about him. There is nothing in what I wrote about Central India (Malwa) which I have

* See also Appendix A.

† The allusion is to the Abyssinian Expedition of 1867-68, in which, but for his employment at Gwalior, Daly would have commanded a brigade.

not told him again and again in the endeavour to make him take a real interest in his rich possessions there. His revenues are some 30 lakhs from Malwa : with liberal nursing in a few years they will spring to 50.

"———— * is a philosopher. He has called upon me and discussed the general question. He says he is as honest as his position admits : that while at Rome he is obliged to do as the Romans do.

"It has been said of the Infidel, where does he get his notion of the God he denies? So of the comparative systems (!) of government in this country. What would happen without the security we give? What did happen in olden time? Pindaries, Dacoits, Largesse—a man's means being the measure of his *contribution!* It is our security which makes natives to think of these things. The happiest rule for the people, that gives contentment without fear, is that administered by one of themselves under our general supervision and protection. Jaora is an instance in point. Our slavery to system frequently works harshly and inflicts suffering, but it is the reliance on our truth and *intention* to do justice which redeems us. In Native States, faith in the Englishman is still strong.

"We have distributed Dinkar Rao's rules of government as much as possible amongst the States of Central India and with excellent effect. Our system, carried out by a well-trained Chief or a minister like Dinkar Rao, would realise Edwardes' notion of a perfect government in a *new* country—that Sir Henry Lawrence should go through the land amongst the people saying what was to be done, and leave Sir John to do it."

Daly had spoken so freely of the Maharaja Scindia that the Government of India imagined that his personal relations with the Chief could not stand the strain, and orders were actually issued for Daly's transfer to another appointment. "I quit this position with regret," wrote Daly to a friend, "I have got

* A leading native official at Gwalior.

on well with Scindia and was gradually acquiring a working influence over him, and despite the unwise publication of my paper, I should, in time, recover any ground that may be lost. Scindia has borne the matter well and honestly. He is too sensible to compare his *administrators* with ours. He has his grievances, and feels, not without bitterness, that we neglected him in days past, and paid no attention to his education and training. He thinks us harsh and comments on our adherence to form at the expense of sympathy."

In point of fact, Scindia, with a large-heartedness that Daly was the first to acknowledge, was at pains to show that he had taken no offence at Daly's free speaking and that he abated not a jot from the confidence which he had learnt to repose in him. The order for transfer was cancelled on a special representation from the Agent to the Governor-General, and Scindia congratulated himself on retaining Daly as his political officer.

Daly went home on sick leave in May 1868; he returned to Gwalior in September, and proceeded to Indore in the following March to officiate for Meade as Agent to the Governor-General. Meade resumed charge at the end of 1869, but was transferred to Hyderabad early in 1870, when D.ly again took up the appointment of Agent to the Governor-General, which he held until his final departure from India eleven years later.

CHAPTER XI

ADMINISTRATION OF CENTRAL INDIA, 1869-1881

Description of the Province and of its condition before Daly assumed
charge ; the famine of 1868-1870 ; relations of Political Officers
with Native States ; Daly's methods of administration and objects ;
annual progress as shown by Reports ; assassination of Lord
Mayo ; the Rewa Chief ; the Opium Trade ; Lord Northbrook's
tour in Central India ; visit to India of the Prince of Wales ; the
Imperial Assemblage at Delhi ; Daly's review of ten years ;
officers who served under him ; his departure.

THE Native States which constitute the province of
Central India cover an area of about 84,000 square
miles, or approximately that of England, Scotland,
and Wales.   The chief administrative authority is
officially styled, "the Agent to the Governor-General
in Central India," and his charge is officially designated "the Central India Agency"; it may be
roughly described as extending from the confines of
Bengal on the east to the Bombay Presidency of the
west, and as bounded on the north by the United
Provinces and Rajputana, and on the south by the
Central Provinces.   When Daly assumed charge,
Central India was divided for administrative purposes
into seven subordinate Agencies, each controlled by
a Political Officer, who acted directly under the orders
of the Agent to the Governor-General.   The province
contained four cantonments, Mhow, Morar, Neemuch,
and Nowgong, which were supervised by the Agent

278

to the Governor-General, who also exercised military control over the local corps in Central India, consisting of the two regiments of the Central India Horse, the Bhopal Battalion, and the Malwa Bhil Corps. The opium revenue of Malwa, which in 1868 amounted to two million pounds sterling, was collected at Indore under the direction of the Agent to the Governor.

The first Administration Report of the Central India Agency was submitted in 1866 by Daly's predecessor, Colonel (afterwards Sir Richard) Meade, who held the post of Agent to the Governor-General for eight years. Meade classified the Chiefships as follows :—Principal States, 4, viz., Gwalior, Indore, Bhopal, Rewa; Secondary States, 23, whereof 2 Mahratta, 2 Muhammadan, 6 Bundela, 12 Rajput, and 1 Gujar; minor and petty States, 44. He estimated the population at over 7½ millions, and the revenues of the Chiefships at rather over 2½ crores of rupees. "Many of the Chiefs," observed Daly a few years later, "wield an influence in the country worthy of all consideration, and far beyond that which income would imply."

No regular census * of Central India was taken until 1881, when the population was returned as 9,261,907; ten years later the census figure was 10,318,812, while at the last census (1901) the enumerated total was 8,628,781. The decrease in 1901 is to be ascribed in large measure to the effects of the famine of 1899-1900; at the same time it is well known that the returns of the two previous

* "Sir John Malcolm in 1823 estimated 98 to the square mile 'as a scale for the present reduced population of Central India.'" *Memoir of Central India, including Malwa*, vol. ii., p. 222.

decades were very unreliable, especially as regards the numbers of the Bhils and other semi-wild tribes.

"The character of the country and of the people inhabiting it," wrote Meade, in 1866, "naturally varies greatly throughout this extensive territory. Nothing can be a greater contrast than the desolate wilds and jungles of the Western Satpuras, and the country extending from them to the Vindhyas—with their savage inhabitants the Bhil tribes, who abhor field, or indeed any manual, labour—and the adjoining richly cultivated plains of Malwa, populated by a thrifty, agricultural people. A great part of Bundelkhand is hilly and unproductive, especially the southern and eastern districts, forming the northern slope of the tableland of the Vindhyas, which throw off offshoots in the form of lower ranges or detached hills, some of the latter of great height, as those surmounted by the celebrated Forts of Kalingar and Ajaigarh. The scenery here is strikingly grand and picturesque, the ghâts being bold and abrupt, and clothed with luxuriant foliage. The greater part of the Rewa has been, till recently, untraversed by Europeans, but the Topographical Survey now in progress will furnish full information."

Malwa stretches from the highlands of the Vindhya Range in a north-easterly direction for nearly 300 miles as far as the river Chambal. This district has long been famous for its equable climate, good crops, and rich soil. It contains the whole of the poppy-growing land from which Malwa opium is exported. It is thickly populated and well-cultivated. Sugar-cane, cotton, wheat, jowari, and the smaller millets are all successfully grown in this favoured district; numbers of rivers and streams, which have their sources in the Vindhyas, run through this area to join various affluents of the Jumna and the Ganges, while lakes, tanks, and numerous wells add greatly to the prosperity and security of the cultivating classes. It has often been said that Malwa is secure from drought. This is a theory advanced by Sir John Malcolm * in his volumes on Central India, and reiterated by his successors. And it was not until 1899 that Malwa lost her fair fame, and fell a victim to the devastating scourge of famine.

The northern districts of Central India are remarkable chiefly on account of the vicissitudes in their conditions. The heat of Gwalior is proverbial; while famine and scarcity have frequently played a disastrous part in the history of the State. Though well populated by as patient and long-suffering a class of cultivators as can be found in any part of India, Gwalior has an unenviable reputation for prolonged droughts; and many years of prosperity are needed to balance the effects of such famines as were experienced in 1868, 1880, 1886, 1897, and 1900.

In Bundelkhand and Rewa the character of the country is hilly; large forests and heavy jungles cover a great portion of this area, and there is a considerable sprinkling of the aboriginal tribes of Bhils and Gonds. In 1871, after a visit to Orchha, during which he composed certain differences between the Chief and his nobles, Daly wrote: " I could not fail to observe that this country of rocks, passes, and forts is populated by thousands who, but for British prestige, would make the old hills ring again with their war cries."

In the Central India of 1868, there was an entire lack of railway communication. The Great Indian Peninsula Railway extended only as far as Khandwa, while the terminus on the northern side of the

* *Memoir of Central India, including Malwa*, vol. ii., p. 42.

province was Agra. In roads also Central India was remarkably deficient. With the exception of the grand trunk road from Bombay to Agra, which passes through Indore, Goona, Sipri, and Gwalior, there was practically not a yard of metalled road in the Agency. Merchandise and goods for export were carried, by devious routes, on the backs of Banjara bullocks; and all journeys were performed on horseback or in carts. Education was almost unknown; the few schools that existed at the large towns, such as Gwalior, Indore, Dhar, and Ratlam, were neglected by the Chiefs, and can hardly be said to have been popular among the people. The administration of justice was marked chiefly by corruption, while the collection of revenue was in many States merely a system of over-assessment and rack-renting, tempered by an occasional remission of uncollected balances. Throughout Bundelkhand, and in many parts of Malwa and Gwalior, gangs of dakoits, emboldened by the supine conduct of native rulers, terrorised the country and collected heavy toll from the villagers, and from such merchants as were bold enough to send their goods through those parts of the country.

In August 1867, when Police Agent at Gwalior, Daly wrote :—

"Colonel Sutherland, Resident at Gwalior, in 1837 described Esaghar, Bhilsa, and Malwa as desolate and miserable. Thirty years have brought no change for the better. Travellers still go armed to the teeth, and in many places the man at the plough has a sword by his side. Traders going from village to village are not safe without an armed Bhil or Sondia. To men accustomed to see districts under British rule such a statement must seem fabulous. It is necessary to live and move in Native States to know the nature of the system under which they exist. The comparison between their method of administration and our own is as St Giles' to St James'."

In reviewing the past condition of Malwa, Daly wrote :—

"Mountstuart Elphinstone, in his report to the supreme Government, 1819-20, on the territory conquered from the Peshwa, describes districts which had once been populous with handsome cities, yielding large revenues to the Muhammadans, now lying desolate and uninhabited through the rapacity of the Mahratta soldiery and the misgovernment of the Peshwa's officers. Men are apt in these days to speak of Elphinstone, but few remember what he wrote of the misery which prevailed, and the dissimulation, mendacity, and fraud taught by extortion, and the sense of oppression and insecurity. Old men still talk of that time, though none can now recognise, in the busy towns now once more spread about the provinces, the picture painted by Elphinstone fifty years ago. If we pass on to Malwa, and take the picture by Malcolm of the same period, the contrast is hardly less remarkable, though under different conditions. In 1817 Holkar's territory was one scene of anarchy from which all government had disappeared. The produce of the country was given over to plunder. Rajput Chiefs and thakurs were consumed by the mercenary bands which they employed to protect them against the Mahrattas. Holkar, Amir Khan (Pindari),* and the Rani of Dhar

* "Amir Khan was a Pathan adventurer, who commenced his career as a private horseman in 1788. After serving first one Chief and then another, he adhered pretty steadily to the family of Jeswant Rao Holkar until 1818, just before the battle of Mehidpur, when he was gained over by the British, under guarantee of holding unmolested his possessions, the value of which was about £200,000 per annum. After this arrangement, he retired into private life and was virtually a prince in his own territory." Sir H. Lawrence's *Adventures of an Officer*, etc., vol. i., p. 10. For a complete account of the Pindaris, see vol. i., chap. x., of Malcolm's *Memoir of Central India, etc*. For the condition of Dhar, see Malcolm, vol. ii., chap. xv.

had 70,000 horse and foot, besides Sibhandis, and no less than 300 field-guns—dependent, or subsistent, on plunder. The revenues of Holkar were less than 4½ lakhs. The Malwa possessions of Daulat Rao Scindia, though free from anarchy, were much disturbed; and Rajput Chiefs were alert to escape from the Mahratta pressure. He had an army of 26,000 regular infantry, 13,000 cavalry, and 400 pieces of cannon, besides Pindaris, ready for the field.

"This was the state of Malwa when the British troops entered Central India in 1817, and, on the 21st December, in the battle of Mehidpur utterly shattered Holkar's army. The victory was so complete that, from that moment, order took root. The distress produced by successive revolutions had become so acute that Chiefs, thakurs, and people alike yearned for peace and the close of the reign of terror. British supremacy was nowhere resisted. Holkar, by the treaty of Mandisor, became one of the independent allies of the British Government. To him, as also to Dhar and Dewas, many estates which had been lost were restored. Malcolm proclaimed every district to be the right of the proprietor in possession, provided he proved himself the friend of peace. The Mahratta Chiefs were thus secured in conquests which, without our protection, they were powerless to hold, and from that date have been accepted as sovereign rulers by Rajput thakurs.

"Malcolm, in writing of these events three years afterwards, says: 'No contrast can be stronger than that which is now presented. The people of Malwa are probably at this moment happier and more contented than they will be hereafter.'

"Fifty years have elapsed since this was written. Malcolm is still remembered with gratitude by the people; who still look to us as the rulers of the country, and pray for our intercession as much as they did in 1818."

In 1868 Central India and Rajputana were visited by a disastrous famine, which grew intense in 1869, and did not disappear until 1870. Daly assumed charge as Agent to the Governor-General, from Meade, in March 1869; it consequently fell to him to record the history of the past year, and he wrote :—

"The exodus from Rajputana, through Malwa, began early in August; families, with their herds and household property, went streaming on for weeks and months in succession; they paused for rest and refreshment only, and then passed on in search of fodder and cheap food. This class, the cultivators of the province, went out to tide over the drought time, and then to return to their homes; overtures were made by States through which they passed to induce them to settle, but hardly one was accepted; when they returned some months afterwards their plight was changed—numbers thinned, means exhausted, the surviving cattle lank and dying, for the rain which was due had not fallen. With that large class below the cultivators and well-to-do inhabitants of villages, which fled from the famine, destitution was normal from the outset. They were without means to travel or strength to labour; they clung about the States of Malwa like locusts; much charity was shown to them. The Public Works Department on the imperial roads was open to all-comers capable in any way of contributing to their own maintenance; thus the lives and self-respect of thousands were saved. The numbers which perished from starvation and exhaustion are not to be computed; there are no statistics to give a clue to this; dead bodies and human bones were found in all directions; parties were constantly moving up and down the roads to bury and burn those who had died by the wayside; in many instances the corpses were left to the jackals and vultures.

"In September the Gwalior Darbar, in view to allay the panic, issued a proclamation urging the village communities to remain in their homes, promising that the first revenue instalment would be postponed, and that assistance, either through the State or through Banias, would be given. This proclamation had a ringing sound, nothing more; moreover, the distress was soon beyond such treatment; to remain in the villages was to meet certain death; wells were dry and water everywhere scarce, fodder was exhausted, and there was no food for man or beast, save that which the jungle gums, roots, and berries supplied.

"In December the highways about Gwalior and the palace gates were crowded with cultivators: whole communities pressed in to appeal against the demand for revenue collections; for the officials had begun to exact payment of the instalment the postponement of which had been promised by proclamation. Up to this time Maharaja Scindia had scarcely realised how terrible was the issue. For several months he had not been able to give his usual attention to public affairs. A dangerous illness prostrated him in August, and he was absent from Gwalior in search of health for upwards of a couple of months afterwards. His opinions soon underwent change; and he directed his Dewan to make a hasty tour through the affected districts. The Dewan quickly returned, bringing with him a harrowing account of what he had witnessed. The Maharaja was now roused: he mounted his horse, and with a handful of followers, for the country was bare, rode from *tahsil* to *tahsil* to see the face of things. What he saw was narrated under his own hand in graphic and striking language.

"I had many long and anxious consultations with Scindia and his Dewan on the measures to be adopted to meet the calamity. The Maharaja was appalled at its extent, and often exclaimed, 'How can I feed a people?' His plan was to put down half a lakh of rupees for distribution amongst the twelve Subhas (divisions), for the purchase of supplies, for deepening wells and tanks, and for relief works. The Sardars and chief men of Gwalior were called upon to feed the thousands thronging the streets in hunger and want. The appeal was liberally responded to by the wealthy community.

"In Bundelkhand distress became visible in September, between which and 31st March last nearly two lakhs were spent by twenty-two States in works of utility and relief. Panna, which was early conspicuous in practical benevolence, Charkhari, Chhattarpur staggered under the burden of relief cheerfully sustained, and the smaller States were not wanting. Rewa, though perhaps slower in taking the field as the darkness gathered, outshone all in bounty. This State is rich, and its riches were nobly used. But the mainstay of the province during this visitation has been the public works of the Government of India. Lakhs of rupees were spent in saving life in Native States, and it was the example of this wakeful munificence before their eyes which roused the Chiefs to a sense of their responsibilities."

Daly's report of the following year (1869-70) was in the same gloomy strain :—

"Within the States of Central India the past year has been marked by all the terrors of famine and disease ; thousands perished from sheer starvation, and thousands from cholera and sunstroke. Villages, and even districts, were depopulated, and there were none left to tell how many of the inhabitants had sunk under the miseries which oppressed them. Scindia computes the casualties in the neighbourhood of Gwalior at 92,987. In Bundelkhand the drought, which began later, lasted longer and was perhaps even more disastrous, for the people are poorer than those of Gwalior ; but the Chiefs of the States, great and small, seem to have given themselves earnestly to relief and measures of precaution. With the exception of a few places on the western border, Malwa suffered not at all from drought, but the streaming crowds from Rajputana and Gwalior brought in their train disease and death. Of the mortality among these wanderers it is impossible to form an opinion. Marwaris, lank and emaciated, came pouring down through every outlet into Western Malwa ; there are no data of their numbers; bodies and bones were found in *nalas*, and on the plains, under trees, and upon the wayside ; and this over a vast space. Even so late as February 1870, an English gentleman, marching through Rajputana to Indore, encountered human beings, living and dead, in every form of misery ; and witnessed scenes too horrible to be described. With the rains of this year (1870) thousands of survivors have found their way back; and even now there may be seen little camps of wayfarers returning to their villages, out of which they came in hundreds. The love of home was strikingly illustrated amongst these people, driven out by drought and famine, pursued by cholera and death: the survivors, in the depth of their misery, thought only of the time of return. No temptations to settle where they found food and kindliness turned them. Scarcely a settler was found. They struggled back, by tens and twenties, along the routes down which they hurried, a few months before, in crowds with their herds. It is pleasant to note the warm and abiding charity of the States in Western Malwa; for months in succession food was distributed at Jaora and Ratlam to thousands, the wealthy opium traders and bankers subscribed liberally, and relief was systematically disbursed under the orders of Hazrut Nur Khan, the Kamdar of Jaora, and Mir Shahamat Ali, the Superintendent of Ratlam. The Maharaja Holkar was also liberal and compassionate. During this year of misery, the dispensaries of Central India have been green spots diffusing food and comfort to the weary.

"Native States are still quivering under the strain; for where famine was heaviest there were no means of alleviating it, neither roads nor approaches. The rail saved Bundelkhand from utter destitution; but Rajputana had no such refuge, hence it was that the population rushed out in panic to starve and die. Salar Jung told Maharaja Holkar that it was the saving power of the rail which had induced him to invite the Government of India to introduce it within the Nizam's territory. He gave an instance which had occurred to himself. Anticipating a dearth of food, he made a large purchase of grain for transport; but· before this could be effected the country had become impassable, and the store rotted, and those for whom it had been provided starved. Salar Jung resolved that, if money could supply an iron way, such a calamity should not recur."

Anyone who compares the arrangements made by the Native States of Central India during the famines

of 1896-97 and 1899-1900 with what occurred in
1868-70, cannot fail to be struck with the advance
made in the thirty years. In the famines of 1896-97
and 1899-1900, Maharaja Sir Madho Rao Scindia
spent upwards of 38 lakhs of rupees (over £250,000)
in direct relief, besides placing 24 lakhs of rupees at
the disposal of the Agent to the Governor-General
for loans on easy terms to neighbouring States,
which found it difficult to bear the strain of a liberal
relief policy. In the year 1896-97 the Maharaja also
remitted arrears of revenue amounting to over 74
lakhs of rupees, of which 60 lakhs were remitted in
commemoration of the Diamond Jubilee, and the
balance on account of famine. In 1869 the States
of Bundelkhand were largely dependent for relief
upon famine works in British India. In 1900 they
spent more than 20 lakhs on famine labour ; throughout Central India the famine relief code of the
Government of India was not only accepted, but
honestly worked up to by the Darbars.

In 1871, prefacing his annual report for the past
year, Daly said :—

"The Administration Reports of Native States
must of necessity widely differ from those which
tell of the workings of British rule. Lieutenant-
Governors and Chief Commissioners lay bare the
state of a province. Defects of law, acts of officials,
high and low, are discussed with a freedom all our
own, and utterly foreign to the comprehension of
chiefs and Darbar officials. A British Political Agent,
save in the special case of a State under temporary
management, has no administrative power. He can
only report a description of life and rule in States in
which he has no executive charge, and in few of
which is there any other law than custom—and that
subject to the caprice of the Chief. The Political
Agent's control is founded on his own personal influ-

T

ence, and the traditional sway of the British Government: except, of course, where marked oppression or disturbance call for the intervention of the Imperial Government. It is only within the last few years that Government, by publishing the annual reports of Political Agents, has kept the public abreast of the current. On the whole the effect has been undoubtedly good. In Scindia's words, 'a lifting up of the purdah (veil) with which Government has hitherto shrouded Native States may startle the public, and disclose things little contemplated'; but it has let in wholesome light and air. While there are rulers who almost resent discussion about their affairs, and affirm that we are bound to be deaf to any wails which arise, there is not one who does not in a measure temper his acts accordingly; and some there are who yearn for honest fame with the public. The unreserved publication of all that a Political Agent to a native court may write of a despotic rule, alien in principle and practice to our own theories, would be as unwarranted and injurious to society as the publication of private correspondence by the Post Office: but frank discussion, in good faith, of things as they are will win and hold its way in the East as well as elsewhere. When Chiefs understand that we have no ulterior motive to serve, that we seek neither land nor subjects, the free ventilation which publicity gives will not fail of beneficial results."

As to the position of the Chiefs, Daly wrote :—

"The ruler himself makes, and at pleasure administers, the law, of which there is no written code, and which is wholly undefined, though in practice justice is ordinarily meted out according to the Shastras, or custom and precedent." This he qualified on another occasion by observing :—"Written laws are of less importance in Native States than the outside world would suppose; their mere absence is no cause of confusion, and their existence is no check upon a despotic Chief whose fiat in all matters is the very essence of his rule. With the most conservative people in the world, usages and traditions form a code from which deviation is rare."

Of the two Mahratta Houses of Scindia and Holkar, he gave this brief summary :—

"The most important in the Agency, in wealth, power, and subjects, the States of Gwalior and Indore have grown strong under British protection since Malcolm's settlement of 1818. Scindia rules over territory in area about the size of Ireland, with a population of 2¾ millions and a revenue of upwards of 1 million. He is free from debt, and has a large cash reserve which is swelling : for his expenditure falls short of his income by probably 30 per cent. His revenue is elastic : for in Dinkar Rao's great settlement of Malwa, which Scindia maintains, the ryots are prosperous ; and in this respect contrast markedly with Holkar's, who are tottering and starving under pressure.

"Scindia's possessions in Malwa form the largest and richest portion of the province, and yield him a revenue of 40 lakhs. But this does not represent half their capacity. There is want of population, and scores of miles are still waste. It is pleasant to note a growing tendency in Scindia to treat his Rajput subjects in Malwa with forbearance. Holkar's example of the reverse has had, at any rate, this effect. Scindia took alarm at the disquietude excited by Holkar's demands for title-deeds from thakurs and zamindars, whose forefathers gave their names to villages before a Mahratta lance was seen above the Vindhyas, and has ordered that no new demands shall be made on thakurs. 'I will have no such cry against me as the country is ringing with against Holkar.'"

These extracts from his first annual reports will suffice to show the spirit in which Daly buckled to his work in Central India. He possessed an extensive knowledge of the history of India generally, and of the States of Malwa in particular. He had a clear and precise conception of Indian character ; and, above all, he possessed a perfect temper, a buoyant good nature, and the faculty of impressing his own high spirits and *bonhomie* upon those with whom he was brought into contact. Personal influence was the keynote of his success; and he avoided most sedulously the system of official correspondence so irksome to native Darbars. If anything serious had to be said, or if any transaction of importance had to be conducted, he would not hesitate to undertake at any season of the year a journey of 400 miles to Gwalior, travelling in the mail-cart, which was the only means of conveyance. There he would discuss matters personally with the Maharaja Scindia, who, under Daly's genial influence, soon cast off the reticence and isolation which for many years had marked his relations with political officers. It is not too much to say that Daly not only succeeded in gaining Scindia's confidence, but, by bringing him out of himself and stimulating his better nature, recovered for him many friendships which he had lost, and restored him to good terms with the officers of the British army serving near his capital. In like manner, by frequent visits to different parts of the Agency, Daly made personal friendships with rulers of various capacities and different characters; and was thus enabled to persuade them to undertake reforms, and to promote the benefits of their people, without resorting to official correspondence or political pressure. To the Rajput thakurs of Central India, Daly always extended especial consideration. "Amongst them," he wrote, "are men of the bluest blood of the Rajputs, relatives of the Rana * (of

* "The Princes of Mewar are styled Ranas, and are the elder branch of the Souryavansi, or Children of the Sun. . . . The Hindu tribes yield unanimous suffrage to the Prince of Mewar as the

Udaipur), whose lands have been in the undisputed possession of their families for many centuries, although the district was often the shuttlecock of conquest."

Daly's great test in estimating the value and the character of every ruler within his political charge was the conduct of the Chief during the trying time of the Mutiny. Throughout his career in Central India he missed no opportunity of drawing attention to loyalty and good services rendered during 1857-58. He made it his habitual practice to bring to favourable notice those Chiefs, or their descendants, who had stood firm at a time when the whole country was ablaze. It was on these grounds, more than for any other reason, that he specially respected Maharaja Jayaji Rao Scindia. He recalled to mind the fact that, when the Gwalior Contingent mutinied, when his own troops had broken out and were joined by the mutineers, and when the Rani of Jhansi was actually knocking at his gates and demanding his assistance in fighting the British, Scindia, with a bare handful of followers, left his capital, rode from Gwalior to Agra, placed himself at the disposal of the officer commanding the Fort, and remained with our troops until Sir Hugh Rose's forces recaptured the Gwalior fortress and restored order in Scindia's capital. In the Maharaja and his able Dewan, Raja Sir Dinkar Rao, Daly always showed the greatest confidence. It is well-known

legitimate heir to the throne of Rama, and style him 'Hinduar Sooraj,' or 'Sun of the Hindus.' He is universally allowed to be the first of the thirty-six royal tribes, nor has a doubt ever been raised respecting the purity of his descent." From *Annals and Antiquities of Rajasthan*, by Lieut.-Col. James Tod (original edition of 1829), vol. i., p. 214.

that on one occasion, at the festival of *Sankarant*, Scindia, in recognition of Daly's warm friendship, went through the form of exchanging head-dresses and binding the wrist thread, in order to prove that he had accepted him into the bonds of brotherhood. And from that date, throughout the years of his residence in Central India, Daly never failed to address the Maharaja Scindia in terms of brotherly affection, and invariably signed himself, in correspondence with him, as "your friend and brother."

Among the Chiefs in Bundelkhand, Daly, acting on the same principle, always upheld the Maharajas of Panna,* Chirkhari,† and Orchha, on account of their loyal and praiseworthy conduct during the Mutiny. In 1869, when he was first acting as Agent to the Governor-General, it fell to his lot to record the death in the previous October of the Secunder Begam of Bhopal. This he did in the following terms :—

"Perhaps in no Native State have the relations with the Government of India been accepted so

---

* Of Panna he wrote in 1871 : "This is a model State, and was made so by the late Maharaja Nirpat Singh, whose death last year called forth the regrets of his people and of the Government of India. When Nirpat Singh succeeded in 1849, Panna was in utter darkness and misrule ; his first step was to abolish *sati*. After ruling twenty-one years he left Panna not only free from disorder and discontent-ment, but conspicuous for the reverse. There was no eye-wash about what he did ; his State in the wilds of Bundelkhand was rarely visited by Englishmen and little known. Aided by an honest minister, he worked out reforms in every part of the Administration. Bundela thakurs and zamindars (landholders), unaccustomed to such a rule, held their Chief in much reverence."

† "The bearing of this State during the Mutiny will long secure that warm sympathy from Englishmen, which Lord Canning in the Cawnpore Darbar proclaimed its due." (From Daly's annual report for 1870-71.)

cordially and firmly as in Bhopal. In the darkest hours of mutiny, with disaffection at her side, nothing turned the Secunder Begam from her fidelity and allegiance. She possessed rare energy of character and capacity for government, and with all her energy and capacity she was true to the British rule. It was her pride to be known as the faithful feudatory of the Queen of England; and almost her last breath was in prayer for the happiness of Her Majesty, her family, and Government. Her Highness's only daughter and successor, the Shah Jehan Begam, has inherited her mother's spirit of loyalty, and has an ardent desire to emulate her fame as a ruler."

The terrible experiences of 1868-69, following as they did on similar experience in Western Malwa, brought closely home to Daly the urgent need for improved communications in Central India. Of the condition in which he found things, a few extracts from his reports will tell. In 1868 he wrote from Gwalior :—

"I am not aware of any work which can be called public being in hand at the cost of the Darbar, nor of there being a mile of metalled road throughout the interior. The fair-weather tracks are of the rudest. There are no roads in Malwa or Esaghar, and the Maharaja is aware that Ujjain, once so rich and prosperous, is daily crumbling away from being cut off from other cities and the main road; and that Esaghar is very desolate. It is quite on the cards that, with one of Scindia's capacity and temperament, Gwalior may one day be as conspicuous in the prosecution of public works as it is now for the absence of them."

In 1869, reviewing the state of the province as Agent to the Governor-General, he wrote :—

"Malwa is without roads; except on the 'gun road,' as the natives call the trunk road, now under within a day's drive of the Great Indian Peninsula Railway. Her Highness has also promised to complete a road to the west, which will link her grain-producing districts with the rail at Ujjain and Indore. The effect of railways on the comfort of the people in Malwa is not to be computed."

In 1878 Daly was able to report that there were 1400 miles of road completed, or under construction by the Public Works Department in Central India, of which only 160 were still unmetalled. In short, he was the *first* to promote railways in Native States, and to induce Chiefs to expend large sums on lines running through their territories. The Government of India, in addressing the Secretary of State in 1878, said :—

"The system of constructing Imperial Public Works in Native States under the Central India Agency with funds supplied in whole or in part by the Chiefs themselves, without interest during the period of construction, was mainly inaugurated by General Daly."

During 1870 and 1871 the affairs of Central India proceeded quietly and without much that is worthy of mark. The annual reports for those years record a general recovery from the famine, and steady progress in the administration of several States. In February 1872, the assassination of Lord Mayo thrilled India with indignation and sorrow.

"His prestige with the Chiefs and Princes of India," wrote Daly, "stood romantically high. He had made their position and personal interests his special study. Hardly any predecessor had seen so much of India, and so carefully marked the characteristics of its native rulers. There was that in his presence and manner which touched Asiatics, and

BHOPAL, FROM THE OLD FORT.

[To face p. 208.

charmed those who came in contact with him, while his character for earnestness commended itself to all. The Chiefs of India mourned for Lord Mayo as for a friend. 'I have made a friend and lost him,' was Scindia's speech."

Scindia's official Gazette of the 18th February contained the following announcement (translated *verbatim* from the vernacular):—

"With the greatest grief and sorrow we announce a heart-rending catastrophe, alas! how lamentable! His Excellency Earl Mayo, K.T., G.M.S.I., Viceroy and Governor-General of India, has suddenly left this transitory scene for the eternal abode, and we his humble admirers are fettered with the chain of grief and desolation. On hearing of this dreadful occurrence His Highness the Maharaja was thrown into grief and sorrow immeasurable. On the 15th and 16th all public offices and bazaars were closed. The striking of gongs, the ringing of bells, and all sounds of joy were stopped: and on each day 49 minute guns were fired by the Darbar artillery. In truth the mourning caused at Gwalior by this life-gnawing occurrence, and the scar of grief and sorrow left on the heart, defy the powers of description. The pen itself weeps bitterly, alas! how unfortunate! With fond expectation His Highness was making arrangements for a camp of exercise to be held near Gwalior; all supplies had been collected there; and from 50 to 60 thousand rupees had been spent: with a stroke of the pen all this has been stopped in consequence of the shock, the great grief, and the sorrow caused to His Highness by the appalling intelligence."

Scindia's grief was reflected in every State in Central India; and Daly received many proofs of the sympathy and sorrow of the ruling Chiefs.

It was in this year (1872) that the affairs of the Rewa State forced themselves into notice. For a long time the Maharaja Raghuraj Singh had failed to pay due attention to his administration. The thakurs, who should have been subordinate to their Chief, held an independent sway, collected excise and other revenue for their own benefit, harboured offenders, and frequently broke out into open revolt. There was no form of government; and the resources of the State were being gradually dissipated. With all his weaknesses and shortcomings the Maharaja of Rewa was a delightful personage. Of enormous frame and great personal courage, he delighted in field-sports, and was perhaps the greatest tiger-slayer of his age. He had a slight smattering of English which he was always anxious to parade; and he was of that cheerful and happy disposition which sets at naught all cares and troubles, and heeds nothing but the pleasures of the present moment. He wasted his money as much in appeasing the wrath of the Brahmans as in providing for his own special delights and absurdities. It is said that during his lifetime the Maharaja was weighed twice against gold, and five times against silver for the benefit of the priests at Allahabad, to whom he also presented such elephants belonging to his State as had shown the white feather during his shooting excursions. His ideas of morality were crude, and he generally referred to any breach of moral discipline by saying: "This, I think, is against your ten orders" the (Commandments).

Daly took special pleasure in the Maharaja, and was always willing to meet him more than half-way in the discussion of his quaint ideas regarding morals, religion, and the best means of administering his State for the benefit of his people. But occasionally it became necessary to speak seriously to His Highness.

In one particular instance Daly was compelled to show the Maharaja some very incriminating papers which bore his signature. The Maharaja affected to be unable to read his own handwriting, and sent for various pairs of spectacles, one after another, with the obvious intention of gaining time. At length, after satisfying himself in this respect, he read the papers out aloud before the Governor-General's Agent; then put them solemnly aside, and said, "This is a very sad case of forgery. I will issue warrant : the man's hand must be cut off."

During each of his tours in this part of the Agency, Daly spent many days in the Rewa State, where he wrote :—

"I was always received by the Maharaja with a display of barbaric splendour hardly to be seen in any other State in Rajputana or Central India. His Highness's Darbar represented a scene of brocade, *kinkhab*, gold, and jewels, which would require the flowery language of Persia and a Persian pen to describe. His palace was worthy of the scene; for its walls and roofs were heavy with ornamentations reflected in scores of mirrors; no less than 200 feudatory barons of Rewa were gathered round their Chief, each clothed in a costly costume, or in ancient armour with breast-plate and buckler, and all adorned with jewels and gold and silver ornaments. The whole scene was one of magnificent Eastern splendour ;—and the town of Rewa, in the midst of which the palace stands, and where this collection of feudatories assembled, is a miserable collection of hovels."

Eventually the Maharaja represented his inability to manage his affairs himself, and requested that a political agent might be appointed to conduct the administration. This change was introduced in 1873, and was attended with the best results. The

Maharaja died in 1880,* having devoted the last few years of his life to the enjoyment of a life in the jungle and the destruction of many tigers.

"Whatever were his failings as a ruler," wrote Daly, "the late Maharaja's benevolent character, his charitable tendencies, and his love of display and hospitality, will long be remembered among his people, by whom he was beloved and reverenced. During a long minority there is every hope that the prosperity of Rewa will be re-established, and that by careful management the resources of the State will be developed."

The young Maharaja was a child of four at his father's death. When he became ruler of the State in 1894, the administration had, for over twenty years, been under the careful control of a succession of able political officers, with results fully commensurate with the hopes that Daly had expressed.

The condition of the Malwa opium trade was a matter that received Daly's early attention. Owing largely to the uncertainty of delivery consequent on

* After the death of the Maharaja, one of the State officials disclosed to the Political Agent the existence of a secret walled-up vault, in which were found two brass vessels containing gold pieces. Among these were fifteen or twenty coins which appeared to be curious, and which were submitted for examination to the late General Sir Alexander Cunningham, then Head of the Archæological Department of the Government of India. He reported that most of the coins were Indo-Scythic, of a more or less familar type, but that one was very rare, being the only specimen which he had ever come across. (The coins were subsequently valued, and General Cunningham was permitted to purchase the rare one for his private collection. It is believed to have been lost in the wreck of the P. and O. s.s. *Tasmania* in 1887). Among the other coins were one of Pertinax, Emperor of Rome from the 31st December 192 to the 28th March 193, and one of Elagabalus, Emperor of Rome from 218 to 222. The latter bore on the obverse the stamped head of an Emperor, with the words *Imp. Antoninus Pius Aug.* ("for he had assumed and polluted that respectable title," Gibbon) ; and on the reverse the words *Adventus Augusti.*

the absence of roads, there was much speculation, and the trade was in an unhealthy state. The general position was thus summed up in one of his first reports :—

"The standard weight of a chest of opium is 141½ lbs., on which an export duty is levied on behalf of the Government of India at the scales. No other opium than that which is intended for export pays duty to Government, or is brought for weighment. We have no concern with its growth, sale, or transport. Our connection with opium grown in Native States begins and ends at the scales : the ryot (peasant) sells as suits his own interest to the China merchant or in his own market; so far it is a free trade. After weighment the trader receives a pass for his chests, and is then free to despatch them to Bombay, how and when he likes."

Up to this time there had been a single Agency, at Indore, for the grant of passes and the collection of revenue; Daly established sub-agencies at Ratlam, Dhar, Bhopal, Mandesor, and also at Udaipur in Rajputana.

"States much covet the presence of Government scales," he wrote; "wherever the opium trade flourishes, there must be merchants of capital, and, as the natives of Malwa say, opium imparts the fragrance of prosperity wherever it has a recognised mart.
"The habit of opium-eating in Rajputana and Central India is now almost universal. It is the stirrup-cup of the Rajput,* and no visitor comes or goes without a draught of the ' Kossumbah ' :—opium

* See, for instance, in chap. xxix., vol. i., of Tod's *Annals and Antiquities of Rajast'han*, the account of how the chivalry of Marwar drank opium together for the last time before their final desperate charge at Mairta upon Scindia's troops under De Boigne. [The notes in the same chapter contain interesting references to De Boigne's career.]

in a liquid form, spiced. Taken moderately, it can hardly be detrimental to health."

In 1874 he reported :—

"A belief is prevalent that the opium revenue is something very precarious; a sort of will-o'-the-wisp, not to be handled and not to be depended upon. A review of its course will show how fallacious this idea is. Variations there are from year to year, due to the peculiarities of the season; but side by side with wheat, hop, and indigo, this variation is slight. Before the repeal of the Corn Laws in England, the price of bread was much more dependent on the weather than opium is in Malwa. Sir John Malcolm remarked, fifty years ago, that though crops in Malwa have been damaged by too much or too little rain, that though they have suffered from biting winds and frosts, the climate is generally so mild and the soil always so rich, with water at command from the many rivers and streams, that there is no record of a complete failure : pressure for food, except from the consequences of war and plunder, was unknown.

"Since 1863 the export duty per chest fixed by the Government of India has not varied, consequently the returns during that period afford complete information on the fluctuations of the trade. These show that this trade, like every other, depends for success on the facilities it enjoys. Within the last thirty years the exports have trebled. In 1850 there was but one place in Malwa to which the merchant could bring his opium for weighment if he desired to export it. There was no made road to Bombay, and thence to China sailing-ships from time to time were irregular in departure. Later, things improved. Roads were growing towards Bombay, monthly steamers had taken the place of the China clippers, and other facilities in like manner had opened. During the last ten years the progress in communications has been marked. The Great Indian Peninsula Railway, step by step, has made its way, and now passes within 80 miles of Indore. The telegraph wire is at every business mart in Malwa, bringing cultivators knowledge which twenty years ago was confined to

HINDOO RAO'S HOUSE AND SIRMOOR BATTALION, 1857.

[Photo Bourne & Sheppard.

[To face p. 304.

merchants and exporters.   Steamships sail from Bombay on fixed dates throughout the year.   These are the things which have led to the development —the steady development—of the opium trade, on which Chiefs and people in Central India depend for their prosperity.

"Prices have been so steadily falling for some years that the great merchants have lost heavily ; and though they recoup themselves to a considerable extent in the exchange, many a big firm has been shaken.   Time bargains occupy as much attention as *bona fide* trade.   It is calculated that these trans-actions reach two millions sterling in the year.

"The flavour and delicacy of opium excite as much attention in the East as do these qualities in the wines of France and Spain in Europe.   A con-noisseur will tell at a glance whether the drug, in its earthen vessel, is the produce of the poppy grown at Mandesor or Ratlam.   The flavour of the poppy juice, like that of the grape, depends on the soil.   Its manu-facture into cakes for packing takes place at a few cities which are more or less famous on that account. It is only opium of the best quality which is fit for the China market.   The high duty prevents the export of any inferior drug, and so preserves the prestige of Malwa in the market.   China takes the new and fresh opium, which is used in a liquid form.   In India, amongst the wealthy, old opium is valued as much as old port at home, and for the same qualities— mellowness and softness.   Opium of a good season and vintage, twenty or twenty-five years old, com-mands a fabulous price, and is only to be had in the houses of the rich.

"Many a *bigah** of the best land is sub-let at prices from Rs. 40 to Rs. 60.   Malcolm estimated the

---

* "The quantity contained in a *bigah*," Daly noted, "was a matter of enquiry before the Committee of the House of Commons on Indian affairs.   A bigah consists of a jarib of 100 hands, but a hand has nothing definite in length.   The length of the hand in the olden days was somewhat significant of the relative strength of Chief and ryot ; where the people held their own it was large, and where the reverse was the case it was small.   In the North-Western Provinces, in common parlance, three bigahs go to an acre."

land-tax or rental of opium lands in Malwa in his day at Rs. 520,000. It is now treble that sum.

"The land-tax of Malwa is unequalled in India, and it is felt that this mainly depends upon the continuance of the opium trade. However this may be, the resources of Malwa are but very partially developed: the people have never recovered altogether from the anarchy which preceded the British supremacy; cities which were once populous and prosperous are still little more than hamlets; and much land is waste. The introduction of railways, now at hand, will, in a few years, work greater changes than those which have been chronicled since Malcolm's time."

All the lines indicated by Daly have been carried out, and the chief towns of Malwa are now in direct railway communication with each other, and with the railway systems to the north and south of Central India.

The autumn of 1875 was famous in Central India on account of the visit of Lord Northbrook, who, accompanied by the Foreign Secretary (Sir Charles, then Mr. Aitchison) and a small staff, passed through Malwa to Rajputana in November.

"His Excellency," wrote Daly, "was the first Viceroy to visit Indore and Malwa. His reception by the Chiefs was most cordial, and the difficulties of the journey and the roughness of the roads only added to the gratification which all felt at seeing a Viceroy who had taken so much trouble to visit them. The Maharaja Holkar gave a grand banquet and illuminated Indore. Lord Northbrook passed on through Dhar, Ratlam, Jaora, and the old city of Mandesor to Neemuch."

This journey was not performed without considerable difficulty, as between Mhow and Dhar—a distance of 40 miles—and again between Dhar and Ratlam—another stage of 50 miles—there were at that time no made roads. The Viceroy was conveyed in a small carriage drawn by troop-horses of the Royal Horse Artillery from Mhow. The Agent to the Governor-General and his staff rode the whole distance, and acted as a volunteer escort to His Excellency; and at each place visited by Lord Northbrook he was met by the political officer of the district, and escorted by a detachment of the Centra India Horse.

"His Excellency was entertained," continued Daly's report, "by the Rajas of Dhar and Ratlam, and by the Nawab of Jaora, at their capitals, in a spirit of the greatest hospitality. Each Chief was anxious that the schools and places of note should be visited by the Viceroy. Ratlam and Jaora have schools which would do credit to any city in British India. And Lord Northbrook gave the cause of education a firm position in Malwa by the interest he everywhere evinced in it. Every Chief and every Thakur pressed forward to pay his duty to the Viceroy."

In education Daly had from the first manifested a most active interest. He instituted the Residency College at Indore, and paid close attention to its work and progress. He took a leading part in the discussion which resulted in the foundation of the Mayo College at Ajmer; it was upon his representations that the Government of India gave their support to the movement of the Chiefs of Bundelkhand who subscribed to found a Rajkumar College at Nowgong in memory of Lord Mayo; and there is hardly a State in Central India which does not point with pride to schools and colleges that owe their origin to his initiative. After his tour in Central India, Lord Northbrook acknowledged in the most handsome manner the efforts which Daly had made and the success which had attended them, and His Excellency gave effect to an undertaking which he had passed while in Central India, whereby the appointment of a British educational officer as Principal of the Residency College at Indore was sanctioned at the expense of Government. This post was first held by Mr Aberigh Mackay, afterwards so well known under his *nom de plume* of Ali Baba, in whose hands the institution made very satisfactory progress. The Maharaja Holkar's sons, Scindia's son Bulwant Rao, the Chiefs of Dewas, Ratlam, Jaora, and Sailana, and the Thakur of Bagli, all attended, and many of the smaller Thakurs sent their relatives.

In 1875-76 the Chiefs of Central India took part in the ceremonials consequent on the visit of His Royal Highness the Prince of Wales. Several, including the Maharaja Scindia, went to Calcutta to assist at the reception of His Royal Highness. The Prince visited Gwalior at the end of January 1876, and spent three days in Scindia's capital.

The Phul Bagh Palace was assigned for the accommodation of the Prince. It stands in an extensive pleasure-ground almost under the south-east bastion of the fortress of Gwalior, and on the site of the building which was erected in 1832 for the reception and entertainment of Lord William Bentinck, then Governor-General of India. It is a handsome double-storied structure in the Italian style of architecture, built of stone on massive arches and buttresses, and enclosing a quadrangle 107 yards square, which is prettily laid out as an English flower-garden, with handsome fountains, statues, and pillars, and English annuals in full bloom. It cost the Maharaja

Scindia not less than 18 lakhs of rupees. When His Highness decided on placing this palace at the disposal of his Royal guest, the building was in the hands of the workmen: it was covered with scaffolding, and the ground strewed with building material. It was feared at one time that it would be impossible to have the palace ready before His Royal Highness's arrival. But the patient energy of the architect, Major Sir Michael Filose, and the unremitting labour of 7000 workmen triumphed, and the palace and its grounds were available on the date fixed.

His Royal Highness drove from Agra, 76 miles; the road was watered for the entire distance. Daly sent the following description of the visit to the Viceroy (Lord Northbrook) :—

"The journey was accomplished pleasantly. The Prince and a suite of twenty-eight left Agra at 8.30: breakfast at Dholpur, thirty-four miles. I had arranged with the Prince and with General Browne * that Scindia, attended by his Dewan only, with the Political Agent and General commanding the district, should be in waiting at the old Residency about five miles from Gwalior. Scindia thus met us at 5 P.M. The Prince took His Highness into his own carriage, in which also were the Duke of Sutherland and myself.

"The Maharaja's regular troops lined the road for a couple of miles, placed at intervals, after which came the Mahratta Horsemen, etc. At Dowlat Rao Scindia's palace, the elephants were in waiting to carry the suite and Sardars in procession. The Prince and Scindia sat on the same golden howdah, with all the emblems of royalty; I sat or stood behind to interpret.

"The passage through the streets to the new palace was magnificent; a mass of people everywhere;

* The late General Sir Samuel Browne, V.C., G.C.B., K.C.S.I.

windows, verandahs, housetops, crammed. A column of Scindia's State followers headed the elephants, occupying half-a-mile in length, behind came the Sardars and English guests and officers. Elephants two abreast, one bearing Sardars, the other Englishmen. The palace was brilliant with illuminations. I will not attempt any description of the finest building in India. Scindia conducted the Prince to the hall, and after the royal suite were introduced to His Highness by the Prince, Scindia presented his Sardars (ten or so). Itr and Pan followed, and Scindia took His Royal Highness to the apartments prepared for him, and thus that day's ceremonies concluded.

"On the morning of the 1st, at eight, the Prince rode to witness Scindia handle troops. Scindia received His Royal Highness with a royal salute. Scindia then marched past at the head of his troops, saluting the Prince. The force on parade consisted of about six thousand cavalry and infantry, two bullock, and two horse batteries. All looked clean and well, and moved *steadily*. The appearance of the troops has wonderfully improved within the last few years. After the march past, Scindia divided his forces, putting half to defend a village which he attacked in person. The Prince was so pleased that he remained on the ground till Scindia pronounced the action over—at noon!

"At 6 P.M. the Prince paid the return visit. The streets were crammed; there was scarcely standing room; everybody striving to catch sight of the Prince; all joyous and orderly. Scindia received His Royal Highness at the carriage. The Darbar hall was full; about forty Sardars were presented by Scindia himself, after which the Maharaja made a short speech, prefacing it by saying to me, 'I will say a few words. Translate sentence by sentence that all may be understood.' . . . 'No language can express the gratitude I feel for the honour the Prince has conferred upon me in thus visiting Gwalior. What can I say? The fame of this day will never die out. I have nothing to offer worthy of the Prince's notice, or of the occasion. I know that it was consideration for me which induced His Royal Highness, despite dust and heat, to remain watching my parade * this morning. I am an uneducated man, knowing little of books, and nothing of the English language. What I did with my troops this morning is an instance, and nothing more, of what may be learnt by observation and labour. When the Prince sees the Queen, beg him to tell her that with hands clasped I am her faithful servant for ever.'

"The foregoing is pretty nearly a translation of the words uttered with strong emotion and glistening eyes. His Royal Highness replied admirably both in *manner* and language. After this, stepping down from the little *dais* on which the chairs of the Prince and himself were placed, Scindia gave His Royal Highness Itr and Pan. Scindia, desirous of doing special honour to his English guests on this occasion, had our chairs in horse-shoe shape on either side of the Prince and himself. The Sardars occupying the whole of the hall below. Major Bannerman and Hope were on the spot with Scindia arranging seats before the Prince arrived.

"The presents were now shown. Arms—matchlock, sword, shield, etc., with two suits of clothing as worn by himself.

"Then came a splendid necklace for the Princess. Pearls 2070, emeralds 3, diamonds (flat) 306, with many small rubies. It can hardly be called a necklace. It is as large as a 'Har' (long garland) of flowers. The pearls are not large but sized, and the diamonds with enamel form knots at an interval of six or eight inches. As a whole, it is the most elegant piece of jewellry conceivable. The Prince was charmed with the offering. Then followed a necklace, presented for the Queen; this was smaller in quantity, pearls large, diamonds large, flat. The

---

* The Maharaja issued the following general order to his army :—

"The march past and the movements on the 1st instant were approved of by Field-Marshal His Royal Highness the Prince of Wales, who highly commended the commanding officers. His Highness the Maharaja has much pleasure in communicating this to commanding officers, in order that they may keep it in joyful recollection, and may continue to discharge their duties in an efficient manner, that the same may redound to their credit and to that of the force."

number, etc., I cannot just now put my hands upon. In money value, Scindia said, there was little difference between them. I fancy that for the Princess may be worth £6000. The Duke of Sutherland put it higher.

"At the banquet that evening Scindia came in after dinner, as at Bombay, with ten of his Sardars. His Highness proposed the Queen's health, and then that of the Prince, reiterating much that he had said in the Darbar. His Royal Highness replied, and very prettily proposed Scindia's health. Thus the ceremonies of that day closed.

"The Prince's departure was fixed for 10.30 the following morning (2nd February). Scindia came to the palace at nine to sit for his sketch. The Prince at 10.15 came into the room in which Hall was sketching him. Scindia brightened up and went to the Prince, and taking his hand walked with him to the carriage. As the Prince took leave, 'I am sorry to see you go, and to think I shall see your face no more. I can hardly expect this. When at home, sometimes think of Scindia, and that all he has, his State and everything in it, is yours.'

"So the Prince's visit terminated. The return journey was easily accomplished. Luncheon at Dholpur, Agra at 6 P.M. Everything connected with the visit was a triumph. Scindia spared nothing; every arrangement was made by himself; his cordial desire was to treat the Prince in a princely way."

The Prince visited Indore in March 1876, just before leaving Bombay on return to England. Holkar, in the cordiality of his reception, was not behind his great Mahratta brother. Indore was illuminated; the streets were thronged; and the Maharaja was devoted to the comfort of his guest. His Royal Highness's attention to Holkar's sons much touched the Maharaja, who expressed an intention of sending one or both by and by to England to renew their expressions of duty and devotion.

Daly thus referred to the subject in his annual report :—

"The event of the year to India—the visit of His Royal Highness the Prince of Wales—specially stirred the hearts of the rulers and princes. Scindia in his palace standing before the Prince speaking burning words with an emotion which touched all who heard him ; Holkar proffering to take ship to Aden to bid His Royal Highness welcome. Chiefs of all ranks evinced the same feeling ; thakurs and men of all degrees and classes praying for standing ground that they might see and bow to the Queen's son, as he passed.

"The feeling displayed towards the Prince of Wales by the Chiefs and people of India is something which cannot be gauged by an Englishman, however broad his experience and thorough his knowledge of the East.

"Before the Prince's arrival in India I consulted with one of the greatest Chiefs as to the course to be adopted in respect of presents and offerings to His Royal Highness : whether it would be wise actually to interdict all offerings, seeing that it would be impossible for the Prince to make returns in any instance of commensurate value. We talked the matter over in all its bearings. My friend in this conversation—who is unsurpassed for astuteness, who is no spendthrift, who is something of a scholar and very much of a financier, not wholly given to sensational sentiments—was decided in his opinion. He said : 'This is an event without precedent. Do not attempt to shape it by anything which has gone before. For the first time during your rule in India, India is to be visited by the Sovereign ; for in the Queen's heir all will see their Sovereign. We, the Chiefs of India, owe it to ourselves to receive the Prince in a manner becoming to us. I could not meet His Royal Highness without an offering : and I cannot present a small offering. Advise Chiefs to present something in their possession—heirlooms, or curios ; and leave the rest to us.'

"This was the spirit which possessed the Chiefs

when laying their offerings before the Prince of Wales. The great rulers gave things of value either from antiquity, tradition, or rarity. No one was content who had not an opportunity to offer some treasured possession.

"Scindia showed me a sash or belt studded with 2070 pearls, and knotted with diamonds and rubies, and asked whether I thought 'that would be a fit offering to the Princess of Wales'; and then pointed to a necklace of large pearls, and said, "and that for the Queen? Her Majesty must not be forgotten.'"

A Chapter of the Star of India was held at Calcutta by His Royal Highness, and was attended by the Maharajas Scindia, Holkar, Rewa, and by the Begam of Bhopal—all of them Knights Grand Commanders of the Order. The Maharaja of Panna, Kashi Rao Dada (brother of Maharaja Holkar), and Ganpat Rao Kharké (Minister of Gwalior), were invested by His Royal Highness with the insignia of Knight Commander of the Star of India. The splendour of that assemblage has been fully described. It was the first occasion when Chiefs of Central India were gathered with their brother Chiefs of other provinces for such a function; they were deeply impressed by the ceremonial, and gratified by the gracious reception accorded to all alike by the Prince.

In the following cold weather occurred another event of great public interest — the Imperial Assemblage.

"The year 1876-77," wrote Daly, "will long be remembered in connection with the event round which the interests of so many were centred. For months before and after the 1st January the great Assemblage and the Proclamation of the assumption by Her Majesty the Queen of England of the title of Empress of India, Kaiser-i-Hind, were subjects for discussion of never-failing interest in the home of every Chief and every thakur throughout Malwa and Bundel-khand. The anxiety of all to be present on the occasion was real ; and it was not without special reason that a single native ruler, great or small, was absent from Delhi. The attendance, indeed, of some of the Chiefs was not effected without a straining of resources, but sacrifices were cheerfully made in the desire which stimulated all to do full honour to the proclamation which they were summoned to celebrate. From the seventy-one Native States comprising Central India, twenty-two Chiefs were present at the Imperial Assemblage, and thirty-six attended the local Darbars held at Indore, Sehore, Dhar, and Agar.

"The meeting of Chiefs and Princes from all parts of Hindustan gave rise to a cordiality in their relations which will long remain an important feature in the results of the Imperial Assemblage. There was an entire abandonment of those scruples regard-ing rank and precedence which have for so many years been the stumbling-block to intercourse. This barrier once broken, Chiefs who had known each other only by reputation, and whose associations were generally those of jealousy and distrust, conversed with friendliness and good humour. The feeling among all was satisfaction and pleasure at the arrange-ments made for their reception and comfort ; and gratitude for the marks of Her Majesty's consideration and grace which all received.

"The honours bestowed were such as would most readily stir the hearts of those upon whom they were conferred. In each case the wish nearest to the heart of the Chief was considered, and, where possible, met. Maharaja Scindia received the distinguished honour of enrolment in the Order of Knights Grand Commander of the Bath, and was at the same time created a General in Her Majesty's Army—an appointment which his love of the army and know-ledge of military matters taught him thoroughly to appreciate. He also received an additional salute of 2 guns. Maharaja Holkar received a similar addition to his salute, and must have felt that the desire of his heart had been sought for and fulfilled, when he learnt that, as an act of grace on the part of Her Majesty the Empress of India, the Government of India were prepared to reconsider the adjustment of the boundary between his territory and Khandesh. Scindia and Holkar were appointed Councillors to the Empress.

"The Begam of Bhopal was charmed with the recognition accorded to her husband, the Nawab Sadik Hussain, and the grant to him of a personal salute of 17 guns. The Maharajas of Rewa and Tehri—Chiefs respectively of the Baghel and Bundela clans—each received an increase of 2 guns to his salute. The Raja of Dhar was enrolled a Knight Commander of the Star of India. The services of the Minister of Jaora, Hazrut Nur Khan, were recognised by the bestowal on him of the C.S.I. Additions of 2 guns were made to the salutes of the Maharaja of Panna, and the Raja of Ratlam; and various tokens of recognition were bestowed upon other Chiefs who attended the Assemblage."

We have recently seen a gathering on more magnificent lines than those attempted at the Imperial Assemblage of 1877. In both cases Delhi was chosen for the ceremonial, and the Coronation Darbar of the 1st January 1903 was held on the same ground as the function of 1877. The arrangements in 1877 were not so complete as those of 1903, nor was the attendance, large as it was, anything like that of the later year. But the Imperial Assemblage was the first pageant of its kind: a new departure for a special and magnificent purpose, which was hailed by all the Chiefs of India as appropriate to the occasion, and as giving them an opportunity, separately and collectively, of testifying their loyalty to the Crown and welcoming their newly created Empress.

It is curious to note that in 1875 Dr J. P. Stratton, Political Agent in Bundelkhand, mentioned in his annual report the remarks of a native Chief on the subject of the title which Her Majesty the Queen, two years later, assumed. It was doubtless some newspaper article or extract of a democratic tendency which led the Chief, who knew English moderately well, to start this subject as he did. In the midst of general conversation he suddenly broke off and said: "There will never be a Republic in England. Will there? That will not be good." A half-laughing reply that "there was not much chance of that," seemed satisfactory to him. And then he went on to say: "Why does not the Queen take the title of Empress of India?" The answer naturally was that Her Majesty was in reality Empress already, whether she formally assumed the title or not. To which the Chief rejoined: "But why not? Why not take the title? It will be good. It will be good specially for the Chiefs of India." Dr Stratton adds, that it had not previously occurred to him to think of native Chiefs wishing for Her Majesty's assumption of that title, or even of their considering it at all: yet when the subject is entered into, the grounds for such views are not far to seek nor difficult to understand.

In his report for the year 1877-78, Daly writes :—

"There is an increasing tendency in the administration of Native States to conform to the general principles of Government in force in British India. The Native States of which Todd and Malcolm wrote exist no longer; the days of strife have passed away, and with them the tyranny and oppression which made life insecure and property the prize of the strong. All the great States are penetrated and swayed to some extent by public opinion; and even where this finds more expression on paper than in acts, the feeling is not less real. The people in Native States do not hesitate to speak of their grievances when pressure is severe. This sign of life is sure evidence of progress. It is well that we should bear in mind that the Native States of this period are in many respects what we make them, and by the continuance of the friendly support which the Government of India now liberally gives to all, they will strengthen in their foundations for good, and in feelings of allegiance to the Empire.

"Dr Stratton remarks on the difficulty of obtaining other than scanty information from which to frame annual reports of the progress made in Native States, and notes that it is only on one or two points of general interest that a Political officer is able to write with assurance. This is very true as regards each year's report: yet the retrospect which the Political Agent makes shows changes which can be wrought in a few years of careful supervision by the exercise of personal influence. When Dr Stratton assumed charge of the Bundelkhand Agency in 1861, the conditions of the Native States were far behind that of the present day. Public works were unknown, communications were few and rough, lawlessness and violence were everywhere rampant, while in many States, owing to bad management, revenue had diminished, and debts increased. There is no State in Bundelkhand which cannot show advantages gained by the friendly advice and support of the Political Agent. Living for nearly twenty years in their midst, and intimately acquainted with the wants and peculiarities of each of the States under his supervision, Dr Stratton has made the best use of his opportunities of working for their good. His efforts have been specially directed towards the improvement of communications and the freedom of traffic. With a valuable practical knowledge of engineering he has given advice in the construction of roads which are already of immense advantage to the Native States; and he has further promoted the cause of prosperity by persuading Chiefs to abolish duties on articles of trade: as a consequence, all the States of Bundelkhand are now as free and accessible to traders as many parts of British territory. In all the States, public buildings, jails, schools, and hospitals have been constructed and maintained; lawlessness has been repressed, and security established. Much remains to be done; but Dr Stratton may congratulate himself on the good which he has brought about, the effects of which will be lasting, and will give a stimulus to those States which are still behindhand to follow the example which they see in others.

"Change to eager eyes, viewing it from day to day, often appears slow amongst a people bound to caste and custom. It is only by looking back that we bring home to ourselves how far away the past is, and how steady has been progress in comfort and security."

The foregoing sketch of Central India under Daly's administration is, perhaps, sufficient to give some idea of the work then devolving upon the Agent to the Governor-General and of the manner in which Daly discharged it. It would be tedious to write in detail of each State. That the objects which Daly placed before himself when he took up his appointment in 1868 were sedulously kept in view, is shown by the following extract from his annual report for 1878-79, which was written when he expected to retire almost immediately. As a matter of fact, owing to the Afghan War, Daly remained in Central India, by the express wish of Lord Lytton, for eighteen months after that report was written, but he did not subsequently refer in direct terms to his general administration of the province.

"As this," he wrote in 1879, "is probably the last annual report that I shall have the honour to submit of the Central India Agency Administration, I propose to make a brief review of the changes that the past ten years, during which I have held the post of Agent to the Governor-General, have worked among the Native States under my charge. With regard to the interior economy of each State it is not necessary that I should write much. The Government of India is fully informed of such political events as have from time to time occurred, and it is sufficient to note that the relations between the Government and the Chiefs of Central India have been maintained in conformity with treaty and agreement, and that the integrity and independence of each State has been preserved.

"The chief incidents of each year have been touched upon in successive annual reports :—the drought and distress of 1868-69, when I first assumed charge of the Agency, followed by famine, disease, and death in the following year ; the efforts made by the Chiefs of Malwa and Bundelkhand to relieve suffering in their States ; then the sorrow which the assassination of Lord Mayo awakened among all classes ; the sympathy that watched the dangerous illness of His Royal Highness the Prince of Wales ; next, the visit of the Duke of Edinburgh ; the Darbars held at Calcutta, Agra, Jubbulpore, Bombay, and Barwai ; Lord Northbrook's tour through Malwa ; afterwards, the arrival of the Prince of Wales in Calcutta, where Chiefs who had never seen each other's faces, and whose ancestors had never met except in battle, pressed in a friendly crowd to bid him welcome ; and his visits to Gwalior and Indore ; the Imperial Assemblage at Delhi, the honours and rewards there bestowed ; the Chapters of the Star of India, and the investiture of the Maharaja Scindia with the dignity of a G.C.B., of the Begam Bhopal with the Orders of G.C.S.I. and of the Imperial Crown. These are passages in the history of Central India during the past ten years.

"I recall, too, with pleasure my annual tours. Visiting Bundelkhand and Malwa alternately, I have had opportunities, such as fall to the lot of few, of making myself acquainted with the people, the country, the traditions, and the customs of each State in Central India. There is not a district or capital I have not visited, not a fortress or stronghold I have not seen ; the rugged passes, the lakes and hills of Bundelkhand ; the alternate jungle and poppy-field of Malwa—are all familiar to me, and I take with me the pleasant remembrance of friendship formed by years of intercourse and personal knowledge with many a Chief, and with nobles and gentlemen, members of their Darbars; and with subjects of their States. But I wish to allude more particularly to the progress which the past decade has brought about in two special matters — I mean with regard to the opening up of the country, and education.

"Ten years ago, the only road worthy of the name in Central India was the Agra and Bombay road, which passes through Gwalior, Goona, and Biaura to Indore, thence by Mhow and Manpur down the southern slopes of the Vindhyas, with a ferry across the Narbudda, and so on by Scindwa and Khargaon into Khandesh. This road bore the traffic which passed through Malwa between Northern and Southern India, and was then, as it always will be, an important military road; but of internal communication there was nothing. The black cotton soil of Malwa was crossed only by country-tracks, rough and difficult at all times, and impassable in the rains. Grain, which sold at Bhilsa and about Bhopal at 50 seers for the rupee, was, from the impossibility of carriage, selling at 8 or 10 seers at Indore, distant barely 100 miles. Opium, which is the trade and wealth of Malwa, with difficulty found its way over the heavy country roads to Indore. In Bundelkhand, things were almost worse : the want of roads and communications was hampering the prospects of the country and preventing trade. There was no passage across the *ghâts*, no means of communication between the East India Railway at Sutna and the garrison of Nowgong, 100 miles away. The railway had not been opened beyond Khandwa, on the Great Indian Peninsula line, and the break between Khandwa and Jubbulpore made it necessary for passengers and traffic passing up country either to travel from Nagpore across country to Jubbulpore, or to go up by the Bombay and Agra road through Indore, leaving the rail at Khandwa.

"My efforts were directed from the first to remedy these defects, and it is due to the liberality and confidence with which the views of Government were met by the Chiefs of Central India that we can now point to the improvements that have taken place. Maharaja Holkar was the first to tender a loan for railway construction through his territory. The million of money he placed at disposal, at 4½ per cent., is now represented by the Holkar State Railway, which connects Indore with the Great Indian Peninsula Rail at Khandwa. This line was difficult of construction, owing to the heavy work in alternately climbing and piercing the Vindhya range and in bridging the great Narbudda near Barwai; but, the work completed, the line is now answering all purposes, and both bridge and *ghât* are monuments of engineering skill. Maharaja Scindia was not slow to follow the example set him. He placed at the disposal of Government altogether a million and a half of money for railways in his territory; the broad-gauge line, connecting Gwalior with Agra, is now nearing completion, while the Scindia Neemuch State Railway carries goods and passengers daily from Indore to the banks of the Sipra, and awaits but a bridge to penetrate Scindia's Malwa capital (Ujjain) and give forth its increase, and through Fatehabad and Barnagar to Rutlam. The extension of the line to Neemuch is being rapidly pushed on, and in a few months it will be ready for traffic. The opening of the line from Ajmer and Nasirabad to Neemuch will complete a chain of railway communication encircling the States of Central India and communicating with every part of Hindustan. Her Highness the Begam of Bhopal, an enlightened ruler, always anxious for the advancement of her State, seeing the advantages of the rail in her neighbours' territories, has been for the last three years in negotiation for the construction of a line to connect her capital with the system of railways. She has now concluded an agreement for a loan of 50 lakhs, and the survey of the line between Itarsi and Bhopal, crossing the Narbudda at Hoshangabad, is being rapidly pushed forward. If, as Her Highness urgently desires, the rail is continued from Bhopal to join the State railway at Ujjain, or, far better, is carried through the grain-producing districts of Bhilsa and, skirting Bundelkhand, to Gwalior, the railway communication of Central India will be complete and trade will have every opening. In Bundelkhand also, though railways are still wanting, much improvement in communications has been effected. The trunk road from Gwalior to Jhansi has been extended to Nowgong, and communication with the East India Railway at Sutna has been opened by a road passing by Panna and Nagode. The Bisramghat road, made by the Panna Chief under Dr Stratton's guidance, is an example of the good work which Native States can accomplish. From Sutna a road has been made for 30 miles to Bela, connecting Rewa, the capital of Baghelkhand, with the rail, and joining the trunk road which passes to Mirzapur. Of roads in Malwa the principal constructed during the last ten years are the Mhow and Neemuch road, passing through Jaora and Ratlam, a branch from Ujjain to Dewas, made with a view to helping the opium trade prior to the opening of the railway, and an extension through Dewas, on the Agra and Bombay road, to Sonkutch, and thence *via* Ashta to Sehore and Bhopal. The Maharaja of Dhar has made an excellent road of 30 miles, connecting his capital with the Mhow and Neemuch road at Ghata Bilode, where the Chambal is crossed by a good iron bridge, and to this point Maharaja Holkar has marked, though not completed, a road 25 miles from Indore. The road from Indore to Khandwa, and the whole length of the Bombay and Agra trunk road, are kept up, and prove useful feeders to the railway."

"Turning to education, I would draw attention to the work done under the supervision of Mr Mackay. In 1868, with the exception of the Maharaja's school in the Indore City, and the Sehore High School, there were hardly any institutions worthy of the name in Central India. Year by year the interest of Chiefs and Darbars in this good work has increased, and the States have vied with each other in the establishment of schools where the children of the country receive cheap and useful education. The Rajkumar School at the Indore Residency has proved of immense benefit to the sons of Chiefs and thakurs. The want of education among the rulers of the country has in past times been a crying evil; the reproach has, to some extent at least, been removed from Central India. It is not alone the advance of education as demonstrated by the establishment of schools in places where the light of knowledge had never before penetrated, to which I would call attention; the collateral advantages of learning have been equally marked. Ten years ago it was the exception to find in a Native State any person, young or old, who could converse with intelligence on general topics, their ideas of things and places were limited to the narrow circle of immediate surroundings; indolence and opium had taken firm hold on the youths of Native States who could afford to be idle, and endeavours to cure this were foiled by the apathy and self-contentment of the people. Learning was a new thing, and, as such, not to be desired, and it was not without trouble and pleading that the cause of education has been advanced. The tide has now fairly turned : a spirit of emulation has now prompted the boys who attend our schools to take the good held out to them, and the results of their training are evidenced by the intelligent interest which all evince in the topics of the day, and by the desire which many have shown to improve themselves by travelling and by seeing places and people their forefathers knew nothing of.

"I would add a few words about the trade in Malwa opium, the revenue from which forms so important a factor in imperial receipts.

"For the ten years ending 31st March 1869, the total number of chests passing the scales was 341,412, the duty realised being Rs. 20,11,04,500. For the ten years ending 31st March 1879, the books show a total export from Malwa of 405,094 chests, representing in duty paid to Government Rs. 24,57,82,725. The improvement, therefore, over the previous decade is 63,682 chests, and a revenue of Rs. 4,46,78,225— in other words, the increase in export is more, on an average, than 500 chests a month, and the yearly revenue to Government has improved by upwards of 44 lakhs of rupees.

"Among the causes of improvement in this important trade I would mention the security of the country and a decrease in highway robbery and violence; inducements held out by Chiefs, to whom land under opium is the chief source of income; improvements in communication, and particularly the facilities which the railway from Indore and Ujjain affords. The establishment of scales at

Ujjain, Jaora, and Udaipur has been the means of drawing the produce of each district to pay export duty to the Government of India without being harassed by the levy of dues by each State through which the opium passed, as was the case when Indore was the only place in Malwa where Government duty could be paid.

"The importance of opium cultivation to the Chiefs of Malwa can hardly be over-estimated; it gives a value to land which no other crop can afford. Wheat and other cereals in the best soil pay from annas 12 to Rs. 3 per bigah; opium yields Rs. 10, Rs. 20, and Rs. 40 for the same measure of land, and in some districts where the advantage of soil and water are great and the opium crop heavy, as much as Rs. 60 per bigah is paid for land under the poppy.

"The principal gainers by the growth of opium are the Maharajas Scindia and Holkar. In Indore territory especially, advantage had been taken of the profits which the trade in opium holds out to increase the assessment on irrigated lands, and Holkar's revenue has, chiefly by this means, steadily increased. Enhanced collections may fairly be estimated at 40 per cent. over those of 1868."

Many are the points of interest and importance which must necessarily receive scant notice in a brief epitome such as the present. Attention was paid to the preservation of objects of archæological interest, in connection with which an indication of the changed conditions now existing is afforded by reading that in 1868 there existed "no local means of photographing *

* The want was specially felt in connection with the splendid ruins at, and near Mandu, to the care and restoration of which, under the direction of Lord Curzon, due attention is now at length being paid. "Yesterday," wrote Daly to a friend in the autumn of 1867, "we were at Nalcha, pitched near the old palace which Malcolm fitted up as a residence, dispossessing in the occupation a tigress which had made a den of one of the rooms. To-day we are in the midst of the ruins of Mandu—broken arches, mosques, palaces, strew the hills for some

such works as may be considered fit objects for the art." Efforts were directed towards persuading Rajput families to curtail the extravagant expenditure upon marriage ceremonies, and the quotation of the prophetic remark made to Daly by a trusted native friend,* who "expressed the hope that British influence will gradually break down the barriers with which Hindu law and custom have blocked the way to alliances in Indian high life." Endeavours were coutinuous to secure the introduction of simple measures for improving the public health, and of vaccination to protect the population against the devastating scourge of small-pox. In these latter aims Daly was supported by an able and devoted body of medical officers, and in particular by Surgeon-Major T. Beaumont, and Lieutenant-Colonels D. Keegan and R. Caldecott, who successively held the appointment of Residency Surgeon at Indore and Administrative Medical Officer in Central India, and through whose efforts great progress was made in the establishment of hospitals and dispensaries throughout the Province.

Among the officers who served under Daly during his tenure as Agent to the Governor-General may be mentioned General the Right Honourable Sir

twenty miles; granite slabs, cunningly carved, ruthlessly cast about, mark the grandeur of the Muhammadans and the destroying hand of the Mahrattas; for the Mahrattas it was who, but a little more than a century ago, thrice gutted the still rich, though fallen Mandu." The palace at Nalcha, to which Daly refers, was originaily built in 1441 by Muhammad Khilji, King of Mandu; it was occupied by Sir John Malcolm, while engaged in the settlement of Malwa, during 1819-20.

* Khan Bahadur Mir Shahamat Ali: "His experience," said Daly, "is varied and deep; it is a well which will always bear dipping into."

Dighton Probyn, G.C.B., G.C.V.O., etc., who commanded the Central India Horse, and held charge of
the Malwa Political Agency during 1868-70; his
successor in that appointment, General Sir John
Watson, V.C., G.C.B., who had joined the 1st Punjab
Cavalry as Adjutant in 1852 ; Colonel Martin, C.B.,
one of Daly's intimate friends, who served with him
in the Central India Horse, and succeeded Watson
in the command; Colonel Sir Edward Bradford,
Bart., G.C.B., G.C.V.O., K.C.S.I., who served in
the Central India Horse and as Political Assistant
at Goona; Colonel Willoughby Osborne, C.B., who
was for many years Political Agent at Bhopal, and
who died while holding the similar post at Gwalior ;
Colonel P. W. Bannerman, one of Daly's most
trusted Political officers, who did conspicuously good
service in Rewa and elsewhere ; Dr J. P. Stratton,
the erudite and energetic Political Agent in Bundelkhand; Colonels A. R. Hutchinson, and E. Impey,
C.I.E., who were each Political Agent at Gwalior ;
General Sir Montagu Gerard, K.C.B., K.C.S.I., who
afterwards commanded the Central India Horse.
Among his Assistants, or Secretaries, at Indore were
Captain Berkeley, now General and C.I.E. ; Captain
West Ridgeway, now the Right Honourable Sir
West Ridgeway, K.C.B., K.C.S.I., lately Governor
of Ceylon; Captain F. H. Maitland, now Earl of
Lauderdale; Lieutenant Barr, now Colonel Sir David
Barr, K.C.S.I., who was Agent to the Governor-
General in Central India from 1894 to 1900, and
subsequently Resident at Hyderabad. Daly's Chief
Engineers and Secretaries for Public Works were
Colonels A. Cadell, L. Russel, and C. Thomason, all
of the Royal Engineers, and Colonel W. S. Trevor,

of the Bengal Engineers—of the latter he wrote in 1875 to Sir George Lawrence :—

"I was about to close this without telling you that W. S. Trevor is here, my P. W. Secretary in place of Cadell. He was with you at Kabul, and remembers every incident there and in the retreat.* He read your book here, and told me that the scenes you described are as clear to him as those around him now. He was eleven years old then, I think. I like him— he is clever and full of soldier-pluck."

With all the officers who served under his orders Daly maintained the most cordial relations of personal friendship. He knew—none better—how trying and anxious were the duties of Political officers in remote places such as Sardarpur, Rewa, and Nowgong; the strain that fell upon all who worked throughout the hot weather in Gwalior, Bundelkhand, and Malwa; and he was ever ready to give them the sympathy, support, and commendation which they needed, and to cheer them with his genial good nature, and kindly spirit. Having an intimate acquaintance with every Chief and thakur, being familiar with the traditions, the customs, and the peculiarities of every State—big or little—it was comparatively easy for Daly, when any doubt or difficulty arose, to grasp at once, correctly and firmly, the salient points of the case, and to give his instructions briefly, concisely, and to the point. But his usual course, when a difficulty arose in any State under his charge, was to go to the spot at once, as fast as trains, or horses, could carry him, meet the Political officer and discuss matters with him, and then take such measures as were necessary to bring about a prompt and satisfactory

* The disastrous retreat of January 1842, fully described in Sir George Lawrence's *Forty-three Years' Service in India.*

settlement. There was no beating about the bush:
no protracted enquiry, no demand for long official
reports—he believed, and the officers who served
under him learned to believe also, in personal
enquiry, frank and friendly advice, a patient hearing
of both sides of the case, and a decision on the
merits — precise, definite, and clear-cut. In the
majority of cases—and they were many—in which
dispute or difference arose, the Chiefs and their
officials accepted Daly's decision without demur—
placing confidence in his judgment, and being assured
that he would suggest nothing that was prejudicial
to their feelings or honour. In this way many
important matters were quietly settled without
unnecessarily causing friction or raising discontent.

Daly was a man of action himself, and required
that all officers serving under him should be as active
and alert as he was: it was one of his well-known
sayings that "a Political officer who couldn't jump
on to a horse and ride 50 miles when duty called him,
wasn't worth keeping." He hated all pomp and
show; and ridiculed the idea of maintaining dignity
by the outward and visible signs or ceremonials, pro-
cessions, formal Darbars, and all functions of a like
nature. Guards of honour, escorts of cavalry, salutes
of guns, he counted as nothing, and he discouraged in
his Political officers and assistants any tendencies
towards that type of mannerism which Ali Babi in his
Twenty-one Days in India alludes to as "paralytic
swagger" and "thirteen-gun tall-talk" — the peculiar
attributes, according to popular view, of Politicals.
"Go, and talk to him" was Daly's standing advice
when a Political officer complained of the difficulty of
getting things done by any Chief: and he gave

practical effect to this theory himself, by *chatting*, confidentially and freely, with any personage who showed disinclination to follow advice or to learn wisdom. Daly was not a profound Oriental scholar ; but he knew the vernacular sufficiently well to bring home his views in the most forcible manner, and withal with so much humour, wit, and common-sense, as to appeal as readily to the most sullen as to the most amenable disposition.

Daly was promoted to Major-General in January 1870, and to Lieutenant-General seven years later. He was made a K.C.B. in 1875, but the honour, as he wrote to his old friend Sir George Lawrence, "came with a deep shadow. The three to whom it would have been joy and pride knew it not." His only brother had died in 1871 ; his wife's mother, to whom he was as a son, followed in 1873 ; finally, after a short illness at Indore, his wife died in October 1874, at Bombay, whither she had been moved in the hope of regaining health from a sea voyage. "My life in India," he said to Sir George, "seems a thing of yesterday, and when I call up the incidents and *time*, it is passing strange, for, until this dark blow came,* I felt

---

* On this sad occasion Maharaja Sir Jayaji Rao Scindia gave a touching proof of the reality of his feeling towards his "brother." He had never met Maharaja Sir Tukoji Rao Holkar of Indore or entered his territories ; proposals for a meeting between the two Chiefs had been frequently made, but had always broken down upon some point of ceremony. But nothing could prevent Sir Jayaji Rao from proceeding to Indore to pay to Daly the visit of sympathy and condolence (Matampursi), which is prescribed by the highest Hindu etiquette. Scindia marched from Khandwa to Indore. He declined to halt at Indore, as he did not consider this seemly in the circumstances ; but remained only a couple of hours, which enabled him to discharge his mournful, though kindly errand. At the first stage from Khandwa, on the banks of Narbada, he and Sir Tukoji Rao Holkar met for the first time in their lives. It is pleasant to add that their relations were

PART OF

CENTRAL INDIA
to illustrate the
LIFE OF GENERAL DALY

Names underlined in blue are mentioned in the book

Scale of English Miles

0   10   20   30   40   50   100   150

no older or colder than when I landed a boy of seventeen."

Of his private life at Indore it is not necessary to say much. He made it his home, and was never so happy as when the house was overflowing with visitors; the memory of his hospitality and of the cheery welcome which was extended to all, is still alive in Central India. With natives his popularity was great, owing to his accessibility to men of every class, and to the sympathetic hearing which he accorded to all.

It was in February 1881 that Daly finally left India, after handing over charge to Mr (now Sir Lepel) Griffin. The Government of India sped his parting with the following notification :—

"His Excellency the Viceroy and Governor-General in Council desires to place on record his high appreciation of the long and distinguished service rendered by Lieutenant-General Sir Henry Daly, K.C.B., C.I.E.,* who vacated on the 10th February his appointment as Agent to the Governor-General in Central India.

"His Excellency the Viceroy is confident that Sir Henry Daly's relinquishment of the important duties which he has for twelve years discharged in Central India will be generally regretted, and by none more than by the Chiefs and people, toward the promotion of whose welfare his exertions have throughout been directed with remarkable energy and success."

thereafter of a friendly character. Twelve years later, when each was in his last illness, they exchanged kindly messages, and it is a curious fact that these two Chiefs, who were by far the most conspicuous figures in Central India, and had both succeeded to the *gadi* in the decade before the Mutiny, died within three days of each other in June 1886.

* Daly was one of the original members of this Order, which was instituted at the Delhi Assemblage on the 1st January 1877, and at first consisted of Companions only.

CHAPTER XII

1881-1895

The Daly College at Indore. Occupations in England. **Master**
of Hounds. Twice contests Dundee. Receives the G.C.B.
Osborne. Second Marriage. Queen Victoria Godmother to
his youngest son. Illness and Death. Character.

AFTER Daly's departure, a movement was set on foot
by the Chiefs of Central India to commemorate in
some visible and substantial manner the services
which he had rendered to the Province. The
Residency College at Indore, which owed its success
to Daly, was conducted in somewhat meagre and
inadequate buildings, and it was felt that the provision
of better accommodation would be an appropriate
tribute to the memory of one who had been the
pioneer of education in Central India. Subscriptions
flowed in, and in due course a handsome building,
bearing the name "The Daly College," and containing a full suite of class-rooms, was erected in a good
position about half a mile from the Residency. The
Hall was opened in November 1885 by the Viceroy,
Lord Dufferin, who concluded his address with the
following words :—

"All Englishmen must be very grateful for the
generous thought which induced the Princes and
Chiefs of Central India, who subscribed for this
institution, to name it after their old friend, Sir

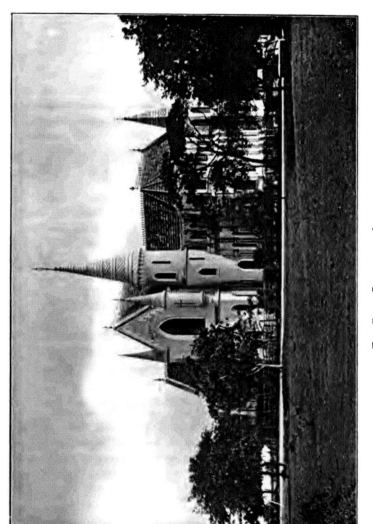

THE DALY COLLEGE AT INDORE.

[*To face p.* 332.

Henry Daly. I am well aware that Sir Henry Daly was one of the most accomplished and high-minded public servants that ever pursued a career of usefulness in India. He was, from first to last, the champion and friend of the Native Princes and the Native States, and I assure you it is very gratifying to us, whose aim and desire is to follow in the footsteps of those who have been most distinguished by their earnest endeavours to do their duty by the people of India, to have such a proof that we are serving a nation who is generous to preserve after their departure such an enduring record of their name and fame as that which you have erected in honour of Sir Henry Daly."

Ten years later, after Daly's death, the present Maharaja Scindia conceived the graceful idea of placing a bust of his father's old friend in the College hall. The work was entrusted to Mr Charles Bates, and, at his untimely death, was in so forward a condition that completion by one of his friends was a matter of no difficulty. From various causes the ceremony of unveiling the bust at Indore was delayed, but it was finally performed in April 1902, when eloquent tributes * to Sir Henry Daly's memory were paid by his old friend and disciple, Colonel Sir David Barr, as well as by the Agent to the Governor-General, Mr C. S. Bayley, and by the Maharaja Scindia.

On his return to England in 1881, Daly divided his time between London and the Isle of Wight. He became Master of the Isle of Wight Foxhounds, and held that post for nearly nine years, during which he was among the hardest riders in the hunting field. He took an active part in local politics and business, and did his full share of magisterial work. He was a member of several Indian Railway Boards, and rendered special aid in the conduct of the affairs

* For the speeches delivered upon this occasion, see Appendix B.

of the Indian Midland Railway. His interest in
Indian questions was fully maintained; he kept up a
wide correspondence with old friends, both English
and native; in 1884 he delivered an interesting
lecture* on "The Punjab Frontier Force," at
the United Service Institution; he was consulted
not infrequently by authorities at the Indian Office
on leading matters of Indian policy; and he gave
much assistance in connection with the celebration of
Queen Victoria's Jubilee in 1887.

In politics Daly, like so many Anglo-Indians, had
no strong party leanings, but he was a follower and
great admirer of Gladstone until the Home Rule
question arose. He then became a Liberal-Unionist,
and in 1886, and again in 1888, he unsuccessfully
contested, in that interest, the Gladstonian stronghold
of Dundee. Here, though an entire stranger when
he arrived a few days before the commencement of
the polling in 1886, he soon won warm friends, and,
at the second contest, the improvement of his position elicited the following letter from the Liberal-
Unionist Whip :—

> "LIBERAL-UNIONIST ASSOCIATION,
> "GREAT GEORGE STREET,
> "WESTMINSTER, *Feb. 14th,* 1888.

"DEAR SIR HENRY DALY,
"I have been hoping to see you
here; but as I have not had that good fortune yet,
I must ask to be allowed to congratulate you most
heartily on your most plucky fight at Dundee. I
assure you our spirits were buoyed up amidst the
disaster at Southwark and the bad luck at Edinburgh

---

* Reproduced as Appendix C. Portions of this lecture have been
incorporated in *Lumsden of the Guides,* by Sir P. S. Lumsden and
G. R. Elmslie, pp. 64 *et seq.* and 255 *et seq.*

by the thought of the great breach which you made in the Gladstonian fortress at Dundee.

"Now your example has helped to storm effectually the weaker fort at Doncaster.—Believe me, Yours very truly, WOLMER."

The Liberal-Unionists of Dundee presented Daly with a very handsome service of plate to commemorate his connection with them.

Daly became a full General in 1888, and was created a G.C.B. in 1889. From Queen Victoria and King Edward (then Prince of Wales) he received many marks of kindness and favour. When the Queen was at Osborne he was frequently invited there, and in August 1889 he wrote the following description of a banquet :—

"I was at dinner at Osborne the day before yesterday. We dined in a splendid tent, I should think seventy or eighty. The Emperor, a strong, jolly fellow, in capital spirits. I was presented to him by the Prince of Wales ; he talked famously, with an accent, but freely and with a thorough understanding. The Queen spoke to me of the Island and the Assembly. The Princess of Wales and the Princess Beatrice also did me the honour of chatting. The scene was an extraordinary gay one: the Germans covered with gold Orders and medals ; H. Bismarck, a strong, thick fellow, speaking much ; all the notables of Germany there. The Queen after dinner proposed 'the health of the Emperor of Germany.' The Emperor rose and proposed 'the Queen.' Nothing more said. Then the Assembly rose, and moved back to the drawing-room ; talking and introducing went on there till 11.30, and, as old Pepys would say, 'then home.'"

Shortly after his final return to England, Daly married again. His second wife, née Coape, was the widow of Mr Stirling Dunlop. His only child by

his second marriage was born in December 1889;
Queen Victoria proposed herself as godmother, and
was present at the christening in Daly's house,
holding and naming the child. Towards the end of
1889 Daly met with a severe fall when hunting, being
thrown on his left shoulder, which had never recovered
from his Delhi wound. He made light of the injury,
and unfortunately refused to lie up; the next few
days happened to involve exceptional physical strain,
and there followed a paralytic stroke. He rallied
from this, and preserved fair health, though greatly
crippled, for some three years; thereafter he sank
gradually, until the end came at Ryde on the 21st
July 1895.

The foregoing pages will have given a tolerably
clear idea of Daly's character. He was of an eager,
bright, joyous, sympathetic disposition. He "warmed
both hands before the fire of life," and loved to make
others enjoy themselves around him. He was overflowing with activity; a grand horseman, and a lover
of horses; in his youth a keen cricketer, and at all
times a supporter and encourager of every manly
sport. He had a rich fund of Irish humour, delighted
in telling and hearing anecdotes, and was an
admirable *raconteur*, being plentifully furnished with
memories of active service and stirring adventure,
and with tales drawn from the lore of Native States.
He was exceptionally well read in historical subjects
and in the lives of great men; he had a strong
memory, and a great aptitude in quotation and in
applying the results of reading and experience; in
writing, he possessed a clear, terse, graphic style,
which was illuminated by his wit and spirits. No
close observer of religious forms, he was deeply

religious at heart; and, as one of his oldest friends observed, his most conspicuous trait was a wide and active, but unostentatious, charity. Upon this subject he wrote to his wife early in 1859: "There is nothing you can lay up for 'my boys' so valuable as a kindly feeling for, and sympathy in, the wants of others: one cannot estimate the good influence on character which such things beget. To my mind, there is no religion so holy as that of helping and comforting our fellow-creatures. I do not mean mere money aid—it is not all of us who can bestow that—but let those who are blessed with the 'talents' use them freely. It is not by storing them for a possible need which may never arise, nor for a time that we may not live to see, that good can come—let us be content to live and do good in our own day."

He was a great favourite in all society, and immensely popular in India with all ranks, creeds, and races. "It was his frank, honest, impartial mind and acts and words," wrote the late Sir Neville Chamberlain, "that won for him the confidence and respect of all he associated with, European or Native. By instinct he fathomed the mind of all classes of Natives; and they at once felt that he judged them rightly. They, on their part, were at once led to trust him; and they accepted him as a just judge, and as a friend who would do his best to see that their rights were respected by the State."

Daly's old regiment, the 2nd Munster Fusiliers (late the Bombay Fusiliers), were quartered at Portsmouth when he died. They sent over a funeral party, and he was borne to his grave by men of the corps which he had joined nearly fifty-five years previously, 6000 miles away.

Y

changes or receives a post without paying *nazarana*, and no doubt the amount of this has great weight in settling the candidate's suitability.

* * * * * * *

" As to the comparative estimation by the people at large, and whether their prosperity and contentment are best promoted under British or native rule, what, let me ask, would cause greater dismay in districts which for years have been under us than the announcement that they were about to be transferred to a Native State— Scindia or Holkar, for instance ? Political officers who have lived amongst Chiefs and thakurs under our guarantee know well the effect of such a threat; but I have never known an instance of discontent on the part of a ryot transferred *by* the Darbar. He has got a fixed lease or settlement in lieu of fixed uncertainty.

* * * * * * *

" I have already made these observations longer than I ought to have done, but the subject bursts with fulness. Let me cast a glance at Malwa. What has caused Scindia's cities of Ujjain and Mandisor year by year to lose wealth, importance, and population ? Mandisor is in the very heart of the poppy-fields, on the banks of a noble river; yet many of its streets are in ruins, and its name is declining. Ujjain, that ancient city, venerated by all Hindus, with the Sipra flowing by its walls and rich land around, is crumbling to the ground, and being yearly deserted by merchants and men of business. On the other hand, why are Ratlam and Jaora, comparatively insignificant States, increasing in wealth and prosperity ? *Because it has chanced to them to fall under British protection.* Within the last forty years, through the heirs of both States being infants on accession, the supervision was assumed by Major Borthwick, one of Sir John Malcolm's assistants. Borthwick delivered over his charge when the time came—Ratlam a busy, handsome city, filled with merchants and traders, prosperity everywhere. After the lapse of a few years, Ratlam again passed into the hands of a child of two or three years old. During the interval dissension and dissipation had destroyed much that Borthwick had built up; but, under British guardianship, more than the old prosperity is reviving. Jaora,

Pishach Mukeshwar Ghat } for Hindus.
Ganesh Ghat

Maulana Ghat, for Muhammadans.

BATHING GHATS, UJJAIN.

[To face p 360

forty years ago, was little more than a village. Under Borthwick's fostering care it became a city, with a rich and well-supplied mart. About two years ago, the Nawab died; his heir is a minor, and thus the State has again fallen under British protection.

•   •   •   •   •   •   *

"The Agent to the Governor-General knows better than I do the utter want of confidence among the natives at large in the promises of any Chief, great or small. I will, however, give an instance in point. About Goona, where I was for many years, scores of square miles of rich land belonging to petty Rajas are lying waste. The Raja of Bhadaura invited my assistance in obtaining cultivators. I spoke to Sikh pensioners of the Central India Horse, and others about to take pension—men always greedy for land—and suggested that they should settle and form villages. The idea thoroughly chimed in with their inclinations, *on one condition*, that I should countersign the engagement between them and the Raja. Without this, despite his liberal offers of years of free tenure and a sanad, not a man would risk his savings or discuss the question. Scindia has long felt the same in many parts."

APPENDIX B.

Speeches delivered on the 2nd April 1902, on the occasion of the unveiling, in the Daly College at Indore, of the bust of Sir Henry Daly, presented by His Highness Maharaja Madho Rao Scindia of Gwalior.

SPEECH by the Honourable Mr C. S. BAYLEY, Agent to the Governor-General.

YOUR HIGHNESSES, LADIES AND GENTLEMEN,—It is with the very greatest pleasure that I welcome you here to-day, for I know nothing more gratifying than to see a large number of persons representative of all classes of our Central Indian community, Chiefs and subjects, Europeans and Indians, officials and non-officials, assembled together to honour the memory of a truly great and good man. That Sir Henry Daly's character and devotion to duty were appreciated by those among whom he moved, the building in which we are met, erected as it was by public subscriptions immediately after his retirement from the service of Government, bears ample and enduring testimony. That the recollection of him remains green among those who had the privilege of knowing him, and that his name is revered by those who, like myself, can judge him only by the fruits which his work has borne, and by the traditions handed down to us by others, is shown by our presence here ; and if further evidence be needed, it is at hand in the bust which has been generously presented to this College by His Highness the Maharaja Madho Rao Scindia of Gwalior, in honour of his father's greatest friend.

It would be impossible for me, within the limits of a short speech, to enumerate Sir Henry Daly's claims to the gratitude of the people of Central India. This much, however, I can say with absolute certainty, that no one who has occupied the post which I have the honour to hold, can fail to be aware of the fact that there is no department of the Administration on which Sir Henry Daly has not left the impress of his clear intellect, his decision and integrity of character, and his excellent judgment of men and things. No one can be much thrown with the Chiefs and people of Central India without observing that the names to which reference in all cases of difficulty is most frequently made, are those of Sir John Malcolm and Sir Henry Daly. To Sir John Malcolm is due the political system of Central India as it exists to-day; but no sooner does any question arise as to the working of that system than an appeal is made to the views held by Sir Henry Daly as the most cogent argument which it is possible to adduce. To us Political officers Sir Henry Daly is a model of all that a Political officer should be: but to all of us alike, whatever our vocation in life may be, he stands forth as a conspicuous example of uprightness, fearlessness, capacity, and kindliness of heart. One can imagine no more appropriate gift to the younger generation of Chiefs and nobles of Central India than the marble image of one whom all must revere, and whose qualities all should strive to imitate.

I esteem it a peculiar privilege that the duty of presiding at the unveiling of this bust should devolve upon me, and I rejoice heartily that the ceremony should be performed by the munificent donor, Maharaja Scindia, in the presence of so many who knew and loved Sir Henry Daly well. It is a matter for regret that His Highness the Maharaja Holkar, who in his younger days knew Sir Henry, and who studied for a while in this College, has been prevented by family bereavement from attending. I am also exceedingly sorry that pressure of official duties has caused the absence of one whom all would have welcomed, and without whom the day's proceedings seem sadly incomplete. I refer to Sir Henry Daly's son, Major Hugh Daly, who served for a while in his father's old regiment, the Central India Horse, and who has in the important position which he has so long held, of Deputy Secretary to the Government of India in the Foreign Department, shown in a conspicuous degree that Sir Henry Daly's talents and political instinct have been handed down unimpaired to his offspring.

I have no wish to take up your time with personal matters, but I cannot avoid a feeling that my own share in this ceremony needs some explanation, I had almost said apology. Many of you are aware that this bust was ordered long ago, at a time when there was every reason to hope that one of the aptest of Sir Henry Daly's pupils and certainly one of the most ardent of his admirers, the one who had the best opportunities for appreciating his merits, my predecessor, Lieut.-Colonel David Barr, would be here to preside over the ceremony of the unveiling. Before, however, the bust arrived from England, Colonel Barr had been selected to fill the arduous and important office of Resident at Hyderabad, and this has necessitated my attempting, I will not say to fill his place, for on an occasion of this kind that is impossible, but to preside over a ceremony which would have been more appropriately conducted by him. Although he cannot be with us in body to-day, he is, I am sure, with us in mind, and he has in answer to a request from me sent the following message, which, with your permission, I will now read to you.

SIR DAVID BARR'S NOTE

I shall be much obliged if you will kindly express to all present my deep regret that I am unable to attend the ceremony of unveiling the bust of my revered friend and master, the late General Sir Henry Daly, G.C.B.

My duties at Hyderabad preclude the possibility of my attendance, and even were it otherwise, I should feel that as I have severed my long connection with Central India, the ceremony is more fittingly conducted by you as the Agent to the Governor-General.

Still, as one of the least of the disciples of the great and good man, whose memory this bust will perpetuate in the College which bears his name and in the place where for twelve years he was the able representative of the Government of India, I hope you will allow me to say how cordially I sympathise with your proceedings, and how entirely my heart is with you on this occasion.

There are still living many of Sir Henry Daly's Political Agents and Assistants. Some of them have risen to high office, and have won honoured names for themselves. I would mention Sir Dighton Probyn, Sir John Watson, Sir Edward Bradford, Sir West Ridgeway, the Earl of Lauderdale, General A. Cadell, General J. C. Berkeley, Colonel Cunliffe Martin, Colonel P. Bannerman, Colonel T. Cadell, Colonel E. A. Fraser, Colonel F. Wilson, Lieutenant-Colonel M. J. Meade—all of whom had the highest regard, esteem, and affection for him, who was their Chief: but I claim the personal distinction of being the only one of Sir Henry Daly's Assistants who served, almost uninterruptedly, under him from his first appointment as Agent to the Governor-General in 1869, to the day when, with a few others, among whom were his dear son George Daly of the Central India Horse, and Dr Caldecott (whose name will, I trust, never be forgotten in Central India), I bade him farewell in February 1881, on board the P. and O. s.s. *Siam*, when he left India for good. For nearly nine years I was Sir Henry's First Assistant, and everything I know of political work, and every success I have attained in my political service, I ascribe to the training and education I received from him, as well as to his never-failing sympathy, kindness, and forbearance towards me personally. As he was to me so he was to all with whom he was brought in touch—bright, genial, considerate. To work under him was a pleasure, for he was not only quick-witted and clever, but had the faculty of grasping his subject, and of arriving at once at a correct judgment. Yet there was no one more appreciative of the efforts of those who worked under his orders, and no one more ready to overlook the blunders of men who had not his constructive genius.

He left his mark on Central India in many directions, but perhaps his efforts in the causes of railway com-

Khuman Singh, Rai Nanak Chand, Mr Krishna Rao Muley, Mr Madge, and a few of the old residents, office clerks, and merchants of Indore, who knew and esteemed Sir Henry Daly, are present with you on this occasion. To one and all I send my greeting and good wishes. With me they share the memory of the soldier-politician whose bust you unveil to-day. With me they recall the services rendered to Central India by him, and his many favours to us all; and though we shall never see again his bright smile, or hear his cheery voice, or admire his lithe, active figure as he rode with the courage and dash of a man of thirty, over any sort of country, and at any sort of pace, yet the marble provided by Maharaja Scindia will bring to our minds the features of one who was our friend and our master—Daly of the Bombay Fusiliers, Daly of the Guides, Daly of Hodson's Horse, Daly of the Central India Horse, and Daly of Central India.

* * * * * * *

Gentlemen, anything that I could add to the words which I have read would but weaken their effect. I leave them with you as a message from a friend whose love for Central India was not less than that of his revered master, and whose memory will, I venture to think, long occupy a place in the minds of the Central Indian Chiefs worthy of one who studied at Sir Henry Daly's feet. I now request Your Highness to unveil the bust.

MAHARAJA SCINDIA'S SPEECH

MR BAYLEY, LADIES AND GENTLEMEN,—I esteem it a great privilege to be present on this occasion to unveil the bust of Sir Henry Daly. I hoped that the Honourable the Agent to the Governor-General would perform the ceremony, but I was asked quite unexpectedly to undertake this honourable task in such a manner that I could not refuse.

My sentiments towards Sir Henry Daly have been exactly expressed by Mr Bayley, and I am sure that all present here who either knew him personally, or are acquainted with his career, will echo them.

The memory of that great and good man, as he has been most appropriately described by Mr Bayley and

BUST OF SIR HENRY DALY. (By Bates.)

THIS BUST IS ERECTED BY MAHARAJA MADHO RAO SCINDIA, G.C.S.I.
IN HONOUR OF
GENERAL SIR HENRY DALY, G.C.B., C.I.E.
AGENT TO THE GOVERNOR-GENERAL IN CENTRAL INDIA FROM 1869 TO 1881
BORN 25TH OCTOBER 1824; DIED 21ST JULY 1895
AND IS PLACED IN THE DALY COLLEGE AS A MONUMENT OF THE AFFECTION AND ESTEEM
IN WHICH HE WAS HELD BY ALL THE CHIEFS AND PEOPLE OF CENTRAL INDIA, AND
IN REMEMBRANCE OF THE FRIENDSHIP, ONLY SEVERED BY DEATH, WHICH
SUBSISTED FOR MORE THAN TWENTY YEARS BETWEEN HIM AND
THE LATE MAHARAJA JAYAJI RAO SCINDIA, G.C.B., G.C.S.I.

[To face p. 848.

Colonel Barr, remains green in the minds of the Chiefs and people of Central India, because so large a part of his service was passed in this part of India, and because he was not only the chief representative of the Imperial Government, but always endeavoured to cultivate the friendship and gain the confidence of those with whom his duties brought him in contact, and by his cordial manner inspired them with love and reverence.

Sir Henry Daly was Political Agent at Gwalior from 1867 to 1870, with intervals during which he was on leave or officiating as Agent to the Governor-General. The period of his service as Agent to the Governor-General is even longer, extending continuously from 1870 to 1881, and he is a conspicuous example of the good effects of a long tenure of office by a man of sympathetic nature. Though I have not met all the Political officers mentioned by Colonel Barr as having served under Sir Henry Daly, still from those whom I have met I have gathered that one and all have entertained the same feelings of affection and regard for his memory as are so eloquently expressed by Colonel Barr.

As to Sir Henry Daly's special connection with Gwalior, I had not, of course, the good fortune to be personally acquainted with him—yet he might have seen me in my childhood; he was my father's greatest friend, and they looked upon each other as brothers.

For myself, since I had the pleasure of making the acquaintance of Major Hugh Daly, whose absence to-day I, in common with Mr Bayley, greatly regret, I have regarded him as my brother.

I trust that though I cannot claim, on account of my youth, the same relationship towards Sir Henry Daly's successors, yet I consider that I have a claim to be looked upon by them in the light of a son.

It has just struck me, ladies and gentlemen, that the proper person to unveil the bust is not my humble self, but Mrs Bayley, and, therefore, as I have not succeeded in inducing Mr Bayley to do it, I beg her to favour me by consenting to my request.

APPENDIX C.

Friday, 27th June 1884.

Lieutenant-General Sir SAMUEL J. BROWNE, V.C., K.C.B., K.C.S.I., late Bengal Staff Corps, *in the Chair.*

THE PUNJAB FRONTIER FORCE.

By Lieutenant-General Sir HENRY D. DALY, K.C.B., C.I.E., Bombay Staff Corps.

THE Council of the Royal United Service Institution has done me the honour to request that I would supply a paper on "The Punjab Frontier Force." The subject is vast; embracing a period of thirty years, during which the Indian Empire was convulsed :—the grand Native Army, of which all were so proud, rich with the glories and conquests of a hundred years—triumphs in all climates, Egypt, Afghanistan, China, and Burma — under Clive, Wellesley, Foote, Pollock, Napier, Gough, and many a good commander—between the dawn and dusk of a May-day in 1857, broke away from their allegiance, rose in arms against us, carrying with them many arsenals and war *matériel* of every description.

The mere recital of the records of the Punjab Force, from the Kohat expedition under Sir Charles Napier, in February 1850, to the glorious defence and glorious death of young Hamilton and Cavagnari's guard of Guides at Kabul, in 1879, would, however compressed, occupy more time than is allotted for such a paper as this. No amount of hard writing could make the catalogue easy reading.

We have the carefully compiled chronicles of Paget, of the exploits of the Force on the North-West Frontier, filling upwards of 450 pages, records of daring service, done with devotion and discipline, under the prestige and leading of Englishmen, by Pathans, Muhammadans of the wildest class and clan—men steeped in blood feuds, traditionally careless of life, hating every dynasty but their own; by Sikhs, descendants of the soldiers of Ranjit Singh, who had wrested Peshawar from the very Pathans by whose side they had been fighting shoulder to shoulder in our ranks.

These chronicles are to us what the chronicles of Froissart were to the soldiers of his time: they bring a glow of pride, testifying to the wondrous power of order and discipline effected by the nerve and brains of a handful of Englishmen.   True it is that many a noble spirit passed away, hallowed in the going; but many remain, pressing to do whatever devotion and duty may.

After I had accepted the invitation to prepare this paper, and began to read the records, reports, and lives of the men who made the history of the time, I felt overwhelmed at the task, and shrank from attempting more than to dot down personal reminiscences, with here and there sketches and anecdotes illustrative of the men and the times—of the deeds done, and the doers.   My own reminiscences have this merit—they carry us back to the earliest stages of the Punjab Force; for I believe Sir John Coke, that rare leader of Pathans, and myself, are the only survival of the original commandants.

Captain Coke and Lieutenant Daly raised the 1st Punjab Infantry and the 1st Punjab Cavalry; and within seven months of their embodiment both corps were reviewed by Sir Charles Napier, and served in the field under his command.   As to Coke's, wrote that heroic soldier to George Lawrence: "I have seen nothing superior to it in drill—it is admirable; and both you and I saw how this brave corps fought under its excellent leader in our five days' campaign."   And in the General Order detailing the fighting, he writes: "As Captain Coke and the 1st Punjab Regiment of Infantry sustained the brunt of this skirmishing, the Commander-in-Chief thinks it due to this admirable young corps, and its excellent leader, to say that their conduct called forth the applause of the whole column."

The stately proclamation of Lord Dalhousie, dated 29th March 1849, recounts how the Punjab became part of the British Empire. The treacherous murder of two British officers at Multan, Vans Agnew and Anderson, in April 1848, was followed within twelve months by the destruction of the Sikh army, the capture of Multan, the battle of Gujerat, and the expulsion of the Afghans across the Indus to the mouth of the Khyber Pass.

Sir Henry Lawrence was placed at the head of the new Government, with unlimited power of selecting the civil and military officers under him; Lord Dalhousie stipulating only for his Agent in the war, Colonel Mackeson.

The defence of the frontier from Hazara to Mithankot, at the junction of the five rivers, was a heavy task to face. It meant the control of lawless tribes, whose trade was warfare and plunder, numbering in all not less than 100,000 fighting men, levying blackmail on travellers and merchants, never combining save against Ranjit Singh or Kabul.

For a thousand years and more the valley of the Indus under the Suleiman range had been studded with a line of forts and towers—ruins of which still remain—as positions and outposts against the ceaseless raids of mountain marauders.

In times not long past, in a country so difficult for military operations—with narrow defiles, mere fissures in the rocks—marauders assembled from long distances, well armed and well mounted, and carrying their food on their backs. They sacked towns, exacted ransoms, murdered Sikh Governor and people, getting back to their fastnesses with impunity.

The first duty which fell on Sir Henry Lawrence was the defence of this trans-Indus frontier, and ten regiments, five of cavalry and five of infantry, were organised for employment.

Before proceeding further, it will be well to turn to the small body of Guides, which owed its origin to Sir Henry Lawrence in December 1846; their organisation must have been in his mind when he conceived the idea of a Frontier Force.

Sir Henry, during the first Afghan War, had seen the difficulties our army, British and native, encountered in the passes, amongst the hill tribes and northern nations, in the absence of guides and interpreters; and he resolved that in the future, within our own ranks, there should be hardy men accustomed to every region and accident of service, and familiar with every village dialect.

The Guides, originally one troop of cavalry and two companies of infantry, were raised by Major-General Sir Harry Burnett Lumsden, then a Lieutenant. Lumsden possessed characteristics for the task in a rare degree: a daring sportsman, full of endurance, hardy and strong of frame, with an instinctive knowledge of men which gave him a power which none under him ever questioned. Life in the Punjab in those times was full of incidents, and few were the days which did not test self-dependence and soldierly intelligence. Henry Lawrence quickly gauged Lumsden's genius. In addition to the strength begotten by the stirring scenes in which he moved, Lumsden breathed among giants—the Lawrences, Edwardes, Nicholson, were his associates.

It is hardly enough to say that on the enrolment of the Guides each man's personal history was known to Lumsden; men from every wild and warlike tribe were represented in its ranks, men habituated to war and sport, the dangers and vicissitudes of border life. Afridis and Gurkhas, Sikhs and Hazaras, Waziris, Pathans of every class, and even Kaffirs, speaking all the tongues of the border, Persian, Pooshtoo, etc., dialects unknown to the men of the plains; in many cases the Guides had a camp language or *patois* of their own. Lumsden sought out the men notorious for desperate deeds, leaders in forays, who

Z

kept the passes into the hills, and lived amid inaccessible rocks. He made Guides of them: tempted by regular pay and enterprise, many joined the corps and became conspicuous for daring and fidelity. On the border, and in the ranks of the Guides, tales, abundant in humour, were told of Lumden's interviews with men who had defied all authority, and had never been seen in the plains but for murder and plunder.

A sketch of Dilawar Khan, who died on the path of duty, a Subadar of the Guides, whose name is familiar in every village between the Khyber and Kashmir, will illustrate this.

When Lumsden first visited Eusafzai in search of recruits—in his own words—"of men accustomed to look after themselves, and not easily taken aback by any sudden emergency," Dilawar Khan was notorious. He had been brought up by Muhammadan priests, and was intended for the priesthood; but kidnapping bankers and rich traders, carrying them across the Indus into Eusafzai, was too attractive in adventure and remuneration, and he forsook the sacred calling.

Dilawar's capital consisted of his sword, a piece of rope, and a huge bullock's skin, which he could inflate at pleasure, and so carry himself and his guests across the sacred river; once there, a message was sent to settle the sum the firm or family would give as ransom for his guest. This was Dilawar's occupation. Lumsden, thinking that Dilawar must have rare local knowledge and pluck to carry on such a trade successfully, sent him an invitation to his camp, promising him a safe return to the hills. The very novelty of the invitation took Dilawar's fancy, and to the astonishment of the chiefs of the district he appeared in camp. Lumsden received him with all courtesy, pointed out that in a short time posts would be so established throughout the country that his calling would be impossible, and the risk of hanging great, and ended his moral by proposing to make him a Guide. Dilawar fairly burst into a fit of laughter at the proposal, and took his departure across the border. Six weeks afterwards he voluntarily turned up at Lumsden's tent, saying he had come to join the Guides, but pleaded hard to be excused the degradation of the "goose step"; but Lumsden held out stoutly for the absolute necessity of his being taught the complete art of war, and finally had the satisfaction of seeing the most dreaded man on the frontier patiently balancing on one leg at his bidding.

Such is Lumsden's own account, and he adds : "About half my first recruits were of this stamp, while the other half were sons or nephews of the chiefs of the district," who sought the Englishmen as representatives of their family, and eventually rose to the higher ranks. So popular became enlistment under Lumsden that thirty or forty young Afridis, or Pathans, fed and clothed by their relatives in the ranks, passed through their drill, awaited vacancies. Great was the excitement at the rifle butts when a vacancy, as a prize, was shot for by these aspirants.

The headquarters of the corps were fixed at Mardan, in the midst of Eusafzai ; a rude fort was constructed, and there in a rich valley, bounded on the north and east by the Swat Mountains, with the Indus and the Kabul Rivers south and west, Lumsden held civil and military sway over a people the Sikhs had failed to subdue, and who had withstood an army with guns led by Ranjit Singh in person.

I have described Lumsden's mode of selecting Afridis and Pathans, to be associated and brought under discipline with Sikhs and other Hindus, and must now give an anecdote of the feeling of this body to Lumsden himself. Sir John Lawrence, as ruler of the Punjab, was wont from time to time to make tours through all parts of the country. On one of his early visits to Mardan, the Chiefs from the hills with their followers, and every village baron, gathered at Mardan to pay the great man obeisance. Revenue assessments and cases were discussed. and appeals received. Lumsden, from early ties, was probably easy in criminal and civil matters with a people whom he found cultivating their fields with sword and matchlock by their side, and who had never paid revenue except by force of arms, and who had no law but tradition and the will of the Kazis. Sir John, though cordially relying on Lumsden's judgment, spent two or three days in cultivating a personal knowledge, as was his habit, with all that came before him, and thus it seemed to the men of the Guides that their leader was harassed by discussions and explanations instead of being with them as usual in the field or at sports.

The night before Sir John was to march with his retinue from Mardan, Lumsden, after Sir John had gone to bed, went outside, and sat on the parapet of the fort. After a while, an Afridi orderly, who always attended Lumsden in sport or fight, crept up to him and said, in a low tone: "Since the great Lawrence came you have been worried and depressed; many have observed this, and that he is always looking at papers, asking questions, and over-hauling your accounts. Has he said anything to pain you? is he interfering with you? He starts for Peshawar to-morrow morning; there is no reason why he should reach it." The incident tells its own tale.

To return to our story. All these men were so welded together by Lumsden that they quailed before no danger, shrank from no raid, however desperate, and bore themselves to their leader against any odds with a fidelity unsurpassed by the Crusaders. In the valley of Peshawar, in 1847, Lumsden's prestige became a proverb, and with his native officers, men of mark and name, the Guides became famous. In the following year Lieutenant Hodson joined the Guides as Adjutant. This was the famous partisan soldier who, after being conspicuous in many a stirring scene, fell at Lucknow in 1858.

During 1848, the year of the rebellion in the Punjab, the Guides under Lumsden and Hodson were repeatedly engaged; their ranks repeatedly thinned, and again and again filled; their pay was above the ordinary scale for native officers and men, and to meet the exposure, and the leading which constant service entailed, the proportion of native and non-commissioned officers was double that of the Line. The corps was self-dependent; they had no carriage save that which was carried by their own mules and ponies ; their pay supplied everything ; extras for foreign service, or any cause, there were none.

It may be thought that I have been too careful in sketching the life and deeds of the Guides through the throes of the Sikhs, on their transition from an independent nation in 1846, to their incorporation with the British Empire in 1849; but this handful of soldiers became the nucleus of the Punjab Force, which, modelled on the Guides, and associated with them in scores of struggles on the hills and in the passes, along a frontier of some 600 miles, became, in May 1857, not only the foundation of the present Bengal army, but, with the exception of the sturdy, heroic Gurkhas, was the only available native force wherewith to stem the tide of sedition which, at a swoop, carried the Sepoy army of Bengal, from Peshawar to Calcutta, into rebellion.

I will now touch upon the constitution of the first regiments of the Punjab Force, five of cavalry and five of infantry, and the organisation is on the same principle to this day. A cavalry corps was composed of a commandant and 3 British officers, 18 native officers, and 588 sabres ; an infantry regiment, with the same proportion of officers and 896 bayonets.

The native officers were the sons or brothers of chiefs and nobles, on or outside the frontier, or Sikhs who had held rank and power in the old army ; men of the family of the ex-Amir of Kabul, the son of the Governor of Jalalabad, who stood by our cause in Sale's defence, were of these. The non-commissioned officers were mostly of the same stamp, serving on to await their promotion to the commissioned rank.

Each corps maintained its own carriage of mules and ponies, and was thus ready at all times to take the field at the shortest notice.

Within a year, each regiment had settled down to guard their portion of the frontier of 500 miles, from Kohat to Mithankot.

Three horse field-batteries, each with five 9-pounders and a 24-pounder howitzer, were attached to the Force.

The batteries were commanded by Bengal Artillery officers who had made their mark during the war. The gunners were Sikhs who had remained faithful. There were also two companies for garrison duty, veterans of the Sikh army. With these batteries were some remarkable Sikh officers, who had served under Avitabile and Van Cortlandt in Ranjit Singh's army, bearing French orders of rank; noble old soldiers they were, with a holy faith in their guns—to them objects of devotion.

The cavalry and infantry force, of necessity hastily organised, was composed in several regiments mostly of men of Hindustan. Life beyond the Indus, away from their families, with harassing duties, and exposure in a climate very different from their own, had no abiding temptation for them : health and spirits gave way ; they longed to return to the plains of India, and be with their own people. Their vacancies were filled on the type of the Guides—the 1st Punjab Cavalry and 1st Punjab Infantry were so from the beginning—and thus it came about that the security of that troubled border was maintained by the descendants of the restless marauders who had roamed and plundered for generations ; and by their side fought Sikhs, their hereditary enemies, still conspicuous for the discipline and daring with which Ranjit Singh had imbued their fathers.

The Punjab Frontier Force in 1852 numbered 11,000 men of all ranks, and 64 guns—including old metal in position on the walls of the forts at Bunnoo and Kohat.

The Bengal army of 1857 was almost entirely drawn from Oudh ; light cavalry, in discipline and horsemanship all that could be desired ; infantry, splendid in physique and perfect in movements, described by no mean judge the gallant old Nott, "noble soldiers whose backs no Afghan had ever seen." Each regiment had some 24 British and from 16 to 20 native officers ; but the native officers, under the system which prevailed, owed their position to length of service only. In the infantry the result was specially conspicuous. Subadars of companies, aged and often toothless, mounted on scraggy ponies, jogged along the line of march. Gallantry in action could hardly win for the Sepoy the badge of a non-commissioned rank. It was with this mass, fresh in discipline, armed to the teeth, steeped in fanaticism, that the Punjab Frontier Force had suddenly to deal.

Mark the contrast in the constitution of the present native army, modelled on the Guides and Punjab Force. Regiments of cavalry and infantry have each a selected commandant and seven British officers. Native officers, numerically as before, often men of birth and position, always men of education; every soldier feels that he bears with him his own fate on the field—that promotion is the sure heritage of skill and valour.

In the majority of regiments, instead of one race, there is an admixture of races—sometimes by troops and companies, sometimes by men antagonistic in religion and caste.

In this commingling of tribes the army has a bond of strength which no temptation has yet shaken.

Sir Hugh Rose bore striking testimony to this as Commander-in-Chief, after the trials and struggles of Umbeyla in 1863: "It was due to the native troops employed, particularly to the regiments organised since 1857, that the Commander-in-Chief should submit to the Government of India a practical proof of their discipline and fidelity. Every effort was made by the Akhund of Swat and the hostile tribes to seduce to their cause their co-religionists in the native regiments opposed to them; but, with the exception of one young Bonair recruit, their sense of duty and discipline kept them true."

The mixture of races in the ranks has proved a political and social safeguard.

Of the fifty fights and expeditions in which the Punjab Force was engaged on the north-west frontier during the ten years Sir Neville Chamberlain exercised command, I will touch on one only—the expedition against the Mahsud Waziris in 1860. This is an illustrative one. The Mahsud Waziris were pre-eminent for plunder and violence, their raids increased year by year in daring, till at last in 1859, after years of immunity, their chiefs brought a body of five or six thousand men into the plains for plunder.

General Chamberlain, who passed down the frontier at this time, wrote to the Government: " In the course of my annual tour, I see much of all classes, and nowhere do I hear the cry for justice till I come within reach of the Waziris. Then commences a train of injuries received and unredressed. There is no more pitiable sight than the tears and entreaties of a family stripped of all their means. Supposing our backwardness to arise from fear, men and women counselled courage, saying, 'We will assist you; they can't stand before guns and percussion arms.'"

This final raid brought their deeds of rapine to a crisis. It was determined to march a column into their strongholds, which no stranger had ever approached — an entangled mass of mountains of five ranges, with their crests rising from 5500 feet to 11,500 feet—accessible only by the defiles of the Suleiman range, channels, by which the drainage from the mountains finds its way to the Indus, varying in breadth from 1000 to 80 yards.

The expedition, composed entirely of soldiers organised and disciplined in the way I have described, without an English bayonet or sabre in the ranks, consisted of—

    Detachments of the Punjab Light Field Batteries: 3 Royal Artillery British officers, 101 fighting men.

    The Peshawar and Hazara Mountain Transport: 6 Royal Artillery officers, 125 fighting men.

    Detachments of Guide, Punjab, Multan Cavalry: 4 British officers, 331 sabres.

    Detachments of Sikh, Guide, Punjab, and Gurkha Infantry: 41 British officers, 4536 men.

In all about 5200 fighting men—Sikhs, Afridis, Gurkhas, and Pathans of every clan—with 64 British officers, of whom 7 were Staff, led by Brigadier-General Sir Neville Chamberlain, whose presence to every man of the Force was a guarantee of success.

On the 17th April 1860, the column entered the Tank Zam defile, a huge ravine, rugged with rocks and boulders, the passage difficult in fine weather—impassable even for elephants after a storm of rain, for the watercourses at the base of the towering mountains, wind for miles before reaching the plains; but selected as the route which afforded the best means of getting up supplies from the rear.

On the 19th, at midnight, the General marched off with the whole of the cavalry, to seize a height, followed by Lumsden with the mountain guns and 2000 infantry.

Now began a series of marches in which miles occupied hours, the safety of followers, supplies, etc., requiring heights on both sides to be crowned until the rearguard came up. In the new ground, day by day, breastworks had to be constructed for night pickets of stones from the hill-sides, palisaded to prevent a sudden rush from overpowering numbers; all tents were struck at dusk; half the men slept accoutred, all in uniform, and the inlying pickets were of necessity strong.

The Waziris, with unity which is proverbial amongst men who subsist almost entirely on plunder from the plains, were gathered, perched on crags and heights, ready for every chance, occasionally fighting with desperation. One chief, seeing an English officer with a few men reconnoitring the ground, shouted to his followers, " Now is the time to die for our faith, and to show the kind of men whose country is invaded." There was no lack of enthusiasm, a desperate rush was made, the gallant fellow died, but not until others had fallen.

The first serious opposition burst out on the 25th : the reveille was just sounding, and all was quiet, when a volley from the pickets and the " fall in " call startled Lumsden's column of 4 field-guns, 100 sabres, and 1200 infantry, which had moved by another gorge. Three thousand Waziris, sword in hand, burst through the pickets, 500 penetrated the camp, where a desperate hand-to-hand struggle ensued; they were driven back, leaving 132 bodies behind them ; no wounded were found, though the number must have been great. Lumsden's loss was heavy also : 21 killed and 109 wounded.

The sick and wounded were now sent back; sixteen

days' supplies, 4000 shoes for the men, and shoes for the horses—for struggling over rocks and boulders had destroyed these—were taken, and arrangements made for an advance on Kani Goram, the capital, hitherto considered inaccessible.

At this time a message came from the Waziris, that they desired a conference; the chief men appeared in camp. The General told them "there was still time to make terms; we had no wish to meddle with their affairs, but we must have security against their plundering and murdering on the British territory, and that unless this was assured their capital would be captured." After much discussion, the maliks (chief men) said: " Why go further? Our people are rough mountaineers, difficult to restrain; blood was fresh, and bodies of relations still unburied in the sun; our country is unfit for an army!" The General replied that it was contrary to our custom to show hostility to the dead, and pointed out to them that many of their dead had been honourably buried by our troops, and that the relations might come and bury the remainder. The Mahsuds, who hold it a sacred duty to bury their dead, seemed touched for the moment; but, depending on their numbers, their crags and mountains, they roughly put aside overtures for peace, and left, warning us of their preparations.

On the 4th May the Force moved forward through a narrow cleft in the rock; 6000 or 7000 of the enemy were in position, the mouth of the pass was closed by an abattis so strong that guns had no effect on it; above the crags and ridges were breastworks of stone, terraced one above the other, thick with Waziris. I will not delay by attempting further description of ground, etc., which well might lead the mountaineers to rely on their courage to maintain it.

The Force was formed into three columns of attack. The right and main attack had to carry breastworks on a crest, the last 12 or 15 feet of which were almost inaccessible, the ground below was broken and cut up with ravines; the attacking party in groups fired from behind rocks, to shelter themselves from the fire and stones hurled from above. Casualties were thick amongst them. The Waziris, seeing this check, leaped from their breastworks, and with shouts, sword in hand, burst through the leading men and reached the mountain-guns and reserve. The ground on which this occurred was visible to both sides; the hills and crags rang with cheers from the clansmen as they watched the glistening swords. Captain Keyes, now Sir Charles Keyes, was with the 1st Punjab Infantry in reserve; putting himself at the head of a handful of men, he cut down the leader of the Waziris, already on the flank of the guns. Thus the tide of triumph was turned. The men of the battery under Captain Butt never swerved; they stood to their guns and fought; the brilliant stroke was over; the Waziris, leaving the ground thick with dead, retreated up the hill, so hotly pursued that the breastwork was carried and the position won.

Our loss was Lieutenant Ayrton, 94th, attached to the 2nd Punjab Infantry, and 30 killed; 84 wounded.

The centre and left attacks were carried with trifling loss, and the stronghold of the Waziris fell into our hands.

During the halt at Kani Goram the soldiers who had won, encamped in order outside the walls, were permitted to visit the town under officers, morning and evening. A Syud, watching the orderly marching of the conquerors about the city, called out to the bystanders, "Well done, British justice!" It is said this remark, testifying to the strength of discipline, touched the English General as much as his military success.

On the 9th May the force marched back by another route towards the plains; and on the 19th, with little molestation, reached Bunnoo, where the column was broken up.

Thus the Force, bearing sixteen days' supplies for 8000 men, led by Sir Neville Chamberlain—of whom it is not fitting to speak in such a paper as this—with a few English officers, marched in triumph through a country which no native power had ever dared to enter—160 miles, through clefts, over crags and mountains peopled by desperate marauders, watching and contesting every peak and point—yet such was the force of discipline and system that three camp followers and as many camels were the only losses *en route*.

The casualties in action were 450 :—

Killed, 1 English officer.
„ 3 non-commissioned officers.
„ 100 men.
Wounded, 346.

I will not speak of Umbeyla in 1863; the expedition of a mixed force, English and native, reinforced as the necessity demanded, commanded also by Sir Neville Chamberlain, until a severe wound compelled him to hand over the command to General Garrock, though he remained in the field, and saw the successful end ; the total casualties were 908 :—

15 British officers killed, 21 wounded.
34 „ soldiers „ 118 „
4 native officers „ 20 „
185 soldiers „ 504 „

Here again many well-known frontier names appeared in a distinguished manner. Wilde, Probyn, Brownlow, Keyes, all added to their reputation.

I will now quit the frontier and turn for a few minutes to the trials and glories of the Punjab Force at Delhi and Lucknow; these have been eloquently described by Kaye and Malleson, and do not call for other mention than bare record here.

Edwardes and the men of might at Peshawar and down the border so stirred the enthusiasm of the chiefs and tribes for our rule that they submitted themselves to organisation, and, proudly taking the place of the Frontier Force, kept the peace themselves, and so admitted of the despatch of regiment after regiment to Delhi.

The first corps to move, being the nearest to the road

was the Guides. Within a few hours of the massacre at
Delhi, cavalry and infantry, 6 officers and about 600 men,
were on the march towards the scene. The grand old
masters of India, the Court of Directors, thus wrote, in
August 1858, of the Guides at Delhi: "The corps, by
the extraordinary alacrity with which they proceeded to
Delhi—marching 580 miles in twenty-one days—in the
months of May and June, turning off the road one night
12 miles to attack mutineers; by their remarkable services
before Delhi, where for nearly four months both officers
and men were constantly in action, sometimes twice a day;
by their singular fidelity, as shown by the fact that not
one man deserted, whilst 350 were killed and wounded;
and by their heroic gallantry having established for themselves the strongest claim to our approbation and favour."

For some weeks after the commencement of operations
at Delhi, the only native troops with the British Force
were the Guides and Charles Reid's Gurkhas, the Sirmur
battalion. During July and August, the 1st, 2nd, and 4th
Punjab Regiments, and 4th Sikh Infantry, squadrons of
the Punjab Cavalry, old border soldiers, with new levies to
meet the casualties of the daily struggles, poured in; and
on the 11th September 1857, some 3000 men of all ranks
of the Punjab Force were in array outside the walls.

On the capture of the city, 28th September, the rolls
were examined, when it was ascertained that the casualties
in the Punjab Force during the operations were little short
of 1000. Of these, 250 were killed, including 9 British and
11 native officers; 16 British and 28 native officers
wounded. No Punjab corps had a complement of more
than 5 English officers; and this number had with some
regiments to be renewed more than once. In the Guides
and 1st Punjab Infantry alone, 6 British officers were
killed, and 11 wounded; some were twice wounded; not
one escaped without a mark.

Of those who fell, I could tell of Lumsden, brother of
the two distinguished soldiers, Sir Harry and Sir Peter;
Travers, brother of the General who won the Victoria
Cross by charging, with four or five Sikh troopers, Holkar's

guns at Indore; Quentin Battye, the pride of the border, the beau ideal of a soldier and horseman, fell amidst the wail of his men, murmuring "Dulce et decorum est pro patria mori!" Murray—young Murray—sorely wounded in the early days of the siege, rejoined the Guides on the morning of the assault, and found his death springing a trench some feet in advance of his eager men.

Many other gallant spirits closed their course, but the names of Quentin Battye, Lumsden, Travers, and Murray were in many mouths, and to this day have a hallowing influence in the ranks in which they died.

The heavy losses caused by the lengthened operations made the pressure great for qualified officers, but the spirit among them was high, and men pressed to serve where duty pointed. As an instance of this, Nicholson, who had marched down with a squadron of Sam Browne's, the 2nd Punjab Cavalry, brother of Brigadier-General John Nicholson—who, as recorded on his tomb, "led the assault of Delhi, but fell in the hour of victory, mortally wounded"—volunteered to join and lead the 1st Punjab Infantry at the storm; because the border men of the regiment knew him, and Major Coke and their own officers were either disabled from wounds or dead. Nicholson lost an arm on this occasion.

Neville Chamberlain, severely wounded in July, had never ceased to cheer the army by his presence, and was the moving spirit in the dark days between the storm and capture, 14th and 20th September.

Coke recovered from his wounds and led a brigade in the subsequent operations in Rohilkhund with marked distinction.

The squadrons of Punjab Cavalry, under Probyn, Watson, and Younghusband; the Sikhs, 2nd and 4th Punjab Infantry, under Wilde, subsequently Sir Alfred, formed part of the column which joined Sir Colin Campbell at Lucknow. The Punjab squadrons were everywhere conspicuous for gallant work; Probyn, Sir Dighton, and Watson, Major-General and C.B., both won the Victoria Cross, and the native officers and men were

worthy of their leaders.   Younghusband was killed during
the advance on Futtehghar.

The 4th Punjab Infantry, at the assault of the Sikan-
drabagh, Lucknow, vied with the 93rd Highlanders ; when
the bugle sound gave the signal for the attack, an eye-
witness wrote : " It was a glorious rush ; on went, in
generous rivalry, the Sikh, Pathan, and Highlander ;
Subadar Gokul Sing, of the Sikhs, mentioned by the
Commander-in-Chief, waving his tulwar above his head,
dashed on five yards in front of his men."

In the succeeding operations at Lucknow, and throughout the campaign, the Punjab Force bore itself with conspicuous glory ; many officers, English and native—in
their gallant leading there was no distinction—fell, or were
disabled.   Wilde was sorely wounded, but recovered, and
in after years distinguished himself on the frontier as the
leader of the force which held him in honour.   Sam Browne,
too—now Lieutenant-General, K.C.B., and K.C.S.I.—performed a gallant feat of arms.   He was in command of a
column, 250 sabres of his regiment and 350 infantry
hastily detached to save an important town in Rohilkhand
from falling into the hands of the rebels.   He found the
enemy in a strong position on a mound, within a short
distance of the threatened city, with a wide tract of inun-
dated ground in front, which prevented attack, or even
approach.   At midnight, with an old woman and boy as
guides, Captain Browne moved his force round the swamp,
and with break of day was in the enemy's rear.   He halted
a breathing space to refresh men and horses, for the march
had been heavy.   The enemy caught sight of him, and at
once turned three 9-pounders into action.   Captain
Browne, seeing a 9-pounder open with grape within 80
yards of his flank, galloped down, sword in hand, on the
gun, attended by his orderly only.   A desperate hand-to-
hand fight ensued—the gun was captured, but not without
terrible wounds to the heroic leader, whose life was saved
by a native officer, an old friend, badly wounded himself,
devotedly rushing with two or three troopers to the rescue.

Sir Samuel Browne's empty sleeve and the Victoria

Cross on his breast, tell of the struggle and honour of that
day. The town was saved, the enemy crushed, and guns
captured. Sir William Mansfield, then chief of the staff,
not wont to be keen of praise, described the affair "as very
brilliant, the attack being made in the most soldierly
manner and *secundum artem.*"

The Punjab Force has, since the time of which I have
been speaking, and since Sir Neville Chamberlain, shattered
with wounds, left the command, maintained its reputation
for discipline and daring. Wilde and Keyes have both
commanded the troops amongst whom they had served
as subalterns.

It was while serving as Brigadier-General, commanding
the Frontier Force, that Roberts began his career of a
General, and developed that capacity for command which
won the love and honour of the soldiers he led over the
Peiwar, at Kabul, and to Kandahar.

In the troubles and triumphs in Afghanistan the Punjab
Force bore an honourable share, with Sir Donald Stewart
on his march from Kandahar, with Roberts at Sherpore,
and in scenes too numerous to mention. In all these
operations the Punjab troops were mingled with the army
at large; but in any case the events are too recent for
more than this general comment.

The Frontier Force, by May 1857, had broadened
into—

Three Horse Field-Batteries, each with a commandant
and subaltern, R.A.

Two Mountain Batteries, each with a commandant and
2 subalterns, R.A.

Five regiments of cavalry.

The corps of Guides.

Four regiments of Sikh Infantry.

Six regiments of Punjab Infantry.

At which, with the exception that the horse field-batteries
have been changed to mountain-guns and one garrison

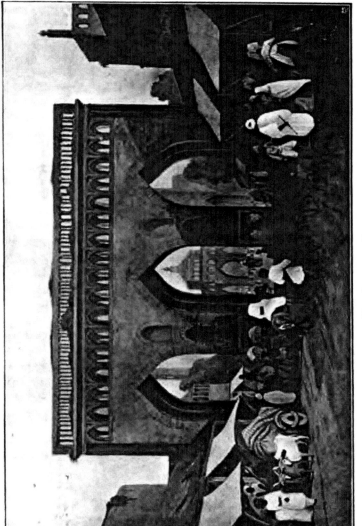

THE LUCKNOW GATES.

[To face p. 368.

company, and the addition of one Gurkha regiment, the Hazara, the force still stands.

The armament has changed with the times. In the early period Brown Bess and the two-grooved rifle did not proudly compete with the long matchlock and Jezail of the Afridi. The cavalry, under the order of their commanders, provided themselves with arms and horses, clothing and equipments; the State supplies were confined to medicine and surgical instruments, and carriage for these only. In the Bengal Irregular Cavalry of that period, the trooper had a matchlock swung at his back. The trooper of the regular regiments bore a heavy carbine, provided by the State, fastened to his saddle. The Punjab Cavalry, following the example of Jacob's Sind Horse, were armed with a light percussion carbine bought by themselves, and carried on their persons, for which the State found ammunition; all wore good swords, and in several regiments half of the men had lances. This order of things, which lasted for many years, has also changed, and the position of the trooper greatly improved; the State now pays him better, and supplies him with an arm of precision free of cost.

The horses of the Punjab Cavalry for a long time were chiefly imported from Afghanistan and Persia: in these countries there are tribes of dealers who, for generations, have been in the habit of bringing strings of horses into India; hardy, clever animals, bearing distinct marks of Arab parentage, well suited to the requirements of the trooper, and costing about £25 on the average.

The Punjab Force, raised under the direct orders of the Governor-General, has never been, as regards the selection of officers for its ranks, and promotion within, subject to the Commander-in-Chief. This, which doubtless seems anomalous to those not familiar with the working and constitution of the Government of India, has proved to possess many advantages, and the force has not suffered in discipline or prestige. The Viceroy has the power of selection from the armies of Bengal, Madras, and Bombay. Wilde and Keyes were both officers of Madras.

2 A

The negotiations with the border tribes, and our relations and treaties with chiefs and rulers, rest with the Viceroy, and are traditionally known to the Punjab Government, through whom work and mediation of varied kinds is conducted. The officers and men of the Force, moving from place to place on a border of 700 or 800 miles, are thus personally imbued with knowledge valuable and almost necessary for life and duty. The work which falls to them could hardly be done in its daily uncertainties by the interchange of regiments of the army at large, and by officers trained merely on the lines of military discipline, moving about under the routine of reliefs.

Discipline and military science being maintained, experience has proved that the State enjoys special advantages from having this border Force at its disposal. On all expeditions, when serving with corps of the Line, the Punjab regiments are subject to the same rules and regulations as others, and no distinction exists between them. There is no jealousy; for the officers are drawn from the army at large, and appointments to the Force are prizes which many seek. With the men, transfers and exchanges are also frequent.

That great administrator, Sir Henry Lawrence, trusted, however, to other means than force for quieting and civilising the trans-Indus territory.

As the first regiments settled down along the border, Sir Henry Lawrence impressed on medical officers the necessity of establishing dispensaries. All officers were specially instructed to seize every opportunity of making these institutions popular. The consequence of this was many a strange scene of war and confidence: men wounded on the hill-side fighting against us were brought to our pickets, and shouts came across the rocks for permission to bring their wounded to our hospital—even while the fight was going on. It so happened that a few days after our first occupation of Kohat, we had many casualties, and many wounded prisoners fell into our hands. Chloroform, then a new introduction in science, was used; and the fame of its soothing power spread far and wide. For months afterwards, men journeyed from long distances, merely to see the Doctor Sahib who sent people to sleep, and then did what he liked with them without giving pain.

The medical officers of the force, upon whose tact and capacity the success of the civilising influence of medicine and surgery depended, were men selected for their energy and ability ; and well and broadly did they lay the foundation of trust in the Englishman's skill and kindliness. As the Chief Commissioner subsequently wrote to Lord Dalhousie, "the presence of such men tends to strengthen our rule." In some cases, the English doctor so won the gratitude of the faithless Afghan that his life would have been safe and his wants attended to, where a dog, outside the camp, would have had no chance.

Vaccination all along the border was another source of power to us. Kafilas from distant countries coming through the passes with their horses, camels, and merchandise, their women and children, were vaccinated by hundreds every year : they too carried the tale of the Englishman's power far and wide ; and Hakims from Kabul and Kandahar came down to be instructed in the Englishman's art of escape from the sore disease, which carried disfigurement and death to so many of their countrymen.

Muhammadan fanaticism, often nurtured to madness by men who, after the commission of crime, have sought refuge from punishment and recognition by their fellows in the solitude of caves and rocks, at the sources of rivers, has many disciples scattered about along the border in places rarely visited by others than those who seek an asylum. These fanatics from time to time come out, sometimes at the bidding of others, sometimes of their own accord, deliberately to murder ; generally the selection falls on some prominent man who is not of the Moslem faith. This to the fanatic is martyrdom. "I have destroyed the infidel ; do with me what you will." So spake the man who calmly stabbed to death, at Peshawar in 1853, the most famous frontier Englishman of his time Colonel Mackeson, whose epitaph, written by the great

Governor-General, the Marquis of Dalhousie, is sculptured on a monument facing the Khyber: "He was the beau ideal of a soldier: cool to conceive, brave to dare, and strong to do. The Indian Army was proud of his presence in its ranks. The reputation of Colonel Mackeson is known to and honoured by all. His value as a political servant of the State is known to none better than to the Governor-General himself, who in a difficult and eventful time had cause to mark his great ability.

"The loss of Colonel Mackeson's life would have dimmed a victory. To lose him thus by the hand of a foul assassin is a misfortune of the heaviest gloom for the Government, which counted him among its bravest and its best."

Mackeson's was a noble nature: death would have been proudly met by him for such an epitaph by such a hand.

Major Adams, an officer of distinction, conspicuous at Peshawar and in Hazara as a Political officer (he was trained in the Guides), was signalled out by a fanatic and openly cut down.

Mecham, a gallant young soldier of artillery, who had served in many fields with honour, was another victim of the assassin on that border.

Healy, Carne, Tapp, good servants of the State, though little known to the outside world, met death in the same foul way, doing their duty.

Godby, of the Guides, and the grand John Nicholson, both were attacked by fanatics. Godby escaped, through the devotion of his men, with a ghastly wound. Nicholson freed himself, and thus describes the scene :—

"I was standing at the gate of my garden with Sladen and Cadell (both General Officers now), and four or five native official attendants, when a man with a drawn sword rushed suddenly up and called out for me. I was wearing a long fur pelisse of native make, which prevented his recognising me at first; this gave time for the only native attendant who had a sword to get between us, to whom he cried out contemptuously to stand aside, saying he had come to kill *me*, and did not want to hurt a common soldier. The relief sentry for the front of my house happening to pass opportunely at this moment, I snatched his musket, and, presenting it at the would-be assassin, told him I would fire if he did not put down his sword and surrender. He replied, 'Either you or I must die'; so I had no alternative, and shot him through the heart, the ball passing through a religious book which he had tied on his chest as a charm.

"The poor wretch was religiously mad; he had disposed of his property in charity the day before he set out for Bunnoo; his religious instructor here has disappeared mysteriously, and got into the hills.

"My police orderly replied to his cry for my blood, 'All our names are Nikhul Seyn here,' and I think would have got the better of him had I not interfered; but I could not allow the man to risk his life when I had such a sure weapon as a loaded musket and bayonet in my hand."

I think I did well to speak of the frontier on which these foul scenes occurred as a "troubled frontier." They are now scenes of the past; resolute rule and the undaunted courage of Englishmen have stamped out the assassin, and put bounds even to Muhammadan fanaticism.

———

Sir H. D. Daly.—There is one remark I should like to make, Mr Chairman. The other day it chanced that I read one of the last letters which the Duke of Wellington wrote from India. It was a letter to Major Shaw, who was the Secretary to the Government, and he said, speaking of returning to Europe and his anxiety to do so: "I have long felt that services in this country, whatever they may be, are not recognised or rewarded on the same scale as services rendered in any other part of the world." I believe that is the same to this day. I have spoken to you of men whose names are known on that border of which I have been speaking, whose names are known throughout India and throughout the Indian army as household words; yet here, barring the great ones, the Lawrences, the Napiers, and perhaps probably Neville Chamberlain, they fall upon the English public coldly and with a chill. Services, as the Duke wrote when Sir Arthur Wellesley in 1805, services in that country are not recognised and rewarded on the scale in which they are in any other part of the world.

INDEX

375

railways, 296-298, 321 ; relations with the Maharaja of Rewa, 299-302 ; on the opium trade of Malwa, 303-306, 324 ; establishes sub-agencies, 303 ; his interest in education, 307, 323 ; on the visit of the Prince of Wales, to Gwalior and Indore, 309-314 ; on the Imperial Assemblage, 314-316 ; result of Dr Stratton's work in Bundelkhand, 317-319 ; his review on the changes in ten years, 319-325 ; officers serving under him, 326-328 ; relations with them, 328 ; method of settling matters, 328 ; dislike of pomp and show, 329 ; promotions, 330 ; K.C.B., 330 ; death of his wife, 330 ; life at Indore, 331 ; popularity, 331, 337 ; departure from India, 331 ; C.I.E., 331 ; tributes to his memory, 332 ; bust unveiled, 333, 342 ; Master of the Isle of Wight Foxhounds, 333 ; his lecture on "The Punjab Frontier Force," 334, 350-374 ; political views, 334 ; contests Dundee, 334 ; General, 335 ; created a G.C.B., 335 ; at Osborne, 335 ; second marriage, 335 ; accident and death, 336 ; character, 336 ; funeral, 337

Daly, Mrs, birth of her second son, 108 ; journey to Lucknow, 108-111 ; on the gaieties at Sekrora, 117 ; the murder of Boileau, 118 *note;* on their visit to Sir H. Lawrence, 121 ; her impressions of the Taj at Agra, 126 ; at Kasauli, 127 ; journey to Multan, 186 ; death, 330

"Daly College, The," erection at Indore, 332, 346

Daly's Grove, 1, 99

Darria Khan, 198

Delama, 236

Delhi, 127 ; outbreak of the mutiny, 131 ; siege, 141-179, 365 ; fall, 144, 179 ; proposed scheme of attack on, 155 ; number of killed and wounded, 170 ; arrival of the siege train, 171, 174 ; plan of assault, 174-176 ; Imperial As-

semblage at, 314, 320 ; Coronation Darbar, 316

Delhi, The Siege of, by One Who Served There, extract from, 141

Dera Ghazi Khan, 15 ; battle of, 18

Dera Ismael Khan, 15, 95

Devil's Bridge, 98

Dewas, 256

Dhar, 283, 306 ; sub-agency at, 303

Dhar, Raja of, honour conferred, 316 ; his construction of road, 323

Dickson, Miss, 121

Dilawar Khan, joins the Guides, 354

Dilkusha Park, 110 ; Palace, 110

Disbrowe, 42

Doalpur, 232

Doon, 130

Dost Muhammad Khan, Amir, 57 *note;* at Peshawar, 115 ; conference with John Lawrence, 115

Dufferin, Lord, at the opening of the Indore Daly College, 332

Dumichand, 193

Dundas, Colonel the Hon. H., 37 ; in command of the force against Multan, 38 ; his character as a soldier, 72

Dundee elections, 334

Dunlop, Mr Stirling, 335

Durriabad, 219

EDWARDES, Colonel Sir Herbert, his operations against Mulraj, 18 ; *A Year on the Punjab Frontier,* 18 *note,* 52 *note;* his camp, 24 ; appearance, 35, 122 ; at Lucknow, 122 ; character, 125, 137, 189 ; at Lahore, 130 ; influence with the Lawrences, 130 ; on the outbreak of Mutiny, 131 ; his wit and humour, 135, 137 ; tact, 137 ; on the delay in attacking Delhi, 162 ; on reinforcements, 164

Ellenborough, Lord, 6 *note*

Elmslie, G. R., *Lumsden of the Guides,* 334 *note*

Elphinstone, Mountstuart, his report on the Native States, 283

Esaghar, 282, 295

FAGAN shot at the siege of Delhi, 176

note; his letter to Lieut. Daly, 61 ; appointed President of a Board for the government of Punjab, 63 ; organises a short frontier tour, 91 ; departure from India, 100 ; at Lucknow, 116, 121 ; his invitation to the Dalys, 120 ; method of entertaining, 121 ; portrait, 124 ; affection for his wife, 124 ; character, 125 ; his appreciation of Daly, 125 *note;* founds Asylum at Kasauli, 128 ; subscriptions to charities, 128 ; death, 167, 168 ; methods of civilising the natives, 370

Lawrence, Sir John, Commissioner of the Jalandar Division, 12 *note;* his character, 13, 129 ; officiates as Resident at Lahore, 14 ; re-ceives a visit from Mulraj, 15 ; conference with Dost Muham-mad, 115 ; at Lahore, 129 ; his Council on the outbreak of Mutiny, 133 ; messages to the Commander-in-Chief, 134 ; on the fighting at Delhi, 144 ; on reinforcements, 152, 163, 165 ; on the plan of assault on Delhi, 179 ; disaffection of tribes, 180 ; as Governor-General, 205

Lawrence, Mrs, escorted to the Sikh camp, 69

Leith, at the siege of Multan, 41, 45 ; wounded, 46

Lerwah, 248

Lloyd, Captain, 34

Longdon, Captain, 25

Loodianah, 158

Lucerne, 98

Lucknow, 110, 190 ; relief of, 181 ; condition after the capture, 200 ; siege, 367

Ludhiana, 139, 190

Lugano, 98

Lumsden, Major-General Sir H. B., his mission to Kandahar, 116, 120 ; probable return, 124 ; his method of raising the Guides, 353-355 ; headquarters, 355 ; relations with his men, 355

Lumsden, killed, 366

Lumsden, Sir P. S., *Lumsden of the Guides*, 334 *note*

Lytton, Lord, 319

MACAULAY, Lord, his description of Fyzabad, 220

Macdowell, second in command of Hodson's Horse, 194

Mackay, Mr Aberigh, Principal of the Residency College, Indore, 308 ; his supervision of education, 323

Mackeson, Colonel, 92 ; his epitaph, 371

Macnaghten, Sir W., 4 *note*

Mahmud of Ghazni, takes the city of Multan, 15

Mahtab Singh, 69, 70

Maitland, Captain F. H., 327. *See* Lauderdale

Malcolm, Sir John, *Memoir of Central India including Malwa*, 279 *note*, 281 *note*, 283 *note;* his estimate of the population of Central India, 279 *note;* on the opium trade of Malwa, 304, 305 ; occupies the Nalcha Palace, 326 *note*

Malines, 99

Mallegaum, 4 *note*

Malleson, Major, 263 *note*

Malta, 3

Malwa, 256 ; famine, 257, 281, 304 ; opium trade, 279, 302-306, 321, 324 ; climate, 280 ; review of the condition, 283, 295 ; construction of railways, 297

Man Singh, Resaldar, at the action of Nawabgunge, 197, 216 *note*

Mandisor, 340 ; sub-agency at, 303

Mandra, 137

Mandu, ruins of, 325 *note*

Mansfield, Lieut.-Gen. Sir William, his rapid promotion, 87 ; char-acteristics, 88 ; on the expected attack of the Mohmands, 89 ; on the management of native tribes, 92-94 ; at Shanklin, 102 ; ap-pointed to the mission at Con-stantinople, 105 ; advice to Daly, 105 ; Major-General, 115 ; Con-sul-General at Warsaw, 115 ; appointed Chief of the Staff to Sir C. Campbell, 173, 189 ; his letter from Fatteh Singh, 207-209 ; K.C.B., 218 ; his views on the reconstitution of the army, 221 ; on the departure of Sir H.

CPSIA information can be obtained at www.ICGtesting.com
Printed in the USA
LVOW11*0907060514

384613LV00013B/242/P